THE COMPLETE GUIDEBOOK TO ROUTE 66

SANTA MONICA TO CHICAGO

by BOB MOORE &
RICH CUNNINGHAM

A Route 66 Magazine Publication

Santa Monica to Chicago

DEDICATED TO THE MEMORY OF
JACK D. RITTENHOUSE,
WHO SHOWED US THE WAY

ISBN 0-9701423-1-5

Copyright © 2003
Route 66 Magazine
PO Box 66
Laughlin NV 89028

All rights reserved.
Without limiting the rights under copyright reserved above,
no part of this publication may be reproduced, stored in a
retrieval system, or transmitted in any form or by any means,
electronic, mechanical, photocopied, recorded, or otherwise
without written permission of the copyright owner.

All odometer readings are accurate for the vehicle used, however
actual readings may vary from vehicle to vehicle. The authors and/or the
Route 66 Magazine Publishing Company will not accept any responsibility
for damage to vehicles or individuals following the directions included herein.
The Road is a living entity and as such listed places may change over time.
Recommendations as to lodging or dining are strictly the opinion of the writer and
do not necessarily reflect the opinion of the publisher or Route 66 Magazine.

FIRST EDITION

5 4 3 2 1

FORWARD!

My dad loved cars.

Cars were a large part of his life.

When I was a kid, Dad had Packard's, Cadillac's, Imperial's, Lincoln's, Studebaker's, and step-down Hudson's - during the time when Hudson's were the top stock-car on the racing circuit. He once participated, as a mechanic, in the famous Carrera Panamericana, or the Mexican Road Race as it was popularly known, under the Lincoln banner. There was a time when our Southern California driveway and carport were home to the Raymond Lowey designed Studebakers. That was during the period when Dad drove the South Bend beauties in the Mobil Economy Run - a balloon-foot exercise in the name of good gas mileage.

But soon he returned to the behemoths he fondly called, "Great road cars." It was important to him how well a car handled out on the road. When he wasn't driving the highways of North America or Mexico, he was an ace mechanic, fixing the internal ills of all types of Detroit iron. Through his innate mechanical skills he learned which cars were well-built, and which were off-the-assembly-line junk.

I was in my teens when I discovered - on my own - that Dad's love affair with the automobile had very little to do with the cars themselves. I found myself, almost mystically, reliving many of the things he had done. During a period when I had no wheels of my own, I spent months hitchhiking from one end of the country to the other - south to north and back, then west to east and back. When wheels were mine once again I discovered the equation:

Car + gas ÷ (Road-out-town) x Map = Going Somewhere

To a hard-core Roadie "going somewhere" is all that matters. Destinations are important only in the context of being someplace to turn around. Roadies seek out maps, highways, and roads, much as coin collectors seek out the elusive 1943 steel penny.

To the Roadie, Route 66 is a major attraction. Along the 2448 miles of the Mother Road from the Pacific Ocean to Lake Michigan, there are sights rarely seen on other highways. The Road is an adventure and along the road are thousands of cafes, motels and tourist stops demanding to be seen and investigated.

The Road offers views of a world missed on the Interstate, as it explores and celebrates the two-lane world of single-story motels, small cafes and stations where gas is still pumped by a guy with BOB stitched on a grease stained blue shirt.

Buckle your seat-belt and leave a big tip for the car-hop as we pull out of the parking lot of Mel's Drive-In and onto the pavement of The Road. Journey with us along Route 66 as we seek out the well-known, the little-known, and the unknown in the world of the Mother Road.

Dad, this one's for you!

Bob Moore

INTRODUCTION

It should be pointed out that this Guidebook is for the Roadies of the world in an attempt to help them find their way along what has been termed The Most Famous Highway in America.

This book is designed to present the road from West-to-East, a new concept in Route 66 Guidebooks, and one that has long been requested, while also providing the traditional East-to-West format.

In traveling the road I attempt to do so as anonymously as possible. I do not announce myself when I enter an establishment (besides, would anyone know me anyway?) - in this fashion I receive the same service and attention as any other "off the highway" Roadie. This allows for an honest evaluation of food, service, and accommodations. I do not accept "comps" or freebies for two reasons:
One, it prevents coloring an evaluation based on receiving something for nothing.
Two, the business owners along the road are there to make money - not give away their product or services.
I have been told about other writers and members of various organizations who not only demand they be comp'ed, but go so far as to threaten a bad review if they are not properly taken care of. In my opinion this is despicable behavior and if you experience this kind of activity I would like to hear about it.
In this edition there will also be more recommendations for dining and lodging. These are truly subjective recommendations based on my personal experience. You may notice quite a few Best Western properties mentioned, this is because in many smaller towns the Best Western is the best place in town - this determination is based on my staying in many of the other motels in a community and finding the B/W to be tops. Please remember that Best Western properties are individually owned and must meet strict standards to maintain the Best Western logo. Up and coming in the world of budget motels is the Microtel Inn chain - offering new, clean rooms in a pleasant atmosphere, you will find some of them recommended as well. Although I do not have extremely high standards - seeking only a clean room, decent service and good food - I nonetheless will point out when a place is unpleasant or if we have received multiple complaints.

A few general hints about traveling the old road.
1. Watch for low gas prices and take advantage of them. Virtually, all gas sold in this country is inspected for quality (only one state, Oregon, does not have a gasoline quality inspection program). So for all intents and purposes gas is gas.
2. Use the octane rating for your vehicle. Check the operators manual and you may be surprised to find you can use a lower octane fuel than you thought. I drive a GMC Yukon XL and the manual recommends 87octane (i.e. regular). I have never had a problem running this fuel. Don't pay for a higher octane than you need - it will do nothing to improve performance.
3. Food is another area that can become extremely subjective - what I like in the way of food you may not. But service is another matter. Over the past few years, I have stopped at a lot of Denny's and found the service has gone straight down the toilet. This observation covers locations throughout California, Nevada, Arizona and all of the Route 66 states. For that reason alone, I cannot recommend any of these restaurants. For breakfast I suggest seeking out a local café with a parking lot packed with local cars - or better yet - pick-ups, this is where you'll want to eat.
4. If you have a positive, or negative, experience at a Route 66 café, motel, or gas station drop me a line and let me know about it. I will check into it and when this book is updated will make use of the information.

The places rated or suggested in this book have been personally visited by yours truly and meet with my standards (such as they are) for a good Route 66 establishment. I do not go on the word of others (although positive or negative word-of-mouth will suggest a visit). A few places may receive negative reviews in these pages, this has been brought about by personal experience, or complaints I've received and followed up on to make my own decision. I do not use a check-list (Is the menu pretty? Did the door open without a squeak? Etc.). I base my opinions on the quality of service, quality of the food, or the cleanliness of the accommodations. As a rule most Route 66 businesses are great, but there are a few bad apples and if they are really bad, they will be mentioned. The fact an establishment does not appear in these pages is not indicative of a problem - most likely I have never stopped there - but please remember I have been traveling the Road since 1989 and have watched many places go downhill, or in some cases never come up. Now for the lawyer's part - these are my personal observations and opinions and may not reflect the opinion of the publisher, editor or any other individual involved in the production of this volume.

So with all of that explained, let's walk to the end of the Santa Monica Pier (it's almost sunset) and get that great shot of the sun dipping into the Pacific, because tomorrow morning, bright and early, we're ON THE ROAD!

ADVENTURE TOURS

In various parts of the book will be sections designated as ADVENTURE TOURS. These are sections of the road chosen for their historical interest. However, in virtually all cases these sections are very rough, usually dirt or extremely damaged pavement and as such are not suggested for the Roadie traveling in a classic (or even new) Corvette.

It should be pointed out that each of these sections will cover all of the problems to be encountered with recommendations for four-wheel drive if necessary.

Conditions can vary from dirt to sand, to extreme hills and, in times of severe weather, deep mud.

When you see the designation ADVENTURE TOUR read the entire section before deciding to drive it, understand all of the problems that may be encountered, and if the suggestion for four-wheel drive only is provided take it seriously.

Now for the stuff that keeps the attorneys happy:

> **SOME OF THE ALIGNMENTS DESCRIBED AS ADVENTURE TOURS MAY REQUIRE OFF-PAVEMENT DRIVING AND MAY NOT BE SUITABLE FOR A STANDARD AUTOMOBILE. SUCH AREAS WILL BE FULLY DOCUMENTED AND ALL CAUTIONS AND POTENTIAL HAZARDS SHOULD BE CAREFULLY OBSERVED BY THE READER. THE AUTHORS, ROUTE 66 MAGAZINE, ITS AGENTS OR ASSIGNEES WILL ASSUME NO RESPONSIBILITY FOR DAMAGE TO EITHER VEHICLES OR INDIVIDUALS WHO CHOSE TO PARTAKE IN ANY OF THE ADVENTURE TOURS OUTLINED IN THIS PUBLICATION.**

HIGHWAY NOTE

As we were going to press, information was received that California is joining the rest of the nation with a uniform numbering system of interstate exits. These numbers will be presented in a south-to-north and west-to-east manner beginning at where the interstate originates in California; for example I-5 will be numbered from the Mexican border north to the Oregon state line. Preliminary information received from CalTrans has been included in the guidebook indicating exit numbers on Interstates 10, 15 and 40 where required. Please note, this project is not due for completion until 2005 and although shown in the guidebook, the exits may not yet be posted.

NOTES FOR THE READER ABOUT MAKING THE GUIDEBOOK AND THE ATLAS WORK TOGETHER:

- The Guidebook text contains hundreds of map references that look like this: **(N117)** or **(A012)**. These references are the ID numbers of waypoints that appear on the maps in the Atlas, so you can read the text and follow your progress (or keep from getting lost!) by using the Atlas.
- Waypoint ID's are prefixed by the first letter of the respective state, except Oklahoma and Illinois which are prefixed by "H" and "L" respectively. This is because of a policy decision not to begin a waypoint with the letters "O" or "I," in order to avoid confusion with the numerals "0" and "1."
- If you can't figure out what map page a waypoint appears on, just look up the waypoint in the table of contents in the Atlas. It lists all the maps and the range of waypoints appearing on each.
- The waypoint numbers are only identification numbers, they are not sequential indicators. The correct sequence for travelers is described in the Guidebook so just follow that. A waypoint shown on the map that doesn't appear in the text you're reading applies to the other direction of travel.

Santa Monica to Chicago

CALIFORNIA

EASTBOUND

Although not a part of Route 66, any trip beginning at the western terminus of The Mother Road should begin with a visit to the Santa Monica Pier the evening before starting that Route 66 Adventure. A photo of the neon sign on the arch leading to the pier, with a spectacular California sunset in the background would be a perfect start for any photo album or Route 66 slide show.

For the true Roadie Route 66 begins at the intersection of Ocean Avenue and Santa Monica Boulevard, for the history buff and Hard-Core Roadie it is known that Route 66 originally did not go to Santa Monica *(ending at Broadway and 7th Street in downtown Los Angeles)* and the final alignment ended at Lincoln and Olympic Boulevards in Santa Monica. But the mystique of Route 66 has us starting at the pacific and running east to Lake Michigan, so that is where we begin - Ocean Ave and Santa Monica Boulevard. In Palisades Park to the west is the Will Rogers Highway dedication plaque *(and a whole lot of street people)* and just across the street is the Belle-Vue Restaurant, serving good food in a California Mission style building since 1937.

As you turn east off of Ocean Avenue and onto Santa Monica Blvd,

ZERO ODOMETER (C001)
Santa Monica was founded in 1872 and for many years was a popular tourist resort with the summer population quadrupling the size of the city. Traveling east, architectural wonders abound along Santa Monica Boulevard. Watch for the beautifully restored Mayfair Theater (1911), the 1924 Steele Building faced with white glazed brick, and further on, the old Cummings Buick showroom is now used to store and display stretch limousines. As you approach I-405, look for the Royal Theater.

   3.8 miles (C002) - Cross under the San Diego Freeway (I-405).
   4.7 miles (C003) - On the hilltop to the left is the Mormon Temple.
   5.8 miles - On the left can be seen the towers of Century City, covering the site of the old 20th Century Fox Studios.
   6.4 miles (C004) - At the corner of Wilshire and Santa Monica is Trader Vic's, an homage to a man's time spent in Polynesia.

BEVERLY HILLS AND HOLLYWOOD
In 1853, one small adobe house stood in the area now known as Beverly Hills and Hollywood. Originally named HOLLYWOODLAND by the wife of real-estate magnate Horace Wilcox in 1887, the new subdivision brought people to the area in large numbers, but it was still considered enough of a boondocks that a 1903 ordinance made it illegal to herd more than 2,000 sheep through town at one time.

A late spring snowstorm in Flagstaff, Arizona pushed Cecil B. DeMille further west, to Southern California where his vision of the future of motion pictures took root in Hollywood. The first motion picture studio began cranking out film at Sunset and Gower when the Nestor Company took over the old Blondeau Tavern and barn.

No trip to this area would be complete without a turn through the streets of Beverly Hills. Buy a "*Map to the Stars Homes*" and see where your favorite stars live or lived. This area developed rapidly as "the" place for movie people because of its proximity to the studios and the ocean.

   9.1 miles (C005) - Barney's Beanery, north side of the street. Serving great road food since 1920. Excellent burgers and "killer" chili.
   West Hollywood and the Formosa Cafe lie ahead. The Formosa is a favorite of the movie crowd. Don't be a Lucy.
   13.2 miles (C006) - Cross Highway 101 freeway.
   14.5 miles - Road curves to the left, stay in the right lane for another curve **(C007)** onto Sunset Boulevard.
   16.5 miles (C008) - A great, old sign atop Jensen's Recreation Building.

LOS ANGELES
A small native-American village named *Yang-na* was discovered by a group of missionaries and explorers under the leadership of Captain Gaspar de Portola in 1769, and was immediately re-named Porciuncula after an Italian chapel. In 1771, Franciscan Padres returned to the area and founded the Mission San Gabriel nine miles to the northeast of the original village. Ten years later, Don Felipe de Neve marched a band of settlers from Mexico and with a few soldiers from the mission founded El Pueblo de Nuestra Señora la Reina de Los Angeles de Porciuncula or The Town of Our Lady the Queen of Angels of Porciuncula.

Each of the founding families was given a plot of land facing the Plaza and for more than a century this was the center of

Santa Monica to Chicago

community life. By 1800, seventy families were busy raising grain and cattle in the town. The first English settler was "pirate" Joseph Chapman captured in 1818. Joseph (*later re-baptized as José*) was a skilled carpenter and erected a church building that faced the Plaza.

Following the Mexican War of 1846-47, California was seized by the United States and the small village became a hell-raising frontier town. Violence was so common the place took on the name Los Diablos (*the devils*). Finally, following a riot in Chinatown in 1871 where 19 Chinese were murdered, the town took stock of itself and decided to improve its image.

The railroad arrived in 1876 as the Southern Pacific pulled into town. In 1885, the Santa Fe reached Los Angeles and started a fare war that makes the airfare battles of today pale by comparison. Travel from Kansas City to Los Angeles started at $100, fell to a low of $5 and for one day, to $1.00! "Kansas City to Los Angeles for a dollar," proclaimed the Santa Fe handbills. he fare wars resulted in a two-year growth spurt that saw the city expand from twelve to fifty thousand people.

The year was 1891 and a single well drilled in the front yard of a home soon grew to more than 1,400 derricks pumping across the city. OIL! Black Gold was a new source of revenue for the growing city.

As the city grew, water became a major problem. In order to push through a multi-million dollar water bond, the city opened fire hydrants dumping water into the sewers and made lawn watering illegal. As the flora wilted under the California sun, a tired and fed-up electorate passed the bond issue. With bond money to burn, Los Angeles turned to the Owens River, 250 miles north, as the new water source for the growing city. With the Owens River water flowing south through siphons and pipelines to Los Angeles, the once green and fertile Owens Valley became, in the words of Will Rogers, "a valley of desolation."

World War Two brought a plethora of soldiers, sailors and marines to the Southland, who, with the end of the war, returned with their families to settle in the warm, sunny clime offered by Southern California. Where once orange groves flourished, homes took over. The neighborhood Mom-and-Pop stores were eclipsed by the strip mall and ultimately huge indoor shopping malls took over and became home to hordes of Valley Girls and Mallrats.

An excellent source of information regarding the various routes across Los Angles County can be found in Scott Piotrowski's book, *Finding the End of the Mother Road - Route 66 in Los Angeles County* (www.66productions.com).

LODGING: Lodging in the area is as wonderfully varied as you can imagine, following are a few of my personal choices. My favorite and home-away-from-home for those L.A. trips is the Argyle at 8358 Sunset Blvd just east of La Cienega (323.654.7100). A beautifully restored art-deco masterpiece (*it was formerly The St. James Club*) The Argyle is centrally located on the famed Sunset Strip with the rooms offering a commanding view of the city, and just a few doors east of The House of Blues. Another Strip hotel that is comfortable and well located is the Best Western Sunset Plaza at 8400 Sunset Blvd (323.654.0750). For a truly eclectic lodging experience nothing can match the Beverly Laurel at 8018 Beverly Blvd (213.651.2441). The rooms are very 50's decor in a well maintained fifties building. On the corner is Swingers Diner - great for a cup of coffee, a croissant and people watching. The Beverly Laurel can be reached from Santa Monica Blvd by going south on Fairfax to Beverly Blvd then a right - the hotel will be on your left. A nice chain property on Santa Monica Blvd is the Comfort Inn at 2815 Santa Monica Blvd (310.828.5517). These are just a few of the thousands of properties in the L.A. area.

DINING: As with lodging there are literally thousands of places to eat in L.A. A few of the more interesting and entertaining are: Pinks Hot Dog Stand - "The Hot Dog of the Stars" at 709 N. La Brea, you will be amazed at who you will see here, a Hollywood favorite since 1939; Another wonderful people watching place, particularly late at night is Barney's Beanery, 8447 Santa Monica Blvd - Great Chili and a multiple page menu that will drive you crazy; Ed Debevic's in Beverly Hills at 134 N. La Cienega a fun atmosphere with good "home-style" food. Be sure to order the small hot fudge sundae. What's not to like in a place with the motto, "Eat and Get Out"; and for that ultimate shake, malt, or burger and fries check out Mel's Drive-In at 8585 W. Sunset Blvd - yep, it's the same Mel's of San Francisco fame. Entertainment at its best with down-home cooking is a must at the House of Blues, 8430 W. Sunset Blvd. Great atmosphere, good food and top entertainment all at this funky place on Sunset. Upscale dining is not my forte, but I have found the *fenix* at the Argyle to be excellent. The French cuisine is superb at Le Dome - 8720 Sunset Blvd. For an interesting experience, in a formal atmosphere (including formal attire), the Russian food at Diaghilev is excellent, 1020 N. San Vicente Blvd. For star watching check out Dan Tana's at 9071 Santa Monica Blvd.

Now, back to the road.

Just past the 110 Freeway (Pasadena Fwy) at

17.8 miles (C009) - Make a left on Figueroa, then continue on Figueroa and enter the Pasadena Freeway.

Originally named The Arroyo Seco Parkway, the Pasadena Freeway opened on the 30th of December, 1940. The age of this freeway can be easily determined by noting the off-ramps that abruptly terminate following a rather hard right turn.

The freeways lend a strange air to travel in Southern California. For speeding Angeleno's, it is not uncommon for them to be unsure of where they are at any given point. Their vehicle insulates them from all but the mindless chatter of talk radio and the concrete stretching ahead, providing a sense of place to only two locations - where they entered the freeway and where they exit. Unless something unexpected happens to the car, forcing them off the freeway, everywhere between the above mentioned two points does not exist.

Santa Monica to Chicago

Continue on the freeway and notice Dodger Stadium on the left as you leave Los Angeles heading for Pasadena. Just before the I-5 interchange cross the Los Angeles River (*Yep, all that concrete is the river*).

Follow the Pasadena Freeway (I-110) into Pasadena where at

26.0 miles (C010) - It becomes Arroyo Boulevard.

27.2 miles (C011) - The historic Santa Fe depot can be seen off to the left, no longer used except for Metro-Link commuter service. This depot was used extensively in early films and by traveling movie stars. It was easier to arrange to shoot scenes here than at the Union Station in downtown Los Angeles, and it provided the movie stars a way to come into town without being mobbed at the station (advance word having been sent out that they were arriving in "Los Angeles").

PASADENA

This area was once part of the San Gabriel Mission, and as Rancho San Pasqual it was granted to an aged housekeeper by the Mission fathers in 1826. When she married, at age 99, the property passed from her hands to her husbands (*married women were not allowed to own property*) and was sold by her stepson in 1839 to two dons who abandoned it within a few years. (*Got that figured out?*)

The Governor granted the land in 1843 to a Mexican Army officer, Don Manuel Garfias. The land title was validated in 1854 and granted a patent by Abraham Lincoln in 1863. Garfias sold the land to Benjamin Wilson, whose name adorns a local mountain, canyon, lake, trail, avenue, and a school. The land was bartered and swapped many times between Wilson and his business associates and in 1873 4,000 acres of the land became the property of Dr. John S. Griffin.

The Winter of 1872 was a harsh one in Indiana and Dr. Thomas Elliot, with a group of friends, founded the California Colony of Indiana in order to get out where the "livin' was easy." Following the sale of the land the exodus of millionaires began. Many of the homes along Orange Grove Boulevard (west of Arroyo Parkway) are the result of the wealthy moving to Pasadena. Incorporated in 1886 and charted by the state in 1901, Pasadena was to become, by the end of the 1930s the richest per-capita city in the United States.

At the intersection of Arroyo and Colorado Boulevard, make a right and

ZERO ODOMETER

0.2 miles (C013) - The Pasadena Post Office is on the left. As you travel east on Colorado Boulevard, take note of the old architecture and magnificent churches that set Pasadena apart from the many design nightmares that typify the architecture of the Los Angeles Basin.

4.2 miles (C014) - Highway Host Motel - cool sign.

6.1 miles (C015) - Make a slight right turn onto Colorado Place and follow through a residential area. **DO NOT** make the left onto Colorado Blvd (**C016E**).

6.8 miles (C017) - Santa Anita Racetrack and a "Y" intersection. Make a left onto Huntington Drive.

7.6 miles (C018) - Railroad overpass.

7.7 miles - Arcadia - The Derby Restaurant on the left is named for the Horse Racing Derby and not the famed Brown Derby of Hollywood fame.

8.0 miles (C020) - Cross under I-210.

8.6 miles (C021) - The Pottery Ranch, here since the 1940s.

Along here are Monrovia and Duarte. Monrovia was platted in 1886 by W. N. Monroe and lots were sold for $100 each. A far cry from today's selling price. Duarte was named for Andres Duarte, the grantee of 4,000 acres of land on this site. He also built a ditch to bring water from San Gabriel Canyon for irrigation of the nearby fields.

11.6 miles (C022) - Intersection with I-605.

10.2 miles (C023) - Original site of the Trails Restaurant.

12.6 miles (C024) - The San Gabriel River. Cross the bridge and the road becomes Foothill Boulevard.

14.1 miles (C025) - Cross under railroad tracks.

AZUSA

The town that used to brag about having everything from "A to Z in the USA." Founded in 1887 during the land boom period and named for an Indian village, *Asukag-na,* once on this site.

15.0 miles (C026) - The Foothill Drive-in Theater. At this writing its future is uncertain, let's hope it remains as one of the last of the truly great drive-ins.

GLENDORA

Founded in 1887 by George Whitcomb who named the town after his wife by combining "glen" and her name "Ledora" into one. Many classic motels along this stretch of the road.

18.3 miles (C027) - On the left the Golden Spur Restaurant. Has operated continuously for more than seventy years. Originally opened as a hamburger stand to serve the local horseback population.

18.8 miles (C028) - Railroad over-crossing

20.2 miles (C029) - San Dimas and the Pinnacle Peak Steak House - be warned, the walls are festooned with neckties, evidence of the "dudes" who entered without first removing their neck appendage.

21.6 miles (C030) - Cross under the freeway.

LA VERNE

Originally named Lordsburg during the land boom of the 1890s. A hotel was built during the land-boom and when the rush died off the town was stuck with the huge white-elephant of a building. New settlers were brought to the area in 1891 by the Santa Fe, and an arriving group of Dunkards (a religious sect) purchased the hotel and renamed it Lordsburg College. When the town name was changed, so was the college, becoming La Verne College.

23.0 miles (C031) - Intersection with La Verne's D Street. One mile south is the 1930s downtown strip that will take you back to a simpler time in our history.

23.9 miles (C032) - On the left is the La Paloma Restaurant, a local favorite for many years. Originally known as Wilson's.

25.8 miles (C033) - On the left is Griswold's Old School House - shopping, dining, etc. on left.

CLAREMONT

Known as the home of the Claremont Colleges, a group of seven colleges located in beautifully preserved settings. Just east as you pass through Upland, you will be on a 1931 section of Route 66 designed with a grass median and eucalyptus trees. After having traveled across hundreds of miles of desert, the westbound Roadie found this to be a welcome respite.

31.2 miles (C034) - Intersection of Euclid and Foothill. A monument to Pioneer women is on the north side. South of here in Ontario was the site of the 4th of July Annual All-States Picnic. People would gather in the large, park-like median of Euclid Avenue under banners for each state of the union and celebrate "old home" times.

31.4 miles (C035) - The Sycamore Inn, built in 1848 as a Butterfield Stage Stop. Check out the Bear Gulch monument on the grounds.

31.6 miles (C036) - Cross under railroad tracks.

32.1 miles (C037) - Intersection with Vineyard. On the northeast corner the former Thomas Winery, now the site of shops and restaurants. On the southwest corner is the 1928 Klusman House (*during the Fall of 2002 - it appears as if it may be targeted for demolition*).

33.2 miles (C038) - Archibald Ave. and the former site of a classic 1920's-style gas station on the northwest corner. Next door was the original Dolly's Diner.

34.2 miles (C039) - The former Virginia Dare Winery. Not restored, but resurrected, as an office and store complex.

36.7 miles (C040) - Cross under I-15 freeway.

39.7 miles (C041) - The Redwing Motel.

40.4 miles (C042) - On the right, the former Bono's Restaurant and Deli, a Route 66 and Foothill Blvd landmark since 1936, closed in 1999 (*rumors abound that it may be re-opening*).

43.2 miles (C043) - The Moana Motel, a nicely maintained motel of the 1950s.

46.2 miles (C044) - At the intersection with Riverside, on the southeast corner, take note of the mosaic on the front of the Washington Mutual building (SE corner) and

ZERO ODOMETER

1.2 miles (C045) - The Wigwam Motel - opened in 1950 the Wigwam was one of those places where the kids always begged Dad to pull in the Roadmaster for the night. Today's business at the Wigwam is not suited to the average Route 66 traveler - so hold out for the Wigwam in Holbrook, Arizona.

SAN BERNARDINO

Named by a group of soldiers, Indians, and missionaries from the San Gabriel Mission to the west. The group entered the valley on May 20th, 1810 - the feast day of San Bernardino de Siena. Rancho San Bernardino was purchased by a group of Mormons for $77,000 in 1852, and they proceeded to lay the city out along the lines of Salt Lake City, Utah. The Mormons remained a strong influence until they were recalled to Salt Lake City by Brigham Young in 1857. San Bernardino is the site of the largest railroad switching center and junction west of Chicago and was the home of the original McDonald's Drive-in at 699 2nd Street (founded by the McDonald brothers).

From here west stretched miles and miles of orange and lemon groves along Route 66. This was the first citrus fruit to be seen by the Dust Bowl refugees and with the magnificent mountains rising to the north and the clear blue skies of more than sixty plus years ago it must have been a breathtaking sight.

2.3 miles (C046) - The road will curve to the left and become 5th Street.

3.3 miles (C047) - Make a left onto Mt. Vernon Ave. Continue north on Mt. Vernon noting the older motels and cafes that indicate this was once a major route through the city.

5.1 miles (C048) - Go straight ahead, the road will then curve to the left under the freeway **(C050)** and become Cajon Blvd.

6.8 miles (C051) - Two older (closed) motels on the left. One is the Palms, the other is the El Cajon.

11.5 miles (C052) - Cross under railroad tracks.

11.7 miles (C053) - Curve to the left.

13.1 miles (C056) - Town of Devore and the northbound on-ramp to the freeway. Straight ahead and on the left is a bar and café where Route 66 dead-ends **(C055)**. Make a gentle right **(C054)** and cross over the freeway. Take the on-ramp to I-215 north and continue north to join I-15 (*less than 1/2 mile*).

MOVE TO THE RIGHT-HAND LANE AS QUICKLY AS POSSIBLE

15.0 Miles (C057) - Take Kenwood Ave. exit, exit 124, turn left and cross under the freeway. West of the freeway, a left at the intersection **(C059)** will take you on a short section (0.7 miles) of the old highway that ends at the freeway **(C058)** with a fence line preventing access.

To continue north on old Route 66, turn right at the intersection and

ZERO ODOMETER

This was known as Upper Cajon Boulevard.

0.3 miles (C060) - Old garage on right.

2.0 miles (C061) - Intersection to the left.

3.6 miles (C062) - Rock wall along left side of roadway, an early rest stop.

3.9 miles (C063) - Intersection to right. Road is closed.

4.5 miles (C064) - Intersection to the left. At this site, behind the boulders, was one of the Federal Highway Camps established to provide the road weary Dust Bowl Survivors with a safe haven, away from Californians who had developed a habit of vandalizing the campsites and parking places of the west-bound travelers.

4.7 miles (C065) - Cross over to the west side of the divided highway. The section to the east was actually the original highway, before the four-lane was put in.

5.7 miles (C066) - End of divided highway.

6.0 miles - Sign on the railroad right-of-way (*to the left*) for Cajon.

6.2 miles (C067) - A great old bridge.

6.4 miles (C068) - If you enjoy watching trains in action, make a left and follow the old highway north for a short distance (*0.4 miles*). This is a great area to stop and watch trains pulling the hill through the Cajon Pass. You'll most likely see many rail-buffs with both still and video cameras along here.

SAFETY NOTE: Be extremely cautious near the tracks - trains coming down the canyon are using dynamic braking and in many cases cannot be heard until they are nearly on you.

6.6 miles - When you are ready to continue north, rejoin the freeway here - the Cleghorn Road exit **(C069)** - and continue the climb. The road up the remainder of the pass is nothing like the old days of two-lane road that taxed a car's cooling system and a driver's nerves, but it is still one heck of climb as evidenced by the the trucks laboring heavily in the far right lanes.

12.7 miles - Hungry? At the top of the pass take the Oak Hill Road exit, exit 138 **(C070)**, make a right and follow the road around to the Summit Inn. This cafe is like a step back in time. Try the Hillbilly Burger for a real treat in a classic Roadie Café atmosphere.

Back on I-15, continue on to Victorville. The original road is under the southbound lanes all the way from the Cajon Summit to Palmdale Road in Victorville (*11.5 miles*).

At Palmdale Road **(C071)**, exit the Interstate.

VICTORVILLE

Originally named Mormon Crossing from 1878 to 1885, it was first changed to Victor, and later Victorville. The town was a rip-roaring mining camp until 1900 when the mines played out. The town left its false-front buildings standing and by 1914 the Wild West look had attracted the Hollywood crowd, who, between 1914 and 1937 made over two hundred films in Victorville and the surrounding area. The California Route 66 Museum is located on D Street in the downtown area.

To travel Route 66 through Victorville take 18 West/Palmdale Road, exit 150, east from I-15 and follow it through town to D Street **(C072)**. Make a left onto D Street and it will cross under the freeway and then become the National Old Trails Highway (*name of the road before Route 66 was designated*). As you cross the Mojave River on a classic old bridge **(C073)**,

ZERO ODOMETER

0.8 miles (C074) - Cross under high-tension lines.

2.0 miles (C075) - Antique Station building with a huge collection of old signs on the walls.
2.6 miles (C076) - Oro Grande, first settled as a gold mining town, then limestone replaced gold as the ore of choice in the 1880s and today the huge Riverside Cement Company plant is the mainstay of the town.
2.9 miles (C077) - Cross under railroad.
3.2 miles - A small canyon area with cement plants.
4.3 miles (C078) - On the left, the Lost Hawg Saloon.
8.4 miles (C079) - Left side of road, cabins, store and gas station, all closed.
9.4 miles - Left side of road, closed cafe/gas station.
9.5 miles - Right side of road, gas station, closed.
10.7 miles (C080) - Right side of road, gas station, closed.
11.7 miles (C081) - Intersection with Silver Lakes Road.
12.1 miles (C082) - Formerly Helendale. Old gas station and store on the right and the railroad marker for Helendale can be seen alongside the tracks.
16.1 miles (C083) - Intersection with Indian Trail.
24.9 miles (C084) - Right side, Dunes, old motel.
27.3 miles (C085) - The remains of the old Lenwood Drive-in Theatre.
28.4 miles (C086) - Right side, an interesting looking building with houses (apartments) that match it to the south. This may have been the old Radio Court motel.
29.8 miles (C087) - Hwy 58 over-crossing.

BARSTOW

Named in 1886 for the then President of the Santa Fe Railroad, William Barstow Strong. The site was unofficially called Waterman Junction following the silver strike of 1881. The Santa Fe had originally planned to build their division point in Daggett (*about five miles east*), but word leaked out and land prices skyrocketed. The Santa Fe then moved to Waterman Junction along the Mojave River and Barstow was born. By the time the name had been chosen, the townsite had hotels, churches and more than enough saloons.

Barstow owes much of its history to the railroads, and the appreciation of that history can be seen at the Barstow Station. Designed after a railroad depot, Barstow Station houses one of the most unique McDonald's I have ever seen. Once served you take your tray load of Big Macs, fries and shakes into a converted passenger car to eat. Barstow Station also houses a series of gift shops with more than enough temptations for any tourist.

Following the advent of the motorcar, Barstow continued to be a central point for travelers and with the arrival of Route 66, it became an important stopping place for road-weary warriors of the Mother Road. Main Street is lined with motels and as you drive from the west end of town to the east the age of the motels becomes quite evident - not so much through disrepair or neglect, but through the architecture.

At 112 E. Main St is the El Rancho Barstow, a classic motel of the old school. The huge neon sign is supported by a pair of twin towers, and that alone takes you back to days gone by. The El Rancho is unique in one other respect - the buildings were constructed in 1944 using railroad ties from the defunct Tonopah and Tidewater railroad, a narrow gauge that ran from Beatty, Nevada to Ludlow, California. Unfortunately, the motel has not been well maintained and cannot be recommended.

Also in Barstow is the beautifully restored Santa Fe Depot and Harvey House, Casa de Desierto. To see this wonder, turn north on First Street to cross over the Santa Fe yard. The depot is on your right. There is also the Barstow Route 66 Museum located in the old depot building.

Barstow is working hard at becoming a Route 66 revival town and in time will succeed, but for now there is really no place I can recommend for lodging (*maybe the Holiday Inn or the Ramada - on a good day - but they are, in my opinion, way overpriced*). The majority of the older motels have not been well maintained and many accept weekly/monthly tenets - a sure sign of a place you do not want to stay. Best bet, call ahead to Ludlow and make reservations at the Ludlow Motel (see below). Reservations must be made, and the keys picked up, at the Chevron Station in Ludlow. Call 760.733.4338.

Leaving Barstow, pass under the freeway on the east end of town and make an immediate left at Main Street **(C089)**. It will be necessary to enter the Interstate ahead, but before doing so, take note of the Greystone Cafe and Bar **(C090)** about half a mile from the turn. You can still see the old stone motel cabins in the rear of the place.

Enter I-40 **(C091)** and stay on the interstate to the Nebo off-ramp, Exit 5, **(C092)**. Take the off-ramp and make a left at the bottom. Follow the road north. On the left will be a road entering the Marine Base, this is old Route 66 - confiscated by the Marines in 1968, this 2.4 mile section is now closed to the public (*you can travel it only as far the gate to the Marine installation*). The road makes a right **(C093)** just past the old road and then follows a series of dips (*whee!*) into Daggett about two miles ahead.

DAGGETT

Santa Monica to Chicago

Originally known as Calico Station, the town became Daggett, in honor of the Lt. Governor of the State, when that designation was submitted to the Post Office in 1883. Once a thriving smelter and Borax stamp mill town for the many mines in the area as well as a terminus for the famous Twenty-Mule Teams from Death Valley, life has now slowed for Daggett. At the intersection, on the southwest corner stands a curved roof building that was once Mrs. Millers Cafe that, in the 1930s, sported a sign proclaiming "All you can Eat!"

To the left and across the tracks can be seen the old Stone Hotel, hopefully to be restored by the San Bernardino County Museum board. This building was formerly known as the Daggett Railroad Eating House.

At the stop sign in Daggett **(C094)**,
ZERO ODOMETER

2.5 miles (C095) - The open area on the left with the tower in the center was part of the California Edison Solar One facility. This was a solar/thermal power plant. The area around the tower once contained hundreds of huge mirrors aligned to point at the large tower. The tower would absorb the heat reflected from the mirrors to superheat a molten salt solution (*a combination of sodium nitrate and potassium nitrate*) used to drive a series of steam turbines to produce power. When this facility was in operation, the large, black tower in the center would glow white-hot. The black on the tower is burned surface from the intense heat. It was a successful experiment, but the continuing availability of cheaper fossil fuels closed it down.

5.4 miles (C096) - The old agricultural inspection station is on the left (*now a private garage*). It was here vehicles entering California had to stop and open all luggage, boxes and whatever else was being carried. It was also here the Joads ("*The Grapes of Wrath*") convinced the officers that grandma was ill and had to be rushed to a doctor, when in fact she was dead.

NEWBERRY SPRINGS

Newberry Springs was once called Water, a simple, but important name in the arid desert. The springs emerged from beneath the black sides of the mountain to quench the thirst of all who happened by. The railroad loaded tanks cars here and hauled the water to the tank at Bagdad for the steam engines.

14.5 miles (C097) - The Bagdad Cafe. This is the location used in the movie, *Bagdad Café*. Good food and friendly atmosphere (*beware of "General" Bob*).
14.7 miles (C098) - Dry Creek Station.
15.5 miles - Old Whiting Bros. Station.
25.8 miles (C099) - Hector Road freeway entrance.
26.3 miles (C100) - Rest area turnout on the right.
27.5 miles (C101) - A maze of high-tension lines cross the highway.
29.0 miles (C102) - Intersection with Pisgah Crater Road.
32.7 miles (C103) - Cross railroad tracks.
35.7 miles - Cross I-40 at Lavic Road **(C104)** and make a right **(C105)** on the frontage road. This section of road from here to Ludlow is not Old 66, it was a service road before the advent of I-40. Old 66 is actually under I-40.
36.6miles - Road surface a little rough (like hell, it's miserable!).
42.6 miles (C106) - Make a right on Cucero Road, cross under freeway and enter

LUDLOW

At the intersection - to leave town - make a left **(C107)** and continue east.

This is where Route 66 meets the Interstate and the place is usually jumping with traffic, at least at the west end of town, where the Chevron station provides an opportunity to re-fuel the Family Truckster, as well as its occupants, provided they want nothing more than a nitrite-charged tube-steak and a Coke. However, across the road is the Ludlow Café, featuring good service and good food, and just to the west is the Ludlow Motel, a small, but extremely clean place (*See the people at the Chevron Station for keys and payment for the motel. Call ahead for reservations at 760.733.4338*). This is a great little motel located in the middle of the Mojave, providing that great desert atmosphere, the sound of trucks on the highway and trains rumbling through what is left of the town.

The east end of town sits quietly, watching the traffic race by on the Interstate and on 66. The old Ludlow Cafe has been effectively vandalized over the years, but still had a enough life in it to serve as a set for the movie *Kalifornia*. It was here that Brad Pitt, as Early Grace, who after murdering a gas station attendant (*at Amboy*), terrorized David Duchovny (Fox *Mulder of "X-Files" fame*), Michelle Forbes, and Julliette Lewis who played Pitt's child-like wife.

Ludlow was once a boomtown. Two narrow gauge railroads served Ludlow from Death Valley where ore was off-loaded into cars of the Santa Fe. Down by the tracks a large building constructed in 1909 once housed the Ludlow Mercantile Company (*the Murphy Bros. were the second owners*), the building has seen the ravages of earthquakes over the past few years and is in danger of collapse. Over the past few years more and more of Ludlow has disappeared to fire and bulldozer, turning it into a scar on the desert with fewer and fewer of the vestiges of the once bustling community.

Santa Monica to Chicago

About two miles east on old 66, as you cross the railroad tracks **(C108)**,
ZERO ODOMETER

From here east the land is quite barren, with the road following the lay of the land. At various places remnants of the old alignment can be seen on either side of the road.

Along this section your maps may show the "communities" of Haynes, Siberia and Klondike. These were names given to equipment locations by the railroad. You have to admit, naming a place in the desert "Klondike" or "Siberia" showed a great sense of humor on someone's part.

10.9 miles (C109) - On the north side can be seen the lone surviving building of Siberia. If you choose to visit, please do not vandalize anymore than has already be done and respect the railroad right-of-way. This was once the site of a few Mom and Pop Cafes and Motor Courts during the 1940s. Originally a water stop for the AT&SF (*now the BNSF*).

18.1 miles (C110) - Bagdad

Amazing! There is nothing left of this once bustling town. There are now only acres of earth scrapped to the bone with one lone tree providing the only clue to the location of Bagdad.

This was once the rail center for the War Eagle and Orange Blossom gold mines located to the north. From 1875 to 1910, huge wagonloads of ore were hauled to Bagdad for transport on the railroad. From 1889 to 1923, the town had saloons, churches, hotels, a school, a Harvey House Restaurant and a Post Office.

Although barren today, memories of the long gone Bagdad Cafe linger on. The movie of the same name was filmed in Newberry Springs, but the essence of the original Bagdad Cafe came through. People from all across the desert would journey to Alice Lawrence's Bagdad Cafe to enjoy an ever-changing tableau of characters provided by the highway, and the only dance floor and juke box for miles in either direction.

The wind, heat, and the lack of water (*Bagdad went from July 1912 to November 1914 without a drop of rain*), combined with the actions of vandals destroyed many of the town's buildings. In 1991, the entire area was scraped clean to be used as a storage facility for a natural gas pipeline running between Bakersfield and Topock.

25.6 miles - Intersection with the road south to Twenty-nine Palms.

26.2 miles (C111) - AMBOY

There used to be two gas stations in Amboy, one on either side of the highway. It didn't mater which one you stopped at, they both charged a high price for gas - up to 49¢ a gallon when the rest of the country was selling at 19¢! Today, the station on the south side of the highway is just memory, but across the highway Roy's Motel, the café, and the gas pumps are the life of Amboy. The motel, a holdover from the 1940s consists of small white cabins equipped with that desert necessity, the swamp cooler. Over the past few years I have received many complaints about Amboy and the actions of the management of the café and motel. I experienced that attitude personally in 2001 and again in 2002 and for that reason suggest only a quick stop to take photos and then move on. Normally, I would suggest buying a meal or a souvenir T-shirt, but the management even gets upset if you want a hamburger, so just don't bother. You may recognize Amboy from hundreds of commercials and ads, which is why they don't care too much for the visiting Roadie - they make thousands off of film companies.

36.1 miles (C112) - The abandoned Roadrunners Retreat Restaurant and gas station. The buildings are of 1960's vintage and at times appear brand new, complete with a stretch of freshly lined asphalt out front. The sprucing up is the result of movie and advertising companies using this site for films and commercials.

37.6 miles (C113) - Chambless. A small desert village that shares it's post office with Cadiz (three miles south). At the east end of Chambless, at Cadiz road,
ZERO ODOMETER

4.2 miles (C114) - Abandoned building and station. This was the community of Summit where gas, food and small cabins were provided. Today, it is the site of the most graffitied building I have ever seen.

11.5 miles (C115) - Remains of the Danby Store and Gas Station.

11.7 miles (C116) - Danby Road intersection.

16.6 miles - Abandoned house on left.

20.8 miles (C117) - Essex. Named by the Santa Fe for no particular reason, well, that's not exactly true. The Santa Fe originally named the water stops and stations in strict alphabetical sequence starting at Amboy. The stops towards Needles were Amboy, Bristol, Cadiz, Danby, Edson, Fenner, Goffs, Homer, Ibis (Ibex) and Java. As the Santa Fe expanded and added more passing tracks, the alphabetical sequence fell apart with the additions of Bannock between Homer and Ibis, Klinefelter between Ibis and Java, and Hartoum between Java and Needles. Over the years, Edson became Essex and Bristol became Bengal.

In 1977, Essex gained fifteen minutes of fame when the town's 35 residents wrote the *Los Angeles Times* claiming to be the only town in America without television. The entire population was invited to the Johnny Carson Show, and a manufacturer in Pennsylvania, who saw the show, donated the translator equipment that brought television to Essex.

23.0 miles (C118) - Junction of Goffs Road and the National Old Trails Highway.
ZERO ODOMETER

Santa Monica to Chicago

From this point there are two routes into Needles. Follow **OPTION TWO** to Goffs to see the original routing of Route 66 or continue on **OPTION ONE** for the 1931 alignment, which will dump you onto I-40 for the final run into Needles.

Both routings will be covered.

First the 1931 alignment:
OPTION ONE - ESSEX - MOUNTAIN SPRINGS ROAD - NEEDLES

0.2 miles - Cross railroad.

6.8 miles - Quarry on the right.

9.8 miles - Turnout for another of the 1958 vintage rest stops.

12.0 miles (C119) - Mountain Springs Road ramp onto I-40. At the top of this hill, was the site of a gas station, cafe and a few tourist cabins. A large cross was erected on the hillside with the sole purpose of getting people to stop and perhaps buy something. This is also the summit of the climb out of Needles for westbound traffic - this location is at an elevation of 2770 feet, nearly 2300 feet higher than the elevation at Needles.

As you descend, notice the traffic pulling the hill westbound. Imagine what it was like for the Dust Bowl refugees pulling this grade in their tired trucks and cars loaded with all of their worldly belongings. Now, add to that vision the fact this was a two-lane road full of trucks, busses and cars.

16.5 miles - Water Road. Power lines from Hoover Dam (*Boulder Dam for us die hard Democrats*) cross the highway here. There used to be housing for power line workers at this location. The eastbound on-ramp is a favorite place for the CHP to use their radar - **WATCH YOUR DOWNHILL SPEED!**

19.7 miles - Off to the left Goffs can be seen in the distance.

21.6 miles - South Pass. Used to be a gas station here - devoured by the Interstate.

23.5 miles - Another steep section of highway, notice westbound trucks struggling to pull the grade.

36.5 miles - Exit I-40 for Needles (exit 139).

PART TWO - ESSEX - GOFFS - NEEDLES

Make certain odometer is zeroed as you make the left turn from National Old Trails Highway onto Goffs Road **(C118)**.

The run from here to Goffs may seem like miles and miles of nothing, but consider the fact that the road is not crowded and the desert has a beauty all of its own. Look for long freight trains along here, both moving and stopped waiting for traffic in the opposite direction.

4.7 miles (C120) - Cross under I-40

5.3 miles (C121) - Fenner and the Oasis. Nice rest stop, decent food, friendly service.

15.4 miles (C122) - **GOFFS**.

When Route 66 was dedicated in 1926, Goffs was there to serve the transcontinental motorist. Goffs was established in 1883 as a siding at the "Top of the Hill" for the Southern Pacific Railway. In 1893, the Nevada Southern built a short line into Goffs from the north. A school was proposed in 1911 to serve the railroad employees, and classes began in a rented building. In 1914, the Goffs School was dedicated. With the advent of diesel engines the Goffs site as a water-stop for trains came to a close and it was the new highway, Route 66, that kept the town going. In December 1931, the new alignment, eight miles shorter, opened and Goffs began its decline. The school closed in 1937. WW-II brought 10,000 soldiers to the area for desert training, but by then there were no businesses to serve them, forcing the schoolhouse into service as a makeshift cafe.

Today, the Friends of the Mojave Road have restored the schoolhouse and additional buildings have been moved to the area for restoration. They are open the first weekend of each month except for July, August and September.

If you have any old highway maps with you, they may indicate various places along the stretch of road from here to Needles. Places you cannot find - Bannock, Klinefelter, Ibis and Piute are a few of the names. These were never towns, or even villages, they were locations named by the railroad for equipment sheds, signal boxes and water towers. Some of the names were those of Santa Fe employees.

23.0 miles (C123) - Here is the location of one of the "towns" mentioned above. Look to the left and a sign by the tracks has "HOMER" printed on it. No store, no gas station, no motel, no zip code - that's Homer, California (*D'OH!*).

27.2 miles (C124) - Bannock - another railroad siding.

29.6 miles (C125) - Make a right onto Hwy 95. This was the site of Arrowhead Junction, a gas station, store and cafe. The location was named Arrowhead Junction because the road to Salt Lake City (today's Hwy 95) was known as The Arrowhead Trail in the 1920s.

33.4 miles (C126) - Not a happy spot. Nothing to see here, but it's mentioned because it is the location where comedian Sam Kinison was killed on April 10, 1992. He was killed by a drunken seventeen-year-old driving a pick-up on the wrong side of the road. Sam was 38 and had been married for less than a week.

34.6 miles (C127) - According to old railroad maps (*and certain high quality Route 66 maps!*) this was the site of Klinefelter, all that remains are some really old palm trees.

35.9 miles (C128) - On the left can be seen (over the dune) an early alignment of 66 (not recommended for travel).
36.2 miles (C129) - Enter I-40 eastbound and continue to Needles.
42.3 miles (C130) - Exit I-40 at River Road.
42.9 miles (C131) - Make a right onto Old Trails Highway.
44.2 miles (C132) - Make a right onto the Needles Highway (*shown on older maps as River Road*).
45.0 miles (C133) - Cross over I-40 and enter.

NEEDLES

Named by a soldier at old Fort Mojave for a group of pointy spires that jut from the Black Mountains of Arizona, visible to the south and east of town.

The city was founded in 1883 with the coming of the railroad and for years the Santa Fe was the principle employer of the city. The town Plaza, between G and H Streets is a virtual oasis in the center of the city with palms, pepper, Palo Verde and tamarind trees providing a spot of much needed shade for the desert community.

The east side of the Plaza is fronted by the deserted El Garces, formerly the Santa Fe Depot and Harvey House. The El Garces is in line for restoration and with luck another beautiful example of the famed Harvey House's will be available for tours.

Entering Needles from the west, you will pass a series of 1950's era motels - The El Rancho, The River Valley Lodge, The Best, and The Diamond Motel. The California Country Kitchen is a great dining stop. Unfortunately, most of the older motels have not been well maintained and some will not honor confirmed reservations (*the River Valley Lodge is one example*) preferring to deal with the weekly stay crowd. Best places to stay are the chain motels and my favorite is the Best Western Colorado River Inn.

Follow Needles Highway under the freeway 2 blocks to the intersection with Broadway **(C134)**. Make a right onto Broadway and pass the Sage and Western motels, a pair from the heyday of Route 66. Broadway becomes an overpass to bridge the railroad. At the base of the overpass on the other side, make a left onto K Street **(C135)**, then a right onto Front Street **(C136)**. Stay on Front Street - the small park just past the railroad underpass (on the left) was where some of the opening scenes of *Two lane Blacktop* were filmed. Make a right on G Street, one block, then left, then a left on F Street, followed by a right on Front Street to go around the El Garces Hotel. (These turns are collectively shown on the map as waypoint **(C137)**.)

Follow Front Street to Broadway **(C138)**, then Broadway out of town.

At the I-40 underpass **(C139)**,

ZERO ODOMETER
4.1 miles (C140) - Left onto Five Mile Road (National Old Trails).
5.7 miles (C141) - Right onto I-40 and continue on Interstate to Park Moabi exit (exit 153).

There are sections of the old highway scattered around the desert, but so much of the area suffers from major washouts caused by thunderstorms it is best to explore only if you have a high-clearance four-wheel drive vehicle.

ADVENTURE TOUR
Please read all admonitions regarding Adventure Tours at front of the book.

CAUTION: If the weather has been raining, or threatening rain DO NOT attempt this tour. Flash floods and washouts will make portions of this virtually impassable.

Just before entering I-40 at the Five Mile Road interchange **(C141)**, at the 5.7 mile point **(ATC01)** is the first opportunity for an Adventure Tour. At the turnout (**ZERO ODOMETER**) on the south side of the road, make a right and follow the dirt road east, then south (it's a curve to the right). This was the National Old Trails Road. At 0.2 miles **(ATC02)** pavement will be encountered. **WATCH YOUR SPEED**, the pavement is very rough and missing in places. **Approximately 2.2 miles (ATC03)** a severe washout. Go to the right to get around it - **DO NOT** drive too close to the washout - it may be undercut.

2.7 miles (ATC04) - Pavement disappears, but will reappear within a quarter of a mile.
4.0 miles - Road is atop a ridgeline.
4.3 miles (ATC06) - Road ends with an overlook of I-40. Notice the great old inlaid rock gutters along the north side of the road along here.

At this point you can return the way you came back to I-40, or if you have a four-wheel drive vehicle and really want an adventure, return about a quarter of a mile and notice the road (dirt) angling off to the south and down **(ATC05)**. Real down! Turn onto this road and, in four-wheel drive, carefully descend the hill (watch for large rocks, washouts and sand). At the bottom **(ATC07)** follow the road to the left through the sandy wash and under I-40.

Santa Monica to Chicago

> **(ATC08)**. After crossing under the Interstate, the road will fork, take the left fork and follow it up onto the pavement. This is the end section of the 1947 alignment of 66 **(C147)**. Follow this road under the railroad tracks, to Park Moabi Road **(C143)**. From here it is possible to follow the road to the old bridge as outlined below, or make a right and go to I-40 eastbound into Arizona.

Heading out of Needles east on I-40 the next opportunity to drive an old section of highway presents itself at the Park Moabi exit **(C142)**. At this exit make a left, cross the Interstate and follow the road down the hill. At the bottom of the hill:
ZERO ODOMETER
And make a right onto the Old Trails Highway **(C143)**.
  1.7 miles - The road ends **(C145)** at the site of the two old bridges across the Colorado. Wait a second - wait a second, I only see one bridge! More about that in a moment.
  The road you just traveled is the 1947 alignment of Route 66. Near the end of the road there is a jog to the right. The highway used to go straight at this point across the Red Rock Bridge **(C144)** into Arizona. The bridge had originally been used by the Santa Fe, but, in 1947, the railroad opened a new bridge, 500 feet upstream, (*yep, there it is on the other side of the Interstate*), as part of a project to double-track and straighten their roadbed and the Red Rock Bridge was abandoned.
  By 1947, the bridge and the old railroad alignment had been donated to Arizona and California, giving Route 66 a new alignment, along the old Santa Fe roadbed. This eliminated the terrible curves and grades motorists had fought since 1916.
  With the opening of I-40, the old bridge was abandoned and then dismantled in 1966 and 1967. The only remains of the Red Rock Bridge are a couple of concrete foundation anchors on the westside of the River. (*The bridge is shown for reference on certain high quality Route 66 maps*).
  The Old Trails Bridge **(C146)**, now a historic landmark and well cared for by PG&E, was, at the time of its opening, the longest three-hinged arch bridge in the country. The bridge was long and narrow, with a hard right turn as you entered California. It was wide enough for cars, but trucks and busses had to cross one at a time.
  As you explore this area where the fictional Joad Family and thousands of others crossed into the promised land of California, there are many memories of the road that once served the traveler. The rock-framed sign with "*Historic Route 66 - Welcome - Turn Right Next Exit*" painted on it was constructed for eastbound traffic on the 1947 alignment and has been re-painted to catch the eye of travelers on I-40.
  Off to the right are remnants of the old highway as it wound along the cliff face and headed up the hill. Walk along this section of road and you will see the laminated board guardrail. Stand here and visualize the tremendous amount of traffic this narrow piece of asphalt once carried. A short walk brings you to a gate and a fence across the road, the old bridge can be seen ahead, around the curve of the hillside.
  The old highway crossed the river, twisted its way along the cliff face, then climbed the hill where the gas compressor station sites. In the early days of Route 66, there was a place called the Teapot Dome on top of the hill. It was a gas station and cafe, supposedly named Teapot Dome because by the time cars made the climb they were "boiling like a teapot." The building had a large teapot mounted on the roof to go along with the name. The old highway then proceeded toward Needles on a route that roughly parallels the 1947 alignment, only on top of the cliff.
  Drive back the way you came and when you reach the intersection with the Moabi Park Road **(C143)**, continue straight (north). A sign warns, "Not a Through Road" - the sign is correct, it will be necessary to return to this point. At the intersection:
ZERO ODOMETER
  1.1 miles (C147) - A severe washout of the pavement here. Road is blocked by large rocks. A dirt road across the washout is to the left. Sandy crossing, not recommended for the average sedan.
  1.5 miles (C148) - You are at the fence line along the freeway, most likely having walked there. From here, the original routing continued straight across what is now the freeway right-of-way and up the hill (*a portion of the pavement can still be seen on the cliff above - see Adventure Tour above*). The curve you are standing on was the 1947 alignment that curved to the right and is now buried beneath the Interstate.
  Return to Park Moabi Road **(C143)**, then up the hill and re-enter I-40 eastbound.
  Crossing the river, California, the first of the eight Route 66 States is behind us, and ahead lies Arizona where the road will eventually reach over 7,000 feet as it winds through ponderosa pine forests.
  Back to the car, the Road awaits.

Santa Monica to Chicago

ARIZONA

EASTBOUND

Arizona beckons with Route 66 rising from an elevation of 505 feet at the Colorado River to over 7,000 feet near Flagstaff. Ahead lies the longest remaining stretch of Old Route 66 left in the country. For the next 170 miles, you will experience Route 66 as it was in the days of the Dust Bowl refugees. Beyond that, we will follow the various alignments of the road as it traverses the high country of northern Arizona.

Take the first I-40 exit (Topock) **(A001)** in Arizona and at the top of the ramp make a left, cross I-40 and make another left and:
ZERO ODOMETER
   0.4 miles - Follow the road to the right under the railroad.
   0.8 miles (A002) -

TOPOCK
   A place with more names than can be imagined. Originally called Needles by Lt. Whipple, the name was changed with the arrival of the railroad in 1883. The railroad brought the need for a post office and with the California town of Needles just a few miles upstream the people of Needles, Arizona decided to change the name to Powell. The post office closed in 1887 and other names for the town came into popular use; Red Rock and Red Rock Crossing being the most popular. In 1903, a new post office and a new name, Mellen, after Colorado Steamboat captain, Jack Mellen. The various permutations of Red Rock would not work as there was already a dearth of Red Rocks in the Territory. In 1909, the post office closed once again and it was 1915 before a population surge demanded another post office. Mellen became a problem (due to the hasty scrawl of telegraph operators) when it was confused with Needles. The railroad had called the place Topock and that was the name that stuck. The name is a contraction of the Navajo *a-ha-to-pak*, meaning water-bridge.
   5.0 miles (A003) - Intersection in Golden Shores, continue straight.
   8.2 Miles (A004) - Historic Route 66 Backcountry Byway turnout. A great photo spot.
   18.8 miles - Up the hill on the right are the foundation remains of Riverside Court - a motel situated a long, long ways from the river.
   22.8 miles (A005) - Intersection, stay right and continue to Oatman
   24.1 miles (A006) - Community of Old Trails. Once a mining community rivaling Oatman. The Old Trails post office was established in February 1916 and discontinued in July of 1925. Name is thought to have come from the fact that both Beale and Sitgreaves passed along the Old Trail through the area.
   25.0 miles (A007) -

OATMAN
   Steep canyon walls rise up either side of the Black Mountains from downtown Oatman. Main Street, Route 66, gives you a feeling of stepping back in time, or possibly into a movie set - which it was, as many scenes in the film *How the West Was Won* were shot here.
   Drive carefully through town as the local burro population makes Main Street their domain. The animals are accustomed to tourists and feed can be purchased at just about any store in town. This is a great place to make a friend for life, or at least until you run out of burro food.
   Originally named Vivian for the Vivian Mining Company, the name was changed in 1909 to Oatman. The name was for a pioneer family attacked by Apaches in 1851 near Gila (*Hee-la*) Bend in southern Arizona. The parents were murdered, the boy severely beaten and left to die, and the two girls kidnapped. The girls were hidden a half-mile north of the present townsite of Oatman, at a spring known locally as Olive Oatman Spring. One of the girls, Mary Ann, died in captivity. Olive was released in 1856 or 1857 (*records are fuzzy*) through the efforts of Henry Grinnell, a local rancher, and she returned to Fort Yuma where her brother was living.
   Oatman was a mining town and as such was a bit of a hell-raiser, but less so than many other mining towns. There was a strong sense of community with high morale and good spirits. Clarabelle Decker, whose family moved to Oatman in 1909, recalled, "There was no crime that I remember in Oatman. Some men drank too much, but everybody was friendly and kind."
   The Oatman Hotel is a landmark for the trivia buff. Following their marriage in Kingman, Clark Cable and Carole Lombard

spent their honeymoon night in the hotel and it is still possible to rent a room - but watch out for Oatie, the resident ghost.

Following the closing of the mines during World War Two, Route 66 kept the town active with seven gas stations, numerous restaurants, cafes, and hotels to serve the motoring public. The Oatman Hill (east of town) was feared by many drivers and considered to be the worst part of Route 66. Jack Rittenhouse, in his 1946 *A Guide Book to Highway 66*, describes a service that, for $3.50, would tow your car over the hill. In *Russ's Bus*, Russ Byrd tells of having to stop his bus near the top to let his riders walk up the hill because the bus could not pull the last section of the grade with a load of passengers.

One afternoon, in October of 1952, the hill became quiet. The new Route 66 ribbon cutting had taken place between Kingman and Topock. The new road ran south from Kingman through Yucca along a relatively flat stretch of country. The day after the opening of the new Route 66 alignment, six of the seven gas stations in Oatman closed, and people began to leave town as more-and-more businesses threw in the towel.

Today, Oatman is a thriving tourist town with a rustic atmosphere. The Main Street burros and Route 66 attract thousands of visitors a year for a chance to take a step back in time.

At the east end of town watch for Carter Lane (on the right) and

ZERO ODOMETER

Drive slowly up the hill, appreciate the desert scenery, the road itself and imagine what it was like to travel this road when it was packed with trucks, busses and cars.

3.0 miles (A008) - The remains of the town of Gold Road.

GOLD ROAD

Originally named Acme with the first post office in 1903. It was renamed Gold Road in 1906. A thriving mining area from early 1900's Gold Road began to die out in the late 'teens and in 1925 the post office closed. 1937 saw a rebirth of the town that lasted through the start of WW-II.

The final blow came in 1949 when the Arizona State Legislature passed a law making business property owners liable for full taxes whether they were doing business or not. This upset the few remaining citizens of Gold Road to the point they literally burned down the town. Many historic buildings were lost, not only in Gold Road but throughout Arizona, because of this short-sighted excuse for revenue enhancement.

The area has been reopened for mining, and tours are offered at the Gold Road Mine where you can get your kicks under 66 (275 feet under to be exact).

As you head on from Gold Road watch on the right for the trees, plants and a small tunnel into the cliff side - this is Onetto Spring.

4.3 miles (A009) - Sitgreaves Pass, also known as Gold Hill Summit. (Elevation 3515 ft). On the left hand side are the foundation remains of a gas station and ice cream parlor that once served the weary traveler at the top of the hill (*as well as offering a place for the car to cool down after the climb*).

Behind the foundations and curving down the north side of the canyon are the remains of the old wagon road.

5.0 miles (A010) - On the right is a small pull-out and 33 steps that lead up to Shaffer Fish Bowl Spring. In the spring, there are a few hearty goldfish and the flowers that surround the rear of the bowl are quite beautiful. Watch for bees around the water in the warm months. From the spring, there is a spectacular view of the road and mountains beyond.

6.8 miles (A011) - Little Meadows on the left, characterized by the tall cottonwood trees and the remains of old buildings.

7.2 miles (A012) - Ed's Camp. One of the great desert "junk-shop" stops of all time. Closed since 1992. Please do not "explore" this area. The owners are very protective - photos from the road are not a problem, but please respect the No Trespassing signs.

8.5 miles (A013) - On the left the ruins of Cool Springs Camp. Once a thriving tourist stop for water on the climb up the hill, there were cabins, a gas station and store at this location. The site was rebuilt in 1992 for the movie *Universal Soldier* then blown up. It amazes me that after filming the entire area was thoroughly cleaned (I saw the spot shortly after the film crew left). Good news though, there are plans to rebuild Cool Springs - COOL!

9.0 miles (A014) - Bureau of Land Management sign designating this section of old Route 66 as a National Historic Byway.

10.6 miles (A015) - In the Rittenhouse Guide Book (page 110), there is a mention of Fig Springs Camp. Today, there is nothing remaining of this site.

22.1 miles (A016) - Make a right toward I-40 on Shinarump Road. Continue under I-40 **(A017)** and make a left onto the frontage road **(A018)**. This area - wrecking yard, truck stop and truck wash - is McConnico, named for S. B. McConnico, Vice President and General Manager of the Arizona and Utah Railroad, a small railroad that connected from here to Chloride in 1899.

27.6 miles (A019) - On the right, across the canyon can be seen the remains of the National Old Trails Highway and the original alignment of Route 66. This road can be reached at the intersection of Andy Devine Blvd and Fourth Street in Kingman.

28.5 miles (A020) - Make a right onto Andy Devine (Old Route 66).

Santa Monica to Chicago

KINGMAN

In 1882, the locating engineer for the railroad, Lewis Kingman, named the community after himself. (*Is that what you do when you're the man who would be king? Ouch!*) At one time the town was called Shenfield Railroad Camp after the contractor who plotted the original townsite.

The years have seen Kingman become a major crossroads as railroad and highway converged to make it the most important city in Mohave County. It is interesting to note, however, that as late as 1940, Kingman streets were mostly unpaved and the comment was made that food and lodging were some of the most expensive anywhere along Route 66.

Kingman has two great Hollywood connections. The first is gravel-voiced Andy Devine, who called Kingman his home (*he was born in Flagstaff, but his family moved to Kingman when he was a year old*). The second connection is the marriage of Clark Gable and Carole Lombard at the Methodist Church.

Kingman embraced their son and named the Main Street of the city after him. Along the length of Route 66, many cities are changing street names to Route 66. As much as I love the highway, I hope that Kingman never changes Andy Devine Blvd.

World War Two brought the Army-Air Force to Kingman with a large base on the site of the present Mohave County Airport. Following the war, Kingman became the storage site for more than 7,000 mothballed aircraft. Many of the planes had never seen combat, and for some inexplicable reason (*Hey, patriotism is all well and good, but a contract's a contract, buddy!*), the factories continued to manufacture aircraft, which were flown straight to Kingman and eventually dismantled as scrap.

A few sights to see in Kingman include Locomotive Park (where Old Route 66 joins Andy Devine Blvd), the Powerhouse which houses the Route 66 Museum, and the Beale Hotel, once owned by Andy Devine's father.

LODGING: Best Western Kings Inn, Best Western A Wayfarers Inn, Quality Inn, Hill Top Motel (classic older motel - nicely maintained). **DINING:** Dambar Steakhouse (Stockman Hill and Andy Devine), El Palacio (4th Street and Andy Devine), Portofino Restorante Italiano (318 Oak Street). 50's Atmosphere: Mr D's Route 66 Diner (105 E. Andy Devine).

At the east end of town, as you pass under I-40 **(A021)**,

ZERO ODOMETER

1.2 miles (A022) - The Skyline Motel. The first motel when entering the town from the east.

14.6 miles (A023) - Valle Vista Country Club development on the left. The orchards you see along here are pecan and pistachio trees.

23.7 miles (A024) - Cross bridge.

24.0 miles (A025) - Hackberry General Store. Lovingly restored by John and Kerry Pritchard, the Hackberry General Store is a must stop. Great photo opportunities abound, along with the opportunity to meet two of the nicest people along the road.

Continue east about 2.5 miles, and as you pass Bert's Country Dancing **(A026)**,

ZERO ODOMETER

2.0 miles (A027) - Valentine

Originally named Truxton Canyon in 1898 when the large Indian School was active. The post office closed when the school moved and the community was given a new name when the Post Office reopened in 1910. The new name was Valentine in honor of the Commissioner of Indian Affairs Robert G. Valentine.

3.7 miles (A028) - Abandoned buildings on the left.

5.5 miles (A029) - Crozier Canyon area. This was the site of a group of tourist cabins, gas station and cafe. All private property, please respect the owners privacy.

6.6 miles (A030) - Original highway on the right.

11.4 miles (A031) -

TRUXTON

Flowing springs brought Lt. Beale to this spot in 1857 and his naming of the area for either his mother (Emily Truxton Beale), his brother (Truxton Beale) or his grandfather (Thomas Truxton). The availability of water also brought the railroad with steam engines thirsty for the precious liquid.

A proposed rail line to the Grand Canyon brought the modern development of Truxton in 1951. D. J. Dilts built a restaurant and gas station in hopes of cashing in on a rail line that never materialized. A stop at the Frontier Cafe is a must for the hungry Roadie. Good food, "Real Home Cooking by the Girls from Oklahoma" and an atmosphere that belies Route 66's reputation for 24 hour a day hustle and bustle is more than enough reason to stop.

Between Truxton and Peach Springs, the road climbs and on the right can be seen vestiges of the old alignment of the highway. Most of these sections are on private land and are inaccessible. As you approach Peach Springs, notice the cattle loading pens on the right side of the highway.

20.1 miles (A032) -

Santa Monica to Chicago

PEACH SPRINGS

Originally named St. Basil's Well by Father Garcès the explorer who arrived in June of 1775. When Lt. Beale arrived with the camel caravan in 1858, he named the area Indian Spring. The name Peach Springs was derived from the large number of peach trees planted in the area by settling Mormons.

Tribal Headquarters for the Hualapai (*wall-a-pie*) are located here.

Once little more than a great place for photographing old motels, gas stations and cafes, with the construction of the Hualapai Lodge, Peach Springs is moving towards becoming a tourist center offering first class accommodations and access to tours and river runs of the Grand Canyon and Colorado. For reservations, call the Hualapai Lodge at 888-255-9550 (AAA and AARP honored).

At the east end of town, where the highway becomes two lanes going up-hill **(A033)**,

ZERO ODOMETER

0.5 miles (A034) - On the left, the southern end of the Grand Canyon can be seen in the distance.

4.4 miles (A035) - Old alignment on the right, not accessible.

10.7 miles (A036) - Grand Canyon Caverns. A Roadie attraction that keeps on going despite the reduction in traffic. A great place to visit and spend an hour or two. Be sure to get a picture with the dinosaur out front. (**NOTE:** The cavern tour can be strenuous for people with heart or walking problems).

At the point the road from the caverns intersects with Old 66,

ZERO ODOMETER

1.6 miles (A037) - On the right, up the slight hill, is the site of Hyde Park. All that remains are the foundations of the store, station and cabins. (*Certain high-quality Route 66 maps show Hyde Park buildings on the north side of the highway also.*) A few rusting cars at the back of the property make interesting photo opportunities. This area was fenced off in 2002 to provide for habitat reconstruction - if the fence is still present do not enter the area.

2.9 miles (A038) - Up the hill on the right, is the site of Deer Lodge Cabins mentioned on page 105 of the Rittenhouse Guidebook.

6.5 miles (A039) - Calvary Hogan Mission.

14.0 miles (A040) - Notice the pole line as it curves off to the left. This was the 1921 alignment of the old highway.

16.0 miles (A041) - Curve to the left.

20.5 miles (A042) - I-40 access underpass.

SELIGMAN

Prescott Junction was the name of this small town in 1882 when the railroad reached this far west. The town was the junction point for the Atlantic & Pacific Railroad and the Prescott & Arizona Central. The present name of Seligman was selected in 1886 for one of the Seligman Brothers, a pair of financiers from New York who were stockholders in the Atlantic & Pacific Railroad. This was, until 1950, the "official" site of the change from Mountain to Pacific Time (*honored primarily by the railroad*).

Seligman is the home of Angel Delgadillo, the founder of the Arizona Historic Route 66 Association. Angel is a man who is driven to do what is right in life, and the loss of Route 66 seemed wrong to him. He sensed a need to preserve what Route 66 meant to America and he set out to do it. Plan some time to visit Angel at his barbershop and Route 66 museum in the center of town.

Be sure to pick up a walking tour map of Seligman and visit the sites listed, particularly the old Harvey House, the Havasu, which closed in 1954. At this writing the Havasu has been purchased and there are plans to restore it, much like the La Posada restoration in Winslow.

LODGING: A great, restored motel is the Historic Route 66 Motel. **DINING:** Westside Lilo's Café - great for Breakfast, Lunch or Dinner (*Beware of the home-made cinnamon rolls - they're as big a mid-fifties Cadillac*). Fast Food and Fun: The Snow Cap.

Night photos of the Copper Cart and the Historic Route 66 Motel sign are naturals for your album of Route 66 memories.

To leave town and stay on Old 66, make a right at the Crookton Road turn-off on the east edge of town **(A043)**. This is not a full right, but a slight bend to the right and:

ZERO ODOMETER

Various sections of the old highway alignment can be seen between here and the joining up with I-40. The old highway went around many of the hills you will cut through and evidence of the old highway will cut back and forth across this later alignment.

3.3 miles (A044) - Old alignment appears on the right hand side.

Enjoy this drive because you will soon leave the quiet of the old highway and have to join I-40. In the distance can be seen the San Francisco Peaks, the highest point in Arizona with an elevation of 12,670 feet (*Mt. Humphries*).

8.2 miles (A045) - Railroad bridge and old highway bridge on the left.

17.5 miles - Cross cattle guard.

Santa Monica to Chicago

17.7 miles (A046) - Curve up and over I-40. This is the Crookton Road interchange.

At this point it will be necessary to join the Interstate. There is a short side tour outlined below, but it will be necessary to return to this point when you're done.

SIDE TOUR

Cross the I-40 overpass **(A046)** and ZERO ODOMETER. On the south side, turn onto the Frontage Road.
0.1 miles - Cross cattle guard.
0.8 miles - Cross cattle guard and pavement becomes rough, this is old Route 66.
1.2 miles - a "Y" in the road, continue straight.
2.2 miles - Large dip in the road.
2.8 miles (A047) - Partridge Creek Bridge, built in 1920s for original highway alignment. Bridge is still in good shape, but the classic thing is the tree growing through the bridge on the west end. A great photo stop.

It is suggested you turn around here and retrace the road back to I-40 **(A046)**. The road ahead is quite rough in spots and the section that would allow you to connect to Ash Fork is now fenced and gated at the railroad crossing.

Continue on I-40 eastbound to Exit 144 **(A048)**. Exit and follow the road into Ash Fork.

ASH FORK

Brought to life by the need for a better site to off-load ore from the mines in Jerome, Ash Fork went from a railroad siding to a full-fledged town in less than a year. 1882 was the year of the request for a station stop by freighters tired of hauling ore up the hill to Williams, and 1883 was the year a post office bearing the name Ash Fork was established. Thomas Lewis opened a store alongside the tracks (on the north side) in 1882 and in 1885 Wells Fargo opened a stage station. Expansion continued north of the tracks until a fire in 1893 destroyed the town. When it was rebuilt, Ash Fork was on the south side of the tracks.

The Santa Fe opened the grand Escalante Hotel in March of 1907 as the Harvey House for Ash Fork. People came from as far away as Prescott (fifty miles of dirt road to the south) to eat at the Escalante and cowboys were known to ride for three days for a warm smile from a Harvey Girl over a dinner unequaled in the area. The Escalante was torn down following the Santa Fe's realignment of the main line (*the Crookton Cutoff*) in 1960.

At the west end of town, make a right onto 8th Street **(A049)**. This will put you on the old alignment as it entered town. This is a turn-around section as access on the west end, past the KOA, is pretty rough.

While in Ash Fork check out DeSoto's Beauty and Barber Shop at 314 W. Lewis **(A050)** (westbound 66). A great 1960 DeSoto sits on top of the roof, and I believe that is Elvis behind the wheel. Been on the Road awhile? Need a haircut? Now's your chance to meet a couple who rescued a decrepit gas station building and made it into a new and viable business - Joe and Edie DeSoto are nice people, tell them Bob says Hi! Also you should stop at the Ash Fork Cash and Carry on west Lewis Avenue for some antique shopping and to meet Frank and Lisa Bohan, a couple of the new generation of Route 66 entrepreneurs.

The old Beale Wagon Road (which stretched from Fort Smith, Arkansas to the Colorado River) can be seen about fifteen miles north of Ash Fork by following First Street north, cross the tracks and stay on Double A Ranch Road (Forest Road 142) out to Russell's Tank. You will cross the new alignment (1960) of the Santa Fe out here as well. The Beale Wagon Road was the first Federally funded road in the Southwest and was built at a cost of $210,000.

Between Ash Fork and Williams are many old alignments of Route 66 that are still accessible and driveable.

From Ash Fork, continue east to Williams. It is quite a climb from here as you rise from Ash Fork at 5,144 feet to Williams at 6,792 feet. The country will change from high desert plains, to juniper, then to the beauty of the mighty Ponderosa Pine.

Leaving Ash Fork eastbound, it will be necessary to re-join I-40 **(A051)**.

ADVENTURE TOUR

Please read all admonitions regarding Adventure Tours at the front of this book.

The following sections of Old 66 are driveable in a standard sedan, but a high clearance vehicle is advised. The pavement is heavily deteriorated in spots so speed should be watched. The final section up Ash Fork hill is unpaved and should not be attempted if it is raining, muddy or there is snow on the ground.

Exit Interstate at the Monte Carlo exit (#149) **(ATA01)**, cross under I-40 and drive across the parking lot of the

truck stop to the northeast side **(ATA02)**. Just past the closed café the old alignment (1932/52) can be seen heading east. At the fence line:
ZERO ODOMETER
- **0.2 miles** - Box culvert and road damage
- **0.6 miles** - Change in road surface.
- **0.9 miles** - Crest of the hill. Stop and look behind you at the view.
- **1.5 miles** - Pavement missing.
- **1.9 miles** - Box culvert with road damage.
- **2.0 miles** - Large section of pavement missing.
- **2.1 miles** - Large section of pavement missing.
- **2.8 miles (ATA03)** - Box culvert, road damage - SLOW.
- **2.9 miles (ATA05)** - Road to the right is FR6 which leads back to I-40. If you do not want to make the climb up Ash Fork Hill, make a right here and follow FR6 for 0.4 mile to I-40. **(ATA04)**.

It will be necessary to return to this point after climbing the hill.
To continue up the hill, at this point:
ZERO ODOMETER
- **0.3 miles (ATA06)** - Box culvert. Just past this point, go straight ahead where FR6 turns to the left.
- **0.4 miles** - Dip, drainage cut, slow.
- **0.5 miles** - Dip, drainage cut, slow.
- **0.8 miles (ATA07)** - Short stretch of pavement leading to box culvert.
- **1.1 miles** - Drainage cut.
- **1.4 miles** - Tight spot, trees on either side.
- **1.5 miles (ATA08)** - End of the road. Fence line and I-40 straight ahead. Great views of the valley from here.

Turn around and backtrack to FR6, make a left on FR6 **(ATA05)** and follow it to I-40 **(ATA04)** and continue eastbound to Williams.

A bike tour is available at 0.2 miles on FR6, a turn-out is to the right and allows for biking the 1921 alignment west for three miles (rough), then back up the 1932 alignment for three miles (steep, but easy).

About halfway up the hill toward Williams, look to the right and you can see the old alignment clinging to the side of the hill. Look closely and you will see where the road crossed the Interstate **(ATA11)** and winds down to the left **(ATA08)**.

Bike and walking tours **(ATA12)** are also available for the 1922/32 sections of road at the Devil Dog exit (#157) on I-40. Maps for these can be obtained at the Visitors Center in Williams (Grand Canyon Blvd and Railroad Ave).

Leave I-40 at Exit 161 **(A052)** for Williams.

WILLIAMS

Nestled among the pines and named for Bill Williams Mountain (*although locals will incorrectly tell you it was named for Mountain Man Bill Williams - the mountain was, the town wasn't*) the town hugs the west shoulder of the mountain named for the famous fur trapper and mountain man. Williams is also known as the Gateway to the Grand Canyon. Just up the road (*thirty miles*) is Flagstaff, a bustling, progressive city, serving the major shopping needs of Northern Arizona, which allows Williams to remain locked inextricably in the early 20th century, shunning progress at every turn.

When I-40 by-passed the town on October 13, 1984 (*the last Route 66 town to be bypassed*), it appeared as if Williams was going to roll over and die. But, in 1989, the Grand Canyon Railway saved the town and annually brings thousands of people to "ride the train to the Canyon." The city has embraced the railway by allowing for major construction of new buildings - a hotel, a restaurant and gift shop, and on the drawing boards a new RV park, all on the railroads property, while allowing the downtown area to deteriorate (*it should be noted even the Grand Canyon Railway is not based in Williams - their headquarters are in Flagstaff*). A community that seems to thrive on the adage *tourist beware,* Williams is a place where gas prices will be considerably lower (*by as much as 50 cents a gallon*) away from the interstate off-ramps (*High Country Market at Route 66 and 1st Street is usually the best price in town*). If you need car repairs, be cautious - a few of the local garages are favorites of the 60 Minutes crews for being rip-off artists. If you need car service, I have found the Chevron on west Route 66 (*next to the Safeway*) to be operated in a fair and honest fashion. Watch out for motel rip-offs as well - some of the owners like to jack their rates sky-high (*particularly if it is late in the evening*) - the best choices would be: for a classic motel - The Westerner; The Route 66 Inn or The Mountainside Inn - for chain

Santa Monica to Chicago

properties - The Best Western Inn of Williams (*a 1000 point B/W property*); The Fairfield Inn. Because of a bogus CANYON FEE the Holiday Inn is not recommended. For a truly enchanting lodging, experience check out The Grand Canyon Retreat at 518 E. Route 66 - intimate and luxurious, yet at a very affordable price (928.635.0905 or www.grandcanyonretreat.com).

To leave Williams on the original alignment from the west, make a left onto Grand Canyon Blvd from downtown. As you cross the railroad tracks,

ZERO ODOMETER

0.1 miles - On the left is the Frey Marcos - the former Harvey House now beautifully restored as a Museum, Depot and Gift Shop. The Grand Canyon Railroad leaves from here for the run to the Canyon.

0.3 miles (A053) - Right onto Edison.

0.5 miles (A054) - Left onto Airport Road.

0.7 miles (A055) - Right on Rodeo Road.

1.0 miles (A056) - Cross tracks, to the right is the Wye ("Y") used for turning the train around.

1.5 miles (A057) - Make a quick right, then left onto the road east.

Leave Williams eastbound by entering I-40 at the Hwy 64 (Grand Canyon Hwy) junction **(A058)**.

Optional tour below is another dirt road experience along the '21 alignment.
To continue the main tour, go to "Onwards To The Deer Farm" below.

OPTIONAL TOUR

Make a right at Echo Canyon Road **(ATA34)** and

ZERO ODOMETER

Immediately make a hard left, do not go through the gate onto private property. Cross cattle guard and continue east-southeast.

0.2 miles (ATA35) - Forest Road to the right, go straight on. If in a passenger car, you might want to walk. This is the '21 alignment.

0.3 miles - Old box culvert, a classic.

0.4 miles (ATA36) - Railroad embankment and end of road. A great place to watch trains pulling the hill heading east.

Return to the highway.

NOTE: Another side trip for the intrepid Roadie, just up the road!

Go past the railroad underpass **(A058)** by one-quarter mile. Turn right at the first possible turn **(ATA33)**, make an immediate left, and:

ZERO ODOMETER

0.2 miles - Yellow line and pavement on left goes under the I-40 embankment. You are on the final alignment of old highway.

0.3 miles - Right turn.

0.5 miles - Curve to the left onto Forest Road 51A- the original alignment is on your right, but it is overgrown and tends to be muddy. You are immediately greeted by a big chuckhole (*or gopher hole - you hit one, then go-fer another*). *(Ouch!)*

1.2 miles (ATA32) - Leave pavement - SLOW, road is heavily rutted. Go straight, road to right goes down to Williams Junction, a depot used when the railroad moved away from Williams with the Santa Fe realignment in 1960/61. There is nothing at the depot site today - totally barren but it is a great place for train spotting (*nearly 70 trains pass this point in any given 24-hour period*).

1.5 miles - Leave the pine forest.

1.7 miles - Good-sized dip in road.

2.1 miles (ATA31) - Take a left onto the access road to the freeway interchange **(A060)**. (*Straight ahead is a continuation of the '21 alignment, but it ends in a private yard, with an overly friendly dog - a very BIG, overly friendly dog.*)

ONWARDS TO THE DEER FARM

NOTE: Part of the old highway between Williams and the Deer Farm is dirt road, although not as rough as most of the Adventure Tours. If you do not want to travel on dirt, enter I-40 east of Williams and continue to the Deer Farm exit **(A067)**.

Continue to the Garland Prairie/Circle Pines Exit (167) **(A060)**, make a left at the top of the ramp and:

ZERO ODOMETER

0.2 miles (A061) - Turn right.

0.8 miles (A062) - Cross cattle guard and you are on the 1931 to 1964 alignment of Route 66.

0.9 miles - Pavement ends.
1.2 miles - Williams City Limits sign.
2.5 miles - Cattle guard.
2.7 miles (A063) - Abandoned building on the right.
3.0 miles - Davenport Lake on the right. The 1941 alignment and I-40 cross the middle of the lake, making for some interesting "ice-driving" in the Winter.
3.6 miles (A064) - Pavement.
4.2 miles (A065) - The Deer Farm. A great Roadie attraction where you can roam the grounds while feeding deer and numerous other animals. We spent about an hour (*not really enough time*) walking the grounds and feeding the deer. I made quite a few "friends for life" as I fed the deer.

Continue east, and at the frontage road/on-ramp stop sign,

ZERO ODOMETER

Do not enter I-40, follow the curve around the on ramp and continue east.

0.4 miles - Great old house on the left. Was once the Wagon Wheel Lodge.
1.1 miles (A068) - Double box culvert and concrete pavement.
2.1 miles - Asphalt pavement.
2.3 miles - Back to concrete pavement. This is the Oak Hill Recreation area, the original ski area for Williams.
3.4 miles (A069) - Garland Prairie Vista Point on the right. By all means pull over here for a fabulous view of the San Francisco Peaks to the east. This is the view seen in thousands of post cards.
5.1 miles (A070) - Large meadow and remains of cabins, etc. (*Could this be the site of Old Maine?*)
6.0 miles (A071) -

PARKS

A small community with a history of many names. Originally named Rhoades when the first post office opened in 1898 (later changed to Rhodes), it was changed to Maine in October of 1907 in remembrance of the battleship sunk in Havana, Cuba.

The community operated as a railway stop until the arrival of the highway. At that point, the town moved two miles east, leaving the original townsite as Old Maine (*shown as Maine Station on the National Old Trails Maps of the 1920's*). At the new townsite, a man named Parks opened a store and post office. In 1907, the government realized the people had changed the name from Rhodes to Maine (*ah, you can't fool the government for long*) and officially changed the name to Maine, only to discover there was already a Maine in the Territory. The end result was another name change to Parks, after the storeowner.

The present store building was constructed in 1910 when the original store burned to the ground. The first alignment of the road went behind the building. When the alignment was changed, in 1931, the new routing went in front of the building. The storeowners took the windows out of what had become the back of the building and moved them to what was to be the front. A roof extension (*the canopy over the gas pumps*) was also added at that time.

6.1 miles (A072) - Double box culvert and the point where the 1941 alignment joins up with the abandoned 1931 alignment (*more about the '31 alignment in a moment*).
6.6 miles (A073) - Entrance to I-40. Dirt road ahead, if you don't want to travel on dirt return to I-40 here.
7.0 miles - Cattle guard. Just past here is the connection for the 1921, 1931 and the 1941 alignments. The 1941-1964 alignment **(A074)** bears to the right (*cannot be seen*) and winds up buried beneath I-40 for the run into Bellemont.
7.2 miles (A076) - Auto Tour sign and turnout. These signs were placed by the Forest Service under the direction of Teri Cleeland of Williams. Pull off here and spend some time exploring.

Immediately south of here, about 150 to 200 feet, can be seen the 1921 alignment **(A075)** of the National Old Trails Road. The road is evident by the cut through the trees.

Straight ahead is the 1931 alignment **(A076)** and a pleasant three-quarter of a mile hike or bike ride. Do not drive on this section.

The old pavement comes and goes along here, trees push their way up through the concrete along the edge of the road. A little over a half mile down the road is the old Springhouse, used when there was a Forest Service Campground here.

At the Auto Tour sign,

ZERO ODOMETER

1.4 miles (A077) - Junction with Forest Road 107, continue straight. As you follow the road up the hill, you can see evidence of the old highway twisting back and forth across the road - look for cuts through the trees. Abandoned businesses and homesteads can be seen along here.

1.9 miles (A078) - Fortynine Hill - This is the site of the highest point on the old highway in Arizona (*until recently it was thought this was the high point on Route 66, but that has proven to be incorrect. So now is the time, kids, to begin guessing where the highest point is. No cheating by looking ahead in the book! The winner gets to pick out the motel stop in Tucumcari!*), topping

Santa Monica to Chicago

out at 7414 feet. The road was moved south with the 1941 alignment to avoid the climb over the pass.

2.4 miles (A079) - Brannigan Park - an open meadow with a few homes and out-buildings.

3.3 miles - Box culvert.

3.5 miles - Cattle guard and return to pavement.

4.9 miles (A080) - Another Auto-Tour sign and pullout.

5.3 miles (A081) - Curve to left. Ahead of you, at this point, the old highway crossed over to the south side in a straight alignment (*the road from here to Trans-Western road is frontage road only*).

7.5 miles - Trans-Western Road and I-40 on-ramp **(A082)**. Cross the Interstate, do not enter I-40, make a right **(A083)** and

ZERO ODOMETER

This is the second alignment of Route 66, there are three alignments along here, the 1st (National Old Trails Road) is to the south and the 3rd is beneath I-40 to the north.

On the left (across the tracks), is the Navajo Army Depot, formerly the Navajo Ordnance depot. This was one of the largest munitions storage areas in the country during World War Two.

BELLEMONT

Named after Belle Smith, daughter of F. W. Smith, superintendent of the Atlantic and Pacific Railroad in 1882. Formerly called Volunteer for a militia encampment at this location in 1863. Volunteer Spring became a water stop for the railroad with the construction of two water tanks. A new Bellemont appears to be in the works on the north side of I-40, with the Truck Stop, the Micro-Tel and a new housing development to the east.

Bellemont is also where weather seems to happen in Northern Arizona - if it's going to snow, it does it in Bellemont; if the wind is going to blow, it does it in Bellemont. The same can be said for heavy rain, sleet and hail. Bellemont - The Weather Capital of Northern Arizona!

0.5 miles (A084) - To the left is a dirt road that leads to what is left of old Bellemont. About a quarter of mile down this road, on the right **(A085)**, is the original alignment of the National Old Trails Road. The cut through the trees to the west shows the alignment of the old highway **(A086)** as it came through town. Not much left of old Bellemont. The newer buildings you see are a Wisconsin Paper warehouse, a warehouse for Canyonlands Publications and an empty building that has yet to be occupied.

The second alignment continues west for 2.5 miles and ends at I-40 **(A087)**, which can be seen through the trees. Many potholes on this section.

Return to Trans-Western Road **(A083)** and continue straight across. This will put you on old concrete pavement (*portions re-paved in 2002*). You will have to return to this spot to get back on I-40.

ZERO ODOMETER

0.5 miles - Grand Canyon Harley-Davidson and the Roadhouse Cafe on the left - a great place to get a new HD shirt.

0.7 miles - Box culvert.

1.3 miles - Remains of an Old Whiting Bros. gas station and motel on the left. The motel cabins were constructed with wood taken from powder boxes at the Army Depot.

1.6 miles - Pine Breeze Inn (*yes, that's a backward "Z" on the west side of the building*). This is where Peter Fonda and Dennis Hopper attempted to stop for the night in *Easy Rider* and were shunned by the motel owner.

1.7 miles - Box culvert.

1.9 miles (A088) - Road ends at I-40 embankment. Turn around and return to Trans-Western Road.

Rejoin I-40 eastbound and leave the Interstate at Exit 191 **(A089)**. This is the old Route 66 alignment into Flagstaff. On this section, at the top of the hill, is Pine Springs, once a major truck stop on the old highway. Continue into Flagstaff and at the junction of Business Route 40 and Arizona 66, make a left and continue through town.

FLAGSTAFF

Film-makers Jesse Lasky and Cecil B. DeMille were disgusted with New York weather and headed west. The train stopped in Flagstaff and the combination of clear air, spectacular mountains and natural beauty made them decide they had found a new home. This where they would make movies! Suddenly, out of the north came a cold wind, followed by an icy rain and soon snow covered the ground in a white blanket. The two men, without a word to each other or anyone else, loaded their gear on the next train and continued west. Perhaps there are some good things to say about those sudden weather changes in the northland of Arizona.

The history of Flagstaff covers the names of virtually every explorer, surveyor and adventurer of the last two hundred years. But, it was during 1876 when the act that would give Flagstaff its name took place. Numerous stories abound, so I'll recount just one: On July 4th, a group of scouts, awaiting settlers coming from Boston, camped at F. W. McMillan's site alongside the spring. To celebrate the Independence Holiday, the scouts stripped a huge pine tree of its branches and tied an American flag to it with strips of rawhide. In the ensuing days, they laid out a townsite, but with the arrival of the settlers and their disappointment with the soil quality, moved on. The huge flagpole became well known all the way from San Francisco to Santa Fe and travelers were told,

Santa Monica to Chicago

"Travel straight west until you come to that flagstaff."

It was to be 1880 before Flagstaff took on an air of permanence when the railroad established a camp near the spring. By 1886, Flagstaff had become the largest city between Albuquerque and Los Angeles on what would later become the Santa Fe railroad. Lumber, cattle, tourists, the college (now Northern Arizona University) and the railroad have been major influences throughout the life of this mountain town.

DINING AND LODGING

Follow Route 66 (*formerly Santa Fe Avenue*) through town and you will see many old motels lining the north side of the street. Lodging can be a crap shoot with the majority of the older motels not being well maintained (*or having their sheets changed*) - best bet in town on 66: the Best Western Pony Soldier at 3030 East Route 66 (800-356-4143), an early 1960's era property that has been very well maintained (*in fact renovations were taking place during the Spring of 2002*). For one of the finest hotels between Chicago and L.A. check out Little America located at exit 198 on I-40, beautiful grounds, fantastic rooms, and a world-class restaurant make this an absolute treat. Near Interstate exits 198 and 195 (*north side of the interstate*) are many chain motels. My personal suggestion: take exit 195 and check out the chain motels in this vicinity - much nicer than those at exit 198. For dining: the Western Gold Dining Room in the Little America Hotel; Busters (excellent seafood) at 1800 S. Milton Rd; La Fonda (Great Mexican food) at 1900 N. 2nd Street in East Flagstaff (*been there since the early 1950's*); Miz Zip's (THE breakfast place) at 2924 E. Route 66, and my personal favorite, Jackson's Grill (*take I-17 south to the first exit, then make a left on Hwy 89A towards Sedona, continue about a half-a-mile, it's on the right*) excellent food, great service, and an amazing wine cellar. One other point - **ALL** Flagstaff restaurants are smoke free! (*Cigarette smoke - not burning bacon...*)

Cross the hill to East Flagstaff and continue east. You can join I-40 at the east end of town, or follow the old highway. If you want to take the old highway (*recommended!*), watch for the Crown Cafe and bear to the right at a slight fork in the road (*sign says LOCAL TRAFFIC ONLY - not LIKELY as long as there are Roadies!*). This road will take you behind the Flagstaff Mall and is the old concrete highway.

At the intersection with the Hwy 89/I-40 access road (Country Club Drive) **(A091)**,

ZERO ODOMETER

- **0.5 miles** - The backside of the Flagstaff Mall. (*No more Sears for you until Albuquerque! Thank God...*)
- **1.1 miles** - Arizona Department of Transportation yard and a change in the road surface.
- **2.4 miles** - Rain Valley Road to the left.
- **3.2 miles** - Road curves to right.

Notice the low cinder hill on the left that is slowly disappearing as THEY obtain volcanic cinders for maintaining secondary roads, and also for ice control on the paved roads in the winter.

- **3.9 miles** - Railway bridge.
- **4.2 miles (A092)** - Turn right onto bridge to eastbound I-40.

The old highway is buried beneath the Interstate so we will use exit numbers to point out interesting areas.

Exit 211 - WINONA (A093)

Made famous by Bobby Troup in his song, "Get Your Kicks On Route 66." Winona was originally called Walnut by the railroad, the name was changed in 1886 (*to date no reason for the name Winona has been found except for anecdotal evidence from Mrs' Myrtle Adams in 1924, "Winona was just another name"*). The original site of Winona is a little north of the existing location. It is said that Billy Adams opened the first tourist court in the country here in the 1920s.

Just north of Winona is a closed bridge on the right side of the road. This bridge was used in the movie *Forrest Gump* when Tom Hanks as Forrest was running across the country. (*Also downtown Flagstaff was featured in the film*).

The original alignment of Route 66 went north from Winona to Camp Townsend (on Hwy 89), then west to Flagstaff. This road is all new pavement with little of the old road flavor left, a detour for the hard-core Roadie only.

Exit 219 - TWIN ARROWS (A094)

A once popular truck stop with a cool diner. Twin Arrows has been closed for quite a few years and will probably never reopen. The land is Arizona State Trust property and the future of the area is tenuous at best, take a photo under the Twin Arrows, they may soon be gone.

As you leave Twin Arrows to re-join I-40, notice the building to the east of the on-ramp. This was the site of Toonerville, an old tourist stop. The owners were murdered during a robbery. A construction company presently uses the building.

Notice how the landscape has changed with the crossing of Canyon Padre. You are heading into the high desert plains of Northern Arizona.

Santa Monica to Chicago

Exit 230 - TWO GUNS (A095)

A left across the interstate will take you out to Canyon Diablo, once considered to be the toughest town in the territory. However, the road is extremely rough and not recommended for passenger cars.

A right will take you to Two Guns. Another right, and if the gate is open, you can drive the old highway alignment to where the station, cafe and tourist attractions were located.

Two Guns is an example of a place built strictly to attract the tourist. Clinging to the rocky edge of Canyon Diablo are numerous small buildings. The building with "Mountain Lions" painted on the front was a small zoo. Walk through the arch and down the steps toward the canyon. Parts of the old cages are still backed up against the bluff. Across the canyon can be seen more rock buildings and structures. The old bridge spanning the canyon was the original alignment of Route 66, the alignment was changed to the road you came in on and the Canyon Diablo bridge for the new alignment can be seen from Milepost 230 on I-40.

If you choose to explore this are, **BE VERY CAREFUL!** Do not attempt to walk across any of the old wooden walkways that span the small canyons, or explore the caves under the various buildings. All of these things were built many years ago and their condition has deteriorated.

Two Guns was named for Two-Gun Miller, who claimed to be an Apache. He killed a neighbor during an argument and was acquitted. Friends of the dead man put "Killed by Indian Miller" on the grave marker. Two-Gun Miller did not take kindly to the epitaph, so he added his own to the marker. He was jailed for defacing a grave. Two-Gun lived for years in a cave alongside Canyon Diablo and didn't give a damn about anyone but himself.

A stop at Two Guns will take you on a mind trip back to what travel along old Route 66 must have been like. A stop at Two Guns was an adventure. The mountain lions, bobcats and coyotes were indeed sad looking behind their chicken-wire enclosures, but to a kid from Illinois or California, Two Guns was the real West.

This place is a tremendous example of what people will do to make a business succeed. As you wander the grounds and look at the buildings, you can only marvel at the amount of rock moved to build this place.

Exit 233 - METEOR CRATER (A096)

Just beyond the gas station/RV park/Curio shop is where Old 66 went through. To the right and left is now private land and it is posted. To the left you could travel the old pavement for 1.5 miles to the backside of the I-40 Rest Area (*there is no access to the Rest Area from this road*).

The large rock tower on the hill was the old Curio Shop and Observatory for Meteor Crater. It was possible to view the crater from a telescope mounted in the tower.

If you have never visited Meteor Crater, it is six miles south of I-40.

Exit 239 - METEOR CITY (A097)

The road in front of Meteor City is the old highway and ends a short distance west. If the place looks familiar you have seen it in dozens of commercials.

Vestiges of the old road can be seen alongside I-40 on both the south and north side. Most of these are inaccessible and are on private land.

Exit 252 - WINSLOW (A098)

A name dispute exists for this city. One claim was by prospector Tom Winslow who, in 1920, claimed Winslow was named for him, the other is the claim it was named in 1881 for General Edward F. Winslow, president of the St. Louis and San Francisco Railroad and was associated with the Atlantic and Pacific Railroad. (*I'll take the railroad story over a prospector (!) anyday...*)

An area about three miles north of town, known as Sunset Crossing, had been in use for years as one of the few safe crossings on the Little Colorado River, a Mormon settlement, Sunset, was on one side of the river and a fort known as Brigham City was built on the other in 1876. By the early 1880s, the Mormon's had given up trying to master the Little Colorado.

With the coming of the railroad and establishment of a terminal, Winslow became a railroad town. Frederick C. Demerest set up a tent to do business with the roadbed laying crews, and by late 1881 he was well established as Winslow's first businessman. He built the Arizona Central Hotel on Front Street.

While in Winslow, stop and have your picture taken at 2nd and Kinsley. This is "*The Standin' on the Corner Park*" and what better place to have your picture taken while, "Standin' on a Corner in Winslow, Arizona (- *What a Fine Sight To See - It's a Girl, My Lord, In A Flatbed Ford - Slowin' Down To Take A Look At Me...*").

Just up the street at 212 Kinsley is the Old Trails Museum. A small but packed-to-the-rafters collection of what makes Winslow a special place. Janice Griffith, museum curator and her staff of volunteers have done a tremendous job of preserving the heritage of the town, the railroad and Route 66.

One of the gems of the city is the La Posada, the beautiful Fred Harvey Hotel designed by famed southwestern architect Mary Colter, who was the Fred Harvey Company chief architect and interior designer from 1902 to 1948 (*for more on Mary Colter read,*

Santa Monica to Chicago

Mary Colter-Builder Upon the Red Earth *by Virginia L. Gratten*). The La Posada has been saved and has undergone extensive restoration. Rooms are open in the hotel (ph: 928.289.4366) and the restaurant is once again a delight, with food and service in the impeccable manner of the old Fred Harvey operation. It is suggested that you make the La Posada Turquoise Room a must for lunch or dinner if you are not staying at the hotel. (*Hint: Try the Prickly Painted Desert Warm Bread Pudding for an amazing desert treat.)*

Other lodging: Best Western Adobe Inn at I-40 exit 253 and Holiday Inn Express at exit 255. The downtown motels have deteriorated badly and I cannot recommend any of them. Dining: since Pete Kretsedemas sold The Falcon it has become a crap shoot as far as food quality is concerned- go to the La Posada and treat yourself.

Continue through town east bound and re-join I-40 **(A099)**.

Exit 264 - HIBBARD ROAD (A100)

This used to connect along the old highway to Winslow, but in 1994, the bridge across the Little Colorado (4.6 miles ahead) was closed and all road maintenance discontinued. In 2002 a fence and locked gate blocked access.

Exit 269 - JACKRABBIT (A101)

"Here it is!" The signs used to tease us for hundreds of miles in either direction and now we're here. Built in 1947 by James Taylor and Robbie Robinson, Jackrabbit has served the traveling community for over half a century. This was a kids "must stop" on the annual vacation trip. Be sure to have your picture taken on the huge Jackrabbit out front - he's not the original, that one had to be replaced after a million kids and a few hundred cars had their way with him. Oh yeah, don't forget to have a cup of Cherry Cider. (W*hat is that stuff?)*

In front of the Jackrabbit make a left and

ZERO ODOMETER

Cruise along east on a quiet section of the old highway. Wave to the passing trains and enjoy the scenery.

3.0 miles - Leave the old pavement.

3.4 miles (A102) - If you stop here and look across the Interstate, you can see where the original road lines up with the pavement across the highway.

4.7 miles (A103) - Cross over I-40 to the north side. A right will take you to Joseph City, but first, make a left back along the old highway. We will return to this spot.

ZERO ODOMETER

0.5 miles - A feed store, but the concrete teepee gives it away as once having been a Route 66 business.

0.7 miles - Ella's Frontier - An old trading post that has seen some major vandalism. There were signs announcing Ella's as The First Trading Post On Route 66 as well as other things of historical (*Roadie-wise*) significance that have been stolen or destroyed.

Return to the I-40 crossover and go straight ahead into:

JOSEPH CITY

Originally founded in 1876 as Allen's Camp (*or Allen City, Allen Camp or Allen's City*) for William Coleman Allen, a Mormon pioneer sent by Brigham Young to establish colonies in Arizona. The first names proposed were Cumorah along with Ramah (*both are location names from the book of Mormon*). In February of 1878, the name was changed to St. Joseph, and the railroad soon requested a change because of the St. Joseph on the rail line in Missouri, the name was changed to Joseph in October of 1878 and to Joseph City in December of 1923. Joseph City is the only survivor of four small Mormon settlements along the Little Colorado River. The other three settlements were Brigham City (originally Ballinger's), Sunset (originally Smith's Camp), and Obed (originally Lake's Camp). Joseph City is also the oldest community in Navajo County.

Today, Joseph City quietly goes about its business with little regard for the passing of Route 66. Things disappear along the Mother Road and if you don't take time to photograph them . . . At the northwest corner of Main and Shelly, there had been a station and store. It was in bad shape, but now it is gone, a vacant field replacing the building - and I never caught it on film. There are still a couple of old buildings at the corner of Main and Richards and the Pacific Motel and Cafe sit across the road from each other and both are closed. Quick, get out the camera!

Continue east through town and at the Cholla Power Plant, re-join eastbound I-40 **(A104)**. There is something about the ponds east of the power plant, with steam rising from them, that bring to mind three-eyed, purple fish, with hands - too many late night movies I guess. (*Way too many...*). Or was it the Simpsons that inspired this vision?

Exit 285 - HOLBROOK (A105)

Once a rough and tumble cowtown Holbrook was named after H. R. Holbrook, the first engineer of the Atlantic and Pacific Railroad. The county seat of Navajo County Holbrook carried the odd distinction, until 1914, as the only county seat in the country without a church.

A visit to the Holbrook Wild West Museum is a must. The exhibits are fascinating, showing the life of settler and cowboy alike. Another must see is the old jail in the basement of the museum. Shipped from the east as one solid unit in 1899 at a cost of $3,000 the jail was used until 1976. A walk through the jail gives you the creeps. It is dark, cold and with a sense of isolation and fear such a place was designed to inspire.

The Holbrook of today is no longer the bustling town of Route 66 days. The streets are quiet, but busy, good food can still be had at Romo's, and Julien's Roadrunner Gift Shop offers up Jackalopes (*no kiddin'*), beautiful jewelry and the largest collection of vintage signs on the road. Another unique treasure in Holbrook is the Wigwam Motel **(A106)**. The invitation to "Sleep in a Wigwam" was every kid's wish on the northern Arizona stretch of Route 66. Opened in 1950 and fully renovated in 1988, the Wigwam has kept pace with the times. The rooms are small, but clean, and a treasure of the heyday of the highway. Call in advance of your visit at 928-524-3048 to make certain the motel is open and to make reservations. Other lodging: Best Western Arizonian Inn - Ramada Limited - Holiday Inn Express. Dining: El Rancho - Butterfield Stage Company - Mesa Italiana.

Continue through town, pass under I-40 and climb the hill to the eastern part of Holbrook, then re-enter the Interstate at exit 289 **(A107)**.

Exit 292 - INTERNATIONAL PETRIFIED FOREST, MUSEUM OF THE AMERICAS, AND DINOSAUR PARK (A108)

What a mouthful, but a great place to visit. All those dinosaurs alongside the highway are a clue to what lies through the gate and in the museum. Note that this is a private development and not affiliated with the US National Park Service, which operates the national park nine miles east of here.

Alongside the highway can be seen vestiges of Route 66.

Exit 294 - SUN VALLEY (A109)

If you follow Sun Valley Road north from the Interstate to Pima Road, you will be on Old 66. The road surface has been completely reworked and there is no hint of the old pavement or highway. Looking west from this intersection, you can see the old alignment going across the plains.

Knife City to the south of the Interstate occupies an old Stuckey's building. If you are into knives, this is a must stop to check out an amazing selection. (*Bought a stainless Spyderco here that I had never seen anywhere else.*)

Exit 300 - GOODWATER (A110) - Do not exit.

Just past the Goodwater on-ramp (westbound), you can see Old 66 climbing the hill to your right. This is on private, fenced land with no access either from here or up ahead.

Between mileposts 300 and 299 off on the right, you can see the bridge culverts for the old road.

Exit 303 - ADAMANA ROAD (A111)

A side trip and return to I-40 will take you to Rocky's Old Stage Station. Exit and go to the south side of the Interstate, the Painted Desert Indian Center is to the right. Make a left and follow the road five miles down, parallel to the freeway, to Rocky's Old Stage Station **(A112)**. The site of an old stage stop built in the 1880s and home to Nyal Rockwell from 1954 when Route 66 was a bustle of activity within a few feet of his door. In 1965, I-40 forever changed his life. The government cut him off completely. The cabins could no longer be rented and the cafe served no one. On the property is a National Old Trails Highway sign erected in the 1920s by the Automobile Club of Southern California to guide travelers along the way. As you drive back up the hill from Rocky's, pause before the top and look back at the road that was once the Main Street of America. You can see the scar of the old alignment as it cuts across the Painted Desert Monument as well as the fence that cut Nyal Rockwell off from the world. (*Rocky and his wife held on there for 30 more years, scraping out a living by running a salvage yard and used car business. It didn't have to be that way...*)

Return to Adamana Road and rejoin the Interstate.

Exit 311 - PAINTED DESERT AND PETRIFIED FOREST (A113)

Turn off here for a look at one of the true wonders of nature. The Painted Desert is a marvel of color, constantly changing as the day passes and the seasons change.

For the Route 66 buff, the old road can be seen about a half mile north of the park entrance gate. The road to the right is Old Route 66. This road is closed to the public, so please respect the signs. However, if you were to receive permission to drive down this road, you would soon be back on the pavement of Old 66 and, sitting off in the distance, you would be able to see The Painted Desert Trading Post standing alone and forgotten on the rise above the Dead River.

Continuing on through the park you will come to Tiponi Point, Tawa Point and Kachina Point. The Painted Desert Inn stands on Kachina Point.

Santa Monica to Chicago

The Painted Desert Inn was built by Herbert D. Lore in 1924. The building housed a lunch counter, an Indian trading post and was Lore's home. Lore had a one-way loop road cleared that connected the Inn to old Route 66. The loop road ran along the rim of the Painted Desert, much as today's road.

The Inn was purchased by the government in 1936, and the CCC set to work enlarging the building. Many problems were encountered in the new construction and it was 1939 before work moved to the interior of the building. Flagstone and oak flooring were laid, the walls were plastered and furniture built. By July of 1940, the Inn was opened for business, and through October of 1942, became a popular place with more requests than the six guest rooms could provide. World War II closed the Inn.

Following the war, the Fred Harvey Company took over the Inn, and in 1948, a series of improvements were begun. A well known Hopi artist, Fred Kabotie, performed his magic and produced the murals that grace the snack bar and dining room. During the 1950s and 60s, the Inn developed structural problems because of the bentonite clay beneath the structure. In 1975, the Inn was placed on the national register of Historic Places and is now a National Landmark.

Continuing through the park, you pass many view points of the Painted Desert. About six miles into the park, and just before you cross I-40, you will see a line of telephone poles. If you stop here, you can see the scar left by Old 66 as it passed through the park. The road surface was removed by the Park Service, but the line of the old highway is still there. Looking west, you can see off in the distance, beyond the Interstate, Route 66 rising on the hill, now a frontage road to I-40. At the base of that hill, is Nyal Rockwell's wrecking yard **(A112)**.

Across the Interstate and beyond the railroad tracks is the entrance to the Petrified Forest. At the Puerco Indian Ruin is where the old entrance to the park used to be located. **VERY IMPORTANT** - remember to take only pictures - no petrified wood - and leave only footprints. (*The park museum maintains a "Guilt Box" display case containing letters of apology and pieces of petrified wood taken illegally - only to be returned years later - sometimes in response to a deathbed request. You don't want to end up on your deathbed worrying about pilfered petrified wood, so just explore the area and appreciate the beauty!*)

Indian lore tells of a tired goddess who placed a curse on the area. She was hungry and tired when she reached here and discovered the logs lying on the ground. She killed a rabbit and attempted to light a fire. The logs were soaked through and would not ignite. In her anger, she turned the logs to stone.

The Petrified Forest was formed over 170 million years ago when giant reptiles and amphibian beasts roamed the area. The huge valley, which covered parts of Utah, Texas and New Mexico filled with water and the giant trees floated into the low lying swamp. Over time, they were eventually covered with three-thousand feet of soil. The trees were gradually turned to stone as mineral-rich soil replaced tree cells. During the period when the Rocky Mountains were formed, the ground was lifted to the point it is today and the erosion by wind and water exposed the "logs."

It is important to note that you must retrace your route through the park in order to continue east on I-40. Exiting the park on the south side will force you to return to Holbrook. (*For another jackalope?*)

Eastbound on I-40 once again.

Exit 320 - PINTA ROAD (A114)

ADVENTURE TOUR

Please read all admonitions regarding Adventure Tours at front of this book

This section covers a stretch of Old 66 that features the Painted Desert Trading Post, a classic bridge across the Dead River and ends at the boundary of the Petrified Forest/Painted Desert. The road is rough in spots with sections of old pavement (complete with white line), and dirt. Can be traveled in a standard vehicle at a slow pace.

CAUTION NOTE: If it has been raining, or is raining, be aware there are sections of mud between I-40 and the old pavement. To avoid getting stuck, drive on the high sides of the road and NEVER venture into a puddle.

To join this section, take Exit 320 (Pinta Road) **(A114)** from I-40 and proceed to the North. Follow the road as it curves to the east then back to the north. At the point where the pavement ends:
ZERO ODOMETER
1.0 miles (ATA41) - This is where Pinta Road crosses old 66. Make a left onto the old pavement.
NOTE: Once you cross the fence line to reach Old 66, you are on Navajo Nation land. Respect the land and remain on the road.
1.4 miles (ATA42) - A box culvert.
1.8 miles (ATA43) - Another culvert.

Santa Monica to Chicago

> **3.6 miles (ATA44)** - The remains of the Painted Desert Trading Post. Graffiti artists (*also known as vandals*) have been at work on the façade of the building. This is a great photo opportunity location.
> **3.8 miles (ATA45)** - Bridge across the Dead River. The old cars dumped on the east side of the river were placed there as a form of erosion control to keep the river from undercutting the bank and washing out the bridge abutments.
> **3.9 miles (ATA46)** - Ranch house to the right. Respect the no trespassing signs.
> The road ahead is overgrown with weeds, but drivable. Thanks to the Park Service putting in a well up ahead this section of the road is once again open to travel (it had been closed at the Dead River crossing for seven or eight years).
> **5.2 miles (ATA47)** - A metal culvert is visible on the left side of the road.
> **5.4 miles** - Pavement actually ends (curious!).
> **5.6 miles** - Fairly rough for the next .2 of a mile, watch your speed.
> **6.2 miles (ATA48)** - Boundary line of the Petrified Forest/Painted Desert. Turn around here and return to Pinta Road, then back to I-40.

Exit 325 - NAVAJO (A115)

Three miles southeast of here is Navajo Springs, the site of the first encampment in what would be Arizona Territory. On December 29, 1863, the territorial gubernatorial party camped here in a blinding snowstorm after being assured by their military escort that Navajo Springs was in what would become Arizona Territory. They had a dinner of freshly killed antelope and toasted the establishment of the new territory with champagne. The flag was raised and John C. Goodwin took the oath of office and became the first governor of the new Arizona Territory.

Side trip! From here it is possible to trace some old, long abandoned sections of the road, but only if you are driving a high clearance vehicle. This road begins just south of Navajo **(ATA51)** and will take you back west and under the freeway to the Pinta Road junction **(ATA41)** **(which actually begins an Adventure Tour!)** and you will re-join I-40 at Exit 320 (Pinta Road) **(A114)**.

Otherwise, back on I-40.

Exit 333 - CHAMBERS (A116)

Straight ahead is the Best Western Chieftain Inn a nice motel with an excellent restaurant - a great breakfast or lunch stop. At the top of the off-ramp, make a left and:

ZERO ODOMETER
    0.5 miles (A117) - Intersection. Make a right. This puts you on the old alignment.
    1.5 miles -

CHAMBERS

Named after Charles Chambers, trading post operator at this location from the late 1870s through 1888. In 1926, the name was changed to Halloysite (*a mineral used in the manufacture of expensive china and mined in the area*). Renamed Chambers in 1930.
    1.8 miles - Garage on right.
    2.9 to 3.1 miles - Garage, junkyard and Appaloosa Corral Bar.
    4.1 miles - Abandoned car wash.
    5.1 miles - Houses on right.
    6.4 miles - On-ramp to I-40 at Sanders **(A118)**.
Continue east on I-40.

Exit 341 - ORTEGA ROAD (A119)

NOTE: This is a dirt road side trip to reach Old 66. If you prefer not to travel on dirt continue on I-40.
Head north to the first road that goes east-west **(A120)**. Make a right and:
ZERO ODOMETER
    0.5 miles (A121) - End of pavement.
    2.8 miles (A122) - Bridge across Querino Canyon, and on the left the remains of the Querino Canyon Trading Post. Building has mostly collapsed.
    3.3 miles (A123) - The New Querino Trading Post. Continue straight ahead.
    4.7 miles (A124) - The Good News Church.
    5.1 miles (A125) - Pavement.
    5.2 miles (A126) - Access to I-40 at Exit 346 (Pine Springs Road), continue straight ahead.

Santa Monica to Chicago

    6.3 miles (A127) - Low spot, warning sign not to cross when flooded. BE CAREFUL!
    7.1 miles (A128) - Fort Courage. No, *'F' Troop* was not filmed here.
    8.1 miles - Housing subdivision.
    10.1 miles (A129) - Indian City and site of Allentown.
        Continue east on the frontage road. The road curves and winds over the hills, following the lay of the land.
    12.5 miles (A130) - Make a right through one of the tunnels, crossing under I-40, then make a left on to the frontage road and follow for about six miles to:

LUPTON (A131)
    Named for G. W. Lupton, the trainmaster at Winslow in the early 1900s.
    Cross under I-40 **(A132)** and follow the frontage road east towards New Mexico. Many trading posts and tourist spots along here.
    The Teepee Trading Post **(A133)** is a sixty-foot tall concrete teepee (tipi) that has drawn tourists for years to buy souvenirs and have a bite to eat, in the café upstairs in the top of the teepee (*at this writing the café is closed, which is okay because the food was just so-so*).
    This ends our trip across Arizona. Just ahead is Mile 0 and the beginning of our journey into the Land of Enchantment - New Mexico.

Santa Monica to Chicago

NEW MEXICO

EASTBOUND

Ahead lies the "The Land of Enchantment." A journey across New Mexico provides an understanding of where the state motto came from. There is truly something mystical and enchanting about this place, and as you follow Route 66 you will see the beauty and also be captured by the wonder that is New Mexico. We are going to discover lost alignments and (for the adventurous) a section of Route 66 that will literally drop you back in time.

At the Arizona-New Mexico Stateline (milepost 0, designated NM 118):

ZERO ODOMETER

0.3 miles (N001) - Chief Yellow Horse Trading Post on the left. Two Guns Miller of Two Guns, Arizona fame, established this trading post.

0.8 miles (N002) - Crumbling remains of a small concrete shack on the left. This was the site of the old Box Canyon Trading Post.

2.7 miles (N003) - This is the spot that started me on my search for the Mother Road in 1989. At this site, in 1950, Director Billy Wilder brought Kirk Douglas, Jan Sterling and a large crew to film *Ace in The Hole* (re-titled *The Big Carnival*). A local trading post, Lookout Point, owned by Leroy Atkinson, was used in the filming and the studio built a group of cliff dwellings into the cliff in the background (the one with the split at the top). In 1953, Atkinson sold the trading post to the Christensens, who renamed it Cliff Dwellings Trading Post and capitalized on the ersatz cliff dwellings. Today, nothing remains of the trading post except a couple of pipes where the gas pumps used to be.

5.0 miles (N004) - St. Catherine's Mission on the right. (*Certain high-quality Route 66 maps show this to be the location of Manuelito, perhaps "Old Manuelito".*)

7.1 miles (N005) - Turn off to Manuelito.

8.0 miles (N006) - Bridge over railroad tracks.

8.4 miles (N007) - Cross under I-40.

8.7 miles (N008) - Entrance to I-40, continue straight.

11.9 miles (N009) - Follow road around the State Truck Inspection Station.

12.8 miles (N010) - Stop sign, make a left, and cross under I-40 (*tunnel is narrow so watch for traffic*).

13.1 miles (N011) - Stop sign, make a right onto the old highway. (*To the left, the old highway will dead-end in 0.6 miles.*) Continue east toward Gallup.

16.3 miles (N012) - Mentmore Road on the left.

16.8 miles (N013) - Truck stops, underpass, and enter Gallup.

GALLUP

Named for Santa Fe paymaster David L. Gallup and founded in 1881. Gallup terms itself The Gateway to Indian Country and the proliferation of Native American jewelry, pottery, art and rug manufacturers attests to that title.

Gallup was home to one of the most unique Harvey Houses in the country, the El Navajo. Designed by famed architect Mary Jane Colter, in a native pueblo design, the El Navajo became the social center of the Gallup area. Opened on May 26, 1923, the El Navajo was a beautiful structure. Alas, declining rail passenger traffic forced an economic decision (*with no regard for the historical significance of the building, unlike Needles California, which resolutely holds on to the El Garces despite not knowing exactly what to do with it*) to close the El Navajo in May of 1957, and the building was destroyed shortly thereafter.

Gallup abounds with restaurants, cafes, and lodging facilities. The following are my choices - **Best place to stay** - The El Rancho Hotel, 1000 East 66 Avenue (505.863.9311). A living piece of history as the Home of the Movie Stars. Be sure to stay in the hotel, if possible, and not the newer motel section. The rooms are named for movie stars and the mezzanine has hundreds of autographed photos. The lobby is a thing of beauty. A true Mother Road classic and a Roadie thanks to Armand Ortega for his restoration of this Queen of the Road. Most of the classic motels suffer from disrepair, so if the El Rancho is not your choice consider the Best Western Inn and Suites on east Route 66; the Micro-Tel Inn, off exit 16; or the Days Inn West, also exit 16.

One of the finest restaurants in Gallup is Dominic's, located downtown at 302 W. Coal Avenue - excellent Italian food in a pleasant atmosphere. Great Mexican Food can be had at Virgie's on the west end of town. A good breakfast, in a old diner atmosphere, is available at the Plaza Cafe (1501 W. 66), also the Ranch Kitchen (3001 W. 66). Fast food cannot be beat at Blake's Lottaburger on the east side of town.

As you cross under I-40 on the east end of town **(N014)**,

Santa Monica to Chicago

ZERO ODOMETER and continue east.

    0.8 miles (N015) - New Mexico State Police, right (*new location, older one is up the road a bit on the left*.)

    2.3 miles (N016) - Sundance road, right.

    3.7 miles (N017) - Left, Red Rocks State Park. A wonderful museum here tracing Southwest Native American Culture. Also rodeo grounds in a natural amphitheater at the base of red rock cliffs.

    4.5 & 4.6 miles (N018) - Cross railroad tracks.

    5.1 miles (N019) - Entrance, right, to Fort Wingate Army Depot. Originally established as Fort Fauntleroy, the name was changed to Fort Lyon when General Fauntleroy joined the Confederate Army (*Talk about goin' South!*). In 1868, when the Navajos returned to the area, troops were moved from the original Fort Wingate at San Rafael and the post was renamed Fort Wingate. General Douglas MacArthur was born here in 1880 and General Blackjack Pershing served here. In 1918, the Army Ordnance Department took over the fort for munitions storage.

    7.7 miles (N020) - Junction with NM 400 and entrance to I-40. Continue straight on NM 118.

    9.0 miles (N021) - Right, remains of old station and a café. Site of Perea Trading Post.

    9.5 miles (N022) - Iyanbito, church mission, left.

    11.0 miles (N023) - Rejoin I-40 at the Iyanbito interchange (Exit 36) and continue east.

Exit 39 - Giant Truck Stop is to the left. One of the largest in the nation. Good food available here.

Exit 44 - COOLIDGE (N024)

Named for a director of the old Atlantic and Pacific Railroad. Old Route 66 is on north side here. Left turn at top of off-ramp. The road going east will dead-end in 0.3 miles. The buildings at the top of the rise were Fred Wilson's Trading Post. The road going to the west will bring you to the site of the old Navajo Trading Company. It will be necessary to return to the overpass to continue east on I-40.

Exit 47 - CONTINENTAL DIVIDE (N025)

This is the separation point for the waters of the continent. Rain (*and beer...*) that falls east of here winds up in the Atlantic. Rain (*and beer...*) to the west flows to the Pacific. There are a few trading posts and gas stations remaining, but long gone is the Top O' the World, a dance hall, bar, tourist court, trading post and boarding house for railroad men. The Top O' the World was one of those places with a rather dingy reputation, sort of like "the old roadhouse out on the highway."

Contrary to popular belief, at 7,263 feet, this was not the highest point on Route 66. For post-1937 highway design, that honor belongs to the stretch between Brannigan Meadow and Parks, Arizona at 7,414 feet. For pre-1937, the honor belongs to the Glorieta Pass area near Pecos, NM at just over 7500 feet. (*Okay, kids, who figured it out first? The winner should start thinking about what motel to pick out in Tucumcari!*) The highest point on I-40 is the Arizona Divide - just west of Flagstaff - at 7,335 feet.

Cross over the freeway to the north frontage road, make a right and this will put you back on Route 66. As you turn onto the old highway (designated NM 122),

ZERO ODOMETER

Cruising this section of highway can be truly enjoyable. Traffic on the Interstate is racing along, fighting the trucks and each other to get "there" first (*and then do what? watch more television?*). You will most likely be all alone, cruising at a comfortable speed and not having to hassle the traffic.

    5.4 miles (N026) - Stop sign and Thoreau. Originally named Mitchell, name was changed with the arrival of the railroad. Most likely named after Henry David Thoreau, but the pronunciation varies across the region. Most commonly heard is "threw."

The town lies north of Route 66 on NM 371. It is the home of Frontier Buckles, the manufacturer of the huge buckles worn by Rodeo champions. Also, the Zuni (*zoo-nee*) Mountain Kachina Company is located here, one of the largest manufacturers of Kachinas in the nation.

    16.0 miles (N027) - Prewitt. Trading post at this location started by R. C. Prewitt, Sr.

    21.0 miles (N028) - The Route 66 Swap Meet, operated by Thomas Lamance. A few thousand license plates offer a glimpse into the past, along with a barn full of collectibles.

    22.9 miles (N029) - Highway divides.

    24.6 miles (N030) - Junction with NM 606.

    25.9 miles (N031) - Bluewater. The Bluewater Trading Company is a sight with the murals stretching from one end of the building to the other.

    26.1 miles (N032) - The Bluewater Motel ruins. Great old sign to photograph.

    31.4 miles (N033) - Milan. A rather new town, incorporated in 1957, and named for Salvador Milan a landowner through his wife Veneranda Mirabal whose father had large holdings in the region.

    33.6 (N034) - Bridge over railroad tracks.

Santa Monica to Chicago

34.6 (N035) -

GRANTS

The railroad arrived and with it the name of the town. The Grant brothers, Angus, Lewis and John, were Santa Fe railroad contractors who maintained a site called Grants' Camp at this location. Also known as Grants' Station, and prior to 1881, Alamitos. Post office was established as Grant in 1882 and the name finally changed in 1936.

A true Route 66 town, Grants offers many older motels along East Santa Fe Avenue, and unfortunately many of them are in poor condition. The best of the older motels is The Sands at 112 McArthur St **(N037)** (*a block off of 66 and quiet*). For more contemporary lodging consider the Best Western Inn & Suites of Gallup and the Holiday Inn Express both at exit 85. One warning about accommodations in Grants: A few of the motels at the Interstate exit offer attractive rates on their signs, but once inside the story is, "We're sold out of those rooms," this took place at 1300 hours, on a weekday, with two cars in the lot. The rooms available are priced as much as forty dollars higher than the sign. This story has been the same since my first overnight stop in 1990 (*have checked back in '92, '93, '96, '98, '99, '00 and '01 and received the same line every time*). Good food can be had at the Uranium Café **(N036)** (*across from the Mining Museum*) where the Yellow Cake pancake more than covers the plate and if you can eat two of them they are free! (*This would be a good warm-up for the 72 oz steak at the Big Texan in Amarillo. More about that later...*)

A must stop in Grants is the Mining Museum. A recreated hard rock mine, underground, awaits you. A tour well worth the time and money.

The landscaped median along Santa Fe Avenue (old Route 66) has been adopted by various businesses as a point of civic pride and the effort has paid off in beautifying the town.

Head east out of Grants, watch for the left turn onto **NM 117 (N038)**, and

ZERO ODOMETER

    3.6 miles (N039) - Bridge over the railroad tracks.

    5.3 miles (N040) - Stuckey's on hill to the right, make a left turn onto NM 124 and

ZERO ODOMETER

As you drive east the road will twist and turn to avoid the lava beds. This area was known as *The Mal Pais*, or (*loose translation*) bad country. Highway engineers had to the swing the road around the lava beds because construction techniques of the 1930s would not allow them to build straight across.

    1.2 miles (N041) - Cross under I-40.

    6.0 miles (N042) - McCarty's (NM 124). Named for a contractor who occupied this site during the construction of the railroad. This was also known as Santa Maria de Acoma, the site of a beautiful replica, on a smaller scale, of the church at Acoma Pueblo. Built in 1933, the church is considered to be an architecturally pure example of Spanish Colonial style.

    7.5 miles (N043) - Cross over I-40.

    10.8 miles (N044) - San Fidel. Originally La Vega de San Jose. Name was changed at the suggestion of Father Robert Kalth. Post office established in 1919.

A quiet town with evidence of old cafes, motels and gas stations. One of the most popular was Ramsey's, famous along the road for excellent biscuits and gravy.

    13.1 miles (N045) - A right here will take you to Sky City Casino, half-a-mile south - if you're into that sort of thing.

At this intersection:

ZERO ODOMETER

    0.3 miles (N046) - On the right, this used to be Obie's Long Branch Saloon, on the left the long abandoned Mt. Taylor Motel.

    0.9 miles (N047) - Villa de Cubero. A gas station, general store and tourist court where Ernest Hemingway supposedly worked on The Old Man and the Sea. Across the road was Gunn's Cafe, a place renowned for good food and friendly service. Side trip! A left here will take you on a short loop through Cubero, which was the original alignment of Route 66 until 1937. You will come out at Budville.

    2.4 miles (N048) - Budville. Named by Bud Rice, whose father built the first garage here in the 1920s. Bud, along with his wife Flossie, ran the best towing business in the country (*and held court as the local justice of the peace at night - speeding tickets anyone?*). Bud was murdered during a hold-up in 1967, and in 1979, Flossie sold the wrecker and closed the garage doors.

    3.3 miles - Access to I-40, continue straight.

    4.3 miles - A group of stone buildings on the left are the remains of an old motel.

    6.1 miles (N049) - Paraje (*Spanish - place, or stopping place*), a Laguna Indian village. The old trading post has a new addition (2002), a painting of the robot Bender from the TV series *Futurama*, and an excellent painting by the way. A right at the intersection will take you to Acoma Pueblo, the Sky City (13 miles).

This is an interesting side trip and should not be missed. However, there are some stringent restrictions placed on tourists. You must buy tickets at the Tribal Center, then board a bus for the tour to the pueblo. Photography is permitted only if a permit has been purchased for EACH camera in use. Waits can be rather extensive for the busses, so plan sufficient time for your visit.

    12.8 miles **(N050)** - Junction with old road into Laguna, make a right.

LAGUNA

Spanish for lake, which has long since disappeared. The church here is one of particular beauty. This is the church used in the Kirk Douglas film *Ace in the Hole* (re-titled *The Big Carnival*). Kirk rushed here to pick up a priest and take him back to the site of the cave-in.

    Winding around the hill at Laguna will lead to the village of New Laguna at milepost 4.2.

    13.1 miles **(N051)** - Cross bridge. In 1952, a gasoline truck went off the road and plunged into the arroyo at this location. The resulting fire destroyed the bridge and closed Route 66 for twelve hours.

    13.3 miles **(N052)** - Ramp leading to I-40, but don't take the freeway. Make a left here onto the frontage road, SLOW DOWN AND WATCH FOR IT, it comes up quickly and is not well marked (the Middle School sign is a good help for spotting this turn). At the turn,

ZERO ODOMETER

The five miles of road from here to Mesita - although one of the most picturesque little sections of Route 66 - winds around the mesas and buttes with a few sharp curves and one steep hill. Imagine driving this section on a rainy night with hundreds of other cars, trucks and busses. (*Plenty of business for Bud Rice, who had the exclusive highway towing contract from Grants to halfway to Albuquerque...*)

    0.6 miles **(N053)** - Old Route 66 to the right. Do not drive it!

    2.0 miles **(N054)** - Deadman's Curve. The road turns 180 degrees here.

    2.7 miles **(N055)** - Owl Rock on the left.

    4.6 miles **(N056)** - Mesita, junction with old road.

> **NOTE:** Options lie ahead as to how to follow various Route 66 alignments. It is strongly suggested you take some time to read all of the information from this point to Santa Rosa in order to make decisions regarding your personal trip across New Mexico. Once those decisions are made you may want to mark out the sections that do not apply to eliminate confusion on the road.

    When you reach Mesita, there are three options for reaching Albuquerque. *(Upon arrival in Albuquerque, you will then have two options for getting to Santa Rosa.)*

    There is a dirt road ahead, so it's decision time. To trace the original route of the old road, use OPTION ONE, which is an Adventure Tour "Red Route." (*Please read all admonitions regarding Adventure Tours at the front of this book.*) OPTION ONE is partially a dirt road, slick and muddy in the winter, and following a rain. If you do not wish to travel on dirt, use OPTIONS TWO or THREE, which are paved.

    OPTION 1 - This option will take you on the old, old alignment - on dirt and long neglected pavement - for 11 miles, then re-join pavement at Correo for NM 6 to Los Lunas, following the Option 2 route.)

    OPTION 2 - This option avoids the dirt and will take you on I-40 to the point where you can follow the original alignment (NM 6) into Los Lunas and avoid the dirt section.

    OPTION 3 - This option puts you on I-40 at Mesita and follows the freeway all the way to Albuquerque. If you do so, once you are beyond Exit 126 (NM 6), you will be traveling the route of the second alignment of the highway (*which is under I-40*).

OPTION #1

The original alignment can be reached by continuing east from Mesita **(N056)** along the north frontage road, then crossing I-40 **(N058)** (*crossover only - this is not an interchange*), making a left onto the south frontage road and following the road as is swings south, then east. There is not a lot to see out here, but sections of old pavement and the ruins of a long closed trading post will be visible as you get close to the bridge across the railroad tracks at Correo. Make a right at the junction with NM 6 **(N060)** and follow directions in OPTION #2 from ZERO ODOMETER immediately below. (*If you do not want to follow the Los Lunas loop, make a left off the dirt road at Correo and take NM 6 north back to the I-40 junction* **(N059)**, *then go on I-40 east into Albuquerque - this follows the route of Option #3.*)

Santa Monica to Chicago

OPTION #2

To avoid the dirt section (*but still go through Las Lunas to Albuquerque*), enter I-40 at Mesita **(N057)** and continue east until you reach Exit 126, the turn off for Los Lunas, NM 6 **(N059)**. Take the off-ramp, at the top make a right, and follow NM 6 south to the crossroads **(N060)** at Correo (*Spanish - mail*), so named because it was the only place for many miles where mail could be dropped. Post Office was established in 1914. Also shown on many old maps as Suwanee (*originally San Jose*), founded in 1902, which is just east of this location.

A left at the Correo crossroads leads to a short section of the second alignment (1937) of Route 66. A gate prevents travel beyond this short section, but the road can be seen heading off to the northeast.

A right at the crossroads is where the dirt road from Mesita (Option #1) connects.

To follow the original alignment (pre-1937) of Route 66, continue east on NM 6 to Los Lunas.

At the crossroads at Correo,

ZERO ODOMETER

2.0 miles (N061) - Suwanee.

6.7 miles (N062) - A large canyon off to the left. Great view.

12.7 miles - The old highway skirts the edge of a hill for 0.1 miles.

At milepost 21.10 an old section of the highway is available to the right. It goes for 2.7 miles and has a couple of deep cuts across the pavement.

14.7 miles - Road mentioned above joins the new pavement.

15.9 miles - Old highway to right.

17.1 miles - Old road rejoin the new.

17.4 miles - Old road meets the new on the right. Do not attempt to drive this section. Many of the bridges have been removed making if impassable. Road climbs and from the new "high" road the old alignment can be seen on the right.

20.3 miles - The old road on the right joins the new road.

25.4 miles (N063) - Bridge ruins to the right.

26.1 miles (N064) - Cross over the railroad.

27.3 miles (N065) - Top of the hill. This is a good place to pull over, get out of the car and appreciate the view of the valley. Thousands of postcards were sold with this view.

31.1 miles (N066) - Cross I-25.

32.8 miles (N067) - Los Lunas and junction of NM 6 and NM 314.

Make a left onto NM 314 and continue north to Albuquerque. More than sixty years have taken their toll along here and there is not much of the old highway to see. Continue to Bridge Blvd in Albuquerque. Make a right onto Bridge Blvd **(N068)**, cross the bridge, and make a left onto 4th Street **(N069)**, heading north to Central **(N070)**. Then a right on Central to 2nd St **(N071)** where you have two choices:

- To follow the first alignment (1926), which will take you through Santa Fe, go to the section below marked Santa Fe Loop Option.
- To follow the second alignment (post-1937), go to the section below marked Post 1937 Alignment Option, which follows the description of the Santa Fe Loop.

OPTION #3

Follow I-40 east from Mesita **(N057)**.

When you reach Rio Puerco, an exit and short stop to photograph the old bridge is worth the time **(N076)**. This bridge was built in 1933 and, at 250 feet, is the longest single-span Parker Through-Truss bridge in the southwest. It was saved through the efforts of the New Mexico Historic Route 66 Association and others working together to hold on to a classic piece of highway architecture.

Take Exit 149 **(N075)** and follow Central Avenue down Nine-Mile Hill into the Rio Grande River valley. This was the second alignment (1937) of Route 66 through the city and Central will continue all the way across town.

You have two choices when you get to Central and 2nd St. in downtown:

- To follow the first alignment (1926), which will take you through Santa Fe, go to the section below marked Santa Fe Loop Option.
- To follow the second alignment (post-1937), go to the section below marked Post 1937 Alignment Option, which follows the Santa Fe Loop Option description.

ALBUQUERQUE

Founded in 1706 by Don Francisco Cuervo y Valdes and named San Francisco de Alburquerque (*yes, that first "r" belongs there*). This city along the banks of the Rio Bravo del Norte (*the name of the Rio Grande at the time*) was named after Don

Santa Monica to Chicago

Francisco's patron saint, Francisco Xavier and the Duke of Alburquerque, the Viceroy of Spain. If you have ever wondered why Albuquerque is known as The Duke City, there is your answer. Almost immediately a problem arose with the name. King Philip V of Spain had not been consulted about the name, so to prevent problems the Viceroy changed it to San Felipe de Alburquerque. Somewhere along the line the first "r" was dropped (*or maybe it fell off*) and the name of the city as we know it today came into being.

The Santa Fe Railroad reached the city in 1881, and the year before, the city, called New Albuquerque was platted two miles east of the present Old Town in preparation for the arrival of the railroad. The first mayor was elected in 1885, and the city was incorporated in 1890.

In 1902, one of the classic Harvey Houses along Route 66 was built. The Mary Jane Colter designed Alvarado served the traveling public with food and lodging in the Fred Harvey tradition, while the fantastic Indian Building displayed and sold only the finest in Native American arts and crafts. Ignoring the historic significance of this building, the shortsighted officials of the city allowed the Alvarado to be destroyed in March of 1970.

Albuquerque is a large city, and as such, does not offer much for the hard-core Roadie. Gang crime is a major problem in the city with tourists quite often being the victims (*those iron fences and gates around the motels aren't purely for decoration*). It is suggested that for overnight plans communities such as Gallup, Grants, Moriarty, Santa Fe, Santa Rosa or Tucumcari be the choice of the Mother Road traveler. For a true New Mexico experience, Santa Fe cannot be beat.

SANTA FE LOOP OPTION

Turn north off Central Ave onto 2nd Street (**N071**) and
ZERO ODOMETER
Make a left on Lomas (**N072**), then a right onto 4th Street (**N073**) and follow it north out of town.
1.1 miles - Cross under I-40.
1.6 miles - 4th jogs slightly to the right.
5.5 miles - 4th jogs right at Ranchitos Road.
7.0 miles - 4th jogs left to meet Alameda Blvd.
8.2 miles - 4th curves to the right and becomes NM 313 (*also known as El Camino Real*) Continue north on NM 313 through Sandia Pueblo, Bernalillo and Algodones. Ahead lays the infamous La Bajada Hill.

One of the major obstacles for the early Route 66 traveler was La Bajada (*Spanish - the descent*) Hill, a volcanic escarpment that neatly separates the North Rio Grande Valley from the South Rio Grande Valley with a 500-foot drop. The original road, built by the Army in the 1860s, featured mind-numbing 28 percent grades. Workers from the Cochiti pueblo and the state penitentiary improved the road beginning in 1908. Considered an engineering marvel when completed in 1922, the new road featured 26 switchbacks, a much improved eight percent grade and dropped the 500 feet in less than two miles. A large sign at the top of the hill warned, "This road is not fool proof, but safe for a sane driver." In 1932, the road was moved about three miles to the east (present location of I-25) and the old switchbacks abandoned.

Modern day Roadies have four options, with Option 2 recommended for most travelers:

> **NOTE:** Options lie ahead as to how to tackle La Bajada Hill. It is strongly suggested you take some time to read all of the information from this point to Santa Fe in order to make decisions regarding your trip.
>
> In general terms, the north end of the La Bajada area is in Santa Fe, beginning at Cerrillos Blvd, near the Santa Fe airport (**N081**). The south end is in Algodones (**N074**), near the turn-off to I-25 exit 248).

OPTION 1 - By-pass La Bajada entirely by joining the Interstate in Algodones for the trip to Santa Fe. (*This option is listed first only because the directions are the simplest.*)

OPTION 2 - Use I-25 and paved NM highways to get to the base of La Bajada Hill, look up at it in wonder and disbelief that people ever managed to traverse it, and then re-connect to I-25 to get to Santa Fe. This option uses paved roads for its entire length except the last 1.4 miles which are on a well maintained dirt road that is very comfortable to drive as long as you are in dry weather. (*If you're squeamish about the last 1.4 miles, you can still see the La Bajada switchbacks in the distance from - you guessed it - 1.4 miles away!*)

OPTION 3 - This is a "Red Route" Adventure Tour that closely follows the pre-1937 alignment, using paved NM highways and maintained dirt roads to get to the base of La Bajada Hill where you can stare up in wonder. You will then re-connect to I-25 to

SANTA MONICA TO CHICAGO

get to Santa Fe. This option requires dry weather.

The route will take you into Indian reservations that tourists rarely travel to. There are some roadside services scattered along the way but the endemic poverty and social difficulties of some of the smaller Indian tribes will be readily apparent. Please conduct yourself with appropriate restraint, as the customs of their lives can be something of an enduring mystery to outsiders.

NOTE: For the adventurous, you can also follow the Mother Road south from Santa Fe to the top of La Bajada Hill and look down onto the Mother Road. Follow the directions listed for La Bajada Option 4 in the Chicago-to-LA directions. For the first part of Option 4, the road is flat (good!) but not very well maintained (bad!). You won't get "stuck" in dry weather but you will have to pick and choose your way across the mesa. The reward is a knockout view of the road and New Mexico stretching out before you.

OPTION 4 - This is a VERY demanding "Black Route" Adventure Tour that includes special precautions described below. Drive to La Bajada Hill using Option 3 and then drive up the hill instead of connecting to I-25. (*Note: Even if you don't take this option, you will undoubtedly gain an appreciation of the challenge simply by reading the instructions!*)

OPTION #1

Just north of Algodones it will be necessary to join I-25. Watch for the large power plant, just before it will be a road to the right leading to I-25 **(N074)**. Take this road for 0.4 miles and enter I-25 northbound at Exit 248 **(N079)**. Continue to Exit 278 - Cerrillos Road **(N080)**, approximately 28 miles north. Take this exit to enter Santa Fe.

Jump to "**Continuation of text following all La Bajada Hill options**" for further directions.

OPTION #2

Just north of Algodones it will be necessary to join I-25. Watch for the large power plant, just before it will be a road to the right leading to I-25 **(N074)**. Take this road for 0.4 miles and enter I-25 northbound at Exit 248 **(N079)**.

Take I-25 north approximately 16 miles to Exit 264 - NM 16 **(ATN72)**. Follow NM 16 west approximately 3.5 miles to the turn-off to Tetilla Park Recreational Area **(ATN68)**.

At the junction, if you look to the south - along the power line - you will see the original track of Route 66 next to the power line. This is a fenced off section and not open to the public. Also, take a minute to read the nearby historical marker explaining the phenomena of the La Bajada escarpment.

Turn right (north) and

ZERO ODOMETER

Follow the road towards the recreational area.

1.0 mile (ATN69) - Unmarked turn-off to the right. Turn onto the well-maintained dirt road.
2.2 miles - La Bajada switchbacks visible on the cliff, dead ahead.
2.4 miles (ATN70) - Cool bridge.
2.5 miles (ATN71) - Just past the bridge, there is a hard right onto the dirt road up La Bajada. This is where Option 2 and Option 3 Roadies turn around and return to the junction with NM 16 **(ATN68)**.

(Option 4 - the Black Route Adventure Tour - begins here for the die-hards!)

Upon reaching the junction, turn left onto NM 16 and return to I-25 **(ATN72)**. Take I-25 north and continue to Exit 278 - Cerrillos Road **(N080)**, approximately 14 miles north. Take this exit to enter Santa Fe.

Jump to "**Continuation of text following all La Bajada Hill options**" for further directions.

OPTION #3

Continue north on NM 313 through Algodones. You will pass the road leading to I-25 **(N074)**. As you go past this intersection
ZERO ODOMETER

0.4 miles (ATN51) - Algodones Power Plant.
2.4 miles (ATN52) - Stop sign, and left turn towards San Felipe. You are now entering the San Felipe Indian Reservation.
5.1 miles (ATN53) - Stop sign in San Felipe pueblo. Go straight. Dirt road begins just ahead.
5.4 miles - Cross wash. Washboard road ahead.
6.6 miles - Graded road begins.
7.0 miles - Cross irrigation aqueduct.
7.4 miles - Cross under power line.
8.1 miles - Cross wash.
9.0 miles (ATN54) - Cross railroad tracks.
9.3 miles (ATN55) - Well-paved road begins, seemingly out in the middle of nowhere. Actually, you have just crossed into the Santo Domingo pueblo and the road improvement is defined by the pueblo boundary.

SANTA MONICA TO CHICAGO

10.2 miles - Cross wash, improved with concrete pad.
10.7 miles - Cross wash, improved with concrete pad.
11.4 miles - Cross wash, improved with concrete pad. Keep an eye out for wandering cows and dogs in this neighborhood.
12.2 miles (ATN56) - Big pavement change, right in middle of Santo Domingo pueblo.
12.5 miles (ATN57) - Another odd pavement change.
12.7 miles (ATN58) - Stop sign in center of Santo Domingo pueblo.
13.3 miles (ATN59) - Access to I-25. Cross under overpass.
13.5 miles - Water tower.
13.7 miles (ATN60) - Town of Domingo. Ruins of Domingo Trading Post, which billed itself as the oldest trading post in the West circa 1881. (*1881? Oldest in the West? Oh well, the Old West is the land of b.s.*) Great picture taking opportunity.
13.8 miles (ATN61) - Bridge destroyed. Must have been a heck of a flood. End of the line for this section of Route 66. The old road crossed the river and headed up the hill onto a long flat mesa. Turn around and return to the I-25 access overpass **(ATN59)** for a detour around the bridge.

The detour begins just before the overpass (at the historical markers), where you make a right **(ATN62)** and
ZERO ODOMETER
Follow the inclined curve up to the stop sign. Turn right at the stop sign **(ATN63)** onto the road to Pena Blanca pueblo.
3.3 miles (ATN64) - Enchanted Farm entrance. Interesting brickwork.
4.2 miles (ATN65) - Pena Blanca post office and well-maintained church.
5.4 miles (ATN66) - Junction with NM 16. Turn right and proceed east.
7.4 miles - Turn-off to Conchiti Dam spillway.
9.4 miles (ATN67) - Conchiti Indian Reservation boundary.
10.8 miles (ATN68) - Turn-off to Tetilla Park Recreational Area. This completes the detour around the washed-out Domingo bridge.

If you look to the south - along the power line - you will see the original track of Route 66 next to the power line. This is a fenced off section and not open to the public. Also, take a minute to read the nearby historical marker explaining the phenomena of the La Bajada escarpment.

Turn left (north) and
ZERO ODOMETER
Follow the road towards the recreational area.
1.0 mile (ATN69) - Unmarked turn-off to the right. Turn onto the well-maintained dirt road.
2.2 miles - La Bajada switchbacks visible on the cliff, dead ahead.
2.4 miles (ATN70) - Cool bridge.
2.5 miles (ATN71) - Just past the bridge, there is a hard right onto the dirt road up La Bajada. This is where Option 2 and Option 3 Roadies turn around and return to the junction with NM 16 **(ATN68)**. Option 4 - the Black Route Adventure Tour - begins here - hang on!

Upon reaching the junction, turn left onto NM 16 and head east for I-25, which you will join approximately 3.5 miles down the road **(ATN72)**.

Take I-25 north and continue to Exit 278 - Cerrillos Road **(N080)**, approximately 14 miles north. Take this exit to enter Santa Fe.

Jump to *"Continuation of text following all La Bajada Hill options"* for further directions.

OPTION #4
This is a "Black Route" Adventure Tour and is the most challenging of any on Route 66, bar none. Fasten your seatbelts, campers, you're in for a ride!

ADVENTURE TOUR

Please read all admonitions regarding Adventure Tours at the front of this book.

It is still possible to make the climb up the old road by high clearance four-wheel drive vehicle. (*Or, as was done in 2001, by bicycle in a combination ride and carry mode. See Route 66 Magazine, Winter 2001/2002.*)

The general admonitions for Adventure Tours all apply to La Bajada, but there are some additional requirements as well:

Santa Monica to Chicago

> 1. The road is largely a rock wash and is not maintained in any fashion. There are parts that will leave you with the impression you are doing cross-country rock-hopping.
> 2. A high-clearance four-wheel drive is required. However, there are limitations on the type of four-wheel drive vehicle that can be used on La Bajada. The most successful traverse is done with a short and narrow (*yes, short and narrow!*) wheel base truck/SUV. The reason is that there are a number of places where the road is narrow, and you have to creep along one side or the other to bypass a difficult washout. High-centering is not nearly the problem that width is - consequently the short/narrow recommendation.
> 3. The side-slope of the roadway is generally well supported. You can thank your ancestors for having constructed the un-mortared flatrock retaining walls that endure to this day. You will see the walls along the way and they will evoke great respect from you.
> 4. The dry-weather requirement was never so important as on La Bajada. The presence of 60-90 degree cuts on the uphill side of the road is an unending source of rockslides and wet weather is one of the demons that starts them rolling.
> 5. You must be physically fit enough to pick up, move, or re-position large rocks at 6000 feet above sea level. Unless you have done this before, you have no idea how exhausting heavy labor is at this altitude.
> 6. There are no trees to speak of next to the road, so winching your way out of difficulty will not be an easy proposition. Large boulders can occasionally substitute but you may find yourself digging a deadman for the winch cable.
> 7. There is no water on the La Bajada road. Bring plenty for yourself and your truck.

Follow Option 2 or Option 3 (above) until you reach the base of La Bajada Hill. Note: If you have a vehicle capable of doing La Bajada Hill, the dirt roads on Option 3 will be a piece of cake.

Mileage below is a continuation from either Option 2 or Option 3.

2.7 miles - Major washout. You will see tire tracks leading to the right to get past the roughest part of the washout. Follow them and rejoin the washout where it eases up a bit.

2.9 miles - End major washout.

3.1 miles - Rock wall.

3.2 miles - Rock wall.

3.3 miles (ATN73) - Fork in the road. The left branch of the fork appears to be the less obvious choice because an apparently impossible washout is visible from the fork, but this branch is the original Mother Road with all the switchbacks. The right fork follows an alignment around the mountain instead of straight up the mountain and is more gradual. The historic significance of this fork is not known but if you follow it you will see evidence of modern activity such as fiber optic cable markers as well as old rock walls. So, is it a later version of Route 66?

The downside to the right fork is that the road is very rough (much worse than the left fork) and almost impassible at one point where it took the author 45 minutes to move 8 feet.

Whichever way you decide to go, at the fork,

ZERO ODOMETER

Left branch route:

Look overhead to see how the power lines go up the mountain. That is general direction you will be following, as the towers parallel the road. Note the very heavy-duty design of the towers. The winds blow very fiercely here.

0.1 miles - Permanent impassible washout on right. The washout must be bypassed by going around on the left and making one steep leap off the bypass onto the Mother Road.

Many switchbacks follow with slow going as you cross washouts and boulders.

0.8 miles - Fenceline

0.9 miles (ATN74) - Top of the hill. Park your truck and turn around for a knockout view of the flatlands below. Ahead, just beyond the top of the hill is the foundation of a ruined building, on the right.

1.4 miles (ATN76) - Junction with right branch road.

(Directions continue at the next "ZERO ODOMETER" below.)

Right branch route:

0.1 miles - Major washout.

0.2 miles - Major washout.

0.3 miles - Fenceline and old style gate. Be sure to close it behind you.

Santa Monica to Chicago

    0.5 miles - Rock wall below.
    0.6 miles - Moderate washout.
    0.9 miles - Very difficult washout, almost impossible to navigate. May require winching.
    1.0 miles (ATN75) - Fenceline and top of the hill.
    1.8 miles (ATN76) - Junction with left branch road.

    Once you have reached the junction of the two branch roads (using either branch),
ZERO ODOMETER
    Keep going north towards Santa Fe, driving next to the power lines.
    0.7 miles - Ranch road to the right.
    1.2 miles - Junction with sign.
    1.9 miles - Cattleguard and fenceline.
    4.0 miles - Cross under power lines.
    4.1 miles - Cattleguard and fenceline.
    5.0 miles (ATN77) - Short stone column on left. Odd.
    5.5 miles - Cattleguard and fenceline.
    5.7 miles - Junction with ranch roads.
    6.0 miles - Short-cuts ahead on the left. It can seem kind of confusing here, with all the roads seeming to go in different directions, but if you drive reasonably straight north, you'll do fine.
    6.4 miles (ATN78) - Road changes to pavement. There is a mine entrance on the left.
    6.9 miles - Cattleguard and fenceline.
    7.5 miles (ATN79) - Junction with NM 300. Turn left and
ZERO ODOMETER
    0.7 miles - Cattleguard and fenceline
    2.4 miles - Santa Fe sewage treatment plant.
    3.2 miles - Junction with NM 599. Go straight.
    4.1 miles - Sign showing Santa Fe County Road "66."
    6.4 miles (N081) - Junction with Cerrillos Road. Turn left and rejoin regular Route 66.

Continuation of text following all La Bajada Hill options:

For instructions on driving through Santa Fe, see DRIVING INSTRUCTIONS below.

SANTA FE
    The capital city of New Mexico, Santa Fe is known as "The City Different" truly lives up to its name as one of the most charming cities along Old Route 66. Founded in 1609 as La Villa Real de la Santa Fe de San Francisco (*The Royal City of the Holy Faith of Saint Francis*), it has been a capital city for nearly 400 years. The flags of four nations - Spain, Mexico, the Confederacy, and the United States have flown from atop the Palace of Governors, the oldest capitol in the country. To walk the streets of Santa Fe is to experience history at virtually every turn. The soft, earthen hued beauty of adobe is everywhere while a cool fall evening will bring the smell of pinion pine wafting on the air from hundreds of fireplaces in the homes where hollyhocks line the patios. This beautiful location at the foot of the Sangre de Christo (*Blood of Christ*) mountains was selected, in 1610, by Don Pedro de Peralta, the first governor, with the intent of being a walled city surrounding a palacio as the seat of government. In 1821, Mexico won its freedom from Spain and Santa Fe became the seat of the Mexican government in the northern territory. In 1846, General Kearny marched troops into Santa Fe and with the name "New Mexico," the territory became a province of the United States with the U.S. flag being raised over the Palace of Governors. In 1862, the Confederate flag flew for just over three weeks from March 10th when General Sibley marched into town trying to find a storehouse for his supplies. On January 12, 1912, New Mexico was admitted to the Union as the forty-seventh state and Santa Fe became the capital of New Mexico.
    LODGING: Lodging in Santa Fe varies from the mundane (Motel 6) up to the finest accommodations you can imagine. For that "Old Route 66 Classic Motel" feel it is hard to beat the El Rey Inn at 1862 Cerrillos Rd (505.982.1931) - a beautifully maintained (with lovely gardens) motel of the old school (dating back to the early 1940's). A more contemporary motel, and one close to the Plaza, is Garrett's Desert Inn at 311 Old Santa Fe Trail (505.982.1851), a nicely maintained 1960's property. Two of my favorite hotels are the Hotel Loretto, 211 Old Santa Fe Trail (*which has recently undergone a multi-million dollar restoration - 505.988.5531*) and The Inn of the Anasazi, 113 Washington Ave (505.988.3030). I should mention that the majority of the chain motels are south on Cerrillos Road.
    DINING: Dining in Santa Fe can be an amazing adventure in experiencing the fantastic tastes of New Mexican cooking.

Santa Monica to Chicago

Around every corner there are wonderful cafes and restaurants to tempt the gourmet hiding in each of us. The taste of Santa Fe can truly be enjoyed at Chef Mark Miller's Coyote Café, 132 Water Street (*the menu is* prix fixe *and reservations are required at 505.983.1615*). The Pink Adobe, housed in a 300 year-old adobe building, is as much a marvel of ambiance as the food is a delight to the palate, located at 406 Old Santa Fe Trail (across from the historic Mission San Miguel). Reservations are suggested at 505.983.7712. For excellent breakfasts, try the Guadalupe Café at 422 Old Santa Fe Trail, and if pizza tempts you for lunch the best in New Mexico can be found at Upper Crust Pizza, 329 Old Santa Fe Trail. One thing about Santa Fe - the competition for fine dining is so fierce you are virtually guaranteed an excellent meal wherever you choose to dine.

Shopping in Santa Fe is an adventure into the world of art and beauty with over 200 galleries. Canyon Road is the major gallery row while Old Town Santa Fe hosts five excellent galleries. A few of the more intriguing galleries are: Thirteen Moons at 652 Canyon Road, specializing in the Art Quilt; The Gaugy Gallery, 418 Canyon Road, devoted to the work of Jean-Claude Gaugy whose style is a sculpture/painting known as "linear/expressionism"; and Kiva Contemporary Art, 102 East Water St, specializing in Native American art.

DRIVING INSTRUCTIONS THROUGH SANTA FE

To drive Old Route 66 through Santa Fe follow Cerrillos Road into the heart of the city. It will jog and become Galisteo Street **(N082)** just before crossing the Santa Fe River. Make a right onto Water Street **(N083)**, followed in four blocks by another right onto the Old Santa Fe Trail **(N084)**.

NOTE: There are Historic Route 66 signs directing a left turn on Bishops Lodge Road into the Plaza - these are not correct - Route 66 never entered the Plaza. The problem with this routing is that if you do enter the Plaza, there are no signs directing you back out to Historic Route 66. If you find yourself in this situation, make a right off of Bishops Lodge Road onto Palace Ave, go one block to Cathedral Place and make a right, go two blocks to Water Street and make a right, one block to The Old Santa Fe Trail and make a left.

NOTE: READ AHEAD TO UNDERSTAND TURNS, ETC. COMING UP

Leaving Santa Fe, continue on the Old Santa Fe Trail, it will become The Old Pecos Trail **(N085)** (*at Berger, where the Old Santa Fe Trail cuts off to the left*). Stay on the Old Pecos Trail to the intersection (with stoplight and left turn lane) of St. Michaels Dr. (west) and The Old Las Vegas hwy (east) **(N086)**. Make a left onto the Old Las Vegas Hwy **(NM 300)** and

ZERO ODOMETER

    3.5 miles - Turn-off to Camp Stony **(N087)**.
    6.9 miles - Junction with US 285 **(N088)** - go straight.
    10.5 miles - Join I-25 North at Exit 294 - Cañoncito **(N089)**.

Crossing here will be the high point of Old 66 (Pre-1937) at Glorieta Pass **(N090)** elevation is 7525 feet. This should put to rest, permanently, the discussion of where the high points of Route 66 are located. A short review for all you geography students:
    1. Pre-1937 - Glorieta Pass, NM - elevation 7525.
    2. Post 1937 through 1941 - Fortynine Hill (between Parks and Brannigan Park) - elevation 7414.
    3. 1941 - 1970s - The Arizona Divide (west of Flagstaff) - elevation 7335.

At Exit 299 (Glorieta) leave I-25 **(N091)** and

ZERO ODOMETER

    1.2 miles - Adobe building on the left.
    5.3 miles - Pecos Village limit (west end).
    6.0 miles (N092) - Right onto NM 63 - the Pecos Hwy. Just ahead on the right is Frankie's Coffee House. Stop for a cup - and if early, breakfast.
    7.0 miles (N093) - Entrance to Pecos Ruins National Monument (*Damn, some idiot had all of the tress in parking lot taken out!*)

At the Monument entrance,

ZERO ODOMETER

    3.2 miles - Rowe, NM.
    3.7 miles (N094) - Turn right and go under freeway.
    4.0 miles (N095) - Left onto NM 34.
    16.8 miles (N096) - Sands, NM - cross over freeway.
    17.7 miles (N097) - Short sidetrip. Make a right turn to San Jose. Follow the road through San Jose, past the town-square (*which looks like something out of a Clint Eastwood spaghetti western*) and post office. Go down a short hill (*look for the Santa Fe Trail marker on the right*) to the old Route 66 Bridge **(N098)**. (*Keep an eye out on the bridge for the boys from "Deliverance" - if*

Santa Monica to Chicago

you hear a banjo - leave!)

Retrace your route back to the highway, make a right turn and

ZERO ODOMETER

0.4 miles - Old alignment (and culvert) from San Jose visible on the right, rising from beneath the Interstate.

8.3 miles (N099) - Bernal, NM

14.3 miles (N100) - Tecolote, NM - Old bridge ruins on the left just before town.

18.8 miles (N101) - Romeoville, NM and junction with I-25 and US 84. Turn right onto US 84, cross over freeway and

ZERO ODOMETER

7.5 miles (N102) - Los Montoyas, NM (*not to be confused with Montoya further east on 66*).

24.0 miles (N103) - County line.

24.4 miles (N104) - Dilia - Great old church here to the right, just off the highway.

42.0 miles (N105) - Junction with I-40 at Exit 256. Cross I-40, make a left and join the Interstate to Exit 267 **(N119)** (see below).

POST 1937 ALIGNMENT OPTION OUT OF ALBUQUERQUE

From Central Ave and 2nd St **(N071)**, continue east on Central out of town to Tramway Road **(N106)**. Cross Tramway and

ZERO ODOMETER

You are on NM 333. About a half-mile on the right is a riding and boarding stable that was once a country and western club run by Dill Bills. His nephew, a kid named Glen Campbell, would occasionally take a turn at the microphone.

2.0 miles (N107) - I-40 access, stay on NM 333.

4.3 miles (N108) - Cross under I-40.

6.8 miles (N109) - Cross NM 337.

7.5 miles (N110) - Continue right onto NM 333.

As you go through Tijeras Canyon, notice the giant rocks. What did it take to put a road through here? The rock in this area is so solid that an explosion of more than a thousand dynamite charges took only twenty minutes to clean up!

8.1 miles (N111) -

TIJERAS

(Spanish - *scissors.*) The name was thought to have been inspired by the canyon's shape. Actually, it was named after a family who lived in the area in 1856. The post office was established here in 1888.

In Tijeras, stay in the right lane to follow NM 333 east out of town and at the junction with NM 337:

ZERO ODOMETER

10.1 miles (N112) - Zuzax. Just a sign on the Interstate now, but once it was a bustling trading post (tourist trap style) offering everything from stuffed rattlesnakes to the infamous cherry cider (*What is that stuff?*). The buildings were surplus barracks from Kirtland Air Force Base while out front a bright yellow Cadillac with the word Zuzax painted on it beckoned to Route 66 traffic. From Santa Rosa to Grants, fences and boulders proclaimed Zuzax to anyone who took the time to look, and it was difficult to overlook this odd word. It was 1972 when I-40 eliminated the trading post, but the name lives on, but what does Zuzax mean? Actually, nothing, it was the creation of Zuzax owner Herman Ardans who wanted something short and faintly Indian sounding for his new tourist attraction in 1954. Kind of like George Eastman and the word Kodak.

13.3 miles - Sedillo, an old trading location named after Pedro de Sedill who arrived in New Mexico prior to the Pueblo rebellion of 1680.

16.2 miles - Barton - Named after an early settler of the area. Post office established in 1908 and closed in 1936.

16.5 miles "Route 66" High School visible on left.

20.1 miles - Edgewood. A once busy shipping point for pinto beans, the area is now primarily a bedroom community for Albuquerque, along with being the headquarters for a religious sect known as the Blackstockings.

21.1 miles - On the left, in the midst of an equipment rental yard, stands a castle tower. This was the dream of a man named Kline. All anyone knows is that he built and lived in the tower while gathering stones for the rest of the building. One day he simply left, and the tower now stands as a memorial to yet another unfulfilled dream.

21.6 miles - An abandoned cafe and store on the left, behind a chain link fence. Barely visible are the words "Kathy, NM" on the front of the building. Nowhere can I find a reference to a Kathy, New Mexico. Another curiosity of the road.

27.7 miles - Follow the road around the curves, make a right (N114), and you are in

MORIARTY

Named after Michael Timothy Moriarty, a local rancher who came to the Estancia Valley in the early 1880s seeking a cure for rheumatism. Post office was established in 1902.

A curious point here. The original (1937) alignment ran two miles north of Moriarty and intersected with NM 41 at a spot called Buford. (Named by H. Crossley after his infant son Buford.) The townsite east and north of Moriarty was owned by Crossley. Today Buford is a part of Moriarty, but early maps, the WPA Guide to New Mexico, and the Rittenhouse Guidebook all make reference to it.

Moriarty has a wonderful museum operated by volunteers. Many older motels, gas stations and cafes spread along the stretch of the wide, wide Main Street that was Route 66. The true heart of Moriarty lies not on old Route 66, but south on NM 41 about a mile. Here are the early buildings of the community where business was conducted prior to the arrival of the highway.

Lodging suggestions: Classic - The Sunset Motel; Modern - Holiday Inn Express.

One of the old tourist traps can still be seen along the old highway about three miles east of town. Take NM 41 north to the first dirt road on the right, take this road around a house and barn and it will put you on Old 66. Three miles east is the site of John Clair's snake pit and tourist trap.

Back in Moriarty it will be necessary to join I-40 to continue east **(N115)**.

Exit 203 - LONGHORN RANCH (N116)

The crumbling remains of The Longhorn Ranch are on the south frontage road (old 66). This was a favorite stopping place for Route 66 travelers, as well as being a Sunday diversion for people from Albuquerque, back during the time when we all took Sunday drives.

The Longhorn Ranch had a Wild West Museum, gas station, curio shop and hotel. There were rides in a genuine stagecoach and an authentic "Old West" atmosphere that was difficult to pass-by.

From here east is the Llano (*yawn-no*) Estacado, or Staked Plain (*not a literal translation*), stretching to Texas. An area so barren that is was said men drove stakes into the ground at regular intervals to guide travelers across the desolate landscape.
The old highway dead-ends in both directions from The Longhorn Ranch.

Exit 218 - CLINES CORNERS (N117)

An example of perseverance in action. Roy Cline built his first station in a town called Lucy (on US 60 between Willard and Vaughn), but he could not make a go of it. So he had the station moved (literally) to Highway 6 (later to become 66). With the paving of the highway Roy bought the land at the junction of 6 and 2. In 1937, the road moved north with the new alignment, so Roy moved the station again. One more time the state moved the highway east and renamed it 285. The station followed and finally settled at the junction of Hwy 285 and I-40 (*a portion of Route 66 still exists in front of the station*).

Cline's Corners has a gift shop full of what author Jean Shepherd called, "Great American Slob Art." I do not recommend the cafeteria.

Exit 234 - Section of old highway runs 0.7 miles east from here on the north side.

Exit 252 - REST AREA (N118)

On the north side of the Interstate bridge can be seen, down below, a partially covered-over Route 66 bridge. The old road is also visible next to the fence line. The road to the Rest Area will cross an old Route 66 bridge. West of the Rest Area, past the entrance to westbound I-40, can be seen the old highway heading up the hill. It will end 0.8 miles ahead, but is a great spot to photograph your Road Cruiser sitting on an old stretch of Route 66.

Exit 256 - VEGAS JUNCTION (N105)

US 84 connecting north to Las Vegas, NM and Santa Fe. **NOTE:** This interchange is the east end of the Santa Fe Loop option.

Exit 267 - COLONIAS (N119)

A section will go east from here (north side) for 2.1 miles. This is an interesting side tour to see how the old road followed the terrain while the Interstate was blasted through the hills.

Exit 273 - SANTA ROSA (N120)

Originally named Aqua Negra Chiquita (Little Black Water), changed to Santa Rosa in 1890 by Don Celso Baca after a chapel built in honor of his mother. The valley of the Pecos River brought the railroads (the Rock Island and the Southern Pacific merged here - but not above the Pecos River as legend tells it) as a watering spot. The water also sent the railroads packing when it was discovered the mineral content fouled the innards of the steam locomotives.

The Club Cafe was a Route 66 mainstay from 1935 until 1992 when it closed. The building is there, but the fat man signs are gone. The Comet Diner has taken up the slack, offering excellent food at good prices. The Sun 'N' Sand Restaurant is a great breakfast stop. Unfortunately Joseph's (up the hill) is not as good as it once was and the service has deteriorated badly. Lodging is best left to the chain operations with many of the older motels suffering from lack of maintenance. Recommendations are either of the Best Westerns in town (The Adobe Inn and the Santa Rosa Inn); the Holiday Inn Express, and the Comfort Inn.

RED ROUTE ADVENTURE TOUR

Please read all admonitions regarding Adventure Tours at the front of this book.

To explore this very old section of highway, at the east end of Santa Rosa (south side of I-40) and just past the underpass, make a left onto the old highway, NM 156 **(ATN01)** (This is near the truck stop at the top of the hill). Follow this road for approximately nine miles east. Watch for a road coming in from the northwest with a cattle guard. Left onto this road and
ZERO ODOMETER
Cross cattle guard (slow, it is in a hole) and continue north-east.
The pavement on this stretch is deteriorating badly. Local efforts at patching are keeping the road passable, but watch your speed and the road.
3.8 miles - A large tree on the left is the perfect place to stop. Shut off the engine, take a stretch and listen to the sounds of silence. I once camped at this location and was amazed at the number of stars that could be seen in a sky so black it seemed to envelop me.
7.2 miles - DANGER! Large washout on left side of road, drive to the right, go slow and you will be fine.
9.7 miles - Rejoin pavement on west side of Cuervo **(ATN02)**. At stop sign make a left and cross under I-40, followed by a right onto Route 66.

If you do not do the Adventure Tour above, at the east side of Santa Rosa, enter I-40 and continue east.

Exit 284 - FRONTIER RANCH (N121)
The remains of the Frontier Museum. Once a thriving tourist trap with stores, gas station and museum. Now a sad reminder of the glory days of Route 66.

Exit 291 - CUERVO (N122)
(Spanish - *Crow or raven*). At the bottom of the exit ramp make a left and cross under I-40. Leave Cuervo heading east on the frontage road (Old 66). This road follows the terrain as you parallel I-40. As you watch the cars, trucks and motorhomes jockeying for position on the "Super Slab" be glad you're alone and cruising the Mother Road.

NEWKIRK (N123)
Your first stop, and another place that came to be because of the railroad. Originally named Conant after James Conant, an early settler. Changed to Newkirk by a settler from Newkirk, Oklahoma. Post office established in 1910. Newkirk is now the jumping off point for boaters heading to Conchas Dam, 23 miles to the north.
Route 66 will cross I-40 and return between here and Montoya.

MONTOYA (N124)
With the arrival of a railroad siding in 1902 the town of Rountree was established here. The name was later changed to Montoya. Post office established in 1902.
Once a bustling cattle community Montoya now sits quietly alongside the formerly busy Route 66. A small cemetery lies on the east end of town. Great photos can be taken by crossing the tracks and visiting the abandoned buildings north of the old highway. An old hotel, garage, and a few other buildings provide a sense of the old west. This is private property, so respect everything you see -and take only photos and leave only footprints.
As you leave Montoya, on the east end of town, at the cemetery:
ZERO ODOMETER
Continue east and enjoy the ride.
5.6 miles - Cross under the Interstate **(N125)**. Go slowly and watch for cattle in the tunnel. (*Honestly! Mooo!*)

SANTA MONICA TO CHICAGO

9.4 miles - Intersection **(N126)**. The road ahead goes onto private land. Make a left and there will be a Stuckey's on the left as you approach I-40. Rejoin the Interstate at the Palomas interchange **(N127)**.

Exit 329 - TUCUMCARI (N128)

A Route 66 classic. Signs up and down the highway promoted "Tucumcari Tonight! - 2000 Motel Rooms." Also known as the town "two blocks wide and 2 miles long."

As you enter the west end of town, the off-ramp from I-40 pulls you to the right onto the big boulevard. Now, although we know you are anxious to get to one of those 2000 motel rooms, there is a short side trip tour at the west end of Tucumcari that you should know about. (*Maybe you could run it after lunch/dinner.*)

If you make a left where you join the boulevard **(ATN011)**, you can follow the old road out to where it dead-ends **(ATN012)** near Tucumcari Metropolitan Park.

Named after Tucumcari Mountain, the flat-topped mountain to the south. The name is one of the mysteries of the West. Legend tells of an Apache maiden, Kari, whose lover, Tocom, was killed by a rival. Upon his death Kari took her life, prompting her father to cry out "Tocom! Kari!" As a point of fact the area is Comanche, not Apache, and the name may be a derivative of the Comanche tukamukaru - to lie in wait for someone or something to approach. This information is based on the mountain being used as a lookout point for Comanche war parties.

City was founded in 1902 following arrival of the railroad. During 1901, the townsite was known as Six-Shooter Siding.

A trip through Tucumcari takes you back to the heyday of Route 66 with the proliferation of motels that still fill the night sky with flaming neon. Few of these motels have been restored to their Route 66 glory and cannot be recommended - a good indicator? If the neon has been restored, then the place is most likely being well maintained. Best classic motel in town is the Blue Swallow **(N130)** (505.461.9849), lovingly restored by Dale and Hilda Baake. The Holiday Inn is one of the better chain motels (*and offers a full breakfast with the room - not just stale rolls and bad coffee*). The Best Western Pow-Wow Inn has long been a Route 66 favorite, dating back to the 1960's.Unfortunately the Best Western Discovery Inn cannot be recommended because of numerous complaints about the management.

Dining - try La Cita (on 1st Street, a block south of Route 66) for your first taste of Tex-Mex cooking. Breakfast is a treat at Dean's on the east side of town *(avoid Denny's - the service is terrible)*. Looking for that perfect souvenir? Check out the Tee Pee curio shop.

Leaving Tucumcari eastbound, cross under the Interstate **(N131)** and

ZERO ODOMETER

Turn left at the frontage road **(N132)** and follow it east. The road will traverse a variety of landscapes as it swings away from the Interstate. This road aptly demonstrates why, with heavy traffic, the old highway was considered so dangerous and became known as "Bloody 66."

2.6 miles (132A) - Big-ass hole under the freeway, north of the old road. Stop and look! Its I-40's one and only built-in tourist trap attraction! And it's free! Except to the taxpayers. (*Actually, the Rock Island Railroad used to go through there, using a rather unusual underpass design.*)

11.8 miles (N133) - Plaza Larga Creek.
12.5 miles (N134) - Revuelto Creek.
13.0 miles - Remains of an old station on the left.
21.0 miles - Enter San Jon.
21.5 miles (N135) - Intersection with NM 39.

SAN JON (*San Hone*)

First building went up in 1902 in anticipation of the railroad, which arrived in 1904. The resulting boom was responsible for the town. The name is possibly an Americanization of the Spanish *zanhon* - deep gully.

East end of town shows how the Interstate can destroy a community with the ruins of the closed gas stations and motels crumbling to dust.

There is a dirt road ahead, so it's decision time. To trace the original route of the old road, use OPTION ONE, which is an Adventure Tour "Red Route." (*Please read all admonitions regarding Adventure Tours at the front of this book.*) OPTION ONE is a dirt road, slick and muddy in the winter, and following a rain. If you do not wish to travel on dirt, use OPTION TWO, which is paved and parallels I-40.

OPTION ONE

If you want to continue straight on the old highway alignment, opposite the I-40 Truck Inspection Station **(ATN30)** (you'll see it on the left, next to the freeway),

ZERO ODOMETER

The pavement will become rough, so take it easy, but it will smooth out *(I promise!)*.
1.6 miles (ATN31) - Pavement ends.
5.4 miles (ATN32) - Remains of Bard. Originally Bard City, founded in 1906.
9.0 miles (ATN33) - Bridge and old pavement.
9.3 miles (ATN34) - Bridge and old railroad bridge to the right.
11.5 miles (ATN35) - Jct with NM 93, old motel on left. This is Endee. Name was adapted from the brand of the ND Ranch in 1882. Endee was so rough it was said a trench would be dug on Saturday afternoon to bury the Saturday Night slow-draw artists on Sundays. Post office established in 1886 and closed in 1955.
15.7 miles (ATN36) - Watch for final alignment of Route 66 coming in on the left and enter Glenrio.

OPTION TWO
At intersection with NM 39 in San Jon make a left, continue across I-40 and make a right onto the frontage road **(N136)**.
24.8 miles (N137) (T*his mileage continues from Tucumcari*) - Dirt road visible to right - south of I-40 - is option 1 alignment from above. Also at this point, you will be able to see the crossover pattern (through I-40, coming in from behind you on the right) of the final alignment as it pointed east from San Jon.
35.7 miles (N138) - Exit 361 - Endee. Cross over I-40 and join Interstate eastbound.

Exit 369 - GLENRIO
A unique blend of the English *Glen* and the Spanish *Rio* provided the name for the last town in New Mexico. Founded when the Chicago, Rock Island and Pacific Railroad built into the area in 1903. Post office established in 1916. The train station was on the east side of town in Texas, while the major portion of the community was in New Mexico at the west end of town. The tracks have long since disappeared, but the right-of-way can still be seen both east and west of town.

Once a major gas, food and lodging stop for the highway, today Glenrio sits on either side of a wide, four-lane remnant of the Mother Road. Major photo opportunities abound in this small town.

In the center of town (a stake in the ground on the north side of the road) is a marker indicating the Texas/New Mexico Stateline. We have completed our journey across New Mexico and what a great journey it was. We will be entering the land of the cowboy next as we head across the Panhandle of Texas.

Join I-40 eastbound and cross into Texas.

Santa Monica to Chicago

TEXAS

EASTBOUND

IMPORTANT DRIVING NOTE: In Texas, exiting traffic from the Interstate has the right-of-way, so there will be a stop or yield sign for traffic on the frontage road. Since you will be on Frontage Roads quite a bit watch for traffic exiting and stop or yield as necessary.

Texas is a place that is truly "bigger than life." Our trip across the Panhandle on Route 66 will touch only a small part of the state, but it will introduce you to the world of Texas - a world of friendly people, grand vistas and, of course, cowboys.

Entering Texas from the West the trip starts in Glenrio at exit 0 **(T001)** on I-40 (*or in the middle of town if coming through from San Jon on the dirt road*).

GLENRIO

Founded in 1903 when the railroad built a siding here. Glenrio is home of the famous "First in Texas/Last in Texas Motel" - the sign is almost gone now, so catch a photo before the weather wipes it out completely.

To continue east it will be necessary to enter I-40. Continue on I-40 to:

Exit 18 - ADRIAN (T003)

Left, cross freeway, then a right at stop sign. This is where Route 66 once again is the road of choice as we leave the Interstate and head east.

Adrian is full of surprises for the photographer in search of old buildings. Look for the Bent Door Cafe, currently closed (*at this writing the building is for sale*). At the east end of town is the Antique Ranch and Café. Great barbeque here, plus the chance to browse some antiques.

At the rodeo grounds **(T004)**,

ZERO ODOMETER

5.9 miles (T005) - Landergin. Shows on some older maps, but was never more than a railroad work camp with a few buildings and no tourist facilities.

9.3 miles (T006) - Curve around rest area.

13.0 miles (T007) - VEGA - The Heart of Route 66 and the geographic center between Chicago and L.A.

A store founded in 1903 was the first building in Vega. A. M. Miller, the stores owner, submitted the name Vega, along with Gusben (for his sons Gus and Stephen). The name Vega, Spanish for meadow, was chosen because it reflected the level land of the countryside.

Lodging: Best Western Country Inn - a 1960's motel, very nicely maintained. A full buffet breakfast at the café next door comes with the room (*the cafe burned in 2002, but may be rebuilt by the time you read this*). The Vega Motel - small, 1940's vintage with nicely restored rooms. Modern motel: Comfort Inn - exit 35 on I-40.

Another great place to photograph the old buildings of a Route 66 town. Also check out Dot's Mini-Museum. North on Hwy 385 is Cal Farley's Boys Ranch.

At the junction of 385 and 66 **(T007)**,

ZERO ODOMETER

Head east out of Vega.

13.1 miles (T008) - Wildorado - pronounced *Will-doe-ray-doe*. The old Jessie's Café (on the south frontage road) has reopened as Randy's (closed Sunday and Monday) and the plethora of pick-ups in the parking lot are a good indicator this a great place to eat. Stop in for lunch or dinner where you will be pleasantly surprised by a menu that is upscale with fresh seafood or steak specials that include a true taste of Texas. Nice folks, good food and a wonderful example of another Route 66 location brought back to life.

A major cattle-feeding operation can be seen on the right (*and because the prevailing wind blows SW to NE at the feedlot, you should be able to enjoy your lunch at Randy's!*), along with the Wind Generator Research Farm.

14.5 miles - Curve to right.

15.0 miles - Cross under bridge.

16.1 miles - Frying Pan Ranch Road.

19.1 miles - On right is the Wind Generator Research Farm.

19.4 miles (T009) -

Santa Monica to Chicago

BUSHLAND
Named for W. H. Bush, landowner, and C. B. Bush, postmaster. Original name was Bush, but changed in 1908 when W. H. took a new wife. She thought Bushland sounded better and when the train station was repainted insisted the new name be placed on the building.

21.0 miles - Stop sign.

24.0 miles (T010) - Arnot Road interchange (I-40 exit 60) and stop sign. Make right, go under I-40, then left onto south frontage road. Stay on frontage road for one mile and the Cadillac Ranch **(T011)** is on the right.

Cadillac Ranch is one of those sites that must be visited and photographed. The concept of Stanley Marsh 3 (*yep, "3"*) as an homage to the American Dream and executed by The Ant Farm, Inc., the Ranch is a salute to the great finned road beasts of the 1940s to the 1960s.

After visiting the Cadillac Ranch, continue east to Hope Road **(T012)**, then left on Hope to Amarillo Blvd **(T013)**. Turn right on Amarillo Blvd and proceed to the intersection of Amarillo Blvd and Soncy **(T014)**. Go straight at the intersection and:

ZERO ODOMETER
Continue east and follow the road as it curves to the north. Notice the old Route 66 motels along here - The Broncho, Sunset and Skyline.

2.2 miles - Large VA Hospital on the left.

2.4 miles (T015) - Watch for 9th Avenue exit and make a right.

AMARILLO
The Spanish word for "yellow" (*pronounced AHM-A-REE-O in Spanish, but AM- A-RILL-O in Texan*) was laid out by Henry B. Sanborn in 1887 near Amarillo Lake. The name came from the yellow color of the lake banks, and the many yellow flowers growing in the area. Sanborn originally named the townsite Oneida, but changed it when the town was designated as the county seat in an election, in which he promised cowboys a town lot each if they would vote for his town.

Prior to Sanborn the area was rife with buffalo. Ragtown, as the camp was known, prided itself on a hotel constructed of buffalo hides - including walls and roof. With the demise of the local buffalo, the grinding and selling of bleached buffalo bones for fertilizer became a big business.

Cattlemen were the next to settle the area. The mighty XIT Ranch, formed from the sale of over 3,000,000 acres of land to finance the State Capitol at Austin, brought in cowboys, ranchers and settlers. Amarillo has served as a shipping point for cattle, farm products, oil and gas over the years. Amarillo is also the primary source for the majority of the worlds helium supply.

A local rancher, J. F. Glidden, invented and patented barbed wire - also known as Devil's Rope. He and H. B. Sanborn were the first to use the wire to fence their ranch properties in 1882. Prior to that time, the wire was used to prevent cattle from straying south during the winter.

Today, Amarillo is a thriving city, confidently facing the future, while still holding to the vestiges of the past.

3.2 miles (T016) - Curve to the left.

3.5 miles - Cross Western. Amarillo Country Club on left.

3.8 miles (T017) - Curve to the right on 6th. This is the San Jacinto Heights section of the city and 6th Street is what is known as Antique Row. A great place to park the car and roam the stores looking for that special collectible. At 2908 West 6th **(T018),** is the Golden Light Cafe, a great Roadie stop for a good old fashioned "slider with fries," be sure to order a Dr. Pepper to go with that burger (*but, damnit, they no longer have DP in bottles!*).

4.7 miles (T019) - The Morning Star Motor Court on the right.

5.2 miles (T020) - Cross under railroad tracks.

6.5 miles (T021) - Make a left onto Fillmore.

Stay on Fillmore north to Amarillo Blvd.

7.5 miles (T022) - Make a right onto Amarillo Blvd (East US 60 and Bus. I-40).

Originally, The Big Texan Steak Ranch was located along this stretch of the old highway, just west of Eastern Ave. With the opening of I-40 on November 15, 1968 at 2 PM, Bob Lee's business went bust. He moved the Big Texan to its present location alongside I-40 (*west of Lakeside Road*). In 1976, he had another set-back when the Big Texan burned to the ground, the fire shut down traffic on I-40 for over two hours. He rebuilt, added a motel with a Texas shaped swimming pool and was back in business. The Big Texan still serves a great steak at a reasonable price, and yes, they still offer the free 72 oz. steak, if you can eat it in an hour with all the trimmings - shrimp cocktail, salad, baked potato and buttered roll. It has been done by one local gent over twenty times, but be warned, it ain't as easy as it looks! When we were there in April of 2002 a dude finished the steak in 17 minutes and even commented, "I ate the gristle too!"

Lodging in Amarillo is pretty much like any good-sized city. Some of the older motels suffer from neglect. A few of my favorites: Best Western Amarillo Inn, 1610 Coulter (806.358.7861). The Big Texan is fun with its Old West façade (*plus it ain't that far to walk, or be carried, after tackling that 72 ouncer!*), (806.372.5000). Comfort Suites, 2103 Lakeview Dr (806.352.8300).

Santa Monica to Chicago

Hampton Inn, 1700 I-40 East, (806.372.1425).

Dining offers just about anything you might want, a few of my favorites - The Big Texan (*of course*), Dyers Barbeque (*good sauce!*), Ruby Tequila's Mexican Kitchen (*kinda Gringo, but good*) and Calico County (*homestyle cookin'*).

For the dedicated Route 66 Roadie, it is possible to explore a portion of the 1940 highway east of town.

12.2 miles (T025) - At Triangle Road and Amarillo Blvd on the east end of town (look for the old Triangle Motel) make a right (this is not a hard right, but a "Y" type intersection). This corner was the original junction of Hwy 60 and 66. The road will go for 0.5 mile.

12.7 miles (T026) - At the Lakeside frontage road, make a right (this is the only turn possible), continue to the stop sign **(T027)**, cross Lakeside and make a left on east-side frontage road and at Triangle Road (13.2 miles) **(T028)** make a right and:

ZERO ODOMETER

1.0 miles (T030) - Intersection with Folsom Road. "Dead End" on sign, because it will.

1.3 miles (T029) - Road ends at airport. The original road went across what are now runways and taxiways. Beyond the hangers in the distance, the road will continue.

Backtrack to Folsom Road **(T030)**, turn right and go north, past the KOA on the right, to Amarillo Blvd **(T031)** and make a right. Continue east and just past the airport watch for entrance to the Texas State Technical Institute. Exit Amarillo Blvd **(T032)** and go south on Avenue B.

This is the site of the old Amarillo Air Force Base where there are many of the old hangers and training buildings. The barracks area was on the left in what now appears to be a large park.

At 8th Avenue **(T033)** (old Route 66) make a right and stop at the gate, the old pavement can be seen continuing on into the airport.

At the gate,

ZERO ODOMETER

Turn around and head east on 8th Ave. (*this was the Amarillo Air Force Base 1st Avenue, the street numbering system was changed in the mid-1990s since the entrance to the facility is now from the north*).

0.4 miles (T034) - Old entrance to Air Force Base as mentioned on page 65 of the Rittenhouse Guide Book.

0.7 miles (T035) - J Street, stop sign and flashing light. Continue straight.

1.7 miles (T036) - Junction of FM 1912, stop light. 8th Avenue becomes FM 2575 straight ahead. Continue straight. (*If you are curious about the "FM" designation on some road signs, it indicates a Farm to Market road*).

3.5 miles (T037) - Enter Carson County.

3.6 miles - Eight trees.

4.0 miles - Farmhouse on left.

5.7 miles (T038) - Junction of FM 2575 (Durrett Road) and Business Loop 40. This is the far east end of Amarillo Blvd, the final alignment of Route 66 through Amarillo. At this intersection, turn right. Enter I-40 **(T039)**, continue to Exit 81 **(T040)**, then join Hwy 2161 east bound. At stop sign at junction with 2161,

ZERO ODOMETER

7.3 miles (T041) - Junction with 207 (north).

CONWAY

A small community with a great old gas station and tourist cabins.

Continue east.

8.2 miles (T042) - Junction with 207 (south) that goes to Claude. The 1926-27 alignment of Route 66 actually went east out of Amarillo on what is now Hwy 287 to Claude, then connected north to Conway.

15.5 miles (T043) -The grain elevators are all that is left of Lark.

22.5 miles (T044) - Junction with Texas 295 and

GROOM

Named for Englishman Colonel B. B. Groom who established a ranch in the area. By the late 1910s, it was a booming community of farmers and ranchers. The area developed into cattle, wheat and maize country. Store fronts, motels, and gas stations provide fine photo opportunities. The film *Leap of Faith*, with Steve Martin, was filmed in Groom, with The Movie Motel (on the west side of town, just east of TX 295) being used as a set.

It will be necessary to head north and join I-40 to continue eastbound. At the Interstate, cross under and check out the "Leaning Tower of Texas." Also here, on the left, is the 190-foot steel cross erected in 1995.

It should be mentioned the original route went from Groom **(T045)** to Jericho, then up the hills to Alanreed and McLean. Much has been written about the Jericho Gap and how to follow it. It should be mentioned that much of the old highway has been obliterated or exists on private and posted land. So we will not go into this routing at any great depth.

Santa Monica to Chicago

24.2 miles (T046) - Return to I-40 eastbound.

Exit 124 - JERICHO (T047)
Turn south here for about one mile to a dirt road, make a right on the dirt road and this is the site of Jericho **(T048)**. The only thing remaining in Jericho are the remains of an old tourist court. One of the great stories of Jericho involves a man working at the gas station when a Model A pulls in, going in reverse. The driver asked for gas and the attendant asked if he was having transmission trouble. The driver said, "Nope, I'm just traveling Route 66 in reverse," got back in the car, put it in reverse and headed out on the highway. Tall story, Texas Tale, or fact?

This area was notorious in the days before the pavement for the gumbo mud that could grab and hold a semi-truck in its goo.

Re-join I-40 eastbound **(T047)**.

EXIT 135 - ALANREED (T049)
A small quiet spot off the Interstate, Alanreed (*sometimes Allanreed*) has the distinction of having had more names than any other Texas Route 66 town. First known as Eldridge (1886), it became Spring Tank, then Springtown because of a large water tank fed by local springs. For a time, it was known as Prairie Dog Town after a large colony of the critters nearby.

But the most interesting name has to be Gouge Eye. A local tale explains the name as follows. A pair of cowboys were having a violent fight in one of the local saloons. This saloon provided a free buffet and in the course of the fight the food was knocked off the bar. Grapes were a featured item and they spread out across the floor. After the fight broke up, a traveler stopped at the saloon and seeing the grapes on the floor asked what they were. He was told there had been a terrible fight and these were the eyes that had been gouged out during the melee. True? Who knows, but a thank you to that great storyteller Delbert Trew for sharing it with us.

It was named Allenreed (1902) in honor of a contracting firm Allen and Reed who were in business when the Rock Island Railroad came into the area, and finally the name Alanreed stuck (*but no one knows why*).

In the center of town, is a nicely restored gas station, thanks to efforts of the volunteers from the Old Historic Route 66 Association of Texas. A left at this intersection will take you north towards I-40. At the I-40 frontage road, 6th Avenue, a right will place you on the 1950's alignment. Just past the intersection is the location of the old Regal Reptile Ranch. If you remember, the ranch's large snake that arched into the blue Texas sky, you can see it again at the Route 66 Museum in McLean.

Return back to old 66, by the restored gas station, make a left and continue east toward McLean. On the east side of Alanreed, at the intersection of FM291 (southbound), on the right is possibly the oldest cemetery on Route 66.

As you near McLean, it's time for a mini-Adventure Tour! On the west side of town, continue to where Old 66 crosses under I-40. As you approach the I-40 under-crossing, notice the road veering back to the right, past an old alignment that ends between two rows of trees **(T052)**. Could be worth a short hike to check it out.

Then, after crossing under I-40, there's a stop sign **(T053)**. For the adventurers, go straight ahead to follow this old section of pavement (*slow, can be rough in spots and/or bad weather*) to where it intersects with the four-lane Route 66 into McLean **(T056)**.

For the less adventurous, make a (hard) left at the stop sign and go west to County Rd 26 **(T054)**. Follow the road to the right and it will take you to the four-lane (final alignment) Route 66 **(T055)** into McLean.

McLEAN
Established as a cattle-loading site around 1900. The townsite was donated by Alfred Rowe, an English rancher, who died on board the Titanic. The town was named after W. P. McLean of the Railroad Commission.

McLean is the home of the Devils Rope & Route 66 Museum **(T058)**. The Route 66 section of the museum has some wonderful artifacts of the Mother Road and is well worth a visit, the Devils Rope section refers to barbed wire and it is absolutely amazing how many variations of barbed wire there have been. Spend some time here, enjoy the exhibits and buy something in the gift shop. This entire museum was built by and is staffed by volunteers, so they can use your purchase to insure the continuing growth of the museum. Another project of the museum has been the restored Phillips 66 gas station **(T057)**. If your are lucky while visiting you may meet Delbert or Ruth Trew, two of my special friends and very special friends of The Mother Road.

The Red River Steak House is a great place to eat, founded by the originator of the K-Bob chain. The Cactus Inn has been nicely restored, but because of numerous complaints concerning the owner we cannot recommend it.

East and north of McLean, during World War II, was a prisoner of war camp where many Germans POW's were interred for the duration of the War.

On the east side of McLean, continue straight at the I-40 access and:

ZERO ODOMETER
- **0.3 miles (T059)** - Stop sign, follow road to the left.
- **2.8 miles (T060)** - Cross County Line Road.
- **5.0 miles (T061)** - At Farm Road 1443 turn right and cross I-40, then left onto the concrete highway **(T062)**.

Santa Monica to Chicago

6.2 miles (T063) - The trees in the median of the highway to the left are what remains of the staggered windbreaks described in Rittenhouse's *A Guide Book To Highway 66*. The trees were planted to slow the north wind, prevent erosion in the summer, and snow drifting in the winter.

9.3 miles (T064) - Farm Road 453.

14.3 miles (T065) - Lela.

18.4 miles - Enter Shamrock.

SHAMROCK

Named for good luck and courage by the first postmaster of the town, George Nickel, an Irish immigrant. Shamrock sits on the eastern edge of the Panhandle gas field and for years was known for the thick black clouds produced by the carbon black plants in the area.

As you drive through Shamrock, it is impossible to miss the U-Drop Inn and Tower Gas station, an art deco masterpiece. As we went to press, we have learned the U-Drop has been purchased by the city. Watch for the future preservation of this icon of the road. Many other buildings in town tried to adopt the U-Drop-Inn "look" by having roof caps placed on them to simulate the deco design.

LODGING: Irish Inn Motel and the Econo-Lodge.

DINING: Mitchell Family Restaurant - go for the chicken fried steak, also a great salad bar. The Dairy Queen - typical Dairy Queen fare, but you have to experience a true Texas phenomenon. Virtually, every town in Texas has a Dairy Queen, and they are the hubs of local activity serving everything from breakfast to dinner.

At the stop light **(T067),** continue straight and,

ZERO ODOMETER

1.5 miles - I-40 access. Do not enter freeway.

4.7 miles (T068) - Stop sign and Farm Road 2168.

6.8 miles (T069) - Stop sign and Farm Road 1802.

8.4 miles (T070) - Classic old bridge.

You will notice the road surface changing from concrete to asphalt and back along here. As the concrete deteriorated over the years it was replaced with the asphalt material.

14.5 miles (T071) - Leave Texas.

It has been a short run across this part of the great state of Texas, but one that introduced us to a new landscape, new people and great food. Oklahoma lies just ahead with nearly 375 miles of Mother Road to explore.

Santa Monica to Chicago

OKLAHOMA
EASTBOUND

During the summer, the raspy sound of cicadas in the large trees alongside the highway will welcome you to the Sooner State **(H001)**. Ahead, there are over 375 miles of Route 66 - covering alignments from 1926 through the mid-1950s. The first stop as we enter Oklahoma is the quiet, nearly deserted town of:

TEXOLA
Bounced back and forth between Texas and Oklahoma, the town now rests a half-of-mile east of Texas. (*Nope, it does not straddle the state line, unlike ol' Glenrio, Texas, back there on the New Mexico line.*) Originally granted to the Choctaw Tribe in 1820, it became part of Greer County, Texas in 1860. Settlement began in the 1880s, and an 1896 Supreme Court decision made it a part of Oklahoma. Over the years, the town has had three names - Texokla, Texoma and Texola.

A photographers dream with many old store fronts, abandoned buildings and just north of 66 on Main Street, the territorial jail - a dismal building for the criminal with nothing but bars between the miscreant and the elements.

After enjoying Texola, in front of Water Hole #2, at Texas Street **(H002)**,
ZERO ODOMETER
2.9 miles - The old highway alignment is on the right, across the gully, and along the tree line.
5.1 miles (H003) - Cross bridge.
6.4 miles - Enter Erick, as highway reduces to two lanes **(H004)**.

ERICK
Founded in 1901 and named after Beeks Erick, a member of the founding townsite company, Erick straddles the 100th Meridian (*once considered as the eastern boundary of Texas*). In the mid- to late-1800s, banks would not loan money to farmers west of the 100th Meridian because that was considered the start of the Great American Desert.

Erick is known for the intersection of Roger Miller Boulevard (Old 66) and Sheb Wooley Avenue (formerly Main Street) **(H005)**. At this location, the buildings on all four corners had diagonal doors facing the intersection, the only place on Route 66 where this occurs. The reason for diagonal doors was to make the building, and thus the business, appear more inviting and friendly for the patron of the store, hotel or bank. There are now only three buildings remaining at this intersection.

Be sure to stop and see Harley and Annabelle at the Sandhills Curiosity Shop, one block south of 66 on Sheb Wooley Ave, two of the most fun lovin' people along the road.

At the east end of town, when you reach the divided highway **(H006)**,
ZERO ODOMETER
1.8 miles - Curve to the left.
4.2 miles (H007) - Four-lane transitions to two-lane.
4.4 miles - Along here, on the left, can be seen abandoned sections of the old highway. The lanes to the north were the original Route 66, the lanes you are driving on were added in the 1950s.
7.2 miles - Curve to the right.
8.8 miles - I-40 moves closer to old highway.
13.0 miles (H009) - Short, sharp right turn down to a divided highway. Make a left across the highway and head north into Sayre. (*Note: This is a nasty little turn followed immediately by a hazardous crossing of a four-lane highway. Be very careful!*)
14.5 miles (H010) - Cross the North Fork of the Red River.
Until 1896, Texas claimed the land west from here. It took six years for the Supreme Court to decide Texas extended to the South Fork of the Red River and not the North Fork.
14.9 miles - Stop light, junction of 66 and 152 **(H011)**.

SAYRE
Founded in 1901 and named after Robert H. Sayre, a stockholder in the railroad.

The courthouse and Main Street were used in filming *The Grapes of Wrath*. The scene is of the Joad's truck turning onto Main Street with the Courthouse in the background. Many people think this was a shot of the state capitol in Oklahoma City.

The famous boxer, Jess Willard, "The Great White Hope" once ran a rooming house here.

At the corner of 4th and Elm **(H012)**, there appear to be a pair of storm cellars on either side of the highway. These are actually entrances to the underground pedestrian walkway that allowed people to cross what was once a busy Route 66 (*these were also used at times as storm cellars during tornado alerts*).

At intersection of BL40 and Hwy 283 **(H013)**, make a right turn and:
ZERO ODOMETER
As you pass the Ford dealer, move to the left lane for a left turn ahead.
- **1.5 miles (H014)** - Left onto frontage road - I-40 is on your right.
- **3.2 miles (H015)** - Stop sign (at truck stop), make right and cross I-40.
- **3.9 miles (H016)** - Left onto Frontage Road.
- **4.9 miles (H017)** - Cross an old yellow bridge. (*Old Yeller, anyone?*)
- **5.2 miles (H018)** - Stop sign, left, cross I-40.
- **5.5 miles (H019)** - Right turn.
- **10.2 miles (H020)** - Stop sign, cross divided highway, turn left onto BL-40.
- **12.6 miles (H021)** - Junction OK 34 and OK 6. There is a motor court and the vacant Queenan Trading Post on the left just before the intersection.
- **13.2 miles** - Curve to the right.
- **14.8 miles** -

ELK CITY

Original name was to be Crone, in honor of a local settler, but the application was mis-read and the town was named Crowe in 1899 at a location three miles south of the present downtown. The name was to be changed to Busch in 1901 in hopes of wooing the St. Louis beer magnate, Adolphus Busch, to build a brewery in the community (*or a least make a contribution to the growing town*). Many members of the town hated the fact their town name was to be derived from a beer label. When the railroad arrived, angry citizens threatened to push the ladder from beneath the sign painter who was putting the hated name on the station. Local residents called the town Elk City, but the name was not officially recognized until 1907.

Throughout the 1930s, 40s and 50s, Route 66 was a major force in the community as thousands of travelers discovered Elk City as a great place to stop for the night. The many motels along 3rd Street (old 66, now BL 40) attest to the popularity of Elk City as a continuing overnight stopping place.

While in Elk City, visit the Old Town Museum complex on the west side of town where the National Route 66 Museum is located **(H023)**. The oil drum Kachinas out front were originally located at the old Queenan Trading Post. Downtown be sure to visit the Anadarko Basin Museum of Natural History in the historic Casa Grande Hotel. Behind the museum is the Parker Rig #114. At 179 feet it is the world's tallest, non-working oil rig.

LODGING: Best Western Elk City Inn (405.225.2331), Knights Inn (405.225.2241), Holiday Inn (405.225.6637).

An old routing of 66 can be found by turning south on Pioneer (Route 66 Museum is on northwest corner) to Broadway, then follow Broadway to Main, make a left on Main to Country Club and make a right on Country Club.

On the east end of town, at the junction with Hwy 34 **(H024)**, make a left, followed by an immediate right to enter the frontage road and:
ZERO ODOMETER
- **2.2 miles** - Curve to the left.
- **2.4 miles (H025)** - Stop sign, continue straight, freeway is on your right.
- **4.8 miles (H027)** - Stop sign and right under I-40.
- **5.1 miles (H028)** - Stop sign and make a left.
- **5.5 miles (H029)** - Cross railroad.
- **5.6 miles** -

CANUTE

Founded in 1902 by a company that specialized in townsites. On the east end of town is the Catholic Cemetery where a hill is topped by a life-sized bronze of Christ on the cross and the Apostle John, Mary the mother of Jesus and Mary Magdalene.

- **6.2 miles (H030)** - Stop sign in middle of town and
ZERO ODOMETER
Make a left and cross I-40.
- **0.4 miles (H031)** - Right turn onto frontage road.
- **2.0 miles (H032)** - Cross bridge.
- **2.6 miles (H033)** - Stop sign, right turn and cross I-40.
- **2.8 miles (H034)** - Left onto south frontage road.
- **3.8 miles** - Cross bridge.
- **4.5 miles (H035)** - Left and cross I-40.
- **4.8 miles (H036)** - Right turn, KOA on left, I-40 on right.

Santa Monica to Chicago

    7.8 miles (H037) - Stop sign and

FOSS
Classified as an official Oklahoma Ghost Town. An abandoned gas station (Kobel's Place) is the only evidence of Route 66 days.

    7.9 miles - Cross bridge.
    8.35 miles - Cross bridge.
    11.6 miles (H038) - Right and cross under I-40, then left onto south frontage road.
    15.2 miles (H039) - **DO NOT** enter I-40.
    15.7 miles - Cross bridge.
    17.1 miles - Cross bridge.
    18.6 miles - Cross under railroad.
    19.1 miles - Water tower on left.
    19.2 miles - Roadside park on right.
    19.5 miles (H041) - Stop sign, then left.
    20.6 miles - Cross under I-40.
    21.6 miles (H042) - Curve to left onto 10th Street.
    21.9 miles (H043) - Right onto Gary Blvd.

CLINTON
The land-rush crowd bypassed this area when the Cheyenne-Arapaho Reservation opened in 1892. Many felt the land was not worth staking out. The Frisco Railway built to the area in 1903 and Clinton was founded. Named after Federal Judge Clinton F. Irwin.

Clinton is the home of the first official state Route 66 Museum at 2229 W. Gary Blvd **(H044)**. Well worth a visit. (*Note that the museum is not on Route 66, as described above in the text. You need to return to downtown to pick-up where you left off.*)

Many sites to see here including McLain Rogers Park with its Route 66 themed miniature golf course.

Recommended lodgings are Best Western Trade Winds (405.323.2610) and the Holiday Inn (405.323.5550), as with many towns the older motels suffer from neglect and disrepair. Dining is good at Branding Iron Restaurant for steaks and Lupita's for Mexican food.

On the east side of town, you cross two bridges with a classic Route 66 motel in between them. The first bridge is the Washita River Bridge **(H045)**. Then comes the Ranch Siesta Motel **(H046)**. Then comes the second bridge, the Turtle Creek Bridge **(H047)** where you:

ZERO ODOMETER
    0.4 miles (H048) - Left across highway, then right.
    1.4 miles (H049) - Make a right and cross I-40 and left onto south frontage road.
    3.5 miles - Ignore Local Traffic Only sign ahead and continue straight.
    5.0 miles (H050) - Arched bridge.
    5.5 miles (H051) - Make a left, cross I-40.
    5.7 miles (H052) - Right onto the north frontage road.
    11.8 miles - Enter Weatherford, this is South 4th Street, continue to the triangle intersection and make a right onto Main Street **(H054)**.

WEATHERFORD
Founded in 1893 and named after US Marshal William J. Weatherford. Astronaut Thomas P. Stafford, commander of the 1975 Apollo-Soyuz mission, was born in Weatherford. A museum of NASA memorabilia is in town.

LODGING: Best Western Mark Motor Hotel (405.772.3325). **DINING:** City Diner at 1231 Main St, cool ambiance, good food.

Continue east on Main Street. At the east end of town, there is a tricky intersection **(H056)**. At the junction with with Washington Street, you make a left - followed by an immediate right - in order to enter the frontage road. To make the two turns successfully, you need to be in the correct left-hand turn lane because there are two of them to choose from. Position yourself in the right-hand of the two left-turn lanes so when you swing through the intersection you will be able to make the hard right onto the frontage road.

But wait, there's more! As you make the turn onto the frontage road,

ZERO ODOMETER
If you mess up the turn, just go on up Washington Street to Davis Street **(H057)** and make a right. You'll rejoin the "real"

Santa Monica to Chicago

Route 66 within a mile at:
- **1.3 miles (H058)** - Stop sign, make a right.
- **2.3 miles (H059)** - Stop sign, continue straight (east) past the I-40 access.
- **3.3 miles** - Under railroad bridge.
- **5.6 miles** - Bridge.
- **6.3 miles (H060)** - Lucille's Historic Route 66 Store, gas station and former tourist court on the left. News of restoration as we go to press. Stop a moment to honor the memory of Lucille and Cheryl Cory, one of the great advocates of the Mother Road who passed way too soon.

HYDRO

An area noted for peanut production and a quiet stop on the old alignment as it is off the later alignment, and away from the Interstate. Be sure to park in the middle of the street, that's what it's there for.
- **6.8 miles (H061)** - Junction of 58, stop sign and optional turn-off to Hydro. Continue east.
- **7.5 miles** - Route 66 curves away from the Interstate.

For the Roadie time has become suspended once again. What year is it? Who is the President? Look, up ahead, is that Rod Serling standing by that abandoned gas station and motel? (*Or is really Anthony "Psycho" Perkins waiting to welcome you to the Bates Motel?*)

- **8.5 miles** - Single arch bridge.
- **9.1 miles (H062)** - Appears to be an old gas station converted to a private home.
- **16.2 miles** - Cross bridge.
- **17.8 miles (H063)** - Abandoned motor court and turn-off for Bridgeport on the left.

Prior to 1933, the road went through Bridgeport to cross the Canadian River. A visit to Bridgeport is to see a modern-day ghost town. As you travel the streets, you wonder about the people who lived here when it was a hustling town on the river and the old highway. Local legend has it that the newspaper in Geary told everyone in Bridgeport to move out because it was going to become a ghost town. So they did, and now it is.

- **18.9 miles** - Cross bridge.
- **19.6 miles (H064)** - Hinton Junction. Go straight, Hwy 281 goes to the right.
- **19.8 miles** - Stop sign.
- **20.2 miles** - Cross small bridge.
- **21.3 miles (H065)** - This is the 3,944 foot, historic 38 span, or "ponies," bridge across the Canadian River. Many stories are told as to why the bridge has 38 ponies, but the true story (*or so I've been told*) is the size of the ponies was the largest that could be handled by the road building equipment in the mid-1930s. "Road Test" hill is straight ahead, the road climbs 150 feet in one mile and was once used by new car owners to see if their car could climb the hill in high gear.
- **22.8 miles (H066)** - Exit pony bridge.

NOTE: Options lie ahead as to how to follow various Route 66 alignments. It is strongly suggested you take some time to read all of the information from this point to El Reno **(N120)** (*which is 22 miles east of the pony bridge*) in order to make decisions regarding your trip across this section of Oklahoma.

When you exit the pony bridge, there are three options for reaching El Reno. To trace the original route of the old road, use **OPTION ONE,** which is an Adventure Tour "Red Route." (*Please read all admonitions regarding Adventure Tours at the front of this book.*) **OPTION ONE** is a dirt road, slick and muddy in the winter, and following a rain. If you do not wish to travel on dirt, use **OPTIONS TWO** or **THREE**, which are paved.

OPTION 1 - This option will take you on the old, old alignment, on a dirt road, from the pony bridge north to Geary with an optional sidetrip to see the old tollbridge crossing to Bridgeport. This option joins the Option 2 route just south of Geary.

OPTION 2 - This option avoids the dirt and will take you directly to Geary on a paved road, then east to Calumet and south to El Reno.

OPTION 3 - This option takes you directly east to El Reno and bypasses Geary and Calumet altogether.

OPTION # 1

This was a 1932/33 temporary road to connect to the suspension bridge at Bridgeport until the pony bridge was completed.
After crossing the 38 pony bridge **(H066)**, make a left at the first intersection **(H067)** and:
ZERO ODOMETER
- **0.4 miles (H069)** - Make a right.

Santa Monica to Chicago

0.5 miles (H070) - Make a left.

1.8 miles - The wide-open country disappears as the road enters a virtual tunnel of trees. If it has been raining be prepared for some slick, red Oklahoma mud ahead. (*I should mention it will take at least five dollars in quarters to get this mud off at the car wash in El Reno.*)

3.0 miles (H071) - The road to the left (optional sidetrip) will take you along the old alignment to the site of the bridge across the river to Bridgeport. The old toll bridge has been gone a long time, but the bridge pilings can still be seen.

4.9 miles - Road to right.

6.0 miles (H072) - Make a left onto Hwy 281 into Geary.

6.2 miles (H073) - Junction of 281 and 270 in Geary, make a right, and join up with the Option #2 description below following "ZERO ODOMETER."

GEARY

Named after Ed Guerrier, a pioneer, it soon became known as Geary. Established in 1898.

OPTION #2 - The 2nd Alignment of the Mother Road

To make the Geary/Calumet loop without driving on dirt, continue straight on 281 north to Geary, past the junction for the El Reno Cutoff **(H068)**. (*Keep an eye out for your mud-laden brethren from Option #1 who will be joining you on Hwy 281 just south of Geary.*)
At the junction with Hwy 270 in Geary **(H073)**, make a right and:
ZERO ODOMETER

6.3 miles - Curve right and cross bridge.

10.4 miles - Cemetery on right.

11.3 miles - Old building on right.

11.4 miles - Curve right.

11.9 miles (H074) - Calumet.

13.4 miles - Six Mile Creek.

24.1 miles (H077) - Intersection, old station on northeast corner.

(Continue at the "In To El Reno" listing, below)

OPTION #3 - The El Reno Cutoff

After crossing the pony bridge **(H066)**, turn right at the first road to the right **(H068)** and
ZERO ODOMETER

1.0 miles - Top of the hill.

1.5 miles - Old gas station on left.

1.7 miles (H075) - Make right onto Spur 281.

4.0 miles (H076) - Make left onto old Hwy 66 (just before I-40 truck stop), and continue on (east) towards El Reno.
Just before the 66 and Hwy 270 junction **(H077)**, notice the early rumble strips of asphalt in the eastbound lanes.

IN TO EL RENO

At junction with 66 and Hwy 270 **(H077)**,
ZERO ODOMETER

1.8 miles - Cross small creek.

4.5 miles (H078) - Fort Reno Visitors Center. Make a left at major intersection to continue east. Road to the west enters Interstate.

7.0 miles - Older motels along here.

EL RENO

Founded when the Rock Island Railroad arrived two months after the land run of 1889. El Reno was the western edge of the land rush. Reno City was originally located on the north side of the Canadian River. The city refused to pay the railroad the bonus it wanted to bring the tracks to the city, so the railroad built on the south side of the river. Then the town moved buildings and all to the new site. One hotel was stranded for a short period in the middle of the river, but continued business as usual until it could be fully relocated.

July of 1901 saw the population of El Reno increase by 145,000 - in one day - when the Kiowa-Commanche Reservation was opened as the last chance for free territory land for settlers. Fortunately most of the influx departed as soon as the lottery drawing for the land was completed.

Santa Monica to Chicago

The Dustin Hoffman, Tom Cruise hit film *Rain Man* was filmed at the Big 8 Motel on the east end of town, standing in for an Amarillo motel. A sign out front proclaimed it "Amarillo's Finest." Don't bother, new owners changed the name to Deluxe Inn (*not even*), trashed the sign, and don't have a clue about any film being shot here.

LODGING: Best Western Inn at Hensley's (405.262.6490) and Days Inn (405.262.8720).

When you cross Four Mile Creek **(H079)**,

ZERO ODOMETER
- **0.7 miles (H080)** - Cross railroad tracks.
- **1.1 miles (H081)** - Right onto Choctaw Avenue.
- **1.2 miles (H082)** - Make a left onto Wade Street (40 BUS) and move to right lane for a right turn.
- **1.3 miles (H083)** - Turn right onto Rock Island. El Reno water tower is on right ahead.
- **2.1 miles (H084)** - Cross over railroad tracks.
- **2.9 miles** - Pass the VFW hall with a WWII bomber out front.

Continue straight out of El Reno, following the curve of the road.

At the junction of 66 and Shepard Ave. **(H085)**.

ZERO ODOMETER
- **2.8 miles** - Huge storage yard for drilling equipment.
- **3.9 miles** - El Reno city limits.
- **4.5 miles** - Three-lane road.
- **5.0 miles** - Cross Purcell Creek.
- **8.4 miles** - Cross Shell Creek.
- **9.6 miles** - Westport 66 housing development (right).
- **10.1 miles** - Cross Garth Brooks Blvd **(H086)**.
- **11.1 miles** -

YUKON

Home of Garth Brooks. Laid out by the Spencer brothers in 1891 and named after the Yukon River in Alaska. The nearby town of Frisco was virtually deserted when the railroad went through Yukon and everyone moved to the new community.

If it is evening check out the Yukon's Best Flour sign at the east end of town. The sign had been dark for years and became a matter of civic pride when it was re-lighted.

At the railroad tracks by the Flour Mill **(H087)**,

ZERO ODOMETER

The following will cover the old alignment through Bethany and Oklahoma City.
- **1.4 miles (H088)** - Make a right onto Mustang Road and then a quick left onto Lakeshore, also designated as NW 36th St.
- **2.8 miles** - Underpass.
- **3.1 miles (H089)** - Stop sign, stay to the left at fork, lake will be on the right.
- **3.5 miles (H090)** - Lakeview Pioneer Home, formerly the Lakeview Courts as shown in the 1940's AAA books.
- **4.8 miles** - Cross steel truss bridge.
- **5.2 miles (H091)** - Make a left, then a right, re-join the 39th Expwy (old Route 66) and continue east.

OKLAHOMA CITY

Oklahoma has the distinction of having the only State Capitol (post-1938) building on Route 66. It is also one of the few towns in the state with no Indian heritage, having started out as a pioneer town.

Many towns are said to have sprung up overnight, but Oklahoma City did so in thirty minutes. At Noon on April 22, 1889, the signal was given thirty miles away for the start of the Great Oklahoma Land Rush, and within fifteen minutes men of the Seminole Land and Town Company were dragging chains on a run. To be honest, over a thousand people camped along the Santa Fe tracks at the projected townsite. This early preparation led to the nickname "Sooner" being given to the early settlers (*Which seems to be another way of saying cheaters.*).

There were numerous routes of 66 through Oklahoma City. To get through the city, we will follow the 1936 route. If you are interested in the other routes, *Oklahoma Route 66* by Jim Ross is a great source book.

To follow the 1936 route, go eastbound on the 39th Expressway and exit at May Avenue **(H092)**. Make a right on May and continue to NW 23rd St. **(H093)**. Follow 23rd St. east to the State Capitol **(H094)**, curve to the north around the Capitol onto Lincoln, heading north toward Edmund.

North Lincoln was once the motel row of Oklahoma City with many of the classic motels lining both sides of the three-mile stretch. Over the past few years, the motels have all disappeared and the only evidence remaining are large lots, some with foundations.

Santa Monica to Chicago

LODGING: I will admit to an aversion to large cities, but Oklahoma City appears to be a relatively "safe" city and I have not heard of a major area of crime against tourists. There are hundreds of properties available in the city and my suggestion is to stick to a major chain. My personal favorite is the Residence Inn at 4361 W. Reno (405.942.4500).

Continue north on Lincoln and join I-44 eastbound **(H100)** - very short trip - stay in the right hand lane, get off at Kelley **(H101)** and make a left to continue north (*option: make right on 50th from Lincoln, east to Kelley, then a left and then north on Kelley*). At 63rd St., a right will take you to the Cowboy Hall of Fame **(H102)** and the County Line Restaurant (*great bar-b-que!*).

The next instructions are a little confusing, so follow carefully. North on Kelley to Memorial Road **(H103)**, right on Memorial, followed by an **IMMEDIATE** left onto the Hwy 77 access road **(H104)**, then left onto 77 **(H105)**. This is Broadway leading into Edmond.

EDMOND

Founded in 1887 as a coal and watering stop for the railroad. Named for a railroad official. Edmond is the site of Central State University and is primarily a college town and bedroom community for Oklahoma City.

At Second Street **(H108)**, make a right and continue east to Arcadia. You will crossover I-35 **(H109)** as you leave Edmond.

With the widening of the road east to Arcadia much of the Route 66 flavor has been lost. The spreading of the suburbs east out of Edmond are responsible.

ARCADIA (H110)

Noted for the Round Barn, built in 1898 by William Odor, and restored by the Arcadia Preservation and Historical Society. Be sure and leave a buck or two to help with their efforts.

HillBillie's Bar-B-Que as you enter town is well worth the stop and the Old Store is worth a photo or two.

At the round barn:

ZERO ODOMETER

3.2 miles (H111) - Left, a great example of a 1920's gas station.

4.7 miles - Historical Marker for the east boundary of the Oklahoma Land Rush of 1889.

5.0 miles - Little Brother's Gas Station on left.

7.1 miles (H112) - Luther. Old station and store on right.

13.1 miles (H113) - Make a left, onto Hwy 66B, and follow the 1926 alignment through Wellston.

WELLSTON (H114)

When bypassed in 1933, the town took their case to the Supreme Court to keep the town on Route 66. They lost.
Founded in 1880 as a trading post by Christian T. Wells on the Kickapoo Indian Reservation. Look for Pioneer Camp with its original sign and marble-eyed Totems.

17.1 miles (H115) - Back on Route 66, make a left. Pioneer Barbecue on left.

17.3 miles - Cross under Interstate.

19.1 miles - Junction with Hwy 177.

20.0 miles (H116) - Cross Deep Creek of the Canadian River. Town of Warwick ahead on left.

21.3 miles - Cross railroad.

23.4 miles - Meramec Caverns sign on barn.

25.4 miles -

CHANDLER

Founded in 1891 and named for George Chandler, Assistant Secretary of State under President Harrison. Chandler is an example of a "tough" town. Virtually, every building in town was destroyed by a tornado in 1897. With the loss of fourteen lives and destruction of all of the community buildings, reconstruction began immediately. The last old-west style gunfight took place here in 1924, and cost the life of lawman Bill Tilghman. He is buried in the cemetery west of town.

There is a hard left to be made when you enter Chandler proper **(H118)**. As you go past the intersection of 7th and Manvel (Manvel is Rt. 66), check out the restored Phillips service station. Great old brick building, getting plenty of care.

East of town check out the Lincoln Motel, built in 1939 **(H119)**.

The Econo-Lodge (405.258.2131) offers decent rooms at a good rate.

Continue east.

30.6 miles -

DAVENPORT (H120)

Founded by Southern Methodists in 1903 with the purchase of a farm and the laying out of a townsite. Oil was discovered in

Santa Monica to Chicago

1924 and the town attempted to grow, but discovery of the Seminole Field to the south doomed the expansion. Main Street is paved with bricks from the local brick plant and is locally known as "Snuff Street" - drive a block and take a dip. Also the site of the world's first round oil tank, built in 1925.

East of town, continue towards

STROUD (H122)

This was one hell-raising town before statehood, with nine saloons dispensing to the many cowboys who brought cattle to Stroud for shipment on the railroad. After statehood, Stroud became a "dry" town and a trading center for the farmers of the area.

An interesting side note - from here to Bristow lies Oklahoma's largest natural gas storage area with more than 75 billion cubic feet deposited in a depleted underground natural gas field.

On the east side of town, don't miss The Rock Café (lunch and dinner only, Tuesday through Saturday), a local classic built from native stone.

The old road can be seen continuing over the hills ahead. It is blocked at various points and some bridges have been removed but parts of it are accessible. There are many short connectors between the old road and the final alignment you're driving on (OK 66).

At the east end of Stroud **(H123)**, at Allied Road (N3570 Road), both the early and final alignments come together. A left turn will take you to the early alignment, which you will be able to see heading east towards the Salt Creek bridge and Depew, but this section is fenced off.

Upon leaving Stroud, at Allied Road,

ZERO ODOMETER

0.6 miles (H124) - Cross Salt Creek and look for old bridge off to left through trees; can be accessed on a short road to the right.

1.1 miles (H125) - Access to old alignment.

2.1 miles (H126) - Old road enters from left.

3.1 miles (H127) - Old road joins at right.

3.3 miles (H128) - You can see where the old road crossed over what is now the new alignment.

3.6 miles (H129) - Cross Camp Creek.

3.8 miles (H130) - Sidetrip! You can drive on the early alignment by making a right at the junction. (**Note:** The markings for this turn may be unreliable and local road conditions should be checked.)

6.0 miles (H131) - Early road sidetrip rejoins final alignment.

7.7 miles (H132) - Intersection and sign for Oakdale Cemetery. Make a left and then a quick right to join the old road, if you wish. Otherwise, just head straight into Depew.

8.2 miles (H133) - Right, then left to join OK 66 into Depew. Old alignment is on the left. Blocked at both ends, cannot be driven.

8.8 miles (H134) - At the convenience store, turn right for old alignment through Depew and

ZERO ODOMETER

Strongly suggest you make this loop into Depew, some of the finest examples of old, preserved architecture are here. The section of road that goes due east from the turn is the original by-pass of the town.

0.3 miles - Left turn onto to Main St.

0.4 miles - Check out the NAPA auto parts store on the right. As you drive along here notice the great old buildings.

0.6 miles - Left turn off of Main Street.

0.8 miles (H135) - Back to 1939 alignment and make a right.

1.3 miles (H136) - Cross Little Deep Creek.

2.0 miles (H137) - Curve to the right.

6.2 miles (H138) - Cross Catfish Creek.

6.6 miles - Old station on right.

7.3 miles -

BRISTOW

Began in 1897 as a trading post on Creek land in the Indian Territory. The railroad pushed west from Sapulpa and assisted in the development of Bristow. Town was founded in 1901 and named after J.L. Bristow, fourth Assistant Postmaster General. Bristow was also the site of Oklahoma's first radio station, KRFU, which became known as the "Voice of Oklahoma." The call letters were changed to reflect the nickname and became KVOO. In 1927, the station moved to Tulsa where it still pumps a strong signal across the plains.

Turn right on 4th Street **(H139)**, follow through town, at Main Street (junction of 66/14/48) make a left **(H140)** and continue

Santa Monica to Chicago

out of town (crossing I-44).

The following section will cover an older alignment of the highway. Just east of Bristow, cross the Sand Creek bridge (**H141**), drive under I-44 (**H142**) and take a right at 211th Street (**H143**), then left onto old pavement and:

ZERO ODOMETER
Follow the road past the cemetery.

    0.1 miles (**H144**) - Cross rusted arch bridge. Rough road surface.

    1.6 miles (**H145**) - Climb rise to intersect highway (this is new alignment of 66). Go straight across the highway and follow old pavement.

    1.9 miles (**H146**) - Stop sign. Make a left. (**NOTE:** This is Oklahoma 48, not old 66).

    3.1 miles (**H147**) - Log cabin on the hill to the right, make a right turn onto the old concrete road surface. This is Bellvue and the road is Old 66. Follow to first stop sign, then continue straight.

    4.1 miles (**H148**) - Stop sign (2nd stop sign on this stretch).

    4.3 miles (**H149**) - Junction with newer alignment of Route 66. Make a left. (*For laughs, watch for the "Bob Moore" mailbox on the right side of the road just after you join the new alignment.*)

    5.1 miles - Old pavement leads off to the right. This area is posted as private property. Please respect.

HEADS UP, KIDS! WATCH FOR THE NEXT MILE-POINT AND TURN - THE ROAD IS NOT MARKED.

    6.6 miles (**H150**) - Make a left onto the old highway.

This road meanders through the trees and over the hills, following the topography. It is one of those sections that drove the moms of this country crazy, yelling at the old man: "You don't HAVE to pass EVERY truck on the road!"

    8.3 miles (**H151**) - Rejoin the highway, make a left.

    8.9 miles (**H152**) - Cross I-44.

    9.6 miles (**H153**) - Cross Polecat Creek.

    11.5 miles (**H154**) - On the right, in front of the Cripple Creek Antique Mall, is a section of old pavement.

    11.9 miles - Curve to left.

    12.7 miles (**H155**) - Cross Little Polecat Creek. Water tower on right.

    13.7 miles (**H156**) - Kellyville. Old alignment on right as you leave town is not driveable.

    14.5 miles - Curve to left.

    16.4 miles (**H157**) - Old store and cabins at turnout.

    17.4 miles (**H158**) - Left onto old highway.

This is one of the best "frozen-in-time" stretches of the Mother Road, as you drive this section, it is almost as if time has stood still. There is little to remind you that you're in the new millennium. The old highway and overhanging mantel of trees remind you of a time when this was the highway through the area. The only thing missing is the massive amount of traffic that traveled this road in its heyday. (*Certain high-quality Route 66 maps will show you that, at times, you're less than 100 yards from the freeway madness of I-44 as you cruise through this section. But you will feel like you're a hundred miles and a hundred years away...*)

    18.3 miles (**H159**) - Cross beneath a classic 1925 railroad bridge.

    20.5 miles (**H160**) - Remains of the TeePee Drive-in Theatre on the right.

    20.6 miles - Road ahead (across bridge) may be closed, if so it will be necessary to cut across the VFW parking lot to rejoin the newer alignment of 66. At top of parking lot make a left.

    20.7 miles (**H161**) - Historic Rock Creek Bridge. Built in 1921 this bridge is a classic. The pavement on the bridge is red brick and makes for some excellent color photographs.

    20.7 miles (**H163**) - Rock Creek. Original road crossed at creek level. Pavement can be seen to the left and down.

SAPULPA

Founded by, and named for, Chief Sapulpa, a Creek Indian, who ran a store and farmed in the mid-1800s about a mile southeast of the present town site. With the arrival of the Frisco Railroad in 1886 Sapulpa became an important cattle shipping and loading center.

Continue into Sapulpa on Dewey, make a left on Mission (**H164**) and continue out of town on 66. Watch for Highway 166, and make a left onto Frankoma Road (**H165**). This is the old alignment of the highway and will lead you into Tulsa on Southwest Blvd.

TULSA

Originally called Tulsey Town after the Creek Tribe of the Tallasse or Tulsey community. Originally from Alabama, the tribe was moved to Oklahoma during the relocation of the 1880s.

First Post Office was established in 1879. Railroad arrived in 1882 and the large cattle drives that used to go to Vinita for loading were brought to Tulsa.

LODGING: As with any large city Tulsa has lodging options stretching from cheap to deluxe. Also, as with any large city I

Santa Monica to Chicago

would recommend staying at a major chain hotel. Many of the older motels are run-down and neglected. A few of my personal choices are: Best Western Trade Winds Central Inn (918.749.5561); Microtel Inn, (918.234.9100); Residence Inn (918.664.7241).

DINING: Many fine restaurants throughout Tulsa. Favorites, Cattlemen's Steakhouse - what else? Good steaks; Chimi's Mexican Restaurant - good food in a casual atmosphere; Ruby's for good home-style cooking, a Tulsa favorite for 30 years.

To drive through Tulsa on the later alignment of Route 66, follow Southwest and cross the river to 12th, just past Riverside after leaving the bridge.

Make a right on 12th **(H167)**, continue up the hill and follow the curve to the left, cross the interstate, curve to the right and stop at the intersection of 11th and Denver **(H168)**. Continue on 11th. Notice it becomes 10th **(H169),** then it swings to the right and becomes 11th once again. **(H170)** (*Whew! Anyone home in the public works department?*)

Once you are on 11th, stay on it all the way across town to 193rd East Ave. **(H171)**. This is a distance of approximately 12 miles.

At 193rd, make a left and continue under I-44. This route will place you on Historic Route 66 to Catoosa. Watch for Cherokee St. **(H172)**, just past the Pizza Hut. Make a right on Cherokee and continue to Antry St. in Catoosa **(H173)**. Make a right here to the first traffic light, then a left onto Oklahoma 66.

CATOOSA

Named after "Old Catoos" the rounded hill just west of town. The name is supposedly a derivation of *Gi-tu-zi* - Cherokee for "Here lives the people of the light" who met on the summit of the hill. The Port of Catoosa (three miles north) is the largest inland seaport in the nation. It is situated at the head of the McClellan-Kerr Arkansas Navigation System and links Tulsa to the world by way of the Mississippi River to New Orleans.

As you cross Spunky Creek **(H174)**,

ZERO ODOMETER

An old piece of the highway exists ahead.

0.4 miles (H175) - Take the road to the right, followed by an immediate left.

0.5 miles (H176) - The Arrowwood Trading Post. Directly across the main road from the trading post is the water park with its famous Big Blue Whale. he park was built by Hugh Davis for his wife who liked to collect whales.

0.9 miles (H177) - Road curves to the left. Watch for old store on the right. Mobilehome park on the left.

1.5 miles (H178) - Re-join Oklahoma 66 and continue east.

Cross the Verdigris River on an ornate arched bridge **(H180)**. Cross the ship channel **(H181)**, a great looking railway bridge is on your left.

Small town is Verdigris **(H182)**. Continue to Claremore.

CLAREMORE

The town found its beginning as an Osage Indian community early in the 19th century. It was named after the Osage chief who founded the town. Claremore was known for more than fifty years for its artesian spring water, discovered by accident in a 1903 during a test drilling for oil.

Claremore is noted as the hometown of Will Rogers, although Rogers stated he was born "half-way between Claremore and Oologah." The Will Rogers Memorial is west of Route 66, (turn left on Will Rogers Blvd).

Claremore was also the home of Andy Payne, the winner of the famous (or infamous) Bunion Derby, actually it was called the Great Transcontinental Footrace of 1928. Payne had entered the race to win the $25,000 grand prize. After nearly three months, 55 of the original 275 runners limped into Madison Square Garden with Andy Payne in the lead. The winners had to wait for nearly a week for the promoter, C. C. Pyle, to make good on the prize money.

LODGING: Microtel Inn, (918.343.2868).

DINING: Hammett House, good down-home cooking and great pies and rolls.

Go through town on Lynn Riggs Blvd if you want to follow the newer alignment. To follow the historic alignment, jog left onto J. M. Davis Blvd **(H184)** and

ZERO ODOMETER

0.4 miles (H185) - Cross Will Rogers Blvd (Memorial is about ten blocks to the left). Across the street, the Dayton Tire Store is an old gas station and garage - nicely preserved. GOOD WORK!

0.6 miles (H186) - For the gun collector the J.M. Davis Gun Museum, with over 6,000 weapons on display, is a must visit.

1.7 miles (H187) - Road curves to the right, becoming Stuart Roosa, and intersects with Lynn Riggs Blvd. Turn left.

Continue east through Sequoyah **(H188)** to Foyil. As you approach Foyil, a road to the right just before the Andy Payne Memorial will take you into town on an historic section of the highway. This road will terminate at the junction of OK 66 and 28A.

To go through Foyil, make a right on Andy Payne Blvd **(H189)** and

ZERO ODOMETER

Santa Monica to Chicago

0.1 miles - Andy Payne Memorial.

0.3 miles - Curve left.

0.75 miles - Stop sign, continue straight.

0.9 miles - Curve to right.

1.1 miles - Stop sign, make left to next stop sign, right onto 66.

An interesting side trip is to Galloway Park four miles east on Hwy 28A. Ed Galloway built a ninety-foot tall Totem pole and other examples of Oklahoma folk art.

At the intersection of OK 66 and 28A **(H190)**,

ZERO ODOMETER

2.5 miles - Old gas station on right.

3.3 miles -

BUSHYHEAD

Named for a chief of the Cherokee Nation.

4.4 miles (H191) - Culvert crossing - WPA/CCC bridge.

4.9 miles (H192) - Culvert crossing - WPA/CCC bridge.

8.0 miles (H193) - Roadside park on left.

9.4 miles -

CHELSEA

Oil was first discovered in Oklahoma Indian Territory just west of here in 1899 and changed the industry of the community forever. Prior to oil, Chelsea had been a prairie-hay shipping and cattle grazing town.

10.2 miles (H194) - Cross Prior Creek.

10.9 miles - Cemetery on left.

14.3 miles (H195) - Country Court motel on right. A motel set in the country to provide a respite for the traveler who may have traveled farther in one day than anticipated.

14.5 miles - Two lane road.

20.3 miles (H196) - White Oak.

21.9 miles (H197) - Junction of 60 and OK 66. OK 66 ends and becomes US 60. Go straight.

23.1 miles (H198) - Junction with Hwy 69. A right turn here will take you to Big Cabin, nice motels and a great truck stop at the turnpike interchange. Ask for Peggy in the gift shop/store.

25.9 miles - Cross Big Cabin Creek.

26.3 miles -

VINITA

Named after Miss Vinnie Ream, a sculptor commissioned to model the life sized statue of Lincoln in Washington D. C. Vinita is one of the oldest towns in Oklahoma. Original settlement was called Downingville, and the name was changed in 1871 with the arrival of the M-K-T and Atlantic & Pacific railroads.

For people interested in such things, the worlds largest McDonalds restaurant (*second largest, now, I believe*) is built on a bridge that spans I-44 a few miles from Vinita (*worth looking at, but that is all, service is terrible*).

Make a right turn at the intersection of Wilson and Illinois **(H200)**.

Head east on US 60 and 69 and, at Bull Creek **(H201)**,

ZERO ODOMETER

0.7 miles (H202) - Cross under I-44.

1.3 miles - Large pecan grove on right.

1.7 miles (H203) - Cross Little Cabin Creek - arched bridge.

4.9 miles (H204) - Junction with OK 82, continue straight.

9.3 miles (H205) - Dead Man's Corner, road curves to left, junction of highways 60/69/85. Old station on left.

13.3 miles - Road curves to the right.

13.9 miles - Old tourist cabins on left.

14.7 miles (H206) - Rest Haven Motel on left.

AFTON

Named after the river Afton from the Robert Burns poem. Some great examples of 1920's architecture here. Notice the bridge on the east end of town with its unique pedestrian walkways, built in 1929. Stop and see Laurel at the Afton Station.

Santa Monica to Chicago

Upon leaving Afton, you have the highly recommended option of experiencing two extremely rare sections of nine-foot roadway. Yes, Virginia, the Mother Road is only NINE feet wide (*sometimes less!*) along these stretches.

If you want to drive "The Sidewalk Highway," as it is known, use **OPTION ONE**, which is an Adventure Tour "Red Route." (Please read all admonitions regarding Adventure Tours at the front of this book.)

OPTION ONE is partially a dirt road, slick and muddy in the winter, and following a rain. However, unlike some of the adventure tours in the Far West, this tour is more like "Adventure Tour Lite" because you are never isolated away from a nearby paved road. The only reason it is an adventure tour is because the old roadway doesn't tolerate wet weather very well, and one of the criteria of this guidebook is that the designated Route 66 must be an all-weather road.

If you do not wish to travel on the narrow road, use **OPTION TWO**.

OPTION #1 - Driving the "Sidewalk Highway"

15.5 miles (H208) - Watch for a half-circle of narrow road on the right. This is a section of the famous eight-foot roadway. Directly across the highway from this section is what appears to be a dirt road. Make a left onto this road and the old pavement will soon appear. As you leave the highway:

ZERO ODOMETER

0.2 miles (H209) - Grade crossing of the railroad. **STOP,** turn off radio, roll down windows, (*stop arguing about driving on dirt roads!*) and proceed with caution.

1.2 miles (H210) - Cross over I-44. Rough pavement.

1.9 miles (H211) - Curve to right.

2.6 miles - End of eight-foot roadway.

2.7 miles (H212) - Junction with stop sign, turn left onto Highway 69. Technical Institute is on your left at the junction.

Continue north toward Narcissa. One mile north of Narcissa is the intersection with E 140 Road **(H215)**. Make a right and you are back on the remaining section of the eight-food wide highway. The road surface is becoming well worn so "Slow" is order of the day.

As you are making your right:

ZERO ODOMETER

1.0 miles (H216) - Curve to the left.

2.0 miles (H217) - Curve to the right.

3.5 miles (H218) -Make a left turn at the junction of E Street SW and E 130 Road, and head north towards Miami.

6.3 miles (H219) - Junction of Steve Owens Blvd. and Main Street in Miami.

OPTION #2 - Skipping past the "Sidewalk Highway"

At Horse Creek Bridge,

ZERO ODOMETER

1.6 miles (H213) - Former site of the Buffalo Ranch. In business from 1953 until 1997, as a tourist stop.

1.8 miles - Cross over railroad bridge.

2.2 miles (H214) - 60 East turns, continue north on 59, 60, & 69.

2.7 miles - Cross under I-44.

8.0 miles - Intersection with Oklahoma 25 - old garage and gas station.

8.1 miles - Narcissa.

9.2 miles - Curve right.

9.6 miles - Curve right.

10.3 miles - Small store on right.

11.5 miles - Curve left.

12.0 miles - Cross railroad.

12.4 miles - Route 66 Steel Building Company and the Frontier Motel. Also intersection with Oklahoma 10 - continue straight.

12.6 miles - Old garage on right.

12.7 miles - Old motor court on left.

12.8 miles - Curve to right. Neosho River Bridge ahead.

14.0 miles (H219) - Corner of Main and Steve Owens Blvd in Miami. Make a left onto Main Street.

MIAMI

For those not familiar with Native American names, this is *MY-AM-AH*. Originally a trading post called Jimtown, it was home to four farmers named Jim (hence the name). A post office was established by Jim Palmer in 1890 and named Miami in honor of Palmer's wife, a Miami Indian.

Santa Monica to Chicago

The Coleman Theater **(H220)**, built in 1929, at the corner of 1st and Main is an excellent example of restoration.
LODGING: Best Western Inn of Miami (918.542.6681).
Head north on Main Street towards Commerce, OK.
Just north of Miami **(H221)** (on the west side of Route 66) is the Miami Municipal Airport which, beginning in early 1941, was home to British Flying Training School #3 where RAF pilots trained during WW-II. Those killed during training are buried in the Grand Army of the Republic cemetery, which lays between Route 66 and the airport.
Short section of divided highway **(H222)** and

ZERO ODOMETER

You are entering Commerce, Oklahoma, the hometown of Mickey Mantle. To your left you will see the home of the fantastic Newell Motor Coach, the real way to travel Route 66. If you have the pocket change I would appreciate it if you would pick one up for me ($750,000 and up) - I'll pay the gas money for delivery.

1.7 miles (H223) - Curve right. In many locations, you will experience this type of curve. If you look closely, you will see the original road went straight, then had a hard turn to the right or left. Later alignments added the curves.
2.4 miles (H224) - Cross Tar Creek.
3.7 miles (H225) - Divided road and junction with Hwy 69. The road now becomes Hwy 69 and 69A ends.
4.9 miles - Cross under railroad.
6.2 miles (H226) - Curve to left.

QUAPAW

Named for the Quapaw Tribe, who originally resided in Arkansas. At the turn of the century, this was a major hay-shipping center. With an abundance of tall prairie grass, the area later became popular for cattle grazing. Around 1907, zinc mining became a mainstay of the area when ore from the Dark Horse Mine began paying off.
Today, Quapaw is quiet, but busy. Many of the building have great murals painted on them. One garage has a painting of an old-style gas station on it. If you frame your photo just right, it looks real.
It is now less than four miles to Kansas. Alongside the road can be seen many large mounds. These are piles of debris from the zinc mining in the area and are called "chat."
What a trip it has been across the great state of Oklahoma. The land has changed from high-country cattle lands, to oil producing areas, to the mining country around Quapaw. The people have made us feel welcome with friendly attitudes and a "come back soon" philosophy that truly makes us want to turn around and head back, but the Road ahead still beckons and who knows what lies around that next corner?

Santa Monica to Chicago

KANSAS

EASTBOUND

Kansas offers but a brief glimpse of herself as we travel the thirteen miles of Route 66 that cut across the south-east corner of the state. But a rich thirteen miles it is.

At the Kansas Stateline **(K001)**,
ZERO ODOMETER

The road travels through mining country here, although the topography is highly deceptive of the mine activity that was carried out far below the ground.

0.5 miles (K002) - Right turn off Military for old highway.

0.9 miles (K003) - Right turn back onto Military.

1.9 miles (K004) - Junction with Hwy 166. Stay on Hwy 69.

BAXTER SPRINGS

A pleasant and bustling community with a busy downtown area. Baxter Springs takes pride in billing itself as "The First Cowtown in Kansas." The cowtown legacy goes back to the 1860s when cattlemen and cowboys from Texas would drive thousands of longhorns to feed on the abundant grasslands of the region. During 1867 and 1868, a boom hit the area as huge cattle drives brought cowboys in unprecedented numbers. With the arrival of the railroad this seemingly quiet community became the "toughest town on earth" and a wide-open, hell-raisin' cowtown.

Once the railroad pushed on to the west Baxter Springs returned to a quieter life.

Prior to the great cattle drives, Baxter Springs was the site of a darker piece of history. On October 6, 1863, the Baxter Springs Massacre took place at what is now the eastern end of 7th Street. During that morning the Federal Garrison, consisting of one company of cavalrymen and 65 to 70 black infantrymen, was attacked by forces led by William Clarke Quantrill, a Confederate guerrilla fighter and pre-war criminal whose "troops" included Jesse James and his brother, Frank. After less than half-an-hour Quantrill's men withdrew, leaving two of their men dead and nine Federal soldiers mortally wounded. Later, on the same day, Major General James G. Blunt approached Baxter Springs en route to his new posting at Fort Gibson. With him where his staff, a detachment of troops and a regimental band. Blunt mistook the departing Quantrill troops for an escort and was soon surrounded and captured. Quantrill sent a message to the garrison asking for an exchange of prisoners. Witnesses claim Quantrill had already killed all of the captives by the time the messenger was dispatched to the garrison.

General Blunt who, with eight men, had escaped Quantrill's band, found eighty-seven of his men dead by gunshots to the back of the head. In Baxter Springs National Cemetery (2 miles west on 166), a monument is dedicated to the men who fell that October day. (*Quantrill was later driven east into Kentucky where he died after a standoff with Union troops in the spring of 1865.*)

2.2 miles (K005) - Baxter Springs Museum one block east, to the right. Cross bridge.

2.5 miles (K006) - Left turn at this intersection to follow old alignment.

2.9 miles (K007) - Road veers to the right around a long curve.

3.3 miles (K008) - Bridge.

5.4 miles (K009) - Stop and check out the Rainbow Arch Bridge on the left, on the old alignment. There has been much controversy over the loss of the old arched bridges throughout Kansas. Heavy lobbying of the Kansas Department of Transportation has resulted in the saving of one and the losing of one in this area.

6.5 miles (K010) - Intersection, stop sign. (Continue straight.)

6.9 miles (K011) - Stop sign, continue on K66 across Alt 400 ahead.

RIVERTON

A river town situated on the west bank of the Spring River. Post office established in 1919. Riverton is the home of the Kansas Historic Route 66 Association, a dynamic group that works with both Missouri and Oklahoma on road preservation projects..

7.8 miles (K012) - The Association is head-quartered in the old Eisler Bros. Store building. While here be sure to visit with Scott Nelson, President of the Association and proprietor of the store.

8.0 miles (K013) - Cross the Spring River. There used to be a marvelous bridge here. It was the Marsh Rainbow Arch Bridge, taken down in 1986. See Michael Wallis', *Route 66 - The Mother Road*, page 82 for a picture of this beauty.

Just before you cross the river, on the left, is the Spring River Inn and on the right is the Empire District Hydroelectric Power Plant. The power plant looks like one of those buildings you would see in a 1930's Universal Pictures horror film.

Santa Monica to Chicago

GALENA

Lead mines caused an explosion in population in 1877 as Galena was born. Over three thousand people moved here in the space of two months. The "hurry-up" factor combined with slag heaps made for a less than attractive town.

One of the more interesting stories is the rivalry between Galena and Empire City to the north. A log wall was built between the two towns, to keep the good citizens of Empire City from venturing to the rough-and-tumble Galena (*or was it the other way around?*). The people of Galena watched as the wall was painstakingly built, and when it was completed, proceeded to burn it to the ground. The Post Office was established in 1877.

Coming into town, a couple of blocks west of downtown is Katy's Cafe (*a good place for lunch*) and the Galena Museum, it's on the right, by the "Old 66" sign. The museum is housed in a restored railroad depot that was moved to this site.

At the intersection with Main Street **(K014),** make a left and
ZERO ODOMETER
  0.5 miles (K015) - A right onto Front Street.

Continue east on Front Street to intersection with Stateline Road **(K016)**.

Cross Stateline Road and you are in Missouri.

Santa Monica to Chicago

MISSOURI

EASTBOUND

Long known as the "Show Me" State, Missouri will share some wonderful sights along Route 66 as we move from the prairies into the hill country. The Ozarks, the Great Arch and a bridge with a bend in the middle are just a sampling of what lies ahead.

Enter Missouri on Old Route 66 from Galena, Kansas and when you cross the Stateline Road **(M001)**:

ZERO ODOMETER

    0.3 miles - Leave the old road surface.

    0.5 miles - Old section of the road can be seen down and to the left. At the T- intersection **(M002)**, make a left onto MO 66 (7th Street into Joplin).

    3.0 miles - Road becomes two-lane.

JOPLIN

Beneath the street lie a labyrinth of mine tunnels that have been filled with water to support the city above.

Originally settled by John C. Cox in 1838, along the banks of Turkey Creek. In 1841, he named the settlement that had expanded around his store, Blytheville, after Billy Blythe, a popular Cherokee. In 1871, Patrick Murphy of Carthage purchased forty acres west of Joplin Creek and platted the town of Murphysburg. A few weeks later John Cox, now Judge Cox, platted the city of Joplin on the east side of Joplin Creek. A rivalry developed between the two towns, so intense that children would stand on opposite sides of the creek and throw rocks at each other.

In March of 1872, the court was petitioned to combine the two cities under a common charter and call it Union City. More problems ensued and in March of 1873, the State General Assembly merged the two towns as the City of Joplin.

This book will cover what is commonly referred to as "Bypass 66." Other routes through the city were known as "City 66" and "Alternate 66." The *Missouri US 66 Tour Book* by Skip Curtis covers these other routes in detail.

Continue through town to Range Line Road (US 71) **(M004)** and make a left onto Range Line.

NOTE: If planning an overnight in Joplin, a right at Range Line to I-44 is where many chain motels will be found.

LODGING: Hampton Inn (417.659.9900); Best Western Hallmark Motor Inn (417.624.8400);Thunderbird Motel (417.624.7600).

DINING: Jim Bob's Steak and Ribs; Golden Ox.

Cross long bridge over railroad tracks.

Continue north on US 71 *(it becomes Madison in Webb City)* to Broadway **(M005)**, then a right onto Broadway to a T-intersection **(M006)**. Broadway jogs to the left for half-a-block on Webb **(M007)** and turns right, headed for Carterville.

WEBB CITY & CARTERVILLE

Both towns were platted in 1875 and were major lead and zinc mining towns. When demand fell off following WW-I, the towns slowed considerably.

Broadway curves left **(M008)**; continue past Ideal Bar and continue through town to a hard right turn in Carterville **(M010)** where Broadway becomes Main Street. Follow Main to Pine **(M011)**.

Left on Pine to the Carterville Cemetery **(M012)** and make a right at the yield sign.

Follow road to 3-way intersection with a Missouri Historic Route 66 sign **(M013)** and make a right, cross over Hwy 71 to frontage road, then left **(M014)**. Just ahead, check out the Route 66 drive-in on the left **(M015)**.

Continue into

CARTHAGE

Platted in 1842 and named for the ancient commercial center in North Africa. In 1864, guerrillas of the Confederacy burned the courthouse, the business section and most of the private residences.

In Carthage, Route 66 becomes Oak St. *(with its own cool railroad bridge* **(M017)** which you follow to Garrison **(M018)**. Make a left at Garrison and go north on Garrison to Central **(M019)**, and turn right on Central. Head east out of town and follow MO 96 as it veers left and cross a railroad bridge **(M020)**. Shortly you will cross the Spring River **(M021)**.

At junction of MO 96 and County Hwy V **(M022)** make a right to follow the old alignment and

ZERO ODOMETER

    1.5 miles (M023) - Jct MO 96 (the last alignment of Route 66), join 96 eastbound.

    1.7 miles - Small gas station on left.

5.4 miles (M024) - Another small station on left.
9.4 miles (M025) - Avilla. Founded in 1858 and named for hometown of the founders.
10.4 miles (M026) - Remains of White Oak Cabins.
11.3 miles (M027) - Cross White Oak Creek.
12.5 miles (M028) - Remains of Stone City.
13.0 miles (M029) - Remains of Log City.
These two towns were resort locations and were named for the building materials used in their respective construction.
14.5 miles (M030) - Plew. Named in 1893 for a local family. Sometimes found on old maps as Plewtite.
16.9 miles (M031) - Remains of Shadyside Camp on right. All stone buildings and cabins.
17.6 miles (M032) - Rescue. Post office founded in 1897.
21.7 miles (M033) - Phelps. Post office in 1857, named for local attorney Bill Phelps.
23.8 miles - Old alignment to the left, over the hill and rejoins at 24.2 miles.
25.6 miles (M034) - Albatross. Named for the Albatross Bus Line that stopped at this spot. Founded in 1926. Junction with MO 39.
26.5 miles - Old gas station to the right.
26.8 miles - Another old station on right.
27.7 miles (M035) - Heatonville. The Castle Rock Cabins were here.
30.3 miles (M036) - Left here onto Old Hwy 66 (Farm Road 2059).
31.7 miles (M037) - Cross "M" at stop sign.
32.4 miles (M038) - Cross Hwy 96 onto Farm Road 2062.
32.5 miles - Road jogs to the left. Now on old pavement.
33.4 miles (M039) - The buildings here are the remains of Spencer. Named in 1868, buildings here date to 1920s.
33.5 miles (M040) - Make a left (onto "N").
34.1 miles (M041) - Intersection with Hwy 96. Cross 96.
34.5 miles (M042) - Turnback Creek Bridge.
34.9 miles (M043) - Paris Springs Junction. Now on MO 266.
35.5 miles (M044) - Stop sign, continue straight. Old station on right.
37.8 miles (M045) - Halltown. Quite a few antique shops here. Curiously, Jack Rittenhouse mentioned antique shops here in his classic 1946 Guidebook to Route 66.
40.3 miles - Junction with "F."
42.2 miles (M046) - Plano and intersection with Farm Road 45. Large stone building on NW corner.
45.7 miles (M047) - Junction with "T." Old gas station on left.
51.9 miles (M048) - Cross under I-44.

SPRINGFIELD

Earliest settlement was by Thomas Patterson in 1821. In 1822, the Delaware tribe claimed the government had given them the lands of Southwestern Missouri. The courts upheld their claim and all the white settlers left the area. In 1830, John Polk Campbell and his brother established a cabin approximately 400 yards north of the present town square.

Like other western Missouri towns Springfield sided with the Confederacy during the Civil War. In August of 1861, the South won the battle of Wilson's Creek and held the city until February of 1862, when Union forces took it back.

LODGING: Best Western Sycamore Inn (Rail Haven) (417.866.1963); Park Inn (417.882.1113); Skyline Motel (417.866.4356). Plus many chain motels, a lot of the older motels suffer from neglect, disrepair or weekly tenets.

DINING: Hemingway's Blue Water Cafe (*check out the aquarium!)*; Trotter's Bar-B-Q; The Shady Inn.

There are three routes through Springfield.

City Route - The 1925 to 1935 Route follows the Chestnut Expressway (Bus. I-44) to College, around the square to St. Louis, left on Glenstone to Kearney, right on Kearney (MO 744).

Alternate 66 went to the public square, then around and north on Bonneville to Commercial, right on Commercial to Glenstone, left on Glenstone to Kearney, right on Kearney.

By-pass 66 - Chestnut Expressway to West By-pass (US 160) **(M049)**, make a left, north 2 miles to Kearney **(M050)**, right on Kearney (MO 744).

At the junction with Kearney and Glenstone **(M051)**,
ZERO ODOMETER
1.4 miles (M052) - Holiday Drive-in Theatre.
4.4 miles (M053) - Junction of OO and 744. Steer right onto OO.

Santa Monica to Chicago

    6.3 miles (M054) - 125 turns to the right, stay straight on "OO."
    7.5 miles (M055) - Strafford - Check out Grandaddy's BBQ at 101 E. Pine St (one block north of Route 66) Good food, friendly people.
    11.9 miles (M056) - Holman.
    15.3 miles (M057) - Red Top Court was here.
    16.0 miles (M058) - Stop sign, without warning, at junction with "B," go straight - stay on "OO."
    20.3 miles -

MARSHFIELD
Named for Daniel Webster's home in Massachusetts. Platted in 1856. The centerpiece of the town is the courthouse built in 1870.
    21.0 miles (M059) - Junction of 38 and "OO." Turn right onto 38 and go straight for one long block to "CC." (*Wake-up! We know you're already tired of the alphabet soup road numbering system but this a busy five-way junction!*)
    21.2 miles (M060) - Junction of "CC" and 38. Turn left onto "CC," also known as Hubble Drive, named for Edwin Hubble, a local boy, who was the first man to prove there were other galaxies. (*He also had his name on the Hubble Space Observatory, which has had a somewhat checkered history.*)
    28.0 miles (M061) - Junction with "M," stay on "CC."
    28.6 miles (M062) - Abbylee Court on the right. This is Niangua.
    31.3 miles (M063) - Sampson and junction with "HH."
    35.1 miles (M064) - Conway, small main street to the right. Junction with "J," stay on "CC."
    40.5 miles (M065) - Phillipsburg, junction with "C." Turn left onto "C" and cross I-44.
    41.0 miles (M066) - Turn right onto "W."
    50.4 miles (M067) - Junction with BL 44, make a very short right, followed by an immediate left onto I-44 frontage road.

LEBANON
Founded with the forming of Leclede County in October of 1849. An example of a city moved because of the railroad. The railroad refused to build in town when the city refused to give them free land for the depot. They built the station one mile from town. The town picked up and moved to the new location, away from the well-drained original site to the mud flats chosen by the railroad.
    The Best Western Wyota Inn (417.532.6171) and the Hampton Inn (417.533.3100) are good bets for lodging. Stonegate Station is good for both American and Italian specialties.
    51.7 miles (M068) - Curve to right.
    52.5 miles (M069) - Cross Jefferson.
    53.2 miles (M070) - Curve to right.
    53.5 miles (M071) - Left turn onto north frontage road and continue east out of Lebanon, watch for a bend in the road near Comer's Motors on the left due to relocation of old highway.
    59.9 miles (M072) - Right onto "F" and cross over I-44.
    60.4 miles (M073) - Left onto Glacierpoint Road, south side of I-44.
    65.3 miles (M074) - Junction of Glacierpoint, "N," and "T." Go straight on "N." (Glacierpoint ends and "T" runs north to the left.)
    66.5 miles (M075) - Junction of "N" and Heartwood Rd. Go straight on Heartwood. ("N" turns right to the south.)
    68.5 miles (M076) - Steel truss bridge across the Gasconade and
ZERO ODOMETER
    1.4 miles (M077) -

HAZELGREEN
Post office established in 1858. Once a bustling tourist town the "new" four-lane Route 66 was built through town. Post Office closed in 1958.
    2.9 miles (M078) - Gascozark. Heartwood Road becomes "AB" at the junction with 133 in Gascozark. Continue east.
    3.5 miles (M079) - Dadtown - Named for "Dad" Lewis who built a general store here in 1903. First silent movies in the area were shown here in a large tent.
    8.9 miles (M080) - Junction of "AB" and "AA." Time for a sidetrip! A left turn onto "AA" will take you along the 1927 routing to Laquey and bring you back to the main highway farther east.
    9.0 miles (M081) - Junction of "AB" and MO 17. "AB" ends. Continue straight on 17.
    11.0 miles (M082) - Junction of 17, "P," and "NN." Continue straight on 17. The sidetrip from Lacquey rejoins the main high-

way here.
12.5 miles (M083) - Left and cross the interstate, then right onto MO 17.
18.0 miles (M084) -

WAYNESVILLE

Jake Bates opened a store here in 1835 and in 1839 the townsite was platted. Named for Revolutionary War General "Mad Anthony" Wayne.

Take BL 44 through town and continue east.

19.2 miles (M085) - St. Robert.
20.1 miles - Cross over I-44.
21.5 miles (M086) - Junction of "Z" and MO 28. Go straight ahead onto "Z."
25.5 miles (M087) - Veer right to follow the old road to the Devil's Elbow. *(Going straight would keep you on the final alignment, but it isn't nearly as much fun!)* Go past Grandview Courts on your left **(M088)** and down the hill to

DEVILS ELBOW

Devils Elbow was named for the bend in the river where lumberjacks had to deal with a devil's worth of logjams that would pile up behind the bend.

26.4 miles (M089) - Vista Point.
26.9 miles (M090) - Village of Devils Elbow.
27.1 miles (M091) - The "Elbow Inn." A nice to place to stop for eats or a soda.
27.5 miles (M092) - Right turn to rejoin final alignment, heading east.
28.0 miles (M093) - Pass through the massive Hooker Cut.

This four-lane section of the Mother Road was the last piece of Route 66 to be replaced by I-44 in Missouri. The Big Cut is a great and magnificent demonstration of the art of road building.

28.9 miles (M094) - Left turn-off for

HOOKER

Originally Pine Bluff, renamed for a local family. Post office established 1900.

29.8 miles (M095) - Road becomes two-lane (rough road!).
30.3 miles (M096) - Junction of "Z" and "J" at I-44 crossover. Turn left and cross the Interstate. Turn right on the North Outer Road East (*say that fast six times!*) This is a twisting section that will result in entering and exiting the Interstate, so follow carefully.

You will pass Clementine - Post Office established 1891.

Continue down into the valley.

NOTE: Watch for the next turn, **DO NOT** continue to Jerome because there is no longer a way to cross the Little Piney River.

33.5 miles (M097) - Entrance to I-44. Make a right, cross interstate, then left onto I-44.

Leave I-44 at exit 176 **(M099)**.

SIDETRIP! If you want to visit old Route 66 sites take a left after exiting I-44, cross the interstate to the north frontage road (known locally as the Sugartree Outer Road), make another left and follow the road for 2.1 miles. The north frontage road dead-ends down at a tan old motel that is now a private residence **(M101)**. For an interesting photo opportunity, drive just past Vernell's Motel to the long abandoned "John's Modern Cabins" **(M100)** which has been the subject of preservation efforts.

Return and cross I-44, make a right on the south frontage road (known locally as the Arlington Outer Road or the Outer Road West). This section is a nice piece of old highway, the pavement is narrow and there are a couple of steep grades to make it interesting. It will take you 2.9 miles along a great stretch of the old highway down to Arlington **(M102)**, a small town that seems to have had problems finding itself. Over the years it has been in St. Louis, Gasconade, Crawford, Pulaski and Phelps counties and for a brief period it was county seat of Crawford County. The main street was cut off by the new highway in the 40s, and in 1946 Arlington was sold to Rowe Crey of Rolla for $10,000. He had plans of developing it into a resort. Today, Arlington sits quietly beneath the Interstate as a fishing and camping spot for those lucky enough to know where it is.

Back at I-44 exit 176 **(M099)**, make a right to re-join old 66, which is County Road 7100.

3.9 miles

DOOLITTLE

Originally Centerville it was renamed in 1946 to honor General Jimmy Doolittle, Medal of Honor winner and WW-II hero. In Doolittle, old Route 66 is named Eisenhower Street.

5.7 miles (M103) - Intersection with "T" in Doolittle and

Santa Monica to Chicago

ZERO ODOMETER
   2.8 miles (M104) - One lane bridge.
   3.9 miles (M105) - Martin Spring.
   Notice the half-curbs along here. These were designed to keep cars in the proper lane by forcing them back into the traffic lanes. A unique concept that failed miserably. The curbs resulted in cars being tipped over or thrown into oncoming traffic.
   This is the end of Ozark Country and from here east is the Big Prairie country.
   5.5 miles -

ROLLA

Founded in 1855 by a group of contractors who were building the railroad. In 1857, Phelps County was organized and Rolla was selected as the county seat. The town was named, according to legend, when John Webber wanted to call it Hardscrabble. E. W. Bishop, a railroad official wanted to call it Phelps Center. George Coppedge won out with the request it be named after his North Carolina home of Raleigh. However, the name wound up being spelled as Coppedge pronounced it, Rolla (Raw-la).
   Downtown is the Uptown Theater (*sorry, I just could not resist that one!*).
   LODGING: Best Western Coachlight Inn (573.341.2511); Zeno's Motel (573.364.1301).
   DINING: Johnny's Smoke Stak - great barbeque; Zeno's Steakhouse.
   Where the frontage road from Martin Spring meets I-44 Exit 184 **(M106)**, veer right onto Kingshighway (I-44 BL) and follow it to Bishop Ave. (US 63) **(M107)**.
   Make a left onto Bishop and follow it as it crosses I-44 **(M108)**. Continue to junction of Road 2000 **(M109)**.
   Make a right onto Road 2000, follow the curve around to the left and continue to Road 2020 **(M110)**. Make an angled left turn onto RD 2020. (*Make this turn or you will end up at a dead-end at Bob's Body Shop next to the interstate!*)
   Continue for 3.4 miles to "V" **(M111)**. Cross "V" and stay on "Old Highway 66 Outer Road" heading east.
   About 1.5 miles down the road, you will see the "Route 66 Motors and General Store" on your left **(M112)**. Classic cars and things for the person who is crazy about cars. A must stop for the traveling Roadie.
   Approximately 4.5 miles east, turn right onto Jefferson Street (US 68) at the I-44 interchange, cross I-44 **(M113)** and enter

ST. JAMES

Originally platted in 1859 by James Wood and was known as Scioto. The name was changed in a matter of months to St. James. The main business district runs at a right angle to the highway.
   Make a left onto "KK" (also known as E James Blvd) **(M114)** and

ZERO ODOMETER
   (**Note:** There is an instruction below regarding the junction with "F." This is County Road "F" **(M118)**, east of Rosati, not "F" Street in St. James **(M115)**.
     4.5 miles (M116) - Junction of "KK" and "U." Go straight on "KK."
     5.7 miles (M117) - Junction of "KK" and "ZZ." Go straight onto "ZZ." "KK" turns south, to the right.
   This is the Rosati area, more a sprawling community of farms rather than a town. Italians settled area around the turn of the century.
   Near Rosati, watch for cars stopping along the interstate and the people crossing over to old 66 (*See how smart you are to be traveling on the Mother Road instead of Insipid-state 44!*) to visit the numerous grape stands along here.
     8.0 miles (M118) - Junction of "ZZ" and "F." Go straight on "ZZ."
     8.9 miles (M119) - Fanning.
     9.1 miles (M120) - Cross junction with "KK."
     12.7 miles (M121) -

CUBA

Founded in 1857 as a farming village and railroad shipping point. The town virtually abandoned its original location near the tracks and moved up to the highway in the 1930s. Route 66 Cafe is in the center of town.
   Classic lodging at the Wagon Wheel Motel (573.885.3411), contemporary lodging at Best Western Cuba Inn (573.885.7707).
   13.7 miles (M122) - Wagon Wheel Motel.
   17.7 miles (M123) - Remains of Hofflins.
   20.7 miles (M124) - Junction with "H." Oak Grove Wayside Park on left.

BOURBON

During the 1850s, Richard Turner sold whiskey to railroad crews from his store. The place was called the Bourbon Store and in time the townsite took on the name.

Santa Monica to Chicago

25.7 miles (M125) - Junction with "C" and "N." Main street is "Old Highway 66."
26.4 miles (M126) - Cross junction with "N" and "J."
30.6 miles (M127) - Slight curve to the right.
31.8 miles (M128) - Stop light at junction with MO 185.

SULLIVAN

Founded as Mt. Helicon in 1856 and renamed in honor of Stephen Sullivan who donated the railroad right-of-way through the village. As a confederate sympathizer, he was hanged along with John Stanton (after whom Stanton is named) for operating the gunpowder factory at Saltpeter Cave (near Meramec Caverns). Some say that Sullivan was saved and lived to an old age.

37.2 miles

STANTON

Originally Reedville, renamed for John Stanton who ran a powder mill here during the 1850s. (*And who, like fellow Confederate gunpowder maker Stephen Sullivan, also ended up on the business end of a noose run by the Union troops.*)

Many great "tourist traps" along here. Check out the Antique Toy Museum, the Jesse James Museum and of course, Meramec Caverns.

The Caverns opened in 1935 as a commercial enterprise of Lester Dill. When originally opened the caverns had parking for 300 cars, electric lighting and a dance pavilion all within the first room. The caverns are located about 3-1/2 miles to the right on Road "W."

Back in Stanton, cross I-44 **(M129)**, then make a right onto North Outer Road East, and at this point:

ZERO ODOMETER

4.2 miles (M130) - Junction with St. Louis Inn Road.
7.4 miles (M131) - Junction with "WW." Go straight ahead on "WW."
8.8 miles (M132) - I-44 interchange at Exit 239. Turn right and cross the interstate.
9.0 miles (M133) - Turn left onto 66/US 30. 66 which becomes Commercial Ave. in St. Clair.
9.1 miles (M134) - Cross junction with US 30 and 47 (slight left) and

ZERO ODOMETER

ST. CLAIR

Once known as Travelers Repose, the name was changed in 1859 when the town citizens grew tired of the town being thought of as a pioneer cemetery or a tavern. Named for a civil engineer of the Frisco Railroad.

10.3 miles (M135) - Junction of 47 and N Commercial Ave. Go straight on N Commercial, past junction with "TT" **(M136)**.
11.9 miles (M137) - I-44 Exit 242. Cross over to the North Outer Road and turn right.
14.9 miles (M138) - Hall's Place.
15.9 miles (M139) - Do not cross Interstate here. (*This is a crossover bridge to the South Outer Road.*) Stay on north side of I-44.
17.0 miles (M140) - Junction of Hwy 50. Cross 50 and go straight ahead on "M"/"AT"(old 66).

> **NOTE: THIS MANEUVER REQUIRES YOUR UTMOST ATTENTION BECAUSE YOU ARE CROSSING FOUR LANES OF A BUSY HIGH-SPEED DIVIDED HIGHWAY. BE CAREFUL!** (*The producers of certain high-quality Route 66 maps almost met their Maker at this intersection!*)

17.8 miles (M141) - Junction with Hwy "O." Go straight.
18.8 miles (M142) - Junction with Hwy "M." "M" veers left from "AT" at this point. Go straight.
20.5 miles (M143) - The Sunset Motel.
21.5 miles (M144) - The Tri-County Restaurant and Truck Stop is the old Diamonds. The building you see here was built after a tremendous fire in 1948 that destroyed the original building. The fire was so intense that all traffic on Route 66 was stopped for hours.
21.8 miles (M145) - Villa Ridge, cross MO 100 and go straight ahead on "AT."
22.5 miles (M146) - Cross I-44. Bridge only - no interchange.
23.4 miles (M147) - The Gardenway Motel, a classic Route 66 motel (*unfortunately cannot be recommended*).
16.2 miles (M148) - The Diamonds Restaurant and Motel. This is the "new" Diamonds.

Santa Monica to Chicago

Cross junction with MO 100 (MO 100 turns left) and:
ZERO ODOMETER
    0.7 miles (M149) - Bridge over railroad tracks. The tracks run through a deep cut here and in the distance can be seen the entrance to a tunnel that runs beneath Gray Summit.
    4.4 miles (M150) -

PACIFIC
Originally named Franklin when founded in 1852. Renamed in 1854 for the ultimate destination of the railroad. Lots of coal trains pass through here. Many silica mines in the area provide fine sand for glassware.
    LODGING: Holiday inn Express (314.257.8400).
    DINING: Sheffield's Grill & Cafe; Monroe's 66 Diner; The Red Cedar Inn.
    4.0 miles (M151) - Monroe's 66 Diner - nice 66 atmosphere and good food.
    5.8 miles (M152) - Red Cedar Inn. Built in 1934 and has been a local favorite for years.
    4.8 miles - Road becomes two-lane.
    5.5 miles (M153) - Eastern Missouri Correctional Center - Don't pick up hitchhikers.
    6.0 miles (M154) - Remains of the Beacon Motel.
    6.3 miles (M155) - Major road cut followed by a bridge.
    7.2 miles (M156) - Allenton. At this point you are required to join I-44 east of Allenton to continue to St. Louis.
    12.8 miles (M158) - Times Beach can be seen off to the left. Visit the Route 66 State Park and Museum here. Times Beach was a summer get-away for the St. Louis crowd. It developed as a promotional stunt by the St. Louis Star-Times in 1925. If you bought a lot, you were given a six-month subscription to the paper. Contests were held with additional lots being awarded as prizes.
    In 1982, Times Beach was declared contaminated by the EPA because dioxin laced oil had been used on the dirt roads in the early 1970s. By 1986 the buy-out of the town was complete, bringing to an end Times Beach.
    From Times Beach into St. Louis, the road is Interstate highway (I-44).

> **NOTE:** Three routes of 66 exist into St. Louis. This book covers what was known as "City 66," the route used from 1933 on. The other routes are covered extensively in *The Missouri Route 66 Tour Book* by Skip Curtis.

    About 10 miles east of Times Beach (**M158**) on I-44, you will come to the interchange with I-270 and it's time to make a decision.
    If you want to use the freeway system to bypass the city, the most common route is to take I-270 north. However, if you see the road is jammed (I-44 to I-270 north), head south on I-270. It will connect with and become I-55. Continue on I-55, cross the river into Illinois, then take I-255 north to I-270, then make the short (4 mile) backtrack to I-270 - Exit 3 where your Route 66 journey will continue at the Chain of Rocks Bridge. The distance around the city is about the same and the traffic moves much faster - even during rush hours.
    If you want to take 66 through the St. Louis, stay on I-44 and go under I-270. Then, **IMMEDIATELY** after the interchange, get off the freeway at exit 277A - MO 366/Watson Road (**M159**). Follow Watson Road towards St. Louis.
    About 5 miles east, at 7755 Watson Rd. in the village of Marlborough, is the site of a very famous Route 66 landmark, the Coral Court Motel. (**M160**). Although now replaced by a housing subdivision, the Coral Court was a great place in its heyday, both architecturally and socially. You can read everything you'd ever like to know about the Coral Court in Shellee Graham's fine book of stories and photographs, *Tales from the Coral Court (*ISBN 1-891442-08-2 or visit www.coralcourt.com). Note: If you are using a contemporary map to supplement your travels, the Coral Court was located where Watson Road is intersected by Oak Knoll Manor Drive.
    Proceed on Watson Road and cross under the Frisco Railroad bridge. At the St. Louis city limit (**M161**), Watson becomes Chippewa Road.
    Continue on Chippewa to the intersection with Jamieson. Just past Jamieson, on the right, is another Route 66 landmark: Ted Drewes Frozen Custard at 6726 Chippewa (**M162**). Stop in for an original treat!
    Follow Chippewa to the intersection with Gravois (**M163**), (pronounced *Grav-oy*). Make the angled left and follow Gravois to where it makes an angled left onto 12th Street (**M164**), which becomes Tucker Blvd a few blocks farther on.
NOTE: There is an I-55 interchange near where the Gravois-to-12th-Street transition occurs. Due to the problems with the McKinley Bridge (see below), you might be wise to join I-55 here and cross the river into Illinois to the interchange with I-255.

Santa Monica to Chicago

Head north on I-255 to I-270, then make the short (4 mile) backtrack to I-270 - Exit 3 where your Route 66 journey will continue at the Chain of Rocks Bridge.

If you want to follow the route through downtown just for kicks (!) (*sorry, Bobby....*), continue on 12th/Tucker, it will pass through downtown, join 13th Street briefly, and then curve left onto Florissant Ave. **(M165)**. One mile later, make a left onto Palm Street (*also marked as Natural Bridge Ave.*) **(M166)**, go four blocks to Salisbury St. **(M167)** and make a right, which will lead you to the McKinley Bridge **(M168)**. But you won't be going to Illinois on the bridge anytime soon, so either backtrack to the I-55 connection at Gravois/12th Street, or return to Florissant Avenue and turn right. From there you can go straight on Florissant for nine miles to I-270 and then head east to Illinois. (*If you're mad for freeways, go about 2 miles to the I-70 interchange, join I-70 west to I-170 north to I-270 east.*)

Now, about the McKinley Bridge. It was built in 1910 by the Illinois Traction System to connect its freight and passenger electric interurban network with St. Louis, and was named for William B. McKinley, the president of the company, not the assassinated president of the United States. (!) The bridge was later converted for railroad and highway traffic and became owned by the city of Venice, Illinois.

Things went pretty much straight down hill from there. Besides suffering the decay of a typical un-maintained piece of urban infrastructure, there was a 1999 audit that revealed a fortune in "diverted" tolls resulting in the City of St. Louis putting a property tax lien on the bridge portion on the Missouri side and threatening to auction it off. Had enough? Well, there's more. There are $4 million in bonds still owed by Venice and the State of Illinois closed the bridge in October of 2001 because it was unsafe.

Okay, now for some good news. Pending a complicated list of negotiations, the bridge is going to be taken over by the State of Illinois and rebuilt as a toll-free bridge to be maintained by both the Missouri DOT and the Illinois DOT. It will have only two traffic lanes, with bicycle lanes along the outside, and will have a connection with I-70 in St. Louis. However, the work - if it starts and is done on schedule - will not be complete until 2006.

Traveling through St. Louis can be a major pain because of traffic and some of you may not want to deal with the city traffic and just skirt around St. Louis. This is not as easy as the maps may make it look. If you plan to use the I-270 loop to avoid the city, expect it to be jammed with traffic from 0600 to 0930 and again from 1400 to 1800.

Coming in from the west, if you see the road is jammed (I-44 TO I-270 north), head south on I-270, it will connect with and become I-55. Continue on I-55, cross the river into Illinois then take I-255 north to Edwardsville. The distance around the city is about the same, and the traffic moves much faster - even during rush hours.

CITY 66 (also known as Alternate 66) -
NOTE: You cannot follow this routing across the McKinley Bridge - it was closed in early 2002, (but set for re-opening).
I-44 exit 277A (Watson Road).
Watson Road east under the Frisco Railroad bridge, Watson becomes Chippewa at the St. Louis City Limits.
At Gravois, angle left onto Gravois.
Veer left onto Tucker.
Road curves onto Florissant.
Left onto Palm (Natural Bridge) to Salisbury, right to McKinley Bridge and cross into Illinois.

ST. LOUIS

Town site was laid out in 1764 by Pierre Laclede and dedicated to St. Louis IX, the name-saint of King Louis XV of France. The first group to use the area were fur trappers followed by settlers from New Orleans. The 1840s saw the city virtually wiped out by fire, flood and a major cholera epidemic. In 1857, the railroad reached St. Louis bringing in the European immigrants to establish the character of the city. 1904 brought the Louisiana Purchase Exposition to the city and America was introduced to a plethora of new products, including the Hot Dog, Ice Cream Cones and Iced Tea. This is the largest city between Chicago and Los Angeles on 66.

LODGING: As with any large city St. Louis offers literally hundreds of lodging choices. I must admit the only hotel I have stayed at in the city is Hyatt Regency St. Louis At Union Station, a very nice hotel, centrally located with so many amenities you virtually never have to leave the property. Suggestion is to stay at one of the major chains, many of the older motels I have inspected suffer from neglect.

DINING: Excellent dining in all parts of the city, personal favorites are Tony's for great Italian at 410 Market St; Ike's Smokehouse for great barbeque (2841 Hwy 100); and for something different the 94th Aero Squadron at 5933 McDonnell Blvd (excellent Sunday brunch).

Missouri has presented us with an amazing combination of sights from the beauty of the Ozarks to the hustle of one of the largest cities in the nation. Now on to the Land of Lincoln and the eastern End of the Mother Road.

Santa Monica to Chicago

ILLINOIS

EASTBOUND

Credit must be given to the Illinois Route 66 Association for having done an excellent job of marking the old highway through the state. Not just the more well known alignments are marked, but the early and optional routes as well. If you are unsure of any of the directions that follow, just look for a Historic Route 66 marker.

Crossing into Illinois on I-270, the first sight will be the Chain of Rocks Bridge (which can be seen to the right, south of the I-270 Bridge). This bridge with the curve in the middle went into service in 1929 and was still operating into the 1960s.

Leave I-270 at Route 3 **(L001)**, heading south toward Granite City. At the first stoplight **(L005)**, make a right onto Chain of Rocks Road. You will cross over the Chain of Rocks Ship Canal **(L004)** on your way to the bridge **(L003)**. The small dirt road a quarter of a mile back to the left will lead to the river **(L002)** and a great waterside view of the bridge and St. Louis across the Mississippi River.

Constructed in 1929 the Old Chain of Rocks Bridge was financed by tolls. The most obvious feature of the bridge is the 22-degree bend in the middle, a compromise between river traffic and the natural geology of the river (*no, it was not caused by Missouri and Illinois engineers making a mathematical error!*). Had the bridge been built straight it would have wound up in an area where there was not solid bedrock for the foundation. The Chain of Rocks below the bridge were a hazard to river navigation until the construction of the Chain of Rocks Canal to bypass the danger. The two castle-like structures visible to the south of the bridge are water intake towers for the Chain of Rocks Water Treatment Facility constructed in 1894 (*and still in use*).

The bridge is now a great walking and bike tour adventure and at a mile in length is the longest pedestrian/bike bridge in the world. TrailNet deserves major kudos for their efforts at restoration and the re-opening of this classic. The bridge was used in the making of the film *Escape From New York* where it became the 69th Street Bridge. Watch for it toward the end of the film.

Return to Route 3 **(L005)** and cross over to continue east on Chain of Rocks Road. This area is great for photographing old motel signs. Road will curve to the right and intersect with Old Alton Road **(L006)**. Make a left and enter the freeway eastbound but don't settle into your seat just yet because you're getting off immediately (*Meaning NOW! The only reason for the freeway hopping is to get you across the Wabash Railroad tracks.*) At the bottom of the ramp make a right, go under the freeway, then another right **(L008)** back onto East Chain of Rocks Road.

There are many older motels along this stretch. Look for the Luna Café **(L009)** as you go by.

At the intersection with Illinois 111 **(L010)**, the abandoned Bel Air Drive-In is on the left and the Hen House Restaurant is on the right. (*Try THAT place on for size if you want a dining adventure, particularly on Friday-all-you-can-eat fish night!*)

Next to the Hen House is the Best Western Camelot Inn (618.391.2262).

As you cross the intersection,

ZERO ODOMETER

    2.1 miles - Cross bridge.

    2.4 miles (L011) - Old, small gas station on right.

    2.9 miles (L012) - Straight across onto Illinois 157 toward Edwardsville.

NOTE: If you have chosen not to explore the old road, take the Edwardsville exit from I-270. Highway 157 is 0.5 miles north of 270, and deduct 3 miles from the following readings.

    3.2 miles - Climb bluff. The area west of here is the eastern edge of what is known as the American Bottom, classed as "flat as a tabletop." The American Bottom extends for nearly one hundred miles along the Mississippi from Alton on the north to Chester on the south.

    6.8 miles (L013) - Cross under railroad bridge.

    7.3 miles (L014) - Curve to left.

EDWARDSVILLE

Town was platted in 1813 and named for Ninian Edwards, Territorial Governor from 1809 to 1818.

    7.8 miles (L015) - Traffic light at a T-intersection, right turn onto St. Louis Street.

    8.2 miles (L016) - Cross downtown intersection with IL 143/IL 159 and continue on IL 157.

    8.6 miles (L017) - Left turn for IL 157.

    16.2 miles (L018) - Town of Hamel and intersection with IL 140.

Sidetrip! (*This one is kind of neat because one option crosses the other. That allows you to mix and match between the two, if you want!*)

Santa Monica to Chicago

OPTION 1 - This option follows the final Rt 66 alignment (1940-1977) and parallels the interstate, taking you through Livingston but bypassing Staunton.

OPTION 2 - This option follows the early alignment, taking you through Staunton but bypassing Livingston. (*Hey, you can't have everything, but there is a doctor there, I presume...*)

OPTION #1

At the intersection with IL 140 in Hamel **(L018)**, go straight ahead and

ZERO ODOMETER

North of Hamel is the St. Paul's Cemetery **(L019)** and St. Paul's Church **(L020)**. The cemetery is notable for its lack of a fence and the church is a very nice Gothic design.

3.9 miles (L021) - Stop at T-intersection and right turn onto Possum Hill Road to stop sign.

4.0 miles (L022) - Stop sign at junction with IL 4. Go straight ahead on the final alignment, along the west side of I-55, which will take you to Livingston. (*This is where the final alignment crosses the early alignment, which is coming from the right on IL 4 and continues past you to the left to Staunton.*)

6.8 miles (L023) - Livingston. Go straight ahead from the stop for two blocks to Church St. and make a right **(L024)**. Follow the curve around to the left onto the frontage road. (At this writing, there was a detour in place affecting the route. If the detour is still in place, you will need to join I-55 in Livingston and continue north to the next exit. There you can re-join Route 66 where it meets the exit access **(L025)**.

12.8 miles (L026) - Junction with Staunton Road. Make a right turn. (*Staunton is to the left from here if you find it calling to you.*)

As you turn at the junction,

ZERO ODOMETER

To continue, jump to the text below labeled "ROAD TO MT OLIVE."

OPTION #2

At the intersection with IL 140 in Hamel **(L018)**, turn right and

ZERO ODOMETER

2.4 miles (L027) - Junction of IL 4 and IL 140, make a left onto IL 4.

5.5 miles (L028) - Cross I-55.

5.7 miles (L022) - Stop sign at junction with Possum Hill Road. Go straight ahead on IL 4 to continue traveling on the early alignment to Staunton. (*This is where the early alignment crosses the final alignment, which is coming from the left on Possum Hill Road and continues past you to the right to Livingston.*)

7.9 miles - Curve left.

8.8 miles - Old roadhouse on left.

9.4 miles - Cross railroad tracks.

10.6 miles (L029) - Curve to right.

STAUNTON

First cabin built here in 1817 by John Wood. The town was platted in 1835.

10.8 miles - Curve to left onto Hackman St.

11.4 miles - Right onto Pearl St.

11.8 miles - Make a left onto Hibbard St. Go one block to Main St. **(L030)**. Then make a right and stay on East Main through town.

12.8 miles (L026) - Junction with freeway access road. Go straight. (*The road to Livingston is to the right from here if you find it calling to you.*)

As you go through the junction,

ZERO ODOMETER

ROAD TO MT OLIVE

1.0 miles - Cross over I-55.

1.3 miles (L031) - Left at stop (*old alignment visible on the right.*)

1.8 miles - Four lanes narrows to two lanes to cross under railroad.

2.0 miles (L032) - Right turn into Mt. Olive on early alignment. Final alignment goes straight ahead, bypassing Mt. Olive, but is uninteresting.

Santa Monica to Chicago

MT. OLIVE

This small, quiet town was the center of coal mining and union activities in the late 1800s and early 1900s. Mt. Olive is the final resting place of Mary Harris, better known as "Mother Jones." Her simple headstone is at the base of the tall monument in the Union Miner's Cemetery on the northwestern edge of town. Mother Jones was a fierce fighter for the rights of miners and children, having once led a march of children on the city of New York protesting child labor.

4.0 miles (L033) - Russell Soulsby's Shell Station. Now closed, but restored by the Illinois Route 66 Association. Was in constant operation from 1926 to 1992.

4.1 miles (L034) - Intersection with Illinois 138. Go straight ahead and make the curving right onto 5th Street, which then curves left as the road leaves town.

6.4 miles (L035) - Stop sign at intersection with final alignment. Turn right.

11.1 miles (L036) - Road 1000/Kruse Road. There is an asphalt plant at this junction, make a right turn onto the early alignment into Litchfield. Like Mt. Olive, the final alignment goes straight ahead.

LITCHFIELD

An old mining town and the center of a coal field that lies beneath six counties. In 1882, Litchfield became the site of the first commercial oil production in Illinois. The small pocket of oil was soon exhausted, but not before guaranteeing Litchfield a place in the history books.

13.0 miles - Route 66 Cafe on left.

Once the site of an old tourist court, the Route 66 Cafe has the look of a 30's cafe, both inside and out. The food is good and the interior a deco influenced eye pleaser.

13.1 miles - Cross tracks (*slow, it's a rough crossing*).

13.3 miles - The Ariston will be on your left. A fine place to dine with excellent food, a wonderful ambiance and great service. Nick Adam is your host.

At the intersection, of IL 16 and old 66 **(L037)**, continue straight and:

ZERO ODOMETER

0.9 miles (L038) - Make right turn onto final alignment, heading north.

1.0 miles - Cross bridge.

1.3 miles - Old section to the right, **DO NOT** take, stay on four-lane. (*Tempting, though...*)

2.7 miles (L039) - Cross under railroad. On the right can be seen old pavement. There would have been a grade crossing here on the old highway.

4.2 miles (L040) - Left and cross I-55.

4.5 miles - Make a right onto west frontage road.

7.7 miles (L041) - Junction with IL 108 (to Carlinville), go straight. Just ahead on the left is a very unique Holiday Inn **(L042)** - it has a lake and a steamboat!

11.0 miles (L043) - Stop at junction with IL 48/ IL127, continue straight.

11.9 miles (L044) - Our Lady of the Highway monument.

13.3 miles - Curve around rest area.

15.2 miles (L045) - Waggoner Road - Continue straight.

19.5 miles - Farmersville, curve left, then straight to stop.

19.9 miles (L046) - Stop and continue straight. (We're given it to you straight, we swear it!)

28.8 miles (L047) - Divernon. Stop sign, then right, cross I-55 **(L049)**, then left and enter the Interstate. Go to Exit 82 **(L050)**, leave the freeway, and at the stop sign at the end of the U-shaped off ramp **(L051)**,

ZERO ODOMETER

Turn left.

0.4 miles (L052) - Turn right onto the frontage road.

2.3 miles (L053) - Stop, continue straight.

2.8 miles (L054) - Glenarm.

7.5 miles (L056) - Cross I-55 and enter interstate northbound at Exit 88.

11.3 miles (L057) - Exit 92A into Springfield on 6th Street.

SPRINGFIELD

The State Capitol of Illinois did not exist when the state was admitted to the Union in 1818. That was the year Elisha Kelly arrived in the Sangammon River Valley in search of game. Impressed with the fertile soil and abundance of game, he returned home and convinced his brother and father to return with him to Illinois. They established a small settlement, and in 1821 when Sangammon County was created it was determined the Kelly settlement was the only place large enough to provide board and lodging for country officials. The name Springfield came from nearby Spring Creek and one of Kelly's fields.

Springfield is the site of the only home Abraham Lincoln ever owned. The National Parks Service maintains the home in a restored 19th century neighborhood. The area provides a step back in time allowing a visit to the homes and streets of a much simpler America.

LODGING: Best Western Lincoln Plaza Hotel (217.523.5661); Hampton Inn (217.529.1100); Mansion View Inn (217.544.7411); Red Roof Inn (217.753.4302).

DINING: The Cozy Dog (*of course*); Chesapeake Seafood House; Cancun Mexican Restaurant (*not bad Mexican food for Illinois*).

As you exit the freeway,

ZERO ODOMETER

Follow BL 55 by going north on 6th Street.

3.3 miles - At Myrtle Street, BL 55 turns right for two blocks.

3.5 miles - Left on 9th St.

6.3 miles - 9th Street angles right onto Peoria Road. Follow it north past the state fairgrounds.

7.7 miles (L058) - Intersection with Taintor Road. (Turning left here puts you on the southbound route.) Follow BL 55 to the right and under the railroad tracks.

9.1 miles - Curve to left. Pioneer Motel on left.

10.2 miles - Cross Sangammon River.

12.3 miles - Old pavement to left.

12.7 miles (L059) - Enter I-55 northbound at Exit 105.

Leave I-55 at exit 109 **(L060)** (Williamsville) and

ZERO ODOMETER

WILLIAMSVILLE

Williamsville has to be one of the most attractive of the small towns encountered on our Route 66 journey. Downtown is pleasantly maintained with nice shops and storefronts. Route 66 does not go into Williamsville, so if you chose to visit, return to the off ramp and continue north from there.

0.1 miles (L061) - Left turn off freeway access road.

5.8 miles (L062) -

ELKHART

At north end of town an old section can be accessed on the right and driven back into Elkhart. This short drive provides a feel for the old highway.

10.1 miles (L063) -

BROADWELL

The Pig Hip Restaurant is on the left **(L064)**. A Route 66 landmark that closed in 1992 but the subject of ongoing restoration work by the Illinois Route 66 Association folks. The Pioneer Motel and gas station also stand abandoned, a monument to the passing of the great highway.

10.2 miles (L065) - Right turn onto frontage road.

Sections of four-lane Route 66 come and go from here to Joliet. In 1943, the State authorized construction of what would be considered as a high-speed, divided highway between Chicago and St. Louis. This new highway would by-pass the towns and provide a faster, more direct route. As we travel north we will leave the four-lane to visit the towns along the way.

13.8 miles (L066) - Right turn onto Lincoln Pkwy.

LINCOLN

The only town named for Abraham Lincoln with his knowledge and consent. He warned the founders that he "never knew anything named Lincoln that amounted to much." The original settlement, west of the present site, was named Potsville. The arrival of the railroad brought both a location and name change.

To take the route through town, make an angled right onto Stringer Ave. from the parkway **(L067)**. Follow Stringer north as it veers left onto Washington. Turn right at 5th Street **(L068)** to the intersection with Logan **(L069)**. Veer left on Logan to a right on Keokuk **(L070)** and then go straight to Kickapoo **(L071)** where you make a left. Follow Kickapoo to the junction with BL 55 **(L072)** and turn right. (*Text continues at "ZERO ODOMETER" below.*)

LODGING: Comfort Inn (217.735.3960).

If you want to take the parkway around the city, just continue north. The parkway will curve around to the right. Just after

Santa Monica to Chicago

passing under the railroad tracks, you will see a section of old pavement on left, two-tenths of mile in length. At the end of the old pavement, on the right, will be the junction with the "through-town" route **(L072)**.

At the junction,

ZERO ODOMETER
- **1.5 miles** - Cross under I-55.
- **2.9 miles** - Two-lane road.
- **5.0 miles** - Cross bridge.
- **6.1 miles (L073)** - Large block culvert on the left was used by farmers for moving wagons and tractors from the fields.
- **7.7 miles (L074)** - Left turn, then curve to right.

ATLANTA

Another town that moved to meet the railroad. In 1854, the village of Newcastle was a mile away from the tracks and a station stop simply known as Zenia. The town packed up and moved. In 1855, the name Atlanta was adopted.

The Public Library is a unique eight-sided white granite building of Neo- Classic design. Built as the library in 1873, it became a museum in 1979. A tall, granite clock tower stands on the corner. The clock, a 1909 Seth Thomas mechanism, was originally the High School clock. An observation window allows you to see the clock mechanism.

Follow Atlanta Road (it curves to the right) to the four-lane **(L075)**, make a left and:

ZERO ODOMETER
- **1.1 miles** - Cross bridge.
- **1.2 miles** - Change in road surface.
- **3.2 miles** - Right curve.

MCLEAN
- **4.1 miles (L076)** - At intersection with US 136 (rail crossing on the left), make a right.
- **4.3 miles** - At Main Street, make a left.

At this intersection is the well-known Dixie Truckers Home **(L077)**, unfortunately both service and food quality has declined in the past few years. Route 66 Museum is across the street in the old McLean railroad depot.

- **4.4 miles** - Go two blocks and make a right onto E. Carlisle Street.
- **4.5 miles** - Go one block and make a left onto N. Steward Road.
- **4.7 miles (L078)** - Curve to right to leave town.
- **5.7 miles** - Curve right, then left.
- **8.9 miles (L079)** - Funks Grove - The home of pure Maple Sirup, yep, that spelling is correct. The more common syrup indicates sugar has been added to the mixture.
- **13.3 miles (L080)** - Junction with Shirley Road.

You have three choices for your trip through Bloomington - Normal:
OPTION 1: Follow the old route all the way through town.
OPTION 2: Take the "in-town" bypass: Veterans Parkway.
OPTION 3: Go completely around the city on I-55.

BLOOMINGTON - NORMAL

A pair of cities that share a common Main Street, only one like it in the country. A university is at each end of Main Street - Illinois State University at the Normal end and Illinois Weslayan at the Bloomington end.

This site was known as Keg Grove when the first settlers arrived in 1822, after a party of trappers hid a keg of whiskey here, and wound up playing absentee hosts to a group of Native Americans who found the booty. Because of the profusion of flowers in the area the name was changed to Blooming Grove, a far better name than the inevitable Keg Town toward which it was heading. (*We're sure the students at both schools do their best to keep the Keg Town spirit alive every Saturday night!*)

LODGING: Hampton Inn (309.662.2800); Jumer's Chateau (309.662.2020); Eastland Suites Hotel (309.662.0000).
DINING: Steak 'N' Shake; Central Station Cafe.

OPTION #1

Continue straight ahead from the Shirley Road junction **(L080)** along the frontage road, which will become Beich Road.
- **3.5 miles (L083)** - T-intersection. Turn right, following Beich Road across I-55.
- **4.1 miles (L084)** - T-intersection with Springfield Road. (*Anyone for tea?*) Make a left onto Springfield Road and follow it around to one nasty little intersection.

Santa Monica to Chicago

4.8 miles **(L085)** - Intersection with Morris Ave., and adjacent to Veterans Parkway intersection with Morris Ave. You need to make a right off of Springfield Road and then make an immediate left onto Veterans Parkway. Careful!
5.5 miles **(L086)** - Junction of Veterans Parkway and Main Street. Make a left onto Main and head into downtown.
9.3 miles **(L087)** - Intersection with Willow Street. Make a right onto Willow.
10.0 miles **(L088)** - Intersection with Linden Street. Make a left onto Linden.
10.2 miles **(L089)** - Intersection with Pine Street. Make a right onto Pine.
11.0 miles **(L090)** - Intersection with Henry Street. Make a left onto Henry. This is a curving left.
11.4 miles **(L091)** - Intersection with Shelbourne. Make a right and follow markers out of town to Towanda **(L094)**.
(Text continues at "TOWANDA" below.)

OPTION #2
Make a right at the Shirley Road junction **(L080)** and enter the interstate **(L081)** heading for Bloomington.
Stay on I-55 to the Veterans Parkway (Exit 157) **(L082)**.
Take the parkway through the city (11 miles) to I-55 Exit 167 **(L092)**.
Join I-55 north to Exit 171 (Towanda) **(L093)** and leave the interstate.
Make a right at the end of the ramp and join 66 in Towanda **(L094)** where you make a left.
(Text continues at "TOWANDA" below.)

OPTION #3
Make a right at the Shirley Road junction **(L080)** and enter the interstate **(L081)**.
Stay on I-55 to Exit 171 (Towanda) **(L093)**.
Make a right after leaving the interstate and join 66 in Towanda **(L094)** where you make a left.

TOWANDA
Indian for "Where we bury our dead." Very small town.
At the stop in the center of town **(L094)**, go straight ahead and
ZERO ODOMETER
0.8 miles - Cross bridge.
2.6 miles - Two lane road.
4.4 miles - Cross bridge.
5.4 miles - Four lane.
6.8 miles - Rough road surface, cross bridge.
7.4 miles **(L095)** - Angled right turn onto two lane, which is Grove Street.

LEXINGTON
Named for the battlefield in Massachusetts and first settled in 1828.
There is an old alignment north of town that can be walked, but not driven. The town uses it for the annual Taste of Country Fair in July. Vintage looking billboards have been erected, making for an interesting walk. Hungry? There's good food and a fun atmosphere at the Shake Shack on Main St.
7.7 miles **(L096)** - Left on Main.
7.8 miles **(L097)** - Right onto highway.
On the north end of town, as you cross bridge **(L098)**,
ZERO ODOMETER
2.0 miles - Grain elevator, right.
4.4 miles - Four lane road.
5.8 miles - Right turn at two-lane road.
6.3 miles - Cross railroad tracks.
6.9 miles - Curve to left.
11.0 miles - Popcorn storage.
11.5 miles - Grain elevators.
12.1 miles - Old bridge.
13.1 miles - McDowell Road on right.
15.3 miles - Old bridge.
16.9 miles - Cross Vermillion River.

Santa Monica to Chicago

CHENOA
Name is Indian for White Dove. Town grew along alignments of the Peoria & Oquawka and the Chicago & Mississippi railroads that met at a four-way crossing in town. Town was laid out by Matthew Scott in 1856.
DINING: Chenoa Family Restaurant
22.9 miles (L100) - Town center turn-off into Chenoa.
33.1 miles (L101) - South end junction of old 66 in

PONTIAC
Founded in 1887 by James Fell and named for the chief of the Ottawa tribe.
On the north end of town, is the Old Log Cabin Inn **(L106)**. The building faces the newer alignment of Route 66, but this was not always the case. Originally, it faced the old highway (which lies behind the building). After construction of the new alignment, the building was lifted and turned 180 degrees and set back down, facing the new alignment of the highway.
The south end junction of old 66 in Pontiac is at the intersection of modern 66 and Reynolds Street **(L101)**. Make a right onto Reynolds.
Turn left at Ladd Street **(L102)**, just before the railroad tracks. After five blocks, you will cross the Vermillion River and the street will angle to the left.
Continue straight about 10 blocks. The street will curve to the right onto West Lincoln Ave. **(L103)** and then curve to the left as it joins Division Street at the North Creek Bridge **(L104)**.
Go straight on Division and follow it around to the right where it will join a long curve to the left, ending at four-lane 66 **(L105)**.
Make a right onto 66 and:
ZERO ODOMETER
3.1 miles - Cemetery on left.
3.5 miles - Bridge on right crosses the tracks to Cayuga.
3.8 miles (L107) - Small bridge and to the right a barn has an ad for Meramec Caverns in Missouri painted on the side. *(There is a turnout here built by the Illinois Association for taking photos of the barn painting)*.
4.4 miles - Two lane road.
6.5 miles - Interesting bridge across railroad on right.
7.3 miles - Four lane road.
8.1 miles - Right onto two-lane road.
9.8 miles (L108) - Right turn into

ODELL
The two-lane highway bypassed Odell early on. Probably because of the proximity of the downtown section to the railroad tracks.
The old road becomes West Street and curves to the left. At the corner of West and Deer Streets is the famous restored Standard Service Station **(L109)**.
Continue on West Street to Prairie Street and make a right.
Go two blocks and turn left just before the railroad tracks. Go straight to join modern 66 on the north end of town **(L110)** and turn right.
10.9 miles - Two-lane road.
12.9 miles - Small bridge.
14.9 miles - Four-lane road.
15.8 miles -

DWIGHT
Make a right onto the two-lane **(L111)** to follow the early alignment through town.
16.1 miles - Curve to left to two-lane bypass. (Straight ahead is the 1918 alignment.)
16.7 miles - Junction with IL 17. Continue straight. The well-known Route 66 Service Station is on the northeast corner.
16.8 miles - Road curves to right onto Waupansie Street.
17.8 miles - Make an angled left just before the railroad tracks.
18.3 miles - Cross east-west railroad tracks.
18.6 miles - Y-intersection. Jog to the right, stop, then go left and parallel the railroad tracks out of town. Do not follow IL 47, which veers left at the Y.
19.5 miles (L112) - Right onto four-lane alignment at the north end of town.

23.6 miles - Two-lane road.
29.3 miles -

GARDNER
As you enter Gardner, you will see an Historic 66 sign pointing to the right, guiding you onto IL 53 **(L113)**. This turn begins a "mini-bypass" of Gardner. It will take you directly east where you make a left turn north onto IL 53. However, if you would like to drive on Main Street, which was a very early routing, go past the IL 53 turnoff and make a right on Main. Go straight to IL 53, make a left, and head north.

At the junction of IL 53 and Main Street **(L114)**,
ZERO ODOMETER
0.5 miles - Follow curve to right. Do not go straight onto Carbon Hill Road.

Look to the left. The road paralleling this road to the west and across the tracks is another alignment of Route 66. This alignment connects with Plainfield and is the starting point for the westerly journey described in Rittenhouse's *Guide Book to Highway 66*. The roads will continue to parallel each other to just north of Braidwood.

3.3 miles (L115) - Braceville.
6.1 miles (L116) - Godley - Once a thriving mining town with twenty-one mines in operation within a mile-and-a-half of town. By 1906, all were shut down.
8.1 miles -

BRAIDWOOD
In 1865, William Henneberry hit a rich vein of coal while sinking a well. By 1880, the population had swelled to 9,000 and long coal trains, up to six a day, pulled out of Braidwood. A few of the older tourist courts and mine structures can still be seen in the area.

Hungry? Check out the Polka Dot Drive-In **(L117)**.
11.6 miles - Coal City Road.
12.8 miles - Bear right and continue north.
13.3 miles - Cross Kankakee River.
13.6 miles -

WILMINGTON
Founded by Thomas Fox as Winchester, but because of a dispute over the name became Wilmington in 1854.
At Junction with 102, continue north.
14.0 miles (L118) - The Launching Pad Cafe with its Gemini giant Statue.
14.2 miles - Cross bridge.
14.3 miles - Curve to left.
14.9 miles - Johnson & Johnson plant on left.
15.8 miles - Four lane.

Notice along here the southbound lanes are the original Route 66. The southbound lanes follow the lay of the land more than the northbound and are also closest to the railroad tracks.

18.7 miles (L119) - Left turn and enter Elwood on Douglas, make a right in town **(L120)** to cross tracks and leave town.
19.5 miles - Intersection with four-lane. Go straight across.
19.6 miles - Curve to left.
20.0 miles - Curve to right onto Mississippi Road.
21.8 miles (L121) - Road curves to left onto Chicago Road.
22.0 miles (L122) - Make a left and join four-lane at Manhattan Road and
ZERO ODOMETER
5.5 miles (L123) - Hwy 52 joins Hwy 53. Continue straight into

JOLIET
The first settler was Charles Reed in 1831 and by 1834 a townsite was platted. The town was known as Juliet, after the Shakespeare character, for a number of years, but became Joliet after it was assumed (*and we know what that means*) the town was named for French explorer Louis Joliet.

In April of 1848 the first ship arrived on the newly constructed canal and was met by the entire town. Joliet became known for its limestone and shipped blocks as far as New York. In 1852, the railroad reached Joliet followed shortly thereafter by the steel industry.

Santa Monica to Chicago

LODGING: Hampton Inn (815.725.3110); Comfort Inn-North (815.436.5141).

After crossing under the interstate, the road goes through a gentle S-curve onto Chicago Street. Go straight.

6.8 miles (L126) - Intersection with Washington Street, make a right and then an immediate left onto Scott Street.

7.6 miles (L129) - Make a left onto Columbia Street which becomes Ruby as you cross the Des Plaines River Bridge.

After crossing the bridge, go up the hill one block and make a right onto Broadway **(L131)**.

Continue north on Broadway through Crest Hill (1.7 miles) to the big railroad crossing **(L132)** and

ZERO ODOMETER

1.1 miles (L133) - Hey, that's not a picnic park on the left. It's Statesville Prison! This is NOT the adopted home of Jake and Elwood Blues - they called Joilet Prison (on Collins Street) home.

1.2 miles - Division Street. State Police Headquarters on the left.

2.1 miles - Junction with Illinois 7.

2.8 miles - Lewis University on the left.

7.5 miles (L134) - Junction of Hwy 53 and Joliet Road, bear right onto Joliet Road.

8.0 miles - White Fence Farm on left.

10.0 miles (L135) - Join I-55 and continue toward Chicago for eight miles.

Sidetrip! If you're hungry and want to enjoy a genuine Route 66 culinary tradition, stop at Del Rhea's Chicken Basket in Willowbrook on your way into Chicago. Take the IL 83 North/Kingery Rd exit from I-55. (It's 6 miles east of Joliet on the interstate.) Go north from the freeway 1/2 mile to Midway Drive and make a right to the T-intersection at Quincy. Make a right and go straight ahead to the frontage road. The Chicken Basket is just to your right at 645 Joliet Road **(L136)**.

Leave I-55 at Exit 276C **(L137)** (**LEFT off ramp**) for Joliet Road.

At the Willow Springs Road intersection **(L138)**,

ZERO ODOMETER

0.2 miles - "Flicks on 66" video store, left.

1.1 miles - Route 66 Cafe & Grill on left.

1.7 miles (L139) - Left onto East Ave (This is a detour around a quarry).

2.3 miles (L140) - Right on 55th St.

3.2 miles (L141) - Veer left and rejoin Joliet Road.

LYONS

Standing at the edge of one of the earliest sites in the state - the portage between the Chicago and Des Plaines Rivers used by Indians and the explorers Marquette and Joliet.

4.8 miles (L142) - Curve left onto Prescott.

5.2 miles (L143) - Curve right onto 43rd St.

5.6 miles (L144) - Cross the Des Plaines River.

6.2 miles (L145) - Left onto Harlem Ave.

6.6 miles (L146) - Right onto Ogden Ave.

CICERO AND BERWYN

It is difficult to tell when you leave one and enter the other. The giant Western electric plant once provided employment for thousands in the area. Berwyn was actually founded as a bedroom community for Chicago in 1890 by a visionary real estate promoter.

8.1 miles (L147) - Bunyon's Café.

10.3 miles - Railroad underpass.

11.3 miles (L148) - Straight through the large intersection of Cermak Rd./Harding Ave./Ogden Ave. (*This is a very large intersection!*)

13.3 miles - Large RR underpass.

13.4 miles (L149) - Veer left on Ogden at Western.

14.3 miles (L150) - Cook County Hospital on right.

14.6 miles (L151) - Right on Jackson Street.

16.1 miles (L153) - Lou Mitchell's Restaurant.

16.4 miles (L154) - Sears Tower.

Lakeshore Drive and Jackson **(L156)**: End of Route 66.

CHICAGO

Santa Monica to Chicago

First explorers to the area were Louis Joliet and Jacques Marquette in 1673. Juan Batiste Point de Sable built the first cabin here in 1779 with Fort Dearborn being established 1804. The town site of modern Chicago was laid out in 1830. With the coming of the railroad connecting to San Francisco in 1869 the city began a boom that never stopped - except for the setback caused by the Great Chicago Fire of 1871 which destroyed virtually the entire city. Rebuilt upon the ashes the city has never looked back.

Chicago is a giant city and as such has giant city problems. Parking is a horror with lots charging outrageous rates (up to $10 an hour) and traffic can be a positive nightmare. My suggestion for ending that Route 66 trip is to stay outside of the city, then drive in early on a Sunday morning to enjoy a few photo ops (*but then we all know how I feel about cities*).

LODGING (in the city): Chicago Hilton (312.922.4400); Four Seasons Hotel (312.280.8800); Days Inn Lake Shore Drive (312.943.9200); Residence Inn (312.943.9800). As with any large city the majority of the older motels have fallen into disrepair, stick with a major chain (*and even that can be a problem at times*).

DINING: Lou Mitchell's (a Roadie classic); Ed Debevic's; Season's Restaurant (in the Four Season); Su Casa (good Mexican food), plus thousands of other choices!

Congratulations, you have traveled the full length of the Mother Road and are now an official Roadie!

Chicago to Santa Monica

when the Nestor Company took over the old Blondeau Tavern and barn.

No trip to this area would be complete without a turn through the streets of Beverly Hills. Buy a "Map to the Stars Homes" and see where your favorite stars live or lived. This area developed rapidly as "the" place for movie people because of its proximity to the studios and the ocean.

20.1 miles (C004) - At Wilshire is the famous Trader Vic's. One man's dedication to his time spent in Polynesia.

22.7 miles (C002) - Cross under the San Diego Freeway (I-405).

As you continue west on Santa Monica, keep your eyes peeled for the marvelous architecture along the way.

SANTA MONICA

Santa Monica was founded in 1872 and for years was a popular tourist resort with the summer population quadrupling the size of the city. Traveling east architectural wonders abound along Santa Monica Boulevard. Watch for the beautifully restored Mayfair Theater (1911), the 1924 Steele Building faced with white glazed brick, and further on the old Cummings Buick showroom is now used to store and display stretch limousines.

26.5 miles (C001) - Ocean Boulevard, and the end of Route 66.

For the true Roadie Route 66 will end at Ocean Boulevard, for the history buff and Hard-Core Roadie it is known that Route 66 originally did not go to Santa Monica (*ending at Broadway and 7th Street in downtown Los Angeles*) and the final alignment ended at Lincoln and Olympic Boulevards in Santa Monica. But the mystique of Route 66 has us starting at Lake Michigan and ending at the Pacific Ocean.

The Belle-vue Restaurant is on the northeast corner and has been serving meals since 1937. Across the street is the Will Rogers plaque, and to the south is the Santa Monica Pier.

Congratulations, you have made the trek all the way from Lake Michigan to the Pacific Ocean on Route 66. You are now an official Roadie and can wear the name proudly.

Chicago to Santa Monica

faced the Plaza.

Following the Mexican War of 1846-47 California was seized by the United States and the small village became a hell-raising frontier town. Violence was so common the place took on the name Los Diablos (*the devils*). Finally, following a riot in Chinatown in 1871 where 19 Chinese were murdered, the town took stock of itself and decided to improve its image.

The railroad arrived in 1876 as the Southern Pacific pulled into town. In 1885, the Santa Fe reached Los Angeles and started a fare war that makes the airfare battles of today pale by comparison. Travel from Kansas City to Los Angeles started at $100, fell to a low of $5 and for one day, to $1.00! "Kansas City to Los Angeles for a dollar," proclaimed the Santa Fe handbills. The fare wars resulted in a two-year growth spurt that saw the city expand from twelve to fifty thousand people.

The year was 1891, and a single well drilled in the front yard of a home soon grew to more than 1,400 derricks pumping across the city. OIL! Black Gold was a new source of revenue for the growing city.

As the city grew, water became a major problem. In order to push through a multi-million dollar water bond, the city opened fire hydrants dumping water into the sewers and made lawn watering illegal. As the flora wilted under the California sun, a tired and fed-up electorate passed the bond issue. With bond money to burn, Los Angeles turned to the Owens River, 250 miles north, as the new water source for the growing city. With the Owens River water flowing south through siphons and pipelines to Los Angeles, the once green and fertile Owens Valley became, in the words of Will Rogers, "a valley of desolation."

World War Two brought a plethora of soldiers, sailors and marines to the Southland, who, with the end of the war, returned with their families to settle in the warm, sunny clime offered by Southern California. Where once orange groves flourished, homes took over. The neighborhood Mom-and-Pop stores were eclipsed by the strip mall and ultimately huge indoor shopping malls took over and became home to hordes of Valley Girls and Mallrats.

LODGING: Lodging in the area is as wonderfully varied as you can imagine, following are a few of my personal choices. My favorite and home-away-from-home for those L.A. trips is the Argyle at 8358 Sunset Blvd just east of La Cienega (323.654.7100). A beautifully restored art-deco masterpiece (*it was formerly The St. James Club*). The Argyle is centrally located on the famed Sunset Strip with the rooms offering a commanding view of the city, and just a few doors east of The House of Blues. Another Strip hotel that is comfortable and well located is the Best Western Sunset Plaza at 8400 Sunset Blvd (323.654.0750). For a truly eclectic lodging experience nothing can match the Beverly Laurel at 8018 Beverly Blvd (213.651.2441). The rooms are very 50's decor in a well maintained fifties building. On the corner is Swingers Diner - great for a cup of coffee, a croissant, and people watching. The Beverly Laurel can be reached from Santa Monica Blvd by going south on Fairfax to Beverly Blvd. then a right - the hotel will be on your left. A nice chain property on Santa Monica Blvd is the Comfort Inn at 2815 Santa Monica Blvd (310.828.5517). These are just a few of the thousands of properties in the L.A. area.

DINING: As with lodging there are literally thousands of places to eat in L.A. A few of the more interesting and entertaining are: Pinks Hot Dog Stand - "The Hot Dog of the Stars" at 709 N. La Brea, you will be amazed at who you will see here, a Hollywood favorite since 1939; Another wonderful people watching place, particularly late at night, is Barney's Beanery, 8447 Santa Monica Blvd - Great Chili and a multiple page menu that will drive you crazy; Ed Debevic's in Beverly Hills at 134 N. La Cienega a fun atmosphere with good "home-style" food. Be sure to order the small hot fudge sundae. What's not to like in a place with the motto, "Eat and Get Out"; and for that ultimate shake, malt, or burger and fries check out Mel's Drive-In at 8585 W. Sunset Blvd - yep, it's the same Mel's of San Francisco fame. Entertainment at its best with down-home cooking is a must at the House of Blues, 8400 W. Sunset Blvd. Great atmosphere, good food and top entertainment all at this funky place on Sunset. Upscale dining is not my forte, but I have found the *fenix* at the Argyle to be excellent. The French cuisine is outstanding at Le Dome - 8720 Sunset Blvd. For an interesting experience, in a formal atmosphere (including formal attire), the Russian food at Diaghilev is excellent, 1020 N. San Vicente Blvd. For star watching check out Dan Tana's at 9071 Santa Monica Blvd.

Now, back to the road.

9.7 miles (C008) - Jensen's Recreation Bldg - great sign on top of building.

Watch for the Hollywood City Limits sign and get in the left lane for a left turn **(C007)** onto Manzanita Street, which almost immediately becomes Santa Monica Blvd.

13.2 miles (C006) - Cross under the 101 freeway, continue west.

17.3 miles (C005) - Barney's Beanery at 8400 Santa Monica. See DINING above.

BEVERLY HILLS AND HOLLYWOOD

In 1853, one small adobe house stood in the area now known as Beverly Hills and Hollywood. Originally named HOLLY-WOODLAND by the wife of real-estate magnate Horace Wilcox in 1887, the new subdivision brought people to the area in large numbers, but it was still considered enough of a boondocks that a 1903 ordinance made it illegal to herd more than 2,000 sheep through town at one time.

A late spring snowstorm in Flagstaff, Arizona pushed Cecil B. DeMille on to Southern California where his vision of the future of motion pictures took root in Hollywood. The first motion picture studio began cranking out film at Sunset and Gower

Chicago to Santa Monica

AZUSA

The town that once bragged about having everything from "A to Z in the USA." Founded in 1887 during the land boom period and named for an Indian village, Asukag-na, once on this site.

6.8 miles (C026) - The Foothill Drive-In Theater, a classic and well-kept drive-in. It's future was uncertain at this writing.

8.3 miles (C025) - Cross under railroad tracks.

9.6 miles (C024) - The San Gabriel River. Cross the bridge and the road becomes Huntington Drive.

10.2 miles (C023) - Site of the Trails Restaurant.

10.6 miles (C022) - Intersection with I-605.

Along here are Monrovia and Duarte. Monrovia was platted in 1886 by W. N. Monroe and lots were sold for $100 each. A far cry from today's selling price. Duarte was named for Andres Duarte, the grantee of 4,000 acres of land on this site. He also built a ditch to bring water from San Gabriel Canyon for irrigation of the nearby fields.

13.6 miles (C021) - The Pottery Ranch, here since the 1940s.

14.2 miles (C020) - Cross under I-210.

14.5 miles (C019) - Arcadia -The Derby Restaurant on the right is like a Horse Racing Derby and is not connected with the Brown Derby of Hollywood fame.

14.6 miles (C018) - Santa Fe overpass.

15.4 miles (C017) - Santa Anita Racetrack.

Bear to the right at this point to Colorado Place which, at Rosemead, becomes Colorado Boulevard **(C015)** and takes you into

PASADENA

This area was once part of the San Gabriel Mission and as Rancho San Pasqual it was granted to an aged housekeeper by the Mission fathers in 1826. When she married, at the age 99, the property passed from her hands to her husbands (*against the law for a married woman to own property*) and was sold by her stepson in 1839 to two dons who abandoned it within a few years. (*Got that figured out?*)

The Governor granted the land in 1843 to a Mexican Army officer, Don Manuel Garfias. The land title was validated in 1854 and granted a patent by Abraham Lincoln in 1863. Garfias sold the land to Benjamin Wilson, whose name adorns a mountain, a canyon, a lake, a trail, an avenue, and a school. The land was bartered and swapped many times between Wilson and his business associates, and, in 1873, 4,000 acres of the land became the property of Dr. John S. Griffin.

The Winter of 1872 was a harsh one in Indiana and Dr. Thomas Elliot, with a group of friends, founded the California Colony of Indiana in order to get out where the "livin' was easy." Following the sale of the land the exodus of millionaires began.

18.8 miles (C014) - Highway Host Motel - cool sign.

22.0 miles (C013) - Pasadena Post Office on right.

22.2 miles (C012) - Left turn onto Arroyo Blvd.

The historic Santa Fe depot **(C011)** can be seen off to the right, no longer used except for Metro-Link commuter service. This depot was used extensively in early films and by traveling movie stars. It was easier to arrange to shoot scenes here than at the Union Station in downtown Los Angeles, and it gave the stars a way to come into town without being mobbed at the station (advance word having been sent out that they were arriving in "Los Angeles").

23.5 miles (C010) - At the intersection with Glenarm, Arroyo becomes the Pasadena Freeway.

Original routing prior to freeway was west on Colorado Blvd into Eagle Rock, then south on Figueroa to Sunset Blvd.

As you enter the Pasadena Freeway,

ZERO ODOMETER

Watch for Dodger Stadium and make certain you are in far right lane to exit freeway at Sunset Blvd.

8.0 miles (C009) - Exit freeway, then left turn across freeway followed by a right onto Figueroa to Sunset. Make a right onto Sunset.

LOS ANGELES

A small native-American village named *Yang-na* was discovered by a group of missionaries and explorers under the leadership of Captain Gaspar de Portola in 1769, and was immediately re-named Porciuncula after an Italian chapel. In 1771, Franciscan Padres returned to the area and founded the Mission San Gabriel nine miles to the northeast of the original village. Ten years later Don Felipe de Neve marched a band of settlers from Mexico and with a few soldiers from the mission founded El Pueblo de Nuestra Señora la Reina de Los Angeles de Porciuncula or The Town of Our Lady the Queen of Angels of Porciuncula.

Each of the founding families was given a plot of land facing the Plaza and for more than a century this was the center of community life. By 1800, seventy families were busy raising grain and cattle in the town. The first English settler was "pirate" Joseph Chapman captured in 1818. Joseph (*later re-baptized as José*) was a skilled carpenter and erected a church building that

Chicago to Santa Monica

by the Dust Bowl refugees and with the magnificent mountains rising to the north and the clear blue skies of sixty plus years ago it was a breathtaking sight.

12.3 miles (C045) - The Wigwam Motel - Opened in 1950 , it was one of those places that made us want to steer Dad's big Buick Roadmaster in for the night. Today's business at the Wigwam is not suited to the average Route 66 traveler.

At the intersection of Riverside and Foothill **(C044)** on the Southeast corner, check out the marvelous mosaic on the front of the Home Savings building and:

ZERO ODOMETER

There are many older motels and highway businesses along here.

3.0 miles (C043) - The Moana Motel - a nicely maintained motel of the 40s and early 50s.

5.8 miles (C042) - Left, Bono's Restaurant and Deli, operated in this spot since 1936, closed in 1999, but rumors are it may reopen.

6.4 miles (C041) - The Red Wing Motel.

9.6 miles (C040) - Cross under I-15 freeway.

12.2 miles (C039) - The Virginia Dare Winery - not restored, but resurrected as a shopping office complex.

12.8 miles (C038) - Archibald Avenue and on the right hand side, a classic 1920's gas station. Dolly's Diner was just to the west.

13.8 miles (C037) - Intersection with Vineyard. On the northeast corner the former Thomas Winery, now the site of shops and restaurants. On the southwest corner is the 1928 Klusman House (*in the Fall of 2002 - it appears as if it may be targeted for demolition*).

14.3 miles (C036) - Cross under tracks.

14.5 miles (C035) - The Sycamore Inn on the right. Built in 1948 as a stage stop. Check out the Bear Gulch monument on the grounds.

14.7 miles (C034) - Intersection of Euclid and Foothill. A monument to Pioneer women is on the north side.

At this point you enter Los Angeles County. An excellent source book for the various routings and history of Route 66 through Los Angeles County is Scott Piotrowski's *Finding the End of the Mother Road-Route 66 in Los Angles County* (www.66productions.com)

CLAREMONT

Known as the home of the Claremont Colleges, a group of seven colleges located in beautifully preserved settings. Just east as you pass through Upland you will be on a 1931 section of Route 66 designed with a grass median and eucalyptus trees. After having traveled across hundreds of miles of desert, the early traveler found this to be a welcome respite.

20.1 miles (C033) - On the right is Griswold's Old School House. A large collection of buildings and shops that offer just about anything on can imagine.

LA VERNE

Originally named Lordsburg during the land boom of the 1890s. A huge hotel was built during the boom and when the rush died off the town was stuck with the huge white-elephant of a building. New settlers were brought to the area in 1891 by the Santa Fe railroad. A group of Dunkards purchased the hotel and renamed it Lordsburg College. When the town name was changed, so was the college, becoming La Verne College.

22.0 miles (C032) - On the right, the La Poloma Cafe, a local favorite. Was known as Wilson's Restaurant for many years.

22.9 miles (C031) - Intersection with La Verne's D Street. One mile south is the 1930's downtown strip that will take you back to a simpler time in our history.

Approaching I-210 freeway entrance, be certain you are in the left lane to avoid the freeway on-ramp and stay on Foothill Blvd. As you cross under the freeway **(C030)**,

ZERO ODOMETER

1.4 miles (C029) - San Dimas - Pinnacle Pete's Steak House - be warned, the walls are festooned with neckties, evidence of the "dudes" who entered without first removing the neck appendage.

A large park is located to the right and up San Dimas Canyon Road.

GLENDORA

Founded in 1887 by George Whitcomb who named the town after his wife by combining "glen" and her name "Ledora" into one. Many classic motels along this stretch of the road.

3.4 miles (C028) - Cross under railroad tracks.

3.6 miles (C027) - On the right, the Golden Spur Restaurant. Operated continuously on this site for over seventy years. Originally opened as a hamburger stand to serve the horseback population.

Chicago to Santa Monica

Wild West look had attracted the Hollywood crowd, who, between 1914 and 1937 made over two hundred films in Victorville and the surrounding area.

Continue on D Street into town then make a right on 7th Street **(C072)** (just past the Route 66 Museum).

To leave Victorville follow 7th Street to I-15 **(C071)**, make a left and enter I-15 southbound. It will be necessary to stay on I-15 to a point about halfway down the Cajon Pass.

Hungry? Is it lunchtime? Pull off 11.5 miles out from Victorville, exit at Oak Hill Road, exit 138, **(C070)** and cross the freeway. Make a right and drive up the hill to the Summit Inn. Try a Hillbilly Burger for a real treat in a classic Route 66 atmosphere. This is Cajon Summit. Retrace the route to the Oak Hills overpass and re-enter I-15 southbound.

Driving down the Cajon Pass today is nothing like the road in years past. Second gear was almost mandatory, unless you wanted to lose your brakes halfway down. The climb up was equally as grueling, taxing a car's cooling system beyond belief. To experience the old road - what is left of it - take the Cleghorn Road exit, exit 129 **(C069)**, just past the truck check station.

Once off the Interstate you immediately feel as if you can relax (*isn't that traffic on I-15 unreal? Then again, most of it's heading to/from the unreal center of the universe: Las Vegas*). At the stop sign, make a right and, if you are a railroad buff, follow with another right **(C068)** for a short run (*0.4 miles*) on a section of the old road and a chance to stop and join the other railroad photographers catching the trains as they climb through the Cajon.

SAFETY NOTE: Be extremely cautious near the tracks - trains coming down the canyon use dynamic braking, and in many cases cannot be heard until they are nearly on you.

Not interested in trains? Okay, at the stop sign (coming from the old road mentioned above),

ZERO ODOMETER

This is Upper Cajon Boulevard.

0.2 miles (C067) - Great old bridge.

0.4 miles - Sign over on railroad right-of-way for Cajon.

0.7 miles (C066) - Road becomes divided. This was the newer alignment of 66. The section to the east (*closed*) is actually the old road.

1.7 miles (C065) - Cross over to east side of divided highway.

1.9 miles (C064) - Intersection to right. At this site, behind the boulders, was one of the Federal Highway Camps established to provide the road weary Dust Bowl survivors with a safe haven, away from Californians who had developed a habit of vandalizing and harassing the campsites and parking places of the west-bound travelers.

2.5 miles (C063) - Intersection to left. Road is closed.

2.9 miles (C062) - Rock wall along right hand side, an early rest stop.

4.5 miles (C061) - Intersection on right.

6.2 miles (C060) - Garage on left.

6.5 miles (C059) - Left at intersection to rejoin Interstate 15 at nearby on-ramp **(C057)**. (Old 66 continues straight for 0.7 mile **(C058)**, but you will have to double back to this spot to rejoin freeway.)

If you would like to continue on into downtown San Bernardino, take the I-215 freeway to the bottom of the canyon (this is the eastside route). Otherwise, take the Glen Helen Parkway exit, exit 122, **(C056)** to follow old business 66 heading toward San Bernardino.

At the bottom of the off-ramp, on the right, is a bar and café where Route 66 dead-ends **(C055)**. Make a left and

ZERO ODOMETER

1.4 miles (C053) - Curve to the right.

1.6 miles (C052) - Cross under railroad tracks.

6.4 miles (C051) - Two older (closed) motels along here. The Oasis and the Palms.

8.1 miles - Pass under freeway. **(C050)**. Road Y's slightly, stay to left and pass under Highland, slow for a hard right and a stop sign. At stop sign **(C049)**, make a left onto Mt. Vernon Avenue. Notice, as you head south, the large number of old motels and tourist courts along this stretch. Virtually, all of them have seen better days, but their presence is a sure sign of this having been a major road into San Bernardino at one time.

10.2 miles (C047) - 5th Street - Make a right. Fifth will curve to the left **(C046)** and become Foothill Boulevard.

SAN BERNARDINO

Named by a group of soldiers, Indians, and missionaries from the San Gabriel Mission to the west. The group entered the valley on May 20th, 1810 - the feast day of San Bernardino de Siena. Rancho San Bernardino was purchased by a group of Mormons for $77,000 in 1852, and they proceeded to lay the city out along the lines of Salt Lake City, Utah. The Mormons remained a strong influence until they were recalled to Salt Lake City by Brigham Young in 1857. San Bernardino is the site of the largest railroad switching center and junction west of Chicago and was the home of the first McDonald's Drive-in.

From here west stretched miles and miles of orange and lemon groves along Route 66. This was the first citrus fruit to be seen

Chicago to Santa Monica

0.1 to 0.2 miles - An odd intersection, so watch your lanes. You will go under the freeway and be turning westerly on Main St.

0.7 miles (C090) - On the left is the Greystone Cafe and bar. You can see the old stone motel cabins in the back of the place.

1.6 miles (C089) - Make a right, pass under the freeway, and you are in

BARSTOW

Named in 1886 for the then President of Santa Fe Railroad, William Barstow Strong. The site was unofficially called Waterman Junction following the silver strike of 1881. The Santa Fe had originally planned to build their division point in Daggett (about five miles east), but word leaked out and land prices skyrocketed. The Santa Fe then moved to Waterman Junction along the Mojave River and Barstow was born. By the time the name had been chosen, the townsite had hotels, churches and more than enough saloons.

Barstow owes much of its history to the railroads and the appreciation of that history can be seen at the Barstow Station. Designed after a railroad depot, Barstow Station houses one of the most unique McDonald's I have ever seen. Once served, you take your tray load of Big Macs, fries and shakes into a converted passenger car to eat. Barstow Station also houses a series of gift shops with more than enough temptations for any tourist.

Following the advent of the motorcar, Barstow continued to be a central point for travelers and with the arrival of Route 66, it became an important stopping place for road-weary warriors of the Mother Road. Main Street is lined with motels and as you drive from the west end of town to the east the age of the motels becomes quite evident.

At 112 E. Main St. is the El Rancho Barstow, a classic motel of the old school. The huge neon sign is supported by a pair of twin towers, and that alone takes you back to days gone by. The El Rancho is unique in one other respect - the buildings were constructed in 1944 using railroad ties from the defunct Tonopah and Tidewater railroad, a narrow gauge that ran from Beatty, Nevada to Ludlow, California. Unfortunately, the motel has not been well maintained and cannot be recommended.

Also in Barstow is the beautifully restored Santa Fe Depot and Harvey House, Casa de Desierto. To see this wonder, turn north on First Street to cross over the Santa Fe yard. The depot is on your right. The Route 66 Museum is also located in the depot building.

Barstow is trying hard to become a Route 66 town and in time will succeed, but for lodging there is really no place I can recommend (maybe on a good day the Holiday Inn or Ramada, but they are overpriced). Most of the older motels suffer from neglect and a poor attitude by the owners.

Stay on Main Street heading southwest, and at the intersection with Avenue J **(C088)**,

ZERO ODOMETER

1.3 miles (C087) - Hwy 58 overcrossing.
2.5 miles - Lenwood.
2.7 miles (C086) - Left side, an old motel or auto court (*perhaps this was the Radio Court*).
3.6 miles - Intersection continue straight.
3.8 miles (C085) - Left side, the remains of the old Lenwood Drive-in Theatre.
6.6 miles (C084) - Left side, old Dunes motel.
15.4 miles (C083) - Intersection with Indian Trail.
19.4 miles (C082) - Site of Helendale, marker can be seen along tracks to right.
19.8 miles (C081) - Intersection with Silver Lakes Road.
20.8 miles (C080) - Left side, closed gas station.
22.0 miles - Left side, closed gas station.
22.1 miles - Right side, closed cafe, gas station combination.
23.1 miles (C079) - Right side, cabins, store and gas station, all closed.
27.2 miles (C078) - Right side, the Lost Hawg Saloon.
29.0 miles - Small canyon area with cement plants.
29.3 miles (C077) - Cross under railroad.
29.6 miles (C076) - Oro Grande.
30.2 miles (C075) - Antique Station, displaying a huge collection of old signs on the exterior walls.
31.4 miles (C074) - Cross under high tension lines. Check out the towers. Really stunning.

Cross the Mojave River on a classic bridge **(C073)** to enter Victorville (this will be D Street).

VICTORVILLE

Originally named Mormon Crossing from 1878 to 1885, it was first changed to Victor, and later Victorville. The town was a rip-roaring mining camp until 1900 when the mines played out. The town left its false-front buildings standing, and by 1914, the

Chicago to Santa Monica

Murphy Bros. were the second owners). Over the past few years more and more of Ludlow has disappeared to fire and bulldozer, turning it into a scar on the desert with less and less of the vestiges of the once bustling community.

Back to the road.

Heading west on the old road in front of the Ludlow Coffee Shop, the highway will dead-end at the Interstate 1.1 miles down. At the end of the road, you can see the old highway across the Interstate.

Return to the Chevron station, turn **(C107)** and cross under I-40, and make a left onto the frontage road **(C106)** and

ZERO ODOMETER

The sign indicates this is the National Trails Highway. This section (up to Lavic Road) is not old 66, it was a service road before the advent of I-40. Route 66 is actually buried beneath the Interstate.

6.0 miles - Road surface becomes a little rough, (*like hell, it's miserable!*).

7.2 miles - New road surface.

8.1 miles - Cross I-40 at Lavic Road **(C105)** and make a right **(C104)** onto Old 66.

10.6 miles (C103) - Cross railroad tracks.

14.3 miles (C102) - Intersection with Pisgah Crater Road.

15.8 miles (C101) - A maze of high tension wires cross over highway.

17.0 miles (C100) - Rest area turnout on the left.

17.5 miles (C099) - Hector Road freeway entrance.

27.8 miles - Whiting Bros station.

28.6 miles (C098) - Dry Creek Station on left.

28.8 miles (C097) - Newberry Springs and the Bagdad Café. This is the location used in the movie, *Bagdad Café*. Good food and friendly atmosphere (*beware of "General" Bob*).

NEWBERRY SPRINGS

Newberry Springs was once called Water, a simple, but important name in the arid desert. The springs emerged from beneath the black sides of the mountain to quench the thirst of all who happened by. The railroad loaded tanks cars here and hauled the water to the tank at Bagdad for the steam engines.

37.9 miles (C096) - The old agricultural inspection station is on the right. It was here all vehicles entering California had to stop and open luggage, boxes, whatever they were carrying. This is where the Joads (*The Grapes of Wrath*) convinced the officers that grandma was ill and had to be taken to a doctor, when in fact, she was dead.

40.8 miles (C095) - The open area on the right with the tower in the center was part of the California Edison Solar One facility. This was a solar/thermal power plant. The area around the tower once contained hundreds of huge mirrors aligned to point at the large tower. The tower would absorb the heat reflected from the mirrors to superheat a molten salt solution (*a combination of sodium nitrate and potassium nitrate*) used to drive a series of steam turbines to produce power. When this facility was in operation, the large, black tower in the center would glow white-hot. The black on the tower is burned surface from the intense heat. It was a successful experiment, but the continuing availability of cheaper fossil fuels closed it down.

42.9 miles -

DAGGETT

Originally known as Calico Station, the town became Daggett, in honor of the Lt. Governor of the State, when the name was submitted to the Post Office in 1883. Once the site of a thriving smelter and Borax stamp mill for the many mines in the area as well as a terminus for the famous Twenty-Mule Teams from Death Valley, life has now slowed for Daggett. At the intersection, on the southwest corner stands a curved roof building that was once Mrs. Millers Cafe that sported a sign in the 1930's proclaiming "All you can Eat!".

To the right and across the tracks can be seen the old Stone Hotel, hopefully to be restored by the San Bernardino County Museum board. This building was formerly known as the Daggett Railroad Eating House.

At the stop sign in Daggett **(C094)**,

ZERO ODOMETER

The road has many dips along here. (*Whee!*)

2.2 miles (C093) - Road curves to the left. The old road curves back to the right. This section of the old road will end at the Marine Corps Depot and is closed to through traffic. It will be necessary to continue on and enter the Interstate for the run into Barstow.

2.5 miles (C092) - Enter I-40 westbound towards Barstow.

Take the Marine Corps Logistics Base Exit, Exit 2, to rejoin the old highway. Make a left at the bottom of the ramp **(C091)** and

ZERO ODOMETER

Chicago to Santa Monica

break up the monotony.

3.5 miles - A hillside on the left has a microwave radio tower on it and in the distance can be seen Bristol Dry Lake, an extremely foreboding sight to the traveler. This lake bed is known for the mirage's it can toss off to bewilder the uninitiated - a beautiful blue water lake, a rising cityscape, huge building and even mountain peaks have been seen across this expanse of dusty powder that can swallow a person to their knees.

9.9 miles (C111) -

AMBOY

There used to be two gas stations in Amboy, one on either side of the highway. It didn't mater which one you stopped at, they both charged a high price for gas - up to 49¢ a gallon when the rest of the country was selling at 19¢! Today the station on the south side of the highway is just memory, but across the highway Roy's Motel, the café, and the gas pumps are the life of Amboy. The motel, a holdover from the 1940's consists of small white cabins equipped with that desert necessity, the swamp cooler. We have received many complaints about Amboy and the actions of the management of the café and motel. I experienced that attitude personally in 2001 and 2002 and for that reason suggest only a quick stop to take photos and then move on. Normally, I would suggest buying a meal or a souvenir T-shirt, but the management even gets upset if you want a hamburger, so just don't bother. You may recognize Amboy from hundreds of commercials and ads, this is why they don't care too much for the visiting Roadie - they make thousands off of film companies. Amboy was on eBay at $1.5 million in April of 2003. No takers.

10.5 miles Intersection with the road south to Twenty-nine Palms.

18.0 miles (C110) -

BAGDAD

Amazing! There is nothing left of this once bustling town. Acres of earth scrapped to the bone with one lone tree provide the only clue to the location of Bagdad.

This was once the rail center for the War Eagle, and Orange Blossom gold mines located to the north. From 1875 to 1910 huge wagonloads of ore were hauled to Bagdad for transport on the railroad. From 1889 to 1923, the town had saloons, churches, hotels, a school, a Harvey House Restaurant and a Post Office.

Although barren today, memories of the long gone Bagdad Cafe linger on. The movie of the same name was filmed in Newberry Springs, but the essence of the original Bagdad Cafe came through. People from all across the desert would journey to Alice Lawrence's Bagdad Cafe to enjoy an ever-changing tableau of characters provided by the highway, and the only dance floor and juke box for miles in either direction.

The wind, the heat and the lack of water (*Bagdad went from July 1912 to November 1914 without a drop of rain*), combined with the actions of vandals destroyed many of the town's buildings. In 1991, the entire area was stripped clean to be used as a storage facility for a natural gas pipeline running between Bakersfield and Topock.

Between here and Ludlow your maps may show the "communities" of Haynes, Siberia and Klondike. Once again, these were names given to equipment locations by the railroad. You have to admit, naming a place in the desert "Klondike" or "Siberia" showed a great sense of humor on someone's part.

25.2 miles (C109) - On the right can be seen the lone surviving building of Siberia. If you choose to visit, please do not vandalize anymore than has already been done and respect the railroad right-of-way. This was once the site of a few Mom and Pop cafes and motor courts during the 1940's. Originally a water stop for the AT&SF (*now the BNSF*).

35.4 miles (C108) - Right curve and cross the railroad tracks.

37.6 miles -

LUDLOW

This is where Route 66 meets the Interstate and the place is usually jumping with traffic, at least at the west end of town, where the Chevron station provides an opportunity to re-fuel the Family Truckster, as well as its occupants, provided they want nothing more than a nitrite-charged tube-steak and a Coke. However, across the road is the Ludlow Café, featuring good service and good food, and just to the west is the Ludlow Motel, a small, but extremely clean place. If it's getting late and you're thinking of staying in Barstow, consider Ludlow instead. (See the people at the Chevron station for keys and payment for the motel. Call ahead for reservations at 760.733.4338).

The east end of town sits quietly, watching the traffic race by on the Interstate and on old 66. The original Ludlow Cafe has been effectively vandalized over the years, but still had a enough life in it to serve as a set for the movie *Kalifornia*. It was here that Brad Pitt, as Early Grace, who after murdering a gas station attendant, terrorized David Duchovny (Mulder of the "X-Files"), Michelle Forbes and Julliette Lewis who played Pitt's child-like wife.

Ludlow was once a boomtown. Two narrow gauge railroads served Ludlow from Death Valley where ore was off-loaded into cars of the Santa Fe. Down by the tracks a large building constructed in 1909 once housed the Ludlow Mercantile Company (*the*

Chicago to Santa Monica

31.2 miles (C121) - Fenner and the Oasis. Nice rest stop, decent food, friendly service.
31.8 miles (C120) - Cross under I-40.
36.5 miles (C118) - Intersection with National Old Trails Road.

From this point, you can make a right and continue towards Essex, or go east eight miles to catch the Mountain Springs Road exit **(C119)**, then double back towards Essex.

OPTION TWO - NEEDLES - MOUNTAIN SPRINGS ROAD - ESSEX

West out of Needles as you enter I-40:
ZERO ODOMETER

You climb steadily after leaving Needles and it seems as if the climb will never end. You climb for 8 miles and then the climb becomes steeper. A truck lane appears on the right and the semi's are working hard to pull this hill.

13.0 miles - Road becomes steeper, the trucks are pulling at about thirty to thirty-five, some even slower.
14.9 miles - South Pass - Used to be a gas station here - eaten by the Interstate.
16.8 miles - Look to the right and you can see the railroad, the old highway and Goffs off in the distance.
20.0 miles - Water Road - Power lines from Hoover Dam cross the highway along here. There used to be houses for the power line workers here.
21.4 miles - Truck lane reappears as we begin the climb again.
24.5 miles (C119) - Mountain Springs Road exit, exit 115. This is the summit at 2770 feet, the vertical climb from Needles has been nearly 2300 feet. There once was a gas station, cafe, and a few cabins at the summit, along with a large cross erected on the hillside. The purpose of the cross was to get tourists to stop and ask questions and hopefully buy something.

Take this exit to get back on Old 66. Make a left at the top of the exit ramp, and, on the center of the bridge,
ZERO ODOMETER

0.7 miles - Turnout on the left. An early rest stop.
7.0 miles - Quarry on the right.
10.8 miles - Cross the railroad tracks. As you come off the bridge, the road joining from the right is the road from Goffs and Fenner **(C118)**.
11.3 miles - Wrecking yard and cafe on the right.
12.9 miles (C117) -

ESSEX

Named by the Santa Fe for no particular reason, well, that's not exactly true. The Santa Fe originally named the water stops and stations in strict alphabetical sequence starting at Amboy. The stops towards Needles were Amboy, Bristol, Cadiz, Danby, Edson, Fenner, Goffs, Homer, Ibis (Ibex) and Java. As the Santa Fe expanded and added more passing tracks, the alphabetical sequence fell apart with the additions of Bannock between Homer and Ibis, Klinefelter between Ibis and Java, and Hartoum between Java and Needles. Also, Edson became Essex and Bristol became Bengal.

In 1977, Essex gained fifteen minutes of fame when the town's 35 residents wrote the Los Angeles Times claiming to be the only town in America without television. The entire population was invited to the Johnny Carson Show and a manufacturer in Pennsylvania, who saw the show, donated the translator equipment that brought television to Essex.

As you leave Essex, notice the road sign on the west end of town. Nothing special about it, but here we will:
ZERO ODOMETER

4.2 miles - Abandoned house on right. Posted area, do not trespass.
9.1 miles (C116) - Danby Road intersection.
9.3 miles (C115) - Remains of Danby Store and Gas Station. Danby is about a mile and a half off the highway on the left.
16.1 miles (C114) - Abandoned building and station. This was the community of Summit where gas, food, and even cabins were provided. Today, it is the site of the most graffitied building I have ever seen.
20.1 miles (C113) - Chambless (Cadiz).

This one is confusing. All of my maps and guides indicate this is Chambless, however, the post office (about a quarter mile from the store/station) has Cadiz on the front.

I know Cadiz itself is three miles out in the desert south of here, but what's with that post office?

Just west of Cadiz is the abandoned Roadrunners Retreat **(C112)** restaurant, and east of it an abandoned gas station. These buildings are of a recent (late 60s) vintage and are often repainted and used for movies, commercials, and print advertising.

As you leave the Roadrunners Retreat:
ZERO ODOMETER

Continuing west there is an area of personal roadside billboards on the right side of the highway. The berm is well peppered for miles with what I would call "stone graffiti" - names, short messages and even a well placed "ROUTE 66" catch the eye and

Chicago to Santa Monica

point **(C137)**.*)*

Continue on F Street to K Street **(C136)** and make a left (*the small park on the right just before K Street was used in the opening scenes of the film Two Lane Blacktop*). Proceed one block and make a right onto Broadway **(C135)**. Cross the overpass to where Broadway ends at a stop sign **(C134)**.

As you drop down off of the overpass, you will see the Sage and Western motels across the street from each other, examples of the motels from the glory days of 66. Unfortunately most of the older motels have not been maintained and some will not honor confirmed reservations (*the River Valley Lodge is one example*). Best places to stay are the chain motels, with my favorite being the Best Western Colorado River Inn. Good eats at the California Country Kitchen.

Make a left onto Needles Highway (*shown on old maps as River Road or sometimes West Broadway*) from Broadway **(C134)** and follow under I-40. Continue out of town over the I-40 bridge **(C133)** (do not enter I-40) and follow the Needles Highway to the "Y" intersection with National Old Trails Highway **(C132)**. Take the left fork onto National Old Trails (*if you go straight you will wind up in Laughlin, Nevada and lose all your money in a slot machine*). Pass the KOA on your right and continue to Park Road **(C131)**, make a left and enter I-40 **(C130)**.

OPTIONAL ROUTES AHEAD

Option One will take you along the pre-1931 alignment of Route 66, part two will cover the post-1931 alignment.

OPTION ONE - GOFFS-FENNER-ESSEX

Take I-40 west out of Needles to the US 95 exit, exit 144. As you travel out of Needles you can see bit and pieces of the old highway off on the right as it followed the railroad tracks. Virtually, all of this road is inaccessible. Exit at Hwy 95 **(C129)**, head north and:

ZERO ODOMETER

Although this seems like miles and miles of nothing but miles and miles, the run through Goffs is interesting. The road is not crowded, and the desert has a lonely beauty all of its own. Stop for awhile at the Goffs General Store. The burgers smell good and the people are friendly. West of Goffs, you have the opportunity to see some lengthy trains both running and sitting waiting to be passed.

0.3 miles (C128) - On the right can be seen (*over the dune*) an early alignment of 66 (*not recommended for travel*).

1.9 miles (C127) - According to old railroad maps (*and certain high quality Route 66 maps!*) this was the site of Klinefelter, all that remains is a grove of really old palm trees.

3.1 miles (C126) - Not a happy spot. Nothing to see here, but this is the location where comedian Sam Kinison was killed on April 10th 1992. Sam was a bit of a wild man, and although he angered many people with his humor, he also made many of us think about that anger. He was killed by a drunken seventeen-year-old driving a pick-up on the wrong side of the road. Sam was thirty-eight and had been married less than a week.

6.9 miles (C125) - Railroad track and a left to Goffs. This was the site of Arrowhead Junction, a gas station, cafe and store. The location was named Arrowhead Junction because the road to Salt Lake City was called the Arrowhead Trail back in the 1920s.

If you have any old maps with you, they may indicate various places along this stretch of road that you cannot find - Bannock, Ibis, Java and Piute are a few of the names on the old maps. These were never towns or even villages. They were locations named by the railroad for equipment sheds, signal boxes and water towers. Many of the names were those of Santa Fe employees. Some of the names are actually humorous as we will see further down the road.

9.3 miles (C124) - Bannock - a railroad siding.

13.5 miles (C123) - Here is one of the "towns" mentioned above. Look to the right and you can see a sign by the tracks that says Homer on it. No store, no gas station, no motel, no zip code - that's Homer, California (*D'OH!*).

21.1 miles (C122) -

GOFFS

When Route 66 was dedicated in 1926 Goffs was there to serve the transcontinental motorist. Goffs was born in 1883 as a siding at the "Top of the Hill" for the Southern Pacific Railway. In 1893 the Nevada Southern built a short line into Goffs from the North. A school was proposed in 1911 to serve the railroad employees and classes began in a rented building. In 1914, the Goffs School was dedicated. With the advent of diesel engines Goffs place as a water-stop for trains came to a close and it was the new highway, Route 66, that kept the town going. In December 1931, the new alignment, eight miles shorter, opened and Goffs began its decline. The school closed in 1937. World War II brought 10,000 soldiers to the area for desert training, but by then there were no businesses to serve them, forcing the schoolhouse into service as a makeshift cafe.

Today the Friends of the Mojave Road have restored the schoolhouse and additional buildings have been moved to the area for restoration. A great place to visit, open first Saturday and Sunday of each month except July-August-September.

Leaving Goffs, cross the tracks, make an immediate left and continue on Goffs Road.

Chicago to Santa Monica

The road to Needles crosses some desolate looking country. At one time, there was a section of redwood plank road along here to compensate for the shifting sands that constantly buried any attempt at building a regular road.

Exit at Five Mile Road **(C141)** and cross the freeway. On the left is a turnout area (dirt) that will access the Adventure Tour below.

ADVENTURE TOUR
Please read all admonitions regarding Adventure Tours at front of the book.
CAUTION: If the weather has been raining, or threatening rain DO NOT attempt this tour. Flash floods and washouts will make portions of this virtually impassable.

Just past the I-40 overcrossing at the Five Mile Road interchange **(C141)**, is the first opportunity for a California Adventure Tour. At the turnout **(ZERO ODOMETER)** on the south side of the road, make a left and follow the dirt road east, then south (it's a curve to the right). This is a section of the Old National Trails Road.

0.2 miles (ATC02) - Pavement will be encountered. WATCH YOUR SPEED, the pavement is very rough and missing in places.

Approximately **2.2 miles (ATC03)** a severe washout. Go to the right to get around it - **DO NOT** drive too close to the washout - it may be undercut.

2.7 miles (ATC04) - Pavement disappears, but will reappear within a quarter of a mile.

4.0 miles - Road is atop a ridgeline.

4.3 miles (ATC06) - Road ends with an overlook of I-40. Notice the great old inlaid rock gutters along the north side of the road along here.

At this point you can return the way you came back to I-40, or if you have a four-wheel drive vehicle and really want an adventure, return about a quarter of a mile and notice the road (dirt) angling off to the south and down **(ATC05)**. Real down! Turn onto this road and, in four-wheel drive, carefully descend the hill (watch for large rocks, washouts and sand). At the bottom **(ATC07)**, follow the road to the left through the sandy wash and under I-40 **(ATC08)**. After crossing under the Interstate, the road will fork, take the left fork and follow it up onto the pavement. This is the end section of the 1947 alignment of 66 **(C147)**. Follow this road under the railroad tracks to Park Moabi Road **(C143)**. From here make a right and return to I-40, retrace the interstate to Five Mile, exit and cross over I-40 to re-join Old Route 66.

Continuing toward Needles, at the dirt turn-out just past the Interstate,
ZERO ODOMETER
    1.3 miles (C140) - Make a right at the "Y" intersection onto Hwy 95.
    5.7 miles (C139) - Cross under I-40 and enter:

NEEDLES
Named by a soldier at old Fort Mojave for a group of pointy spires that jut up from the Black Mountains of Arizona, visible to the east and south of Needles.

Needles was founded in 1883 with the coming of the Santa Fe railroad and for years, the Santa Fe was the principle employer in the town. The town Plaza, between G and H Streets, is a virtual oasis in the center of the city with palms, pepper, Palo Verde and tamarind trees providing the much needed shade for a desert community.

The east side of the Plaza is fronted by the deserted El Garces, formerly the Santa Fe depot and Fred Harvey House. Here is a great example of the marvelous buildings erected to serve a slower moving touring population.

As you enter town from the east, you drop off a mesa covered with the "modern" stores and stations we are used to seeing, but once closer to the river and rail yard, you will find the Needles of years gone by. The Route 66 motel beckons with a sign shaped like an arrow, pointing to the motel that is just off the old road, the motel is no longer open for overnight stays, it is presently used for long term patrons.

A drive along Broadway is a step back in time. The motels, storefronts and cafes of the heyday of highway travel dot the city from one end to the other.

Watch for the intersection with Front Street **(C138)**, and make a slight right onto Front down to F Street.

Turn left at F Street for one block, then a right, followed by another right onto G Street and then a left back onto Front Street - this takes you around the El Garces Hotel, the old Needles Harvey House. (*These turns are collectively shown on the map as way-*

Chicago to Santa Monica

CALIFORNIA

WESTBOUND

It is necessary to enter California on the interstate freeway. The old bridge is no longer used for vehicles and the 1947 alignment highway bridge is gone.

As you sweep across the Colorado River, there is not a great deal to see, though the original bridge is still there to the left.

Climbing the hill into California, there is an exit for the Moabi Regional Park, exit 153 **(C142)**. Take this exit, make a right at the top, and follow the road down to where it intersects with the Old Trails Highway **(C143)** and

ZERO ODOMETER

At the bottom of the hill, there is a sign for the PG&E Topock Compressor Station on the Old Trails Highway. Make a right and follow the road.

1.7 miles (C145) - The road ends at the site where the two old bridges crossed the Colorado. Wait a minute, I only see one bridge! More about that in a moment.

This road was the 1947 alignment of Route 66. Near the end of the road there is a jog to the right. The highway went straight, at this point, across the Red Rock Bridge **(C144)** to Arizona. The bridge had originally been built by the Santa Fe as a railroad bridge. In 1945, the railroad opened a new bridge 500 feet upstream from the old one as part of a project to double track and straighten the roadbed, and the Red Rock Bridge was abandoned.

By 1947, the bridge and the old railroad alignment, had been donated to Arizona and California, giving Route 66 a new alignment - along the old railroad roadbed - into the Golden State and eliminating the terrible curves and grades motorists had fought since 1916 when the Old Trails Arch Bridge was dedicated.

The Red Rock Bridge was dismantled in 1966-67 with the opening of the Interstate highway over the Colorado. The only remains of the Red Rock Bridge are a couple of concrete foundation anchors on the westside of the river. (*The bridge is shown for reference on certain high quality Route 66 maps*).

The Old Trails Bridge **(C146)**, now a historic landmark and well cared for, was, at the time of its opening in 1916, the longest three hinged arch bridge in the country. The bridge was long and narrow, with a hard right turn as you entered California. It was wide enough for two cars, but trucks and buses had to cross one at a time.

As you walk this area where the fictional Joad family, and thousands of others crossed into the promised land, you can see the rock framed sign with "Historic Route 66 - Welcome - Turn Right Next Exit" painted on it. This sign was constructed for the traffic on the 1947 alignment and has been recently repainted in hopes of catching the eye of the Interstate highway traveler. I remember when the sign read, "Breathe Deeply, Folks. Soon be in Arizona."

Off to the right of the sign are the remnants of the old highway as it wound along the cliff face and headed up the hill. Walk down this section of road and you will find a laminated board guardrail. Standing here it is hard to imagine the tremendous amount of traffic this narrow piece of asphalt once carried. A short walk will bring you to a gate and fence across the road, the old bridge can be seen ahead, around the curve of the hillside. The old highway crossed the river, twisted its way along the cliff face then climbed the hill to where the gas compressor station stands. In the early days of 66, there was a place called Teapot Dome on top of the hill, a gas station-cafe kind of a place. Supposedly, it was named Teapot Dome because by the time cars made the climb they were "boiling like a teapot." The building had a large teapot mounted on top to go with the name.

Head back on the road you came in on.

When you reach the intersection with the Park Moabi Road **(C143)**,

ZERO ODOMETER

and continue straight-ahead (north). A sign warns "Not A Through Road" (*the sign is correct, you will have to return to this point in order to rejoin the Interstate*).

1.1 miles (C147) - A severe washout of the pavement here. Road is blocked by large rocks. A dirt road across the washout is to the left. Sandy crossing, not recommended for the average sedan.

1.5 miles (C148) - You are at the fence line along the freeway, most likely having walked there. From here, the original routing continued straight across what is now the freeway right-of-way and up the hill (a portion of the old pavement can still be seen on the cliff above - see Adventure Tour below). The curve you are standing on was the 1947 alignment that curved to the right and is now buried beneath the Interstate.

Return to the Park Moabi Exit access road **(C143)** and then up the hill to the Interstate on-ramp **(C142)**. It will be necessary to take the Interstate west to the Five Mile Road exit, exit 148 **(C141)**.

Chicago to Santa Monica

Originally named Vivian for the Vivian Mining Company, the name was changed in 1909 to Oatman. The name was for a pioneer family attacked by Apaches in 1851 near Gila (*Hee-la*) Bend in southern Arizona. The parents were murdered, the boy severely beaten and left to die, and the two girls kidnapped. The girls were hidden a half-mile north of the present townsite of Oatman, at a spring, known locally as Ollie Oatman Spring. One of the girls, Mary Ann, died in captivity. Olive was released in 1856 or 1857 (records are fuzzy) through the efforts of Henry Grinnell, a local rancher, and she returned to Fort Yuma where her brother was living.

Oatman was a mining town and as such was a bit of a hell-raiser, but less so than many other mining towns. There was a strong sense of community with high morale and good spirits. Clarabelle Decker, whose family moved to Oatman in 1909, recalled, "There was no crime that I remember in Oatman. Some men drank too much, but everybody was friendly and kind."

The Oatman Hotel is a landmark for the trivia buff. Following their marriage in Kingman, Clark Cable and Carole Lombard spent their honeymoon night in the hotel.

Following the closing of the mines during World War Two, Route 66 kept the town active with seven gas stations, numerous restaurants and cafes, and hotels to serve the motoring public. The Oatman Hill (east of town) was feared by many drivers and considered to be the worst part of Route 66. Jack Rittenhouse, in his 1946 *A Guide Book to Highway 66*, describes a service that, for $3.50, would tow your car over the hill. In *Russ's Bus,* Russ Byrd tells of having to stop his bus near the top to let his riders walk up the hill because the bus could not pull the last section of the grade with a load of passengers.

One afternoon, in October of 1952, the hill became quiet. The new Route 66 ribbon cutting had taken place between Kingman and Topock. The new road ran south from Kingman through Yucca along a relatively flat stretch of country. The day after the opening of the new Route 66 alignment, six of the seven gas stations in Oatman closed, and people began to leave town as more-and-more businesses threw in the towel.

Today, Oatman is a thriving tourist town with a rustic atmosphere. The Main Street burros and Route 66 attract thousands of visitors a year for a chance to take a step back in time.

At the south end of town, in front of Cactus Joe's,
ZERO ODOMETER

1.0 miles (A006) - Community of Old Trails. Once a mining community rivaling Oatman, the Old Trails post office was established in February 1916 and discontinued in July of 1925. Name is thought to have come from the fact that both Beale and Sitgreaves passed along the Old Trail through the area.

2.3 miles (A005) - Fork, take a left.

14.6 miles (A004) - Historic Route 66 Backcountry Byway sign. Great place for photos.

17.8 miles (A003) - Intersection, stop, then continue straight.

24.2 miles (A002) -

TOPOCK

A place with more names than can be imagined. Originally called Needles by Lt. Whipple, the name was changed with the arrival of the railroad in 1883. The railroad brought the need for a post office and with the California town of Needles just a few miles upstream the people of Needles, Arizona decided to change the name to Powell. The post office closed in 1887 and other names for the town came into popular use; Red Rock and Red Rock Crossing being the most popular. In 1903, a new post office and a new name, Mellen, after Colorado Steamboat captain, Jack Mellen. The various permutations of Red Rock would not work as there was already a dearth of Red Rocks in the Territory. In 1909, the post office closed once again and it was 1915 before a population surge demanded another post office. Mellen became a problem (due to the hasty scrawl of telegraph operators) when it was confused with Needles. The railroad had called the place Topock and that was the name that stuck. The name is a contraction of the Navajo *a-ha-to-pak*, meaning water-bridge.

24.6 miles - Left turn under the railroad, follow the frontage road up and across I-40 **(A001)**.

25.0 miles - Make a right on frontage road and go west to the original Old Trails Bridge **(C146)** built in 1917.

The bridge is now used by Pacific Gas and Electric for a gas transmission pipe. The final alignment of Route 66 crossed due west on a bridge that no longer exists. The pilings for the old bridge can be seen across the river. This bridge was the Red Rocks Bridge deeded to Arizona and California when the railroad straightened their alignment and built the new railroad bridge that is north of the Interstate.

Be considerate in this area. It is private property, so take pictures only and do not attempt to go out on the old bridge.

This ends our trip across Arizona. What a trip! Sights, sounds, people, and places will long live in our memories of this wonderful excursion down one of the longest remaining sections of Route 66 in the Nation.

Chicago to Santa Monica

A few sights to see in Kingman include Locomotive Park (where Old Route 66 joins Andy Devine Blvd), the Powerhouse, home of the Route 66 Museum, and the Beale Hotel, once owned by Andy Devine's father.

LODGING: Best Western Kings Inn, Best Western A Wayfarers Inn, Quality Inn, Hill Top Motel (*classic older motel - nicely maintained*). **DINING:** Dambar Steakhouse (Stockman Hill and Andy Devine), El Palacio (4th Street and Andy Devine), Portofino Restorante Italiano (318 Oak Street). 50's Atmosphere: Mr D's Route 66 Diner (105 E. Andy Devine).

As you leave town, at the junction with Andy Devine and Old Route 66 (A020) (across from Locomotive Park and just past the Powerhouse),

ZERO ODOMETER

0.5 to 1.0 miles (A019) - The road you see across the canyon is the original alignment of the National Old Trails Highway.

Once you leave the canyon, quite a few old Route 66 businesses can be seen. Some of the buildings have been re-used, others abandoned, and others bulldozed to the ground. This area - wrecking yard, truck stop and truck wash - is McConnico, named for S. B. McConnico, Vice President and General Manager of the Arizona and Utah Railroad, a small railroad that connected from here to Chloride in 1899.

4.9 miles (A018) - Stop sign. Turn right on Shinarump Road, cross under I-40 (A017) and make a left onto Oatman Road (A016).

18.0 miles (A015) - In the Rittenhouse guide (page 110) mention is made of Fig Springs Camp. Today, there is nothing remaining of this tourist stop.

19.6 miles (A014) - Bureau of Land Management sign designating this section of old Route 66 as a National Historic Byway.

20.1 miles (A013) - The ruins of Cool Springs Camp. Once a thriving tourist stop for water on the climb up the hill, there were cabins, a gas station, and store at this location. The site was rebuilt in 1992 for the movie "Universal Soldier" then blown up. It amazes me that after filming the entire area was thoroughly cleaned (*I saw the location shortly after the film crew left*). For a time the area was totally trashed and the pit filled with oil cans and used oil. I sometimes wonder if we aren't the trashiest people on Earth. The good news though, Cool Springs has been cleaned up and rebuilt.

21.4 miles (A012) - Ed's Camp. One of the great desert "junk-shop" stops of all time. Closed since 1992. Please do not "explore" this area. The owners are very protective - photos from the road are not a problem, but please respect the No Trespassing signs.

21.8 miles (A011) - Little Meadows on the right, characterized by the tall cottonwood trees and the remains of old buildings.

23.6 miles (A010) - On the left is a small pull-out and a set of steps leading up the hill. At the top is Shaffer Fish Bowl Spring. In the spring, there are a few hearty goldfish and the flowers that surround the rear of the bowl are quite beautiful. Watch for bees around the water in the warm months. Looking back down the hill is a breathtaking view of the road and the mountains beyond.

24.3 miles (A009) - Sitgreaves Pass, also known as Gold Hill Summit. (Elevation 3515 ft). On the righthand side can be seen foundations of the old gas station and ice cream parlor that served the tired motorist at the top of the hill.

Also, back behind the foundations can be seen the remnants of the old wagon road clinging to the north side of the canyon.

25.4 miles (A008) - Down the hill and through the remains of

GOLD ROAD

Originally named Acme with the first post office in 1903. It was renamed Gold Road in 1906. A thriving mining area from early 1900's Gold Road began to die out in the late 'teens and in 1925 the post office closed. 1937 saw a rebirth of the town that lasted through the start of WW-II.

The final blow came in 1949 when the Arizona State Legislature passed a law making business property owners liable for full taxes whether they were doing business or not. This upset the few remaining citizens of Gold Road to the point they literally burned down the town. Many historic building were lost, not only in Gold Road but throughout Arizona, because of this short-sighted excuse for revenue enhancement.

The area has been reopened for mining and tours are offered at the Gold Road Mine, where you can get your kicks under 66 (*275 feet to be exact*).

28.4 miles (A007):

OATMAN

Steep canyon walls rise up either side of the Black Mountains from downtown Oatman. Main Street, Route 66, gives you a feeling of stepping back in time, or possibly into a movie set - which it was, as many scenes in the film *How the West Was Won* were shot here.

Drive carefully through town as the local burro population makes Main Street their domain. The animals are accustomed to tourists and feed can be purchased at just about any store in town. This is a great place to make a friend for life, or at least until you run out of food.

As you approach Truxton, on the left can be seen the old alignment coming down the hill. There is no access to this section, private, fenced land.

8.4 miles (A031) -

TRUXTON

Flowing springs brought Lt. Beale to this spot in 1857 and his naming of the area for either his mother (Emily Truxton Beale), his brother (Truxton Beale) or his grandfather (Thomas Truxton). The availability of water also brought the railroad with steam engines thirsty for the precious liquid.

A proposed rail line to the Grand Canyon brought the modern development of Truxton in 1951. D. J. Dilts built a restaurant and gas station in hopes of cashing in on a rail line that never materialized. A stop at the Frontier Cafe is a must for the hungry Roadie. Good food, "Real Home Cooking by the Girls from Oklahoma" and an atmosphere that belies Route 66's reputation for 24 hour a day hustle and bustle is more than enough reason to stop.

In front of the Frontier Cafe,

ZERO ODOMETER

5.0 miles (A030) - Original highway on the left, do not enter, private land.

6.1 miles (A029) - Crozier Canyon area. This was the site of a group of tourist cabins, gas station and cafe. All private property, respect the owners privacy.

7.8 miles (A028) - Right, abandoned buildings.

9.5 miles (A027) -

VALENTINE

Originally named Truxton Canyon in 1898 when the large Indian School was active. The post office closed when the school moved and community was given a new name when the Post Office reopened in 1910. The new name was Valentine in honor of the Commissioner of Indian Affairs Robert G. Valentine.

11.1 miles (A026) - Bert's Country Dancing.

13.6 miles (A025) -

HACKBERRY

The Hackberry General store has seen an amazing restoration. A great photo stop and be sure to say hi to John and Kerry. As you leave the Hackberry General Store, make a right and:

ZERO ODOMETER

0.3 miles (A024) - Cross bridge.

5.6 miles - Old Stuckey's building on left, but it has a new incarnation.

9.3 miles (A023) - Valle Vista Country Club development. The orchards you see along here are pecan and pistachio trees.

20.3 miles - Route 66 Swap Meet on the right.

22.6 miles (A022) - The Skyline Motel. The first motel when entering town from the east.

24.0 miles (A021) - Cross under I-40 and appreciate the lack of Interstate clutter you have seen for the last 175 miles (Flagstaff to Kingman).

KINGMAN

In 1882, the locating engineer for the railroad, Lewis Kingman, named the community after himself. (*Is that what you do when you're the man who would be king? Ouch!*) At one time the town was called Shenfield Railroad Camp after the contractor who plotted the original townsite.

The years have seen Kingman become a major crossroads as railroad and highway converged to make it the most important city in Mohave County. It is interesting to note, however, that as late as 1940 Kingman streets were mostly unpaved and the comment was made that food and lodging were some of the most expensive anywhere along Route 66.

Kingman has two great Hollywood connections. The first is gravel-voiced Andy Devine, who called Kingman his home (*he was born in Flagstaff, but his family moved to Kingman when he was a year old*). The second connection is the marriage of Clark Gable and Carole Lombard at the Methodist Church.

Kingman embraced their son and named the Main Street of the city after him. Along the length of Route 66 many cities are changing street names to Route 66. As much as I love the highway, I hope that Kingman never changes Andy Devine Blvd.

World War Two brought the Army-Air Force to Kingman with a large base on the site of the present Mohave County Airport. Following the war, Kingman became the storage site for more than 7,000 mothballed aircraft. Many of the planes had never seen combat, and for some inexplicable reason (*hey, a contract's a contract, buddy!*), the factories continued to manufacture aircraft, which were flown straight to Kingman and eventually dismantled as scrap.

Chicago to Santa Monica

Make a right onto Crookton Road (if returning from Tour above, continue across I-40) and:
ZERO ODOMETER
    0.2 miles - Cross cattle guard.
    9.5 miles (A045) - Railroad bridge and old highway bridge on right.
    To the left can be seen the old alignment in sections as it travels around the hills you are cutting through.
    14.4 miles (A044) - More evidence of old alignment on the right.

SELIGMAN
Prescott Junction was the name of this small town in 1882 when the railroad reached this far west. The town was the junction point for the Atlantic & Pacific Railroad and the Prescott & Arizona Central. The present name of Seligman was selected in 1886 for one of the Seligman Brothers, a pair of financiers from New York who were stockholders in the Atlantic & Pacific Railroad.

Seligman is the home of Angel Delgadillo, the founder of the Arizona Historic Route 66 Association. Angel is a man who is driven to do what is right in life, and the loss of Route 66 seemed wrong to him. He sensed a need to preserve what Route 66 meant to America and he set out to do it. Plan some time to visit Angel at his barbershop and Route 66 museum in the center of town.

Be sure to pick up a walking tour map of Seligman and visit the sites listed, particularly the old Harvey House, the Havasu, which closed in 1954. At this writing the Havasu has been purchased and there are plans to restore it, much like the La Posada restoration in Winslow.

LODGING: A great, restored motel is the Historic Route 66 Motel. **DINING:** Westside Lilo's Café - great for Breakfast, Lunch or Dinner. (*Beware of the home-made cinnamon rolls, they're as big as mid-fifties Cadillac*). Fast Food and Fun: The Snow Cap.

Night photos of the Copper Cart and the Historic Route 66 Motel sign are naturals for your album of Route 66 memories.

On the west end of town, as you cross under the Interstate access **(A042)**,
ZERO ODOMETER
    4.5 miles (A041) - Curve to the right.
Notice the old pole line on your right and the evidence of the '21 alignment along the hillside.
    6.5 miles (A040) - Pole line meets up with the present alignment.
    9.0 miles - Beautiful Hawk sitting on pole cross-arm. Hope he's still there when you go by.
    16.5 miles (A039) - Calvary Hogan Mission.
    20.1 miles (A038) - The site of Deer Lodge Cabins mentioned on page 105 in the Rittenhouse Guidebook to Highway 66.
    21.4 miles (A037) - On the left, up off the road. This was the site of Hyde Park. All that remains are foundations for the store, station, and cabin. (*Certain high-quality Route 66 maps show Hyde Park buildings on the north side of the highway also.*) A few rusting cars at the back of the property make interesting photo opportunities.
    23.0 miles (A036) - Grand Canyon Caverns.

A Roadie attraction that keeps on going despite the moving of the Road. A great place to visit and spend on hour or two. Be sure and get a picture with the dinosaur out front.

At the intersection with the Grand Canyon Caverns road,
ZERO ODOMETER
    6.3 miles (A035) - Old alignment on left - not accessible.
    10.2 miles (A034) - On the right, the southern end of the Grand Canyon can be seen in the distance.
    11.2 miles (A032) -

PEACH SPRINGS
Originally named St. Basil's Well by Father Garcès the explorer who arrived in June of 1775. When Lt. Beale arrived with the camel caravan in 1858, he named the area Indian Spring. The name Peach Springs was derived from the large number of peach trees planted in the area by settling Mormons.

Tribal Headquarters for the Hualapai (*wall-a-pie*) are located here.

Once little more than a great place for photographing old motels, gas stations and cafes, with the construction of the Hualapai Lodge, Peach Springs is moving towards becoming a tourist center offering first class accommodations and access to tours and river runs of the Grand Canyon and Colorado. For reservations call the Hualapai Lodge at 888-255-9550 (AAA and AARP honored).

At the west end of town, at milepost 103,
ZERO ODOMETER
    0.4 miles - Cattle loading pens.
    1.6 miles - Old alignment goes up and around hill on the right and crosses back just past the second cut ahead.

> **ZERO ODOMETER**
> **0.3 miles (ATA06)** - Box culvert. Just past this point, go straight ahead where FR6 turns to the left.
> **0.4 miles** - Dip, drainage cut, slow.
> **0.5 miles** - Dip, drainage cut, slow.
> **0.8 miles (ATA07)** - Short stretch of pavement leading to box culvert.
> **1.1 miles** - Drainage cut.
> **1.4 miles** - Tight spot, trees on either side.
> **1.5 miles (ATA08)** - End of the road. Fence line and I-40 straight ahead. Great views of the valley from here.
>   Turn around and backtrack to FR6, make a left on FR6 **(ATA05)** and follow it to I-40 **(ATA04)** and continue westbound to Ash Fork.
>   A bike tour is available at 0.2 miles on FR6, a turn-out is to the right and allows for biking the 1921 alignment west for three miles (rough), then back up the 1932 alignment for three miles (steep, but easy).

Exit 146 on I-40 **(A051)** for

ASH FORK

Brought to life by the need for a better site to off-load ore from the mines in Jerome, Ash Fork went from a railroad siding to a full-fledged town in less than a year. 1882 was the year of the request for a station stop by freighters tired of hauling ore up the hill to Williams, and 1883 was the year a post office bearing the name Ash Fork was established. Thomas Lewis opened a store alongside the tracks (on the north side) in 1882 and in 1885 Wells Fargo opened a station. Expansion continued north of the tracks until a fire in 1893 destroyed the town. When it was rebuilt Ash Fork was on the south side of the tracks.

The Santa Fe opened the grand Escalante Hotel in March of 1907 as the Harvey House for Ash Fork. People came from as far away as Prescott (fifty miles of dirt road to the south) to eat at the Escalante and cowboys were known to ride for three days for a warm smile from a Harvey Girl over a dinner unequaled in the area. The Escalante was torn down following the Santa Fe's realignment of the main line (the Crookton Cutoff) in 1960.

While in Ash Fork check out DeSoto's Beauty and Barber Shop at 314 W. Lewis **(A050)** (westbound 66). A great 1960 DeSoto sits on top of the roof, and I believe that is Elvis behind the wheel. Been on the Road awhile? Need a haircut? Now's your chance to meet a couple who rescued a decrepit gas station building and made it into a new and viable business - Joe and Edie DeSoto are nice people, tell them Bob says HI!

Also, you should stop at the Ash Fork Cash and Carry on west Lewis Avenue for some antique shopping and to meet Frank and Lisa Bohan, a couple of the new generation of Route 66 entrepreneurs.

The old Beale Wagon Road (which stretched from Fort Smith, Arkansas to the Colorado River) can be seen about fifteen miles north of Ash Fork by following First Street north, cross the tracks and stay on Double A Ranch Road (Forest Road 142) out to Russell's Tank. You will cross the new alignment (1960) of the Santa Fe Railroad (*now BNSF*) out here as well. The Beale Wagon Road was the first federally funded road in the Southwest and was built at a cost of $210,000.

At the west end of town, make a left onto 8th Street **(A049)**. This will put you on the old alignment leaving town. This is a turn-around section as access on the west end, past the KOA, is pretty rough.

Join the Interstate on the west end of Ash Fork **(A048)** and continue to the Crookton Road interchange **(A046)**.

Exit 139 - CROOKTON ROAD (A046)

There is a short side tour outlined below, but it will be necessary to return to this point when you're done.

> ### SIDE TOUR
>
> Cross the I-40 overpass **(A046)** and ZERO ODOMETER. On the south side, turn onto the Frontage Road.
> **0.1 miles** - Cross cattle guard.
> **0.8 miles** - Cross cattle guard and pavement becomes rough, this is old Route 66.
> **1.2 miles** - a "Y" in the road, continue straight.
> **2.2 miles** - Large dip in the road.
> **2.8 miles (A047)** - Partridge Creek Bridge, built in the 1920's for original highway alignment. Bridge is still in good shape, but the classic thing is a tree growing through the bridge on the west end. A great photo stop.
>   It is suggested you turn around here and retrace the road back to I-40 **(A046)**. The road ahead is rough in spots and the final section that would allow you to connect to Ash Fork is now fenced and gated at the railroad crossing.

Chicago to Santa Monica

1.4 miles - On the right is the Frey Marcos - the former Harvey House now beautifully restored as a Museum, Depot and Gift Shop. The Grand Canyon Railroad leaves from here for the run to the Canyon.

1.5 miles - Cross tracks and you're in Williams.

WILLIAMS

Nestled among the pines and named for Bill Williams Mountain (*although locals will incorrectly tell you it was named for Mountain Man Bill Williams - the mountain was, the town wasn't*) the town hugs the west shoulder of the mountain named for the famous fur trapper and mountain man. Williams is also known as the Gateway to the Grand Canyon. Just up the road (*thirty miles*) is Flagstaff, a bustling, progressive city, serving the major shopping needs of Northern Arizona, which allows Williams to remain locked inextricably in the early 20th century, shunning progress at every turn.

When I-40 by-passed the town on October 13, 1984 (*the last Route 66 town to be bypassed*) it appeared as if Williams was going to roll over and die. But, in 1989, the Grand Canyon Railway saved the town and annually brings thousands of people to "ride the train to the Canyon." The city has embraced the railway by allowing for major construction of new buildings - a hotel, a restaurant and gift shop, and on the drawing boards a new RV park, all on the railroads property, while allowing the downtown area to deteriorate (*it should be noted even the Grand Canyon Railway is not based in Williams - their headquarters are in Flagstaff*). A community that seems to thrive on the adage *tourist beware,* Williams is a place where gas prices will be considerably lower (*by as much as 50 cents a gallon*) away from the interstate off-ramps (*High Country Market at Route 66 and 1st Street is usually the best price in town*). If you need car repairs, be cautious - a few of the local garages are favorites of the 60 Minutes crews for being rip-off artists. If you need car service, I have found the Chevron on west Route 66 (*next to the Safeway*) to be operated in a fair and honest fashion. Watch out for motel rip-offs as well - some of the owners like to jack their rates sky-high (*particularly if it is late in the evening*) - the best choices would be: for a classic motel - The Westerner; The Route 66 Inn or The Mountainside Inn. For chain properties - The Best Western Inn of Williams (*a 1000 point B/W property*); or The Fairfield Inn. Because of a bogus CANYON FEE the Holiday Inn is not recommended. For an enchanting experience check out The Grand Canyon Retreat at 518 E. Route 66 - intimate and luxurious, yet at a very affordable price (928.635.0905 or www.grandcanyonretreat.com).

Continue west on Railroad Avenue to enter I-40 **(A052)**.

There are bike and walking tours **(ATA12)** available for the 1922/32 sections of road at the Devil Dog exit (#157) on I-40. Maps for these can be obtained at the Visitors Center in Williams (Grand Canyon Blvd and Railroad Ave).

About halfway down the hill toward Ash Fork, look to the left and you can see the old alignment clinging to the side of the hill. Look closely and you will see where the road crosses the Interstate **(ATA11)** and winds down to the right **(ATA08)**. The Adventure Tour (below) will allow you to drive u Ash Fork Hill.

ADVENTURE TOUR

Please read all admonitions regarding Adventure Tours at the front of this book.

The following sections of Old 66 are driveable in a standard sedan, but a high clearance vehicle is advised. The pavement is heavily deteriorated in spots so speed should be watched. The final section up Ash Fork hill is unpaved and should not be attempted if it is raining, muddy or there is snow on the ground.

Exit Interstate at the Monte Carlo exit (#149) **(ATA01)**, cross under I-40 and drive across the parking lot of the truck stop to the northeast side **(ATA02)**. Just past the closed café the old alignment (1932/52) can be seen heading east. At the fence line:

ZERO ODOMETER

0.2 miles - Box culvert and road damage.
0.6 miles - Change in road surface.
0.9 miles - Crest of the hill. Stop and look behind you at the view.
1.5 miles - Pavement missing.
1.9 miles - Box culvert with road damage.
2.0 miles - Large section of pavement missing.
2.1 miles - Large section of pavement missing.
2.8 miles (ATA03) - Box culvert, road damage - SLOW.
2.9 miles (ATA05) - Road to the right is FR6 which leads back to I-40. If you do not want to make the climb up Ash Fork Hill, make a right here and follow FR6 for 0.4 mile to I-40. **(ATA04)**

It will be necessary to return to this point after climbing the hill.
To continue up the hill, at this point:

Chicago to Santa Monica

At the Deer Farm, make a right and
ZERO ODOMETER
    0.2 miles (A064) - Pavement ends.
    1.0 miles - Davenport Lake on the left. The '41 alignment and I-40 cross the middle of the lake, making for some interesting "ice-driving" in the winter.
    1.4 miles (A063) - Abandoned building on left.
    1.6 miles - Cross cattle guard.
    2.9 miles - Williams City Limits sign and gravel paving changes color.
    3.2 miles - Pavement.
    3.3 miles (A062) - Cross cattle guard.
    3.9 miles (A061) - Turn to the left.
    4.0 miles - This is the Interstate entrance **(A060)** to continue on into Williams. See Optional Tour below for an early road experience into Williams.
    Take exit 165 **(A059)** to go into Williams. Make a left at the stop sign. As you follow the curve towards town, notice the old road on your left.

Optional tour below is another dirt road experience along the '21 alignment. To continue the main tour, go to "Cross Under Railroad" below.

OPTIONAL TOUR

    Dirt road ahead. On top of freeway overpass **(A060)** at the Garland Pines/Circle Pines sign,
ZERO ODOMETER
    Do not enter freeway, continue straight ahead.
    0.2 miles (ATA31) - Take a right onto Forest Road 51A. (*A left here is also the '21 alignment, but it ends in a private yard, with an overly friendly dog - a very BIG, overly friendly dog.*)
    0.5 miles - SLOW, road is heavily rutted.
    0.6 miles - Good-sized dip in road.
    0.8 miles - Enter the pine forest.
    1.1 miles (ATA32) - Pavement - go straight, road to left goes to Williams Junction, a depot used when the railroad moved away from Williams with the Santa Fe realignment in 1961. There is nothing at the depot site today - totally barren - but it is a great place for train spotting (*nearly 70 trains pass this point in any given 24-hour period*).
    1.8 miles - Big chuckhole (*or gopher hole - you hit one, then go-fer another) (Ouch!*) and curve to the right - the original alignment goes straight, but it is overgrown and tends to be muddy.
    2.0 miles - Left turn onto final alignment of old highway.
    2.1 miles - Yellow line and pavement continues to the right and under the I-40 embankment.
    2.3 miles (ATA33) - Right at stop sign, followed by immediate left onto the new road leading into Williams.

NOTE: Another side trip for intrepid Roadie, continuing the above directions.
    2.9 miles (ATA34) - Make a left onto Echo Canyon Road followed by another left (almost a full 180 degrees), do not go through the gate onto private property. Cross cattle guard and continue back east-southeast.
    3.1 miles (ATA35) - Forest Road to the right, go straight on. If in a passenger car, you might want to walk. This is the '21 alignment.
    3.2 miles - Old box culvert, a classic.
    3.3 miles - Railroad embankment and end of road. A great place to watch trains pulling the hill heading east.
Return to the highway.

CROSS UNDER RAILROAD
    To enter Williams on the original alignment from the east, go under the railroad **(A058)** make a right on Rodeo Road **(A057)** (just before the hill leading into town) follow with an immediate left, then
ZERO ODOMETER
    0.5 miles (A056) - Cross tracks, to the left is the Wye ("Y") used for turning the train around.
    0.8 miles (A055) - Stop, then left on Airport Road.
    1.0 miles (A054) - Right onto Edison.
    1.2 miles (A053) - Left onto Grand Canyon Blvd.

Chicago to Santa Monica

2.9 miles (A078) - Fortynine Hill - This is the site of the highest point on the old highway in Arizona (*until recently it was thought this was the highest point on Route 66, but that has been proven to be incorrect as we saw back at Glorieta Pass in New Mexico*), topping out at 7414 feet. The road moved to the south in 1941 with the new alignment to avoid the climb over the pass.

4.4 miles (A077) - Junction with Forest Road 107.

4.8 miles (A076) - Curve to left and right and the second.
Auto Tour sign. Pull off here and spend some time exploring.

Immediately south of here, about 100 feet (*sorry, I'm rotten at distances - time to get a map!*) can be seen the 1921 alignment (National Old Trails Road) **(A075)**. The road is evident by the cut through the trees.

Straight ahead, beyond the fence, is the 1931 alignment **(A076)** and a pleasant three-quarter of a mile hike, or bike ride, will take you a step back in time. The pavement comes and goes along here, trees push their way up through the concrete along the edge of the road.

A little over a half a mile (*0.6 to be exact*) is the old Springhouse, used when there was a Forest Campground at this location. This is a great spot to have a light snack or lunch.

Return to your vehicle at the Auto Tour sign for more driving along The Mother Road. As you pull out on the road:
ZERO ODOMETER

Back on the road the curve between the auto Tour sign and the cattle guard is the connector **(A074)** between the '21/'31 and the '41 alignment.

0.1 miles - Cattle guard.

0.5 miles (A073) - Entrance to I-40 - **DON'T DO IT!**

0.9 miles (A072) - Double box culvert and point where the '41 alignment (the one you're on) joins up with the '31 alignment (the one you walked). (*Got it?!*)

1.0 miles (A071) -

PARKS

A small community with a history of many names. Originally named Rhodes when the first post office opened in 1898 (later changed to Rhoades), it was changed to Maine in October of 1907 in remembrance of the battleship sunk in Havana, Cuba.

The community operated as a railway stop until the arrival of the highway. At that point, the town moved two miles east, leaving the original townsite as Old Maine (*shown as Maine Station on the National Old Trails Maps of the 1920s*). At the new townsite, a man named Parks opened a store and post office. In 1907, the government realized the people had changed the name from Rhodes to Maine (*ah, you can't fool the government for long*) and officially changed the name to Maine, only to discover there was already a Maine in the Territory. The end result was another name change to Parks, after the storeowner.

The present store building was constructed in 1910 when the original store burned to the ground. The first alignment of the road went behind the building. When the alignment was changed (*the 1931 alignment*) the highway was behind the building, the storeowners took the windows out of what had become the back of the building and moved them to what was to be the front. A roof extension (*the canopy over the gas pumps*) was added.

1.7 miles (A070) - Meadow and remains of cabins, etc. (Could this be the site of Old Maine?)

2.6 miles - Concrete pavement. Take note of the narrow road surface and lack of a shoulder.

3.6 miles (A069) - Garland Prairie Vista Point on the left.

By all means pull over here for a fabulous view of the San Francisco Peaks to the east. This view has been seen in thousands of post cards.

3.7 miles - Asphalt pavement and the Oak Hill recreation area, the original Williams ski area.

5.0 miles - Concrete pavement.

5.5 miles - Hill into Pittman Valley.

6.0 miles (A068) - Double box culvert and asphalt pavement. In the early days, you could find a gas station with tourist cabins along here.

6.6 miles - Great old house on the right.

6.7 miles - Curve to right around Interstate off ramp.

7.2 miles (A066) - Go past the access road to the freeway interchange and make an immediate left onto Deer Farm Road.
DO NOT continue straight unless you have a burning need to visit County Road 74. Route 66 can be found by following Deer Farm Road.

Curve to the right, and you will be back on old 66.

Be sure and stop at the Deer Farm **(A065)**. We spent about an hour (*not really enough time*) walking the grounds and feeding the deer. I made quite a few "friends for life" as I fed the deer.

NOTE: Leaving the Deer Farm west, dirt road lies ahead. If you do not want to travel on dirt, return east and enter I-40 for the run into Williams (exit 165) **(A059)**.

Chicago to Santa Monica

Mexican food) at 1900 N. 2nd Street in East Flagstaff (*been there since the early 1950's*); Miz Zip's (THE breakfast place) at 2924 E. Route 66, and my personal favorite, Jackson's Grill (*take I-17 south to the first exit, then make a left on Hwy 89A towards Sedona, continue for about a half-a-mile, it's on the right*) excellent food, great service, and an amazing wine cellar. One other point - **ALL** Flagstaff restaurants are smoke free! (*Cigarette smoke - not burning bacon...*)

On the west side of Flagstaff, at the junction of Business Route 40 and Arizona 66 (*Barnes and Noble bookstore on the right*) make a right and

ZERO ODOMETER

0.6 miles - Enter the pine forest.

1.4 miles - On the left is the Kit Carson Campground.

1.9 miles - At the top of the hill is Pine Springs, once a major truck stop on the old highway.

3.7 miles - At junction with freeway ramp, continue straight.

4.0 miles - At the sign for the Naval Observatory, continue straight and enter I-40 **(A090)**.

Exit I-40 at Trans-Western Road (exit 185) **(A082)**, make a left and cross Interstate. At the Bellemont sign,

ZERO ODOMETER

Cross cattle guard and turn right **(A083)**. This is the 2nd alignment of the old highway. There are three alignments along this section, the 1st - the National Old Trails Road alignment - is south, and the 3rd is beneath the Interstate. On your left, across the tracks is the Navajo Army Depot, formerly called the Navajo Ordnance Depot, it was one of the largest munitions storage areas in the U.S. during the Second World War.

0.5 miles (A084) - To the left is a dirt road that leads to what is left of Bellemont. About a quarter of a mile down this road, on the right **(A085)**, is the original alignment of The National Old Trails Road (early Route 66), the cut through the trees to the west **(A086)** shows the alignment of the old highway.

BELLEMONT

Named after Belle Smith, daughter of F. W. Smith, superintendent of the Atlantic and Pacific Railroad in 1882. Formerly called Volunteer for a militia encampment at this location in 1863. Volunteer Spring became a water stop for the railroad with the construction of two water tanks.

Straight ahead on the 2nd alignment watch for potholes as the road is deteriorating rapidly. The road will go for 2.5 miles and ends at I-40 **(A087)**, which can be seen through the trees.

Return to the Trans-Western Road intersection **(A083)** and go straight across (heading east).

ZERO ODOMETER

0.5 miles - Grand Canyon Harley Davidson and the Roadhouse Cafe on the left - great place to get that new H-D T-shirt.

0.7 miles - Cross box culvert.

1.3 miles - Old Whiting Bros. gas station on the left. The motel portion of this site was constructed with wood from powder boxes taken from the army depot.

1.6 miles - Pine Breeze Inn - (*Yes, that's a backward "Z" on the west side of the building*) station and old cabins. Part of *Easy Rider* was filmed here.

1.7 miles - Box culvert.

1.9 miles (A088) - Road ends at I-40 embankment. Turn around and return to Trans-Western Road.

NOTE: Dirt road ahead as you continue west on the old alignment. If you prefer not to travel on dirt, join I-40 at this location and exit at Parks (exit 178) **(A073)**.

Cross I-40 **(A082)** and make a left onto the frontage road and:

ZERO ODOMETER

2.0 miles (A081) - Curve to right. Behind you, at this point, the old highway crossed over to the south side in a straight alignment.

2.4 miles (A080) - Auto-Tour sign. One of the many signs placed by the Forest Service. As you pull back onto the road,

ZERO ODOMETER

1.3 miles - Cross cattle guard and begin dirt section.

There are spots with pavement underneath.

1.5 miles - Box culvert.

2.4 miles (A079) - Brannigan Park.

The road climbs through the forest, and, if you look closely, you can see where the original road twisted back and forth, across this well maintained and straightened road.

railroad, the name was changed in 1886 (*to date no reason for the name Winona has been found except for anecdotal evidence from Mrs. Myrtle Adams in 1924, "Winona was just another name"*). The original site of Winona is a little north of the existing location. It is said that Billy Adams opened the first tourist court in the country here in the 1920's.

Just north of Winona is a closed bridge on the right side of the road. This bridge was used in the movie *Forrest Gump* when Forrest (Tom Hanks) was running across the country.

The original alignment of Route 66 went north from Winona to Camp Townsend (on Hwy 89), then west to Flagstaff. This road is all new pavement with little of the old road flavor left, a detour for the hard-core Roadie only.

Time for a side trip! After all that Interstate, how about some very old pavement for boredom relief?

Leaving Winona, you can continue on to Camp Townsend but the best route is to continue west on the Interstate, where we will get off and take old 66 into Flagstaff.

Back on I-40 (westbound).

Exit 204 - WALNUT CANYON (A092)
Take this exit and continue straight ahead. Walnut Canyon is to the left.

As you pass the bridge to eastbound I-40,

ZERO ODOMETER
0.4 miles - Cross a cattle guard and continue straight. You are now on a concrete road surface - this is Old Route 66 into Flagstaff.

0.7 miles - Railway bridge.

1.0 miles - Road curves to left. Straight ahead is Mt. Eldon, off to the left are the San Francisco Peaks, the highest point in Arizona.

Notice the low cinder hill on the right that is slowly disappearing as volcanic cinders for maintaining secondary roads, and also for ice control on the paved roads in the winter are taken from the mountain.

1.8 miles - Rain Valley Road to the right.

3.1 miles - Arizona Department of Transportation yard and a change in the road surface.

3.7 miles - The backside of the Flagstaff Mall.

4.2 miles **(A091)** - At the goofy intersection make a left to join Highway 89 and enter East Flagstaff (*also known as Sunnyside*).

FLAGSTAFF
Film-makers Jesse Lasky and Cecil B. DeMille were disgusted with New York weather and headed west. The train stopped in Flagstaff and the combination of clear air, spectacular mountains and natural beauty made them decide to stay. This is where they would make movies! Suddenly, out of the north came a cold wind, followed by an icy rain and soon snow covered the ground in a white blanket. The two men, without a word to each other or anyone else, loaded their gear on the next train and continued west. Perhaps there are some good things to say about those sudden weather changes in the northland of Arizona.

The history of Flagstaff covers the names of virtually every explorer, surveyor and adventurer of the last two hundred years. But it was during 1876 when the act that would give Flagstaff its name took place. Numerous stories abound, so I'll recount the most popular one: On July 4th, a group of scouts, awaiting settlers coming from Boston, camped at F. W. McMillan's site alongside the spring. To celebrate the Independence Holiday the scouts stripped a huge pine tree of its branches and tied an American flag to it with strips of rawhide. In the ensuing days, they laid out a townsite, but the arriving settlers were disappointed with the soil quality and moved on. The huge flagpole became well known all the way from San Francisco to Santa Fe and travelers were told, "Travel straight west until you come to that flagstaff."

It was to be 1880 before Flagstaff took on an air of permanence when the railroad established a camp near the spring. By 1886, Flagstaff had become the largest city between Albuquerque and Los Angeles on what would later be the Santa Fe railroad. Lumber, cattle, tourists, the college (*now Northern Arizona University*) and the railroad have been major influences throughout the life of this mountain town.

DINING AND LODGING
Follow Route 66 (*formerly Santa Fe Avenue*) through town and you will see many old motels lining the north side of the street. Lodging can be a crap shoot with the majority of the older motels not being well maintained (*or having their sheets changed*) - best bet in town on 66: the Best Western Pony Soldier at 3030 East Route 66 (800-356-4143), an early 1960's era property that has been very well maintained (*in fact renovations were taking place during the Spring of 2002*). For one of the finest hotels between Chicago and L.A. check out Little America located at exit 198 on I-40, beautiful grounds, fantastic rooms, and a world-class restaurant make this an absolute treat. Near Interstate exits 198 and 195 (*north side of the interstate*) are many chain motels. My personal suggestion: take exit 195 and check out the chain motels in this vicinity - much nicer than those at exit 198. For dining: The Western Gold Dining Room in the Little America Hotel; Buster's (excellent seafood) at 1800 S. Milton Road; La Fonda (Great

Leaving Winslow westbound **(A098)** you will see the old pavement on your right. It is not accessible - a gate at exit 245 blocks the road.

About 1.2 miles beyond exit 245 on I-40 you can see the frontage road curve off to the right. At that location, was the Hopi House Trading Post.

Exit 239 - METEOR CITY (A097)

The road that heads west out of Meteor City is Old 66, but it deadends a short distance ahead. This road can be seen on your left (westbound) from I-40.

Back on I-40, just before the Rest Area (milepost 235), you will cross a bridge over the railroad tracks, off to the right and down you can see the old alignment of 66. This section is on private land and is not accessible.

Exit 233 - METEOR CRATER (A096)

Just beyond the gas station/RV Park/Curio Shop is where Old 66 went through. To the right and left is private land and it is posted. To the left you could travel the old pavement for 1.5 miles. This will bring you to the backside of the Rest Area (*there is no access to the Rest Area from this road*).

The large rock tower on the hill was the old Curio shop and Observatory for Meteor Crater. It was possible to view the crater from a telescope mounted in the tower.

If you have never visited the Meteor Crater, I suggest you do so. It is an interesting and educational side trip.

Back on I-40 the old alignment of 66 can be seen off to the left, following the pole line. The road is on private land.

Exit 230 - TWO GUNS (A095)

A right will take you out to Canyon Diablo, once considered to be the toughest town in the territory. However, the road is extremely rough and not recommended for passenger cars.

A left will take you across the interstate to Two Guns. A right, and if the gate is open, you can drive the old highway alignment to where the station, cafe and tourist attractions were located.

Two Guns is an example of a place built strictly to attract the tourist. Clinging to the rocky edge of Canyon Diablo are numerous small buildings. The building with "Mountain Lions" painted on the front was a small zoo. Walk through the arch and down the steps toward the canyon. Parts of the old cages are still backed up against the bluff. Across the canyon can be seen more rock buildings and structures. The old bridge spanning the canyon was the original alignment of Route 66, the alignment was changed to the road you came in on and the Canyon Diablo bridge for the new alignment can be seen from Milepost 230 on I-40.

If you choose to explore this are, **BE VERY CAREFUL!** Do not attempt to walk across any of the old wooden walkways that span the small canyons, or explore the caves under the various buildings. All of these things were built many years ago and their condition has deteriorated.

Two Guns was named for Two-Gun Miller, who claimed to be an Apache. He killed a neighbor during an argument and was acquitted. Friends of the dead man put "Killed by Indian Miller" on the grave marker. Two-Gun Miller did not take kindly to the epitaph, so he added his own to the marker. He was jailed for defacing a grave. Two-Gun lived for years in a cave alongside Canyon Diablo and didn't give a damn about anyone but himself.

A stop at Two Guns will take you on a mind trip back to what travel along old Route 66 must have been like. A stop at Two Guns was an adventure. The mountain lions, bobcats and coyotes were indeed sad looking behind their chicken-wire enclosures, but to a kid from Illinois or California, Two Guns was the real West.

This place is a tremendous example of what people will do to make a business succeed. As you wander the grounds and look at the buildings, you can only marvel at the amount of rock moved to build this place.

Back on I-40 and at milepost 230 cross Canyon Diablo, off to the left can be seen the second bridge built to span Canyon Diablo on Route 66.

Exit 219 - TWIN ARROWS (A094)

A once popular truck stop with a cool diner. Twin Arrows has been closed for quite a few years and will probably never reopen. Take a photo under the Twin Arrows, they may soon be gone.

As you leave Twin Arrows to re-join I-40, notice the building to the east. This was the site of Toonerville, an old tourist stop. The owners were murdered during a robbery. A construction company presently uses the building.

Just west of Twin Arrows, the road crosses Canyon Padre and the landscape changes dramatically. We are entering the juniper and pine region and beginning the climb to Flagstaff.

Exit 211 - WINONA (A093)

Made famous by Bobby Troup in his song, "Get Your Kicks On Route 66." Winona was originally called Walnut by the

Chicago to Santa Monica

2.8 miles - A feed store, but the concrete teepee gives it away as once having been a Route 66 business.

3.0 miles - Ella's Frontier - An old trading post that has seen some major vandalism. There were signs announcing Ella's as The First Trading Post On Route 66 as well as other things of historical (*Roadie-wise*) significance that have been stolen or destroyed.

Return to the I-40 crossover.

Cross the freeway **(A103)** and make a right on the frontage road.

ZERO ODOMETER

1.1 miles (A102) - A slight jog to the left puts you back on the original alignment of 66. If you stop here and look backwards across the Interstate, you can see where the road lines up with the pavement across the Interstate.

1.5 miles - You are now on the old road surface.

4.5 miles (A101) - Here it is! Jackrabbit, Arizona.

JACKRABBIT

"Here it is!" The signs used to tease us for hundreds of miles in either direction and now we're here. Built in 1947 by James Taylor and Robbie Robinson, Jackrabbit has served the traveling community for over half a century. This was a kids "must stop" on the annual vacation trip. Be sure to have your picture taken on the huge Jackrabbit out front - he's not the original, that one had to be replaced after a million kids and a few hundred cars had their way with him. Oh yeah, don't forget to have a cup of Cherry Cider. (*What is that stuff?*)

Rejoin I-40.

Exit 264 - HIBBARD ROAD (A100)

This used to connect along the old highway to Winslow, but in 1994, the bridge across the Little Colorado (4.6 miles ahead) was closed and all road maintenance discontinued. There is now a gate across the road and access to the old road is denied.

Exit 257 - AZ 87 AND HISTORIC ROUTE 66 (A099)

Make a left and cross the Interstate and at bottom of ramp is the intersection with Old 66. A left will take you about a half a mile down to the Minnetonka Trading Post.

The outside, front wall of the trading post is made entirely of petrified wood. Inside, the east room was originally a line shack built by the Hash Knife Outfit.

A right at the intersection will take you into Winslow.

WINSLOW

A name dispute exists for this city. One claim was by prospector Tom Winslow who, in 1920, claimed Winslow was named for him, the other is the claim it was named in 1881 for General Edward F. Winslow, president of the St. Louis and San Francisco Railroad and was associated with the Atlantic and Pacific Railroad. (*I'll take the railroad story over a prospector (!) anyday...*)

An area about three miles north of town, known as Sunset Crossing, had been in use for years as one of the few safe crossings on the Little Colorado River, a Mormon settlement, Sunset was on one side of the river and a fort known as Brigham City was built at on the other in 1876. By the early 1880s, the Mormon's had given up trying to master the Little Colorado River.

With the coming of the railroad and establishment of a terminal, Winslow became a railroad town. Frederick C. Demerest set up a tent to do business with the roadbed laying crews, and by late 1881 he was well established as Winslow's first businessman. He built the Arizona Central Hotel on Front Street.

While in Winslow, stop and have your picture taken at 2nd and Kinsley. This is "*The Standin' on the Corner Park*" and what better place to have your picture taken while, "Standin' on a Corner in Winslow, Arizona (- *What a Fine Sight To See - It's a Girl, My Lord, In A Flatbed Ford - Slowin' Down To Take A Look At Me...*").

Just up the street at 212 Kinsley is the Old Trails Museum. A small but packed-to-the-rafters collection of what makes Winslow a special place. Janice Griffith, museum curator and her staff of volunteers have done a tremendous job of preserving the heritage of the town, the railroad and Route 66.

One of the gems of the city is the La Posada, the beautiful Fred Harvey Hotel designed by famed southwestern architect Mary Colter, who was the Fred Harvey Company chief architect and interior designer from 1902 to 1948 (*for more on Mary Colter read,* Mary Colter-Builder Upon the Red Earth *by Virginia L. Gratten*). The La Posada has been saved and has undergone extensive restoration. Rooms are open in the hotel (928.289.4366) and the restaurant is once again a delight, with food and service in the impeccable manner of the old Fred Harvey operation. It is suggested that you make the La Posada Turquoise Room a must for lunch or dinner if you are not staying at the hotel (*hint: try the Prickly Painted Desert Warm Bread Pudding for an amazing desert treat*). **Other lodging**: Best Western Adobe Inn at I-40 exit 253 and Holiday Inn Express at exit 255. **Dining:** Since Pete Kretsedemas sold The Falcon it has become a crapshoot - go to the La Posada and treat yourself.

Chicago to Santa Monica

Just past the Goodwater on-ramp (westbound), you can see Old 66 climbing the hill to your right. This is on private, fenced land with no access either from here or up ahead.

Between mileposts 300 and 299 off on the right, you can see the bridge culverts for the old road.

Exit 294 - SUN VALLEY (A109)

If you follow Sun Valley Road north from the Interstate to Pima road, you will be on Old 66. The road surface has been completely reworked and there is no hint of the old pavement or highway. Looking west from this intersection, you can see the old alignment going across the plains.

Exit 292 - INTERNATIONAL PETRIFIED FOREST, MUSEUM OF THE AMERICAS, AND DINOSAUR PARK (A108)

What a mouthful, but a great place to visit. All those dinosaurs alongside the highway are a clue to what lies through the gate and in the museum. (*Note that this is a private development and not affiliated with the US National Park Service, which operates the national park nine miles east of here.*)

Exit 289 - HOLBROOK (A107)

Once a rough and tumble cow town Holbrook was named after H. R. Holbrook, the first engineer of the Atlantic and Pacific Railroad. The county seat of Navajo County Holbrook carried the odd distinction, until 1914, as the only county seat in the country without a church.

A visit to the Holbrook Wild West Museum is a must. The exhibits are fascinating, showing the life of settler and cowboy alike. Another must see is the old jail in the basement of the museum. Shipped from the east as one solid unit in 1899 at a cost of $3,000 the jail was used until 1976. A walk through the jail gives you the creeps. It is dark, cold and with a sense of isolation and fear such a place was designed to inspire.

The Holbrook of today is no longer the bustling town of Route 66 days. The streets are quiet, but busy, good food can still be had at Romo's, and Julien's Roadrunner Gift Shop offers up Jackalopes (*no kiddin'*), beautiful jewelry and the largest collection of vintage signs on the road. Another unique treasure in Holbrook is the Wigwam Motel **(A106)**. The invitation to "Sleep in a Wigwam" was every kid's wish on the northern Arizona stretch of Route 66. Opened in 1950 and fully renovated in 1988, the Wigwam has kept pace with the times. The rooms are small, but clean, and a treasure of the heyday of the highway. Call in advance of your visit at 928-524-3048 to make certain the motel is open and to make reservations. Other lodging: Best Western Arizonian Inn - Ramada Limited - Holiday Inn Express. Dining: El Rancho - Butterfield Stage Company - Mesa Italiana.

A short section of Old 66 can be found on the west end of town by making a left (westbound) just past the new park and rest area. Follow that with a right and you are on old 66 for about a mile before the road ends at the embankment for I-40.

Back to I-40 **(A105)** at the west end of town.

The Cholla Power Plant looms to the west. There is something about the ponds east of the power plant, with steam rising from them, that bring to mind three-eyed, purple fish, with hands - too many late night movies I guess. (*Way too many...*)

Exit 277 - JOSEPH CITY (A104) At top of ramp, turn right and
ZERO ODOMETER

Originally founded in 1876 as Allen's Camp (*or Allen City, Allen Camp or Allen's City*) for William Coleman Allen, a Mormon pioneer sent by Brigham Young to establish colonies in Arizona. The first names proposed were Cumorah along with Ramah (*locations mentioned in the Book of Mormon*). In February of 1878, the name was changed to St. Joseph, and the railroad soon requested a change because of the St. Joseph on the rail line in Missouri, the name was changed to Joseph in October of 1878 and to Joseph City in December of 1923. Joseph City is the only survivor of four small Mormon settlements along the Little Colorado River. The other three settlements were Brigham City (originally Ballinger's), Sunset (originally Smith's Camp), and Obed (originally Lake's Camp). Joseph City is also the oldest community in Navajo County.

Today, Joseph City quietly goes about its business with little regard for the passing of Route 66. Things disappear along the Mother Road and if you don't take time to photograph them . . . At the northwest corner of Main and Shelly had been a station and store. It was in bad shape, but now it is gone, a vacant field replacing the building - and I never caught it on film. There are still a couple of old buildings at the corner of Main and Richards and the Pacific Motel and Cafe sit across the road from each other and both are closed. Quick, get out the camera!

The main street through town was Route 66.

0.6 miles - Historical marker erected in 1952 by the Daughters of Utah Pioneers tells how Joseph City was founded and that it is the oldest Mormon community in Arizona.

1.5 miles - The Pacific Cafe and Motel sit across the road from each other, harkening back to the days when 66 was a viable entity. Closed in 1992.

2.3 miles - This is where you turn left to cross the freeway **(A103)**, but first, go straight ahead. We will come back here.

right and past the large radio tower is Old 66, the extension of the road you were on that ended at the Dead River. This road is closed to the public, so please honor the signs. However, if you were to receive permission to drive down this road, you would soon be back on the pavement of Old 66 and, sitting off in the distance, you would be able to see The Painted Desert Trading Post standing alone and forgotten on the rise above the Dead River.

Continuing through the Monument, you will come to Tiponi Point, Tawa Point and Kachina Point, the Painted Desert Inn stands on Kachina Point.

The Painted Desert Inn was built by Herbert D Lore in 1924. The building had a lunch counter, an Indian Trading Post and Lore's home. Lore had a one way loop road cleared that connected the Inn to Old Route 66 (This loop road went down to the intersection). The loop road ran along the rim of the Painted Desert, much as the today's road.

The Inn was purchased by the government in 1936, and the CCC (*Civilian Conservation Corps*) set to work enlarging it. Many problems were encountered in the new construction, and it was 1938 before work moved to the interior of the building. Flagstone and oak flooring were laid, the walls plastered and furniture made. The furniture designs were provided by Park Architects and included Indian designs carved into the heavy pieces.

By July of 1940, the Inn was opened for business and through October of 1942 the Inn was a popular place with more requests than space for the six guest rooms that featured a double bed and fireplace. WW-II closed the Inn.

After the war, the Fred Harvey Company took over, and in 1948, a series of improvements were underway. A well-known Hopi artist, Fred Kabotie, performed his magic and produced the murals that may be seen in the snack bar and dining room.

During the 50s and on into the 60s, the Inn developed structural problems because of the bentonite clay beneath. In 1975, the Inn was placed on the register of Historic Places and is now a National Landmark.

Continuing through the park, you pass many other viewpoints of the Painted Desert. About six miles into the park and just before the Interstate, you will see a line of telephone poles. If you stop here, you can see the scar left by Old 66 as it passed through the park. The Park Service removed the road surface, but the line of the old highway is still there. Looking west from here, you can see off in the distance, beyond the Interstate, Route 66 rising on the hill, a frontage road to I-40. At the base of that hill is a wrecking yard, we'll learn more about that in a bit.

Across the Interstate and beyond the railroad tracks is the entrance to the Petrified Forest. At the Puerco Indian Ruin is where the Park entrance used to be located. **VERY IMPORTANT** - remember to take only pictures - no petrified wood - and leave only footprints. (*The park museum maintains a "Guilt Box" display case containing letters of apology and pieces of petrified wood taken illegally - only to be returned years later - sometimes in response to a deathbed request. You don't want to end up on your deathbed worrying about pilfered petrified wood, so just explore the area and appreciate the beauty!*)

Indian lore of this area tells of a tired goddess who cursed the area. She was hungry and tired when she discovered the logs lying on the ground, she killed a rabbit and tried to light a fire. The logs were soaked through and would not ignite. In her anger, she turned the logs to stone.

This forest was formed over 170 million years ago when large reptiles and amphibian beasts roamed the area. The valley, which covered parts of Utah, Texas and New Mexico, filled with water and giant trees floated into the low lying swamp, and were eventually covered with over 3000 feet of soil. The trees turned to stone by the action of mineral rich soil replacing the tree cells. During the period when the Rocky Mountains were formed, the ground was lifted to the point it is today, and erosion by wind and water exposed the "logs."

Back on I-40.

Exit 303 - ADAMANA ROAD (A111)

Exiting here will result in your having to return for continued travel. Cross under the freeway and go to the south side of the Interstate, the Painted Desert Indian Center is to the right.

Heading back east from the Painted Desert Indian Center, the frontage road is Route 66. This is a great section of road to drive. It is still in excellent shape and it gives you a feel for the later alignment and how if followed the land instead of cutting through it. Five miles down this road is Rocky's Old Stage Station **(A112)**. The site of an old stage stop built in the 1880s and was home to Nyal Rockwell from 1954 when Route 66 was a bustle of activity within a few feet of his door. In 1965, I-40 forever changed his life. The government cut him off completely. The cabins could no longer be rented and the cafe served no one. On the property is a National Old Trails Highway sign erected in the 1920s by the Automobile Club of Southern California to guide travelers along the way. As you drive back up the hill from Rocky's, pause before the top and look back at the road that was once the Main Street of America. You can see the scar of the old alignment as it cuts across the Painted Desert Monument as well as the fence that cut Nyal Rockwell off from the world. (*Rocky and his wife held on there for 30 more years, scraping out a living by running a salvage yard and used car business. It didn't have to be that way...*)

Return to Adamana Road and rejoin the Interstate.

Exit 300 - GOODWATER (A110) - Do not exit.

Chicago to Santa Monica

Continue on I-40.

Exit 325 - NAVAJO (A115)

About three miles southeast of here is Navajo Springs, the site of the first encampment in Arizona Territory. The date was December 29, 1863. The territorial gubernatorial party camped here in a blinding snowstorm after being assured by their military escort that Navajo Springs was in Arizona. They had a dinner of antelope, freshly killed, and toasted the establishment of the new territory with champagne. The flag was raised and John C. Goodwin took the oath of office and became the first Governor of the new Arizona Territory.

Side trip! From here it is possible to trace some old, long abandoned sections of the road, but only if you are driving a high clearance vehicle. The road begins just south of Navajo **(ATA51)** and will take you west and under the freeway to the Pinta Road junction **(ATA41)** (*which actually begins an Adventure Tour!*) and you will re-join I-40 at Exit 320 (Pinta Road) **(A114)**.

Otherwise, back on I-40.

Exit 320 - PINTA ROAD (A114)

ADVENTURE TOUR

Please read all admonitions regarding Adventure Tours at front of this book

This section covers a stretch of Old 66 that features the Painted Desert Trading Post, a classic bridge across the Dead River and ends at the boundary of the Petrified Forest/Painted Desert. The road is rough in spots with sections of old pavement (complete with white line), and dirt. Can be traveled in a standard vehicle at a slow pace.

CAUTION NOTE: If it has been raining, or is raining, be aware there are sections of mud between I-40 and the old pavement. To avoid getting stuck, drive on the high sides of the road and **NEVER** venture into a puddle.

To join this section, take Exit 320 (Pinta Road) (A114) from I-40 and proceed to the North. Follow the road as it curves to the east then back to the north. At the point where the pavement ends:

ZERO ODOMETER

1.0 miles (ATA41) - This is where Pinta Road crosses old 66. Make a left onto the old pavement.

NOTE: Once you cross the fence line to reach Old 66, you are on Navajo Nation land. Respect the land and remain on the road.

1.4 miles (ATA42) - A box culvert.

1.8 miles (ATA43) - Another culvert.

3.6 miles (ATA44) - The remains of the Painted Desert Trading Post. Graffiti artists (*also known as vandals*) have been at work on the façade of the building. This is a great photo opportunity location.

3.8 miles (ATA45) - Bridge across the Dead River. The old cars dumped on the east side of the river were placed there as a form of erosion control to keep the river from undercutting the bank and washing out the bridge abutments.

3.9 miles (ATA46) - Ranch house to the right. Respect the no trespassing signs.

The road ahead is overgrown with weeds, but driveable. Thanks to the Park Service putting in a well up ahead this section of the road is once again open to travel (it had been closed at the Dead River crossing for seven or eight years).

5.2 miles (ATA47) - A metal culvert is visible on the left side of the road.

5.4 miles - Pavement actually ends (curious!).

5.6 miles - Fairly rough for the next .2 of a mile, watch your speed.

6.2 miles (ATA48) - Boundary line of the Petrified Forest/Painted Desert. Turn around here and return to Pinta Road, then back to I-40.

Exit 311 - PAINTED DESERT AND PETRIFIED FOREST (A113)

A turn-off here will provide you a look at the true wonders of nature at work. The Painted Desert is a marvel of color, constantly changing as the day and the seasons pass.

For the Route 66 buff, the old road can be seen about a half mile north of the park entrance gate. The road going off to the

Chicago to Santa Monica

ARIZONA
WESTBOUND

You may enter Arizona on Old Route 66 from Gallup, or on I-40. As you enter Arizona the road surface goes from so-so to What the Hell! If using the Interstate, take the Lupton exit **(A132)** and backtrack to Mile "0" on the north frontage road. Then:
ZERO ODOMETER
    0.2 miles (A133) - The Teepee Trading Post. A sixty foot tall concrete teepee (*tipi*) has drawn tourists for years to buy souvenirs and to have a meal upstairs, in the top of the teepee (*at this writing the café is closed - no big loss, the food was just so-so*).
    0.3 miles - Make a left and pass under I-40 **(A132)**.
    0.4 miles - Make a right onto the old highway. This is Lupton **(A131)**. Originally a cattle town, now supported by tourists. Named for G. W. Lupton, the trainmaster at Winslow in the early 1900s.
    0.7 miles - Trading post on the right. The road is paralleling the Interstate. Notice how the road follows the lay of the land instead of blasting its way though the hills.
    4.6 miles - A closed building on the left appears to have been a trading post or restaurant. Keep your eyes open for livestock on the road. This is open range country.
    5.9 miles (A130) - Make a right and cross under I-40 in one of the two tunnels (suggest right one) to the 1931 alignment on the north side of the Interstate. This is a great old section of road as it dips and rises following the lay of the land.
    8.3 miles (A129) - Indian City and the site of Allentown. Continue west on the frontage road (Old 66).
    10.3 miles - Housing subdivision. Lots of billboards for Fort Courage - The Home of F- Troop!.
    11.3 miles (A128) - Fort Courage (*No, kids, F-Troop was not filmed here, another internet legend*). Continue on frontage road.
    12.1 miles (A127) - Low spot, warning sign not to cross when flooded. **BE CAREFUL!**
    13.2 miles (A126) - Access to I-40 at Exit 346 (Pine Springs Road).
NOTE: The road ahead is packed dirt. It is well maintained and passable, but if you would rather not travel on dirt, rejoin I-40 here and continue to Exit 339 (Sanders) **(A118)**.
    13.3 miles (A125) - Pavement ends.
    13.7 miles (A124) - The Good News Church.
    14.1 miles (A123) - The New Querino Trading post, large metal building on the right.
    14.6 miles (A122) - On the right, the remains of the old Querino Trading Post, and the bridge across Querino Canyon.
    16.9 miles (A121) - Pavement returns as frontage road.
    17.4 miles (A120) - Turn left and return to I-40 at Exit 341 (Ortega Road) **(A119)**.

Exit 339 - SANDERS (A118)
    Named for an early trader in the area.
    After exiting:
ZERO ODOMETER
    Continue on north frontage road.
    1.3 miles - Houses on right.
    2.3 miles - Abandoned car wash.
    3.3 to 3.5 miles - Garage, junkyard and the Appaloosa Corral Bar.
    3.9 miles - I-40 curves to left.
    4.9 miles - Garage on left.

CHAMBERS
    Named after Charles Chambers, trading post operator at this location from the late 1870s through 1888. In 1926, the name was changed to Halloysite (*a mineral used in the manufacture of expensive china and mined in the area*). Renamed Chambers in 1930.
    6.1 miles (A117) - Intersection. Make a left and go to I-40. The frontage road, to your right, will end with an abandoned gas station and church on the right.
    Across I-40 is the Best Western Chieftain Inn, a nice motel and good restaurant.
    Rejoin I-40 here **(A116)** and continue west. Just past the McCarrel Road exit the old highway goes around a hill on the left (south side of I-40). This part of the road is on private land and has been fenced off.

Chicago to Santa Monica

Chicago to Santa Monica

GALLUP

Named for Santa Fe paymaster David L. Gallup and founded in 1881. Gallup terms itself The Gateway to Indian Country and the proliferation of Native American jewelry, pottery, art and rug manufacturers attests to that title.

Gallup was home to one of the most unique Harvey Houses in the country, the El Navajo. Designed by famed architect Mary Jane Colter, in a native pueblo design, the El Navajo became the social center of the Gallup area. Opened on May 26, 1923 the El Navajo was a beautiful structure. Alas, declining rail passenger traffic forced an economic decision (*with no regard for the historical significance of the building, unlike Needles California, which resolutely holds on to the El Garces despite not knowing exactly what to do with it*) to close the El Navajo in May of 1957 and the building was destroyed shortly thereafter.

Gallup abounds with restaurants, cafes, and lodging facilities. The following are my choices - Best place to stay - The El Rancho Hotel. A living piece of history as the Home of the Movie Stars. Be sure to stay in the hotel, if possible, and not the newer motel section. The rooms are named for movie stars and the mezzanine has hundreds of autographed photos. The lobby is a thing of beauty. A true Mother Road classic and a Roadie thanks to Armand Ortega for his restoration of this Queen of the Road. Most of the classic motels suffer from disrepair, so if the El Rancho is not your choice consider the Best Western Inn and Suites on east Route 66; the Micro-Tel Inn, off exit 16; and the Days Inn West, also exit 16.

One of the finest restaurants in Gallup is Dominic's, located downtown at 302 W. Coal Avenue - excellent Italian food in a pleasant atmosphere. Great Mexican Food can be had at Virgie's on the west end of town. A good breakfast, in an old diner atmosphere, is available at the Plaza Cafe (1501 W. 66), and a good steak can be had at Butcher Shop Restaurant. Fast food cannot be beat at Blake's Lottaburger on the east side of town.

Leaving Gallup on the west end, at the underpass for I-40 **(N013)**,

ZERO ODOMETER

0.5 miles (N012) - Mentmore Road on the right.

3.5 miles (N011) - Stop sign. Straight ahead the old highway will dead-end in 0.6 miles. Make a left to cross under I-40, narrow tunnel so watch for traffic.

3.8 miles (N010) - Make a right.

4.7 miles (N009) - Follow road around the State Truck Inspection Station.

8.0 miles (N008) - Entrance to I-40 on right, continue straight.

8.3 miles (N007) - Cross under I-40.

8.5 miles (N006) - Bridge over railroad tracks.

9.2 miles (N005) - Turn off to Manuelito.

11.5 miles (N004) - St. Catherine's Mission on the left. (*Certain high-quality Route 66 maps show this to be the location of Manuelito, perhaps "Old Manuelito".*)

13.5 miles (N003) - This is the spot that started me on his search for The Mother Road. At this site, in 1950, Billy Wilder brought Kirk Douglas, Jan Sterling, and a large crew to film *Ace in the Hole* (re-titled *The Big Carnival*). A local trading post, Lookout Point, was used in the filming and a group of cliff dwellings were built into cliff in the background (the one with the large split at the top). In 1953, the Atkinsons sold the trading post to the Christensens who renamed it Cliff Dwellings Trading Post and they capitalized on the ersatz cliff dwellings. Today, nothing remains of the trading post or the cliff dwellings.

15.7 miles (N002) - Crumbling remains of a small concrete shack on the right. This was the site of the old Box Canyon Trading Post.

16.2 miles (N001) - Fort Yellow Horse Trading Post on the right. Two Guns Miller of Two Guns, Arizona fame, established this trading post.

16.5 miles - New Mexico/Arizona State Line.

time and money.

The landscaped median along Santa Fe Avenue (old Route 66) has been adopted by various businesses as a point of civic pride and the effort has paid off in beautifying the town.

At the west end of town, as you cross over the railroad tracks **(N034)**,

ZERO ODOMETER

Cruising this section of highway can be truly enjoyable. Traffic on the Interstate is racing along, fighting the trucks and each other to get "there" first (*and then do what? watch more television?*). You will most likely be all alone, cruising at a comfortable speed and not having to hassle the traffic.

MILAN (N033)

A rather new town, incorporated in 1957, and named for Salvador Milan a landowner through his wife Veneranda Mirabal whose father had large holdings in the region.

7.5 miles (N032) The Bluewater Motel ruins.

7.7 miles (N031) - Bluewater. The Bluewater Trading Company is decorated with murals.

9.4 miles (N030) - Junction with NM 606.

10.7 miles (N029) - Divided highway ends.

12.6 miles (N028) - The Route 66 Swap Meet, operated by Thomas Lamance. A few thousand license plates offer a glimpse into the past, along with a barn full of collectibles.

17.6 miles (N027) - Prewitt. Trading post at this site started by Robert C Prewitt, Sr.

28.2 miles (N026) - Thoreau. Originally named Mitchell, name was changed with the arrival of the Santa Fe. Likely named after Henry David Thoreau. Pronunciation of the name varies, most often heard is "threw."

The town lies north of Route 66 on NM 371. It is the home of Frontier Buckles, the manufacturer of the huge buckles worn by Rodeo champions. Also, the Zuni (*zoo-nee*) Mountain Kachina Company is located here, one of the largest manufacturers of Kachinas in the nation.

33.5 miles (N025) - The Continental Divide. This is the separation point for the waters of the continent. Rain (*and beer...*) that falls east of here winds up in the Atlantic. Rain (*and beer...*) to the west flows to the Pacific. There are a few trading posts and gas stations remaining, but long gone is the Top O' the World, a dance hall, bar, tourist court, trading post and boarding house for railroad men. The Top O' the World was one of those places with a rather dingy reputation, sort of like "the old roadhouse out on the highway."

Contrary to popular belief, at 7,263 feet, this was not the highest point on Route 66. For post-1937 highway design, that honor belongs to the stretch between Brannigan Meadow and Parks, Arizona at 7,414 feet. For pre-1937, the honor belongs to the Glorieta Pass area near Pecos, NM at just over 7500 feet. The highest point on I-40 is the Arizona Divide - just west of Flagstaff - at 7,335 feet.

It will be necessary to westbound rejoin I-40 here.

Exit 44 COOLIDGE (N024) - Named for a director of the old Atlantic and Pacific Railroad. A pair of righthand turns will take you back east for 0.3 miles to a dead-end. The buildings at the top of the rise were Fred Wilson's Trading Post. Back at the intersection continue straight, past the abandoned building at the low point then up the hill. At the 0.5 mile point is the old Navajo trading company. Straight ahead is the entrance to I-40.

Exit 39 - The huge Giant Truck Stop on the right offers good food and other necessities.

Exit 36 - IYANBITO (N023) - Exit here. When you're at the end of the off-ramp and back on the old highway into Gallup:

ZERO ODOMETER

1.5 miles (N022) - Iyanbito, church mission, right.

2.0 miles (N021) - Old foundation on the left is the site of the Perea Trading Post.

3.3 miles (N020) - Junction with NM 400 and entrance to I-40. Continue straight on NM 118.

5.9 miles (N019) - Entrance, left, to Fort Wingate Army Depot. Originally established as Fort Fauntleroy, the name was changed to Fort Lyon when General Fauntleroy joined the Confederate Army (*Talk about goin' South!*). In 1868, when the Navajos returned to the area, troops were moved from the original Fort Wingate at San Rafael and the post was renamed Fort Wingate. General Douglas MacArthur was born here in 1880 and General Blackjack Pershing served here. In 1918, the Army Ordnance Department took over the fort for munitions storage.

6.4 & 6.5 miles (N018) - Cross railroad tracks.

7.3 miles (N017) - The road to Red Rock State Park. A wonderful museum here tracing Southwest Native American Culture. Also rodeo grounds in a natural amphitheater at the base of red rock cliffs.

8.7 miles (N016) - Sundance road, right.

10.2 miles (N015) - New Mexico State Police, right (new location, older was back down the road a bit on the right).

10.8 miles (N014) -

Chicago to Santa Monica

At the middle school in Laguna **(N052)**, make a right and
ZERO ODOMETER
    1.1 miles (N051) - Cross bridge. In 1952, a gas truck went off the road here and plunged into the arroyo. The resulting fire closed Route 66 for twelve hours.
    1.3 miles (N050) - Junction with old road into Laguna, make a left.

LAGUNA
    Spanish for lake, which has long since disappeared. The church here is one of particular beauty. This is the church used in the Kirk Douglas film *Ace in the Hole* (re-titled *The Big Carnival*). Kirk rushed here to pick up a priest and take him back to the site of the cave-in.
    Winding around the hill at Laguna will lead to the village of New Laguna at milepost 4.2.
    7.0 miles (N049) - Paraje (*Spanish - place, or stopping place*), a Laguna tribal village. Old trading post has a new addition (2002), a painting of the robot Bender from the series TV *Futurama*, and an excellent painting by the way. A left at the intersection will take you to Acoma Pueblo, the Sky City (13 miles).
    This is an interesting side trip and should not be missed. However, there are some stringent restrictions placed on tourists. You must buy tickets at the Tribal Center, then board a bus for the tour to the pueblo. Photography is permitted only if a permit has been purchased for EACH camera in use. Waits can be rather extensive for the busses, so plan sufficient time for your visit.
    8.5 miles - A group of stone buildings on the right could be the remains of an old motel.
    9.5 miles - Access to I-40, continue straight.
    10.8 miles (N048) - Budville. Named by Bud Rice, whose father built the first garage here in the 1920s. Bud, along with his wife Flossie, ran the top towing business in the country (*and held court as the local justice of the peace at night - speeding tickets anyone?*). Bud was murdered during a hold-up in 1967 and in 1979 Flossie sold the wrecker and closed the garage doors.
    Side trip! A right here will take you on a short loop through Cubero on the 1937 alignment.
    12.2 miles (N047) - Villa de Cubero. A gas station, tourist court and general store. This is where Ernest Hemingway supposedly worked on *The Old Man and the Sea*. Across the road was Gunn's Cafe, a place renowned for good food and friendly service.
    12.8 miles (N046) - On the left was Obie's Longbranch Saloon, on the right, the long abandoned Mt. Taylor Motel.
13.1 miles (N045) - A right here will take you to Sky City Casino, half-a-mile south - if you're into that sort of thing.
    15.3 miles (N044) - San Fidel. Originally La Vega de San Jose. Name was changed at the suggestion of Father Robert Klath. Post office established 1919.
    18.5 miles (N043) - Cross over I-40.
    20.2 miles (N042) - McCarty's. Named after a contractor who occupied site during construction of the Santa Fe Railroad. Also known as Santa Maria de Acoma. This is the site of a beautiful replica, on a smaller scale, of the church at Acoma Pueblo. Built in 1933, the church is considered to be an architecturally pure example of Spanish colonial style.
    Driving west from here the old road twists and turns to avoid the lava beds. This area was known as The Malpais or evil country. The highway engineers had to swing the road around the lava beds because the construction equipment of the '30s was not modern enough to allow them to go straight through.
    24.9 miles (N041) Cross under I-40.
Continue to the top of the hill and make a right on NM 117 (old 66) **(N040)**.
    27.8 miles (N039) - Bridge over the railroad tracks and cruise on into Grants **(N038)**.

GRANTS
    The railroad arrived and with it the name of the town. The Grant brothers, Angus, Lewis and John were Santa Fe railroad contractors who maintained a site called Grants' Camp at this location. Also known as Grants' Station and prior to 1881, Alamitos. Post office was established as Grant in 1882 and the name finally changed in 1936.
    A true Route 66 town, Grants offers many older motels along East Santa Fe Avenue, and unfortunately many of them are in poor condition. The best of the older motels is The Sands at 112 McArthur St **(N037)** (*a block off of 66 and quiet*). For more contemporary lodging consider Best Western Inn & Suites of Gallup and the Holiday Inn Express both at exit 85. One warning about accommodations in Grants: A few of the motels at the Interstate exit offer attractive rates on their signs, but once inside the story is, "We're sold out of those rooms," this took place at one in the afternoon with two cars in the lot. The rooms that are available are priced as much as forty dollars higher than the sign. This story has been the same since my first overnight stop in 1990 (*have checked back in '92, '93, '96, '98, '99, '00 and '01 and received the same line every time*). Good food can be had at the Uranium Café **(N036)** (across from the Mining Museum) where the Yellow Cake pancake more than covers the plate and if you can eat two of them they are free! (*Remember the 72-oz free steak contest in Amarillo? If you flunked that one, you get a "second chance" here...*)
    A must stop in Grants is the Mining Museum. A recreated hard rock mine, underground, awaits you. A tour well worth the

suggested that for overnight plans, communities such as Gallup, Grants, Moriarity, Santa Fe, Santa Rosa or Tucumcari be the choice of the Mother Road traveler. For a true New Mexico experience, however, Santa Fe cannot be beat.

Two routes exist out of Albuquerque:
The Las Lunas Option (immediately below) is the earlier routing, pre-1937. This route travels south along the Rio Grande River before swinging west.
The Nine Mile Option (see farther down below) is the later routing, west on Central Avenue, past Old Town, across the Rio Grande, and west up Nine Mile Hill to join I-40.

LOS LUNAS OPTION
To follow the old route, turn south on 4th Street from Central **(N070)**, (this is a left turn heading west and a right turn heading east) and follow it to Bridge Blvd **(N069)**. Make a right and cross the bridge, then make a left onto Isleta Blvd, Hwy 314 **(N068)**. Follow this south into Los Lunas. In Los Lunas, make a right onto NM 6 **(N067)** and

ZERO ODOMETER
Continue out of town and cross I-25 **(N066)**. This is the pre-1937 routing of 66. The route was changed in 1937 to climb Nine-Mile-Hill, and oddly enough, that route - prior to Route 66 - was NM 6.
Climb out of the Rio Grande Valley and notice how the landscape changes.

5.5 miles (N065) - Top of the hill. Pull over, get out of the car and look back at the wonderful view of the valley.
6.7 miles (N064) - Cross over the railroad.
7.4 miles (N063) - Bridge ruins to the right.
12.5 miles The old road meets the new. Do not attempt to drive this section. Many bridges have been removed, stay on the "high" road and look for the old highway to the left.
26.1 miles (N062) - Large canyon on the right. Great view.
30.8 miles (N061) - Suwanee (originally San Jose).
32.8 miles (N060) - Crossroads at Correo (*Spanish - mail*), so named because it was the only place for many miles where mail could be dropped. Post office established in 1914. Also shows on some of maps as Suwanee (originally San Jose), 1902, which was just east of this location.

A right at this crossroads will take you on a short section of the second alignment of Route 66. This was the post-1937 alignment. A gate prevents travel beyond this short section, but the road can be seen heading off to the northeast.
If you don't mind traveling dirt roads, it is possible to follow the old alignment into Mesita. (*If you would rather not travel on dirt, stay straight on NM 6 to I-40* **(N059)**, *then west to exit 117 - Mesita* **(N057)**.)
To travel the old alignment, make a left at the crossroads and over the bridge. Across the bridge are the remains of an old trading post. It is 11 miles from here to Mesita **(N056)** and the road traverses a land that is changing once again as you enter a desert full of color. (*Along the way, you will cross over I-40* **(N058)** *but this is not an interchange.*)

NINE MILE HILL OPTION
Continue west on Central Avenue through the city. As you approach Old Town there are quite a few older motels with cool signs. Cross the Rio Grande and start the climb up Nine Mile Hill, at the top of the hill enter I-40 westbound **(N075)**.
As you come down the hill towards Rio Puerco, a short stop to photograph the old bridge is worth the time **(N076)**. This bridge was built in 1933 and, at 250 feet, is the longest single-span Parker Through-Truss bridge in the southwest. It was saved through the efforts of the New Mexico Historic Route 66 Association and others working together to hold on to a classic piece of highway architecture.

NOTE: Ignore the large "Historic Route 66" sign at exit 126 **(N059)** - this will lead you back in a circle to the east on NM 6 to Los Lunas and Albuquerque. (*You would find yourself in a permanent loop - trapped forever on the same section of Route 66, a real Twilight Zone experience, for sure!*)

MESITA
Leave I-40 at exit 117 - Mesita **(N057)**, and turn right to the old road junction **(N056)**. Make a left and

ZERO ODOMETER
The five miles of road from Mesita to Laguna - although one of the most picturesque little sections of Route 66 - winds around the mesas and buttes with a few sharp curves and one steep hill. Imagine driving this road, at night, in the rain, with a few hundred other cars, trucks and buses.

1.9 miles (N055) - Owl Rock on the right.
2.6 miles (N054) - Deadman's Curve. The road turns 180 degrees here.
4.0 miles (N053) - Old Route 66 comes in on the left. Do not drive it!
4.6 miles - Laguna

Chicago to Santa Monica

Clair's snake pit and tourist trap.

On the west end of town, just past the Route 66 Shopping Center and the Rip Griffin Truck Stop **(N114)**, make a left, followed almost immediately by a right and curve around to the old road. You are now back on Route 66 and
ZERO ODOMETER

6.1 miles - An abandoned store and cafe on the right, barely visible are the words, "Kathy, NM" on the front of the building. There is no mention in any reference to Kathy, NM. Another mystery of The Mother Road.

6.6 miles - On the right, in the midst of an equipment rental yard, stands a castle tower. The dream of a man named Kline. All anyone knows is he built and lived in the tower while gathering stone for the rest of the castle. One day he walked away, and the tower now stands as a memorial to another unfulfilled dream.

7.6 miles - Edgewood - A once busy shipping point for Pinto Beans, Edgewood is now a bedroom community for Albuquerque, along with being the headquarters of a religious sect known as the Blackstockings.

11.2 miles - "Route 66" High School visible on right.

11.5 miles - Barton - Named for a local settler, post office established in 1908 and closed in 1936.
From here the road begins to climb.

14.4 miles (N113) - Sedillo - An old trading location named after Pedro de Sedillo who arrived in New Mexico prior to the Pueblo Rebellion of 1680.

17.6 miles (N112) - Zuzax - Now just a sign on the Interstate, but once this was the site of a bustling trading post serving everything from stuffed rattlesnakes to the infamous Cherry Cider. (*What is that stuff?*) The buildings were surplus barracks from Kirkland Air Force Base and a bright yellow Cadillac with the word ZUZAX painted on it beckoned to Route 66 traffic.

It was 1972 when I-40 eliminated the trading post, but the name lives on. What does Zuzax mean? Nothing, it was the creation of Zuzax founder Herman Ardans who wanted something short and faintly Indian sounding for his new tourist attraction in 1954. Kind of like George Eastman and the word Kodak.

19.6 miles (N111) -

TIJERAS

(*Spanish - scissors.*) The name was thought to have been inspired by the canyons. Actually, it was named after a family who lived in the area in 1856. The post office was established here in 1888.

The remainder of the trip down the canyon offers wondrous views and appreciation of the art of road construction. The canyon was so difficult to cut through and the rock so solid that over a thousand charges of dynamite, set off at one time, resulted in a clean-up of less than twenty minutes.

20.2 miles (N110) - Left onto NM 333.

20.9 miles (N109) - Cross NM 337.

23.4 miles (N108) - Cross under I-40.

25.7 miles (N107) - I-40 access, stay on NM 333.

On the left, as you make the final run down the canyon, is a riding stable that was once a country and western night club run by Dick Bills. His nephew, Glen Campbell, would occasionally take a turn at the microphone.

27.7 miles (N106) - Tramway Road, continue straight across onto Central Avenue for the trip across

ALBUQUERQUE

Founded in 1706 by Don Francisco Cuervo y Valdes and named San Francisco de Alburquerque (*yes, the first "r" belongs there*). This city along the banks of the Rio Bravo del Norte (*the name of the Rio Grande at the time*) was named after Don Francisco's patron saint, Francisco Xavier and the Duke of Alburquerque, the Viceroy of Spain. If you have ever wondered why Albuquerque is known as The Duke City, there is your answer. Almost immediately a problem arose with the name. King Philip V of Spain had not been consulted about the name, so to prevent problems the Viceroy changed it to San Felipe de Alburquerque. Somewhere along the line the first "r" was dropped (*or maybe it fell off*) and the name of the city as we know it today came into being.

The Santa Fe Railroad reached the city in 1881, and the year before, the city, called New Albuquerque was platted two miles east of the present Old Town in preparation for the arrival of the railroad. The first mayor was elected in 1885 and the city was incorporated in 1890.

In 1902, one of the classic Harvey Houses along Route 66 was built. The beautiful Mary Jane Colter designed Alvarado served the traveling public with food and lodging in the Fred Harvey tradition, while the fantastic Indian Building displayed and sold only the finest in Native American arts and crafts. Ignoring the historic significance of this building, the shortsighted officials of the city allowed the Alvarado to be destroyed in March of 1970.

Albuquerque is a large city and as such does not offer much for the hard-core Roadie. Gang crime is a major problem in the city with tourists quite often being the victims (*those iron fences and gates around the motels aren't purely for decoration*). It is

the intersection with Alameda Blvd:
ZERO ODOMETER
- **1.5 miles** - Ranchitos Road.
- **5.4 miles** - 4th Street jogs slightly left.
- **5.9 miles** - Cross under I-40.

At Lomas and 4th Street (**N073**) in downtown Albuquerque, make a right onto Lomas, followed by a left onto 6th (**N077**) to Central Ave (**N078**).

At the intersection with Central Ave, it's time for a decision:

A right turn will put you on the final alignment of Route 66 out of Albuquerque, and up Nine Mile Hill (*see Nine Mile Hill Option below*).

A left will lead you back to 4th Street where can follow the pre-1937 alignment through Los Lunas, to the south of Albuquerque. See Las Lunas Option following the Albuquerque section (*Be sure to read it!*) at the end of the description of the Post-1937 Alignment. (*Got all that? There will be a quiz in 10 minutes!*)

POST 1937 ALIGNMENT TO ALBUQUERQUE

Continue west on I-40 to:

Exit 252 - Rest Area (N118)
On the north side of the Interstate bridge can be seen, below, a partially covered old Route 66 bridge. The old road is still visible next to the fence line. The road to the Rest Area also crosses an old bridge and just past the entrance to I-40 on the west end, the old highway can be seen heading up the hill. This section ends 0.8 miles ahead.

Exit 218 - CLINES CORNERS (N117)
An example of perseverance in action. Roy Cline built his first station in a town called Lucy (on US 60 between Willard and Vaughn), but he could not make a go of it. So he had the station moved (literally) to Highway 6 (later to become 66). With the paving of the highway, Roy bought the land at the junction of 6 and 2. In 1937, the road moved north with the new alignment, so Roy moved the station again. One more time the state moved the highway east and renamed it 285. The station followed and finally settled at the junction of Hwy 285 and I-40 (part of Route 66 still exists in front of the station).

Cline's Corners has a gift shop full of what author Jean Shepherd called, "Great American Slob Art." I do not recommend the cafeteria.

Exit 203 - LONGHORN RANCH (N116)
The crumbling remains of The Longhorn Ranch are on the south frontage road (old 66). This was a favorite stopping place for Route 66 travelers, as well as being a Sunday diversion for people from Albuquerque, back during the time when we all took Sunday drives.

The Longhorn Ranch had a Wild West Museum, gas station, curio shop and hotel. There were rides in a genuine stagecoach and an authentic "Old West" atmosphere that was difficult to pass-by.

From here east is the Llano (*yawn-no*) Estacado, or Staked Plain (*not a literal translation*), stretching to Texas. An area so barren that is was said men drove stakes into the ground at regular intervals to guide travelers across the desolate landscape.

Route 66 dead-ends in both directions from the Longhorn Ranch.

Exit 196 - MORIARTY (N115)
Named after Michael Timothy Moriarty, a local rancher who came to the Estancia Valley in the early 1880s seeking a cure for rheumatism. Post office was established in 1902.

A curious point here. The original (1937) alignment through here ran two miles north of Moriarty and intersected with NM 41 at a spot called Buford. (Named by H. Crossley after his infant son Buford.) The townsite east and north of Moriarty was owned by Crossley. Today, Buford is a part of Moriarty, but early maps, the WPA Guide to New Mexico, and the Rittenhouse Guidebook all make reference to it.

Moriarty has a wonderful museum operated by volunteers. Many older motels, gas stations and cafes spread along the stretch of the wide, wide Main Street that was Route 66. The true heart of Moriarty lies not on old Route 66, but south on NM 41 about a mile. Here are the early buildings of the community where business was conducted prior to the arrival of the highway.

Lodging suggestions: Classic - The Sunset Motel; Modern - Holiday Inn Express.

One of the old tourist traps can still be seen along the old highway about three miles east of town. Take NM 41 north to the first dirt road on the right, take this road around a house and barn and it will put you on Old 66. Three miles east is the site of John

Chicago to Santa Monica

2.0 miles - Cattleguard and fenceline.
2.5 miles **(ATN77)** - Short stone column on left. Odd.
3.4 miles - Cattleguard and fenceline.
3.5 miles - Cross under power lines.
5.6 miles - Cattleguard and fenceline.
6.3 miles - Junction with sign.
6.8 miles - Ranch road to the right.
7.5 miles **(ATN76)** - Fork in the road. One branch goes to the left. Main road goes straight ahead.

The right branch of the fork goes straight ahead and continues to follow the power lines to the top of La Bajada Hill. This branch is the original Mother Road, with all the switchbacks ahead. (*You wouldn't believe you were heading for the top of a hill, given how flat the road is, but you will soon see what all the talking is about!*)

The left branch follows an alignment around the mountain instead of straight up the mountain and is more gradual. The historic significance of this fork is not known but if you follow it you will see evidence of modern activity such as fiber optic cable markers as well as old rock walls. So, is it a later version of Route 66?

The downside to the left fork is that the road is very rough (much worse than the right fork) and almost impassible at one point where it took the author 45 minutes to move 8 feet.

Whichever way you decide to go, at the fork,
ZERO ODOMETER
Right branch route:
0.5 miles **(ATN74)** - Top of the hill. Park your truck and look around for a knockout view of the flatlands below. Just as you arrive at the edge, you will pass the foundation of a ruined building, on the left.

Look overhead to see how the power lines go down the mountain. That is general direction you will be following, as the towers parallel the road. Note the very heavy-duty design of the towers. The winds blow very fiercely here.

Many switchbacks follow with slow going as you cross washouts and boulders.

0.6 miles - Fenceline
1.3 miles - Permanent impassible washout. The washout must be bypassed by going around on the right by making one steep leap off the Mother Road onto the bypass.
1.4 miles **(ATN73)** - Junction with left branch road.

Left branch route:
0.8 miles **(ATN75)** - Fenceline and top of the hill.
0.9 miles - Very difficult washout, almost impossible to navigate. May require winching.
1.2 miles - Moderate washout
1.3 miles - Rock wall below.
1.5 miles - Fenceline and old style gate. Be sure to close it behind you.
1.6 miles - Major washout.
1.7 miles - Major washout.
1.8 miles **(ATN73)** - Junction with right branch road.

Once you have reached the junction of the two branch roads (using either branch),
ZERO ODOMETER
0.1 miles - Rock wall.
0.2 miles - Rock wall.
0.4 miles - Major washout. You will see tire tracks leading to the left to get past the roughest part of the washout. Follow them and rejoin the washout where it eases up a bit.
0.6 miles - End major washout.
0.8 miles **(ATN71)** - Bottom of the hill and a hard left onto the dirt road leading away from La Bajada. (This is where Option 2 and Option 3 Roadies turn around and return to the junction with NM 16 **(ATN68)**).

It is up to you to whether to follow Option 2 or Option 3 from this point south to Algodones. Check out the descriptions of the two options to help you make the decision. **Note:** If you have a vehicle capable of doing La Bajada Hill, the dirt roads on Option 3 will be a piece of cake!

Continuation of text following all La Bajada Hill options:

Follow NM 313 through Algodones, Bernalillo and Sandia Pueblo. The road will curve to the right and become 4th Street. At

Chicago to Santa Monica

10.9 miles (**ATN52**) - Stop sign, and right turn towards Algodones. You are now leaving the San Felipe Indian Reservation.
11.3 miles (**ATN51**) - Algodones Power Plant
Continue south on NM 313 to Algodones. You will pass the road leading to I-25 (**N074**).

Jump to "**Continuation of text following all La Bajada Hill options**" for further directions.

OPTION #4

This is a "Black Route" Adventure Tour and is the most challenging of any on Route 66, bar none. Fasten your seatbelts, campers, you're in for a ride!

ADVENTURE TOUR

Please read all admonitions regarding Adventure Tours at the front of this book.

It is still possible to make the drive down the old road by high clearance four-wheel drive vehicle. (Or, as was done in 2001, a climb by bicycle in a combination ride and carry mode. See Route 66 Magazine, Winter 2001/2002.)

The general admonitions for Adventure Tours all apply to La Bajada, but there are some additional requirements also:

1. The road is largely a rock wash and is not maintained in any fashion. There are parts that will leave you with the impression you are doing cross-country rock-hopping.

2. A high-clearance four-wheel drive is required. However, there are limitations on the type of four-wheel drive vehicle that can be used on La Bajada. The most successful traverse is done with a short and narrow (yes, short and narrow!) wheel base truck/SUV. The reason is that there are a number of places where the road is narrow, and you have to creep along one side or the other to bypass a difficult washout. High-centering is not nearly the problem that width is - consequently the short/narrow recommendation.

3. The side-slope of the roadway is generally well supported. You can thank your ancestors for having constructed the un-mortared flatrock retaining walls that endure to this day. You will see the walls along the way and they will evoke great respect from you.

4. The dry-weather requirement was never so important as on La Bajada. The presence of 60-90 degree cuts on the uphill side of the road is an unending source of rockslides and wet weather is one of the demons that starts them rolling.

5. You must be physically fit enough to pick up, move, or re-position large rocks at 6000 feet above sea level. Unless you have done this before, you have no idea how exhausting heavy labor is at this altitude.

6. There are no trees to speak of next to the road, so winching your way out of difficulty will not be an easy proposition. Large boulders can occasionally substitute but you may find yourself digging a deadman for the winch cable.

7. There is no water on the La Bajada road. Bring plenty for yourself and your truck.

In Santa Fe, at the junction of NM 300 and Cerrillos Road (**N081**), turn right onto NM 300 and
ZERO ODOMETER
   3.2 miles - Junction with NM 599. Go straight.
   4.0 miles - Santa Fe sewage treatment plant.
   5.7 miles - Cattleguard and fenceline.
   6.4 miles (**ATN79**) - Junction with County Road 56C. Turn right and
ZERO ODOMETER
   0.6 miles - Cattleguard and fenceline.
   1.1 miles (**ATN78**) - Go straight ahead as road changes to dirt. The paved road leads to a mine entrance on the right.
   1.5 miles - Short-cuts ahead on the right. It can seem kind of confusing here, with all the roads seeming to go in different directions, but if you drive reasonably straight south, you'll do fine.
   1.8 miles - Junction with ranch roads.

Chicago to Santa Monica

Upon reaching the junction, turn left onto NM 16 and return to I-25 **(ATN72)**.

Take I-25 south and continue to exit 248 - Algodones **(N079)**. After leaving the freeway, turn right at the end of the ramp and go 0.4 miles to the junction with NM 313 **(N074)**. Turn left and you will be back on Route 66 for the trip into Albuquerque.

Jump to "**Continuation of text following all La Bajada Hill options**" for further directions.

OPTION #3

Continue on Cerrillos Road and enter I-25 **(N080)** for approximately 14 miles to to Exit 264 - NM 16 **(ATN72)**. Follow NM 16 west approximately 3.5 miles to the turn-off to Tetilla Park Recreational Area **(ATN68)**.

At the junction, if you look to the south - along the power line - you will see the original track of Route 66 next to the power line. This is a fenced off section and not open to the public. Also, take a minute to read the nearby historical marker explaining the phenomena of the La Bajada escarpment.

Turn right (north), and

ZERO ODOMETER

Follow the road towards the recreational area.

2.0 miles (ATN69) - Unmarked turn-off to the right. Turn onto the well-maintained dirt road.
2.2 miles - La Bajada switchbacks visible on the cliff, dead ahead.
2.4 miles (ATN70) - Cool bridge.
2.5 miles (ATN71) - Just past the bridge, there is a hard right onto the dirt road up La Bajada. This is where Option 2 and Option 3 Roadies turn around and return to the junction with NM 16 **(ATN68)**. (*Option 4 - the Black Route Adventure Tour - begins here for the die-hards!*)

At the junction, Route 66 lays straight ahead beyond the fence line (*as noted above*), so you will begin a detour at this point. Upon reaching the junction, turn right onto NM 16 and

ZERO ODOMETER

1.4 miles (ATN67) - Conchiti Indian Reservation boundary.
3.4 miles - Turn-off to Conchiti Dam spillway.
5.4 miles (ATN66) - Junction with NM 16. Turn left and proceed south.
6.6 miles (ATN65) - Pena Blanca post office and well-maintained church.
7.5 miles (ATN64) - Enchanted Farm entrance. Interesting brickwork.
10.8 miles (ATN63) - Left turn, just before overpass leading to I-25. Sign indicates turn-off to Domingo and Santo Domingo pueblo. Follow the inclined curve down to the stop sign **(ATN62)**. Route 66 is the highway that crosses in front of you.

Turn left onto the road to Domingo. (Santo Domingo is a right turn.) As you make the left turn

ZERO ODOMETER

0.2 miles - Water tower.
0.4 miles (ATN60) - Town of Domingo. Ruins of Domingo Trading Post, which billed itself as the oldest trading post in the West circa 1881. (*1881? Oldest in the West? Oh well, the Old West is the land of b.s.*) Great picture taking opportunity.
0.5 miles (ATN61) - Bridge destroyed. Must have been a heck of a flood. End of the line for this section of Route 66. The old road crossed the river and headed up the hill onto a long flat mesa. Turn around and head south down the highway to the Santo Domingo pueblo. As you cross under the I-25 access overpass **(ATN59)**,

ZERO ODOMETER

0.6 miles (ATN58) - Stop sign in center of Santo Domingo pueblo.
0.8 miles (ATN57) - Odd pavement change, right in the middle of Santo Domingo pueblo.
1.1 miles (ATN56) - Another odd pavement change.
1.9 miles - Cross wash, improved with concrete pad. Keep an eye out for wandering cows and dogs in this neighborhood.
2.6 miles - Cross wash, improved with concrete pad.
3.1 miles - Cross wash, improved with concrete pad.
4.0 miles (ATN55) - Well-paved road ends, seemingly out in the middle of nowhere. Actually, you have just crossed out of the Santo Domingo pueblo and the road improvement is defined by the pueblo boundary.
4.3 miles (ATN54) - Cross railroad tracks.
5.2 miles - Cross wash.
5.9 miles - Cross under power line.
6.3 miles - Cross irrigation aqueduct.
6.7 miles - Graded road ends. Washboard road ahead.
7.9 miles - Cross wash. Graded road begins, but becomes pavement as you enter San Felipe pueblo.
8.2 miles (ATN53) - Stop sign in San Felipe pueblo. Go straight.

Chicago to Santa Monica

> **NOTE:** If you plan to tackle La Bajada Hill. It is strongly suggested you take some time to read all of the information from this point to Algodones (approximately 28 miles south of Santa Fe) in order to make decisions regarding your trip. In general terms, the north end of the La Bajada area is in Santa Fe, beginning at Cerrillos Blvd, near the Santa Fe airport **(N081)**. The south end is in Algodones **(N074)**, near the turn-off to I-25 exit 248). Modern day Roadies have four options, with Option 2 recommended for most travelers:.

OPTION 1 - By-pass La Bajada entirely by joining the Interstate in Santa Fe for the trip to Algodones. (This option is listed first only because the directions are the simplest.)

OPTION 2 - Use I-25 and paved NM highways to get to the base of La Bajada Hill, look up at it in wonder and disbelief that people ever managed to traverse it, and then re-connect to I-25 to get to Algodones. This option uses paved roads for its entire length except the last 1.4 miles which are on a well maintained dirt road that is very comfortable to drive as long as you are in dry weather. (*If you're squeamish about the last 1.4 miles, you can still see the La Bajada switchbacks in the distance from - you guessed it - 1.4 miles away!*)

OPTION 3 - This is a "Red Route" Adventure Tour designed to keep you as close as possible to the original pre-1937 alignment into Algodones. This option requires dry weather. First, you will use I-25, paved NM highways, and a short section of well-maintained dirt road to get to the bottom of La Bajada Hill (*where you can stare up in amazement*). Then you will follow paved highways and maintained dirt roads into Algodones.

The route will take you into Indian reservations that tourists rarely travel to. There are some roadside services scattered along the way but the endemic poverty and social difficulties of some of the smaller Indian tribes will be readily apparent. Please conduct yourself with appropriate restraint, as the customs of their lives can be something of an enduring mystery to outsiders.

NOTE: For the adventurous, you can first follow the Mother Road south from Santa Fe to the top of La Bajada Hill and look down onto the Mother Road but you will have to backtrack to Santa Fe to continue.

To do this, follow the directions listed for the first part of La Bajada Option 4 (below). The road is flat (good!) but not very well maintained (bad!). You won't get "stuck" in dry weather but you will have to pick and choose your way across the mesa. The reward is a knockout view of the road and New Mexico stretching out before you.

OPTION 4 - The first part of this option is really more like a "Red Route" Adventure Tour, as noted above in Option 3. But the second part is a very demanding "Black Route" Adventure Tour that includes special precautions described below. (*Note: Even if you don't take this option, you will undoubtedly gain an appreciation of the challenge simply by reading the instructions!*)

OPTION #1

Continue on Cerrillos Road and enter I-25 **(N080)** for approximately 28 miles to exit 248 - Algodones **(N079)**. After leaving the freeway, turn right at the end of the ramp and go 0.4 miles to the junction with NM 313 **(N074)**. Turn left and you will be back on Route 66 for the trip into Albuquerque.

Jump to "**Continuation of text following all La Bajada Hill options**" for further directions.

OPTION #2

Continue on Cerrillos Road and enter I-25 **(N080)** for approximately 14 miles to to Exit 264 - NM 16 **(ATN72)**. Follow NM 16 west approximately 3.5 miles to the turn-off to Tetilla Park Recreational Area **(ATN68)**.

At the junction, if you look to the south - along the power line - you will see the original track of Route 66 next to the power line. This is a fenced off section and not open to the public. Also, take a minute to read the nearby historical marker explaining the phenomena of the La Bajada escarpment.

Turn right (north), and

ZERO ODOMETER

Follow the road towards the recreational area.

    1.0 mile (ATN69) - Unmarked turn-off to the right. Turn onto the well-maintained dirt road.

    2.2 miles - La Bajada switchbacks visible on the cliff, dead ahead.

    2.4 miles (ATN70) - Cool bridge.

    2.5 miles (ATN71) - Just past the bridge, there is a hard right onto the dirt road up La Bajada. This is where Option 2 and Option 3 Roadies turn around and return to the junction with NM 16 **(ATN68)**. (*Option 4 - the Black Route Adventure Tour - begins here for the die-hards!*)

Chicago to Santa Monica

For instructions on driving through Santa Fe, see **DRIVING INSTRUCTIONS** below.

SANTA FE
    The capital city of New Mexico, Santa Fe is known as "The City Different" truly lives up to its name as one of the most charming cities along Old Route 66. Founded in 1609 as La Villa Real de la Santa Fe de San Francisco (*The Royal City of the Holy Faith of Saint Francis*), it has been a capital city for nearly 400 years. The flags of four nations - Spain, Mexico, the Confederacy, and the United States have flown from atop the Palace of Governors, the oldest capitol in the country. To walk the streets of Santa Fe is to experience history at virtually every turn. The soft, earthen hued beauty of adobe is everywhere while a cool fall evening will bring the smell of pinion pine wafting on the air from hundreds of fireplaces in the homes where hollyhocks line the patios. This beautiful location at the foot of the Sangre de Christo (*Blood of Christ*) mountains was selected, in 1610, by Don Pedro de Peralta, the first governor with the intent of being a walled city surrounding a palacio as the seat of government. In 1821, Mexico won its freedom from Spain and Santa Fe became the seat of the Mexican government in the northern territory. In 1846, General Kearny marched troops into Santa Fe and with the name "New Mexico," the territory became a province of the United States when the U.S. flag was raised over the Palace of Governors. In 1862, the Confederate flag flew for just over three weeks from March 10th when General Sibley marched into town trying to find a storehouse for his supplies. On January 12, 1912, New Mexico was admitted to the Union as the forty-seventh state and Santa Fe became the capital of New Mexico.

    LODGING: Lodging in Santa Fe varies from the mundane (Motel 6) up to the finest accommodations you can imagine. For that "Old Route 66 Classic Motel" I feel it is hard to beat the El Rey Inn at 1862 Cerrillos Road (505.982.1931) - a beautifully maintained (with lovely gardens) motel of the old school (dating back to the early 1940s). A more contemporary motel, and one close to the Plaza, is Garrett's Desert Inn at 311 Old Santa Fe Trail (505.982.1851), a nicely maintained 1960's property. Two of my favorite hotels are the Hotel Loretto, 211 Old Santa Fe Trail (*which has recently undergone a multi-million dollar restoration - 505.988.5531*) and The Inn of the Anasazi, 113 Washington Ave (505.988.3030). I should mention that the majority of the chain motels are south on Cerrillos Road.

    DINING: Dining in Santa Fe can be an amazing adventure in experiencing the fantastic tastes of New Mexican cooking. Around every corner there are wonderful cafes and restaurants to tempt the gourmet hiding in each of us. The taste of Santa Fe can truly be enjoyed at Chef Mark Miller's Coyote Café, 132 Water Street (*the menu is prix fixe and reservations are required at 505.983.1615*). The Pink Adobe, housed in a 300 year-old adobe building, is as much a marvel of ambiance as the food is a delight to the palate, located at 406 Old Santa Fe Trail (across from the historic Mission San Miguel). Reservations are suggested at 505.983.7712. For excellent breakfasts, try the Guadalupe Café at 422 Old Santa Fe Trail, and if pizza tempts you for lunch the best in New Mexico can be found at Upper Crust Pizza, 329 Old Santa Fe Trail. One thing about Santa Fe - the competition for fine dining is so fierce you are virtually guaranteed an excellent meal wherever you choose to dine.

    Shopping in Santa Fe is an adventure into the world of art and beauty with over 200 galleries. Canyon Road is the major gallery row while Old Town Santa Fe hosts five excellent galleries. A few of the more intriguing galleries are: Thirteen Moons at 652 Canyon Road, specializing in the Art Quilt; The Gaugy Gallery, 418 Canyon Road, devoted to the work of Jean-Claude Gaugy whose style is a sculpture/painting known as "linear/expressionism"; and Kiva Contemporary Art, 102 East Water St, specializing in Native American art.

DRIVING INSTRUCTIONS THROUGH SANTA FE
    To drive Old Route 66 through Santa Fe, follow the Old Santa Fe Trail into the heart of the city. Just across the Santa Fe River, make a left onto Water Street **(N084)**, followed in four blocks by a left onto Galisteo **(N083)** that will jog slightly to become Cerrillos Road **(N082)** leading south out of the city.

NOTE: There are Historic Route 66 signs directing a right turn on Bishops Lodge Road into the Plaza - these are not correct - Route 66 never entered the Plaza. The problem with this routing is that if you do enter the Plaza, there are no signs directing you back out to Historic Route 66. If you find yourself in this situation, make a right off of Bishops Lodge Road onto Palace Ave, go one block to Cathedral Place and make a right, go two blocks to Water Street and make a right, then five blocks to Galisteo and make a left. Galisteo will merge into Cerrillos Road. Continue on Cerrillos Road.

    Ahead lays the infamous La Bajada Hill - one of the major obstacles for the early Route 66 traveler was La Bajada (*Spanish - the descent*) Hill, a volcanic escarpment that neatly separates the North Rio Grande Valley from the South Rio Grande Valley with a 500-foot drop. The original road, built by the Army in the 1860's, featured mind-numbing 28 percent grades. Workers from the Cochiti pueblo and the state penitentiary improved the road beginning in 1908. Considered an engineering marvel when completed in 1922, the new road featured 26 switchbacks, a much improved eight percent grade and dropped the 500 feet in less than two miles. A large sign at the top of the hill warned, "This road is not fool proof, but safe for a sane driver." In 1932, the road was moved about three miles to the east (present location of I-25) and the old switchbacks abandoned.

Chicago to Santa Monica

tion below marked Santa Fe Loop Option.

Continuing straight on I-40 will follow the second alignment (post-1937), straight to Albuquerque. For this route, see the section below marked Post 1937 Alignment Option, which follows the description of the Santa Fe Loop.

My suggestion is that, if time allows, take the Santa Fe Loop to see one of the most enchanting cities in the world.

SANTA FE LOOP OPTION

EXIT 256 (N105) - Vegas Junction
Take exit and head north on US 84. As you connect with 84,
ZERO ODOMETER
    17.5 miles (N104) - Dilia - a great old church here, on the left, just off the highway.
    18.0 miles (N103) - County line.
    34.6 miles (N102) - Los Montoyas, NM (not to be confused with Montoya further east on 66).
    42.0 miles (N101) - Romeoville and junction with US 84 and I-25. Cross over freeway, make a left on the north frontage road and
ZERO ODOMETER
    4.5 miles (N100) - Tecolote, NM - As you leave town, look to the right, old bridge ruins.
    10.5 miles (N099) - Bernal, NM.
    18.4 miles - as you descend the hill, look to the left and you can see the remains of the old alignment and a culvert coming up from San Jose.
    18.8 miles (N097) - Short side trip - make a left to San Jose. Follow the road through San Jose past the town square (*which looks like something from a Clint Eastwood spaghetti western*) and the post office. Go down a short hill (look for the Santa Fe Trail marker on right) to the old Route 66 bridge **(N098)**. (*Keep an eye out on the bridge for the boys from "Deliverance" - if you hear a banjo - leave!*)

Retrace the road back to the highway. Make a left onto the highway and
ZERO ODOMETER
    0.7 miles (N096) - Cross freeway to Sands, NM.
    13.7 miles (N095) - Right off of NM 34 and cross under freeway.
    14.0 miles (N094) - Left onto NM 63.
    14.5 miles - Rowe, NM.
    17.7 miles (N093) - Entrance to Pecos Ruins National Monument (*Damn, some idiot took all of the trees out of the parking lot!*).

When leaving (or passing by) at the park entrance,
ZERO ODOMETER
    0.5 miles - Pecos, NM - Watch for Frankie's Coffee House on the left. Stop for a cup.
    1.0 miles (N092) - Intersection with NM 50, make a left turn onto NM 50.
    1.7 miles - West end of Pecos Village.
    5.8 miles - Adobe building on right.
    7.0 miles - Enter I-25 southbound at Exit 299 **(N091)** and continue to Exit 294 **(N089)**.

Crossing here will be the highest elevation point of Old 66 (Pre-1937) - at Glorieta Pass **(N090)**, elevation is 7525 feet. This should put to rest, permanently, the discussion of where the high points of Route 66 are located. A short review for all you geography students:
    1. Pre-1937 - Glorieta Pass, NM - elevation 7525.
    2. Post 1937 through 1941 - Fortynine Hill (between Parks and Brannigan Park, AZ) - elevation 7414.
    3. 1941 - 1970s - The Arizona Divide (west of Flagstaff) - elevation 7335.

Exit 294 (N089) - Cañoncito
Exit I-25 and continue south on the Old Las Vegas Highway and
ZERO ODOMETER
    3.6 miles - Junction with US 285 **(N088)** - continue straight.
    7.0 miles - Turn off to Camp Stony **(N087)**.

Remain on The Old Las Vegas Hwy to the intersection with The Old Pecos Trail and St. Michaels Dr. (Old Las Vegas Hwy becomes St. Michaels) **(N086)**. Make a right onto the Old Pecos Trail and follow it into Santa Fe. The Old Pecos Trail will become The Old Santa Fe Trail at the intersection with Berger **(N085)**.

Chicago to Santa Monica

CUERVO (N122)
(*Spanish - crow or raven*) A point to turn off for a Mother Road Adventure Tour after exploring the small town. At the west end of town, on the south side of the Interstate is a road that runs west/southwest. If you don't mind broken pavement and have a high clearance vehicle, this is a side-trip not to be missed.

> ### ADVENTURE TOUR
>
> **Please read all admonitions regarding Adventure Tours at the front of this book**.
> To explore this very old section of highway, at the west end of Cuervo (south side of I-40) and just past the underpass, make a right onto the old highway and
> **ZERO ODOMETER**
> The pavement on this stretch is deteriorating badly. Local efforts at patching are keeping the road passable, but watch your speed and the road.
> **2.5 miles - DANGER!** Large washout on right side of road, drive to the left, go slow and you will be fine.
> **5.9 miles** - A large tree on the left is the perfect place to stop. Shut off the engine, take a stretch and listen to the sounds of silence. I once camped at this location and was amazed at the number of stars that could be seen in a sky so black it seemed to envelop me.
> **9.7 miles** - Cross cattle guard (*slow, it is in a hole*) and make a right onto NM 156 for the run into Santa Rosa (about nine miles).

If you would rather not travel this section, rejoin the Interstate and continue to Santa Rosa **(N120)**.

Exit 284 - FRONTIER MUSEUM (N121)
The remains of the Frontier Museum. Once a thriving tourist trap with stores, gas station and museum. Now a sad reminder of the glory days of Route 66.

SANTA ROSA (N120)
Originally named Aqua Negra Chiquita (Little Black Water), changed to Santa Rosa in 1890 by Don Celso Baca after a chapel built in honor of his mother. The valley of the Pecos River brought the railroads (*the Rock Island and the Southern Pacific merged here - but not above the Pecos River as legend tells it*) as a watering spot. The water also sent the railroads packing when it was discovered the mineral content fouled the innards of the steam locomotives.

The Club Cafe was a Route 66 mainstay from 1935 until 1992 when it closed. The building is there, but the fat man signs are gone. The Comet Diner has taken up the slack, offering excellent food at good prices. The Sun 'N' Sand is a great choice for breakfast. Unfortunately, Joseph's (*up the hill*) is not as good as it once was and the service has deteriorated badly. Lodging is best left to the chain operations with many of the older motels suffering from lack of maintenance. Recommendations are either of the Best Westerns in town (The Adobe Inn and the Santa Rosa Inn), the Holiday Inn Express, and the Comfort Inn.

Leaving Santa Rosa, it will be necessary to join the Interstate. As you head west, various sections of the old road can be seen on either side of I-40. We will cover some of the more interesting sections next.

> **NOTE:** Options lie ahead as to how to follow various Route 66 alignments. It is strongly suggested you take some time to read all of the information from this point to Mesita **(N057)** (which is forty miles west of Albuquerque) in order to make decisions regarding your trip across New Mexico. Once those decisions are made you may want to mark out the sections that do not apply to eliminate confusion on the road.

Exit 267 - COLONIAS (N119)
A section of the old highway goes east for 2.1 miles. This side tour allows you to experience how the highway followed the land, while the Interstate was blasted through the hills.

At the junction with NM Highway 84 (Exit 256) **(N105)**, a decision must be made:
Turning north on 84 will follow the first alignment (1926), which will take you through Santa Fe. For this route, see the sec-

Chicago to Santa Monica

18.4 miles (N132A) - Big-ass hole under the freeway, north of the old road. Stop and look! Its I-40's one and only built-in tourist trap attraction! And it's free! Except for the taxpayers. *(Actually, the Rock Island Railroad used to go through there, using a rather unusual underpass design.)*

21.0 miles - Turn right from frontage road intersection **(N132)** and pass under I-40 **(N131)** into

TUCUMCARI

A Route 66 classic. Signs up and down the highway promoted "Tucumcari Tonight! - 2000 Motel Rooms." Also known as the town "two blocks wide and 2 miles long."

Named after Tucumcari Mountain, the flat-topped mountain to the south. The name is one of the mysteries of the West. Legend tells of an Apache maiden, Kari, whose lover, Tocom, was killed by a rival. Upon his death Kari took her life, prompting her father to cry out "Tocom! Kari!" As a point of fact the area is Comanche, not Apache, and the name may be a derivative of the Comanche tukamukaru - to lie in wait for someone or something to approach. This information is based on the mountain being used as a lookout point for Comanche war parties.

City was founded in 1902 following arrival of the railroad. During 1901, the townsite was known as Six-Shooter Siding.

A trip through Tucumcari takes you back to the heyday of Route 66 with the proliferation of motels that still fill the night sky with flaming neon. Few of these motels have been restored to their Route 66 glory and cannot be recommended. A good indicator, if the neon has been restored, then the place is most likely being well maintained. Best classic motel in town is the Blue Swallow **(N130)** (505.461.9849), lovingly restored by Dale and Hilda Baake. The Holiday Inn is one of the better chain motels (*and offers a full breakfast with the room - not just stale rolls and bad coffee*). The Best Western Pow-Wow Inn has long been a Route 66 favorite, dating back to the 1960s. Unfortunately, the Best Western Discovery Inn cannot be recommended because of numerous complaints about the management.

DINING: Try La Cita (on 1st Street, a block south of Route 66) for your last taste of Tex-Mex cooking. Breakfast is a treat at Dean's on the east side of town (*avoid Denny's - the service is terrible*). Looking for that perfect souvenir? Check out the Tee Pee curio shop.

As you leave Tucumcari, it will be necessary to join the Interstate at exit 329 **(N129)**. However, there's always time for a side-trip!

When you reach the west end of the city **(ATN011)**, the entrance to westbound I-40 pulls the boulevard to the left. However, you can follow the old road out to where it dead-ends **(ATN012)** by going straight ahead towards the Tucumcari Metropolitan Park.

Re-trace your path and join the Interstate westbound. Between mile posts 324 and 323 can be seen the remains of an old Route 66 bridge off to the left in a small valley.

Seven miles west of Tucumcari, the road climbs the Bluffs of the Llano Estacado marking the western edge of the Staked Plains.

At the Palomas exit **(N127)**, leave I-40, cross the Interstate and continue past the Stuckey's. The road that intersects is Old 66, make a right. **(N126)** (*The road to the left is private land.*)

ZERO ODOMETER

The road twists and climbs over the terrain and can provide some truly awesome views.

4.5 miles - Cross under I-40 **(N125)**. Go slow and watch for cattle in the tunnel (*honestly! Mooo!*).

10.1 miles -

MONTOYA (N124)

With the arrival of a railroad siding in 1902 the town of Rountree was established here. The name was later changed to Montoya. Post office established in 1902.

Once a bustling cattle community Montoya now sits quietly alongside the formerly busy Route 66. A small cemetery lies on the east end of town. Great photos can be taken by crossing the tracks and visiting the abandoned buildings north of the old highway. An old hotel, garage, and a few other buildings provide a sense of the old west. This is private property, so respect everything you see and take only photos and leave only footprints.

NEWKIRK (N123)

Following the faded white line and chip-sealed road from Montoya brings you to Newkirk, another of the small towns born because of the railroad.

Founded in 1901 and originally named Conant after a local rancher, it was changed to Newkirk by a settler from Newkirk, Oklahoma. Post office established in 1910.

The road surface undulates and runs parallel to the Interstate from Newkirk to Cuervo. As you observe the trucks and cars jockeying for position on the "super-slab," be glad you are alone and cruisin' The Mother Road.

Chicago to Santa Monica

NEW MEXICO

WESTBOUND

Ahead lies the "The Land of Enchantment." A journey across New Mexico will give you an understanding of where the state motto came from. There is truly something mystical and enchanting about this place, and as you follow Route 66 you will see the beauty and also be captured by the wonder that is New Mexico. We are going to discover lost alignments and (for the adventurous) a section of Route 66 that will literally drop you back in time.

Exit I-40 for

GLENRIO

Founded in 1903 when the railroad built a siding here. Glenrio is home of the famous "First in Texas/Last in Texas Motel" - the sign is almost gone now, so catch a photo before the weather wipes it out completely.

Route 66 had more than one incarnation across New Mexico, and we will attempt to cover as many of them as possible. On the west end of Glenrio (**ATN36**), at a fence line across the old highway, can be seen the remains of the final alignment of Route 66, cutting down the hill, across an old bridge, and up the hill on the opposite side of the Interstate.

There is a dirt road ahead, so it's decision time. To trace the original route of the old road, use OPTION ONE, which is an Adventure Tour "Red Route." (*Please read all admonitions regarding Adventure Tours at the front of this book.*) OPTION ONE is a dirt road, slick and muddy in the winter, and following a rain. If you do not wish to travel on dirt, use OPTION TWO, which is paved and closely parallels I-40.

OPTION ONE

At the Texas/New Mexico line marker, about halfway through town on the north side of the road

ZERO ODOMETER

Head west, leave pavement, curve slightly to the left - the fenced off final alignment of 66 will be on the right (**ATN36**).

4.2 miles (**ATN35**) - Endee - Name was adapted from the brand of the ND ranch in 1882. Endee was so rough, it is said a trench was dug each Saturday to bury the slow-draw artists on Sunday. Post office established 1886, closed 1955.

6.4 miles (**ATN34**) - Bridge and old railroad bridge to the left.

6.6 miles (**ATN33**) - Bridge and old pavement.

10.2 miles (**ATN32**) - Remains of Bard, originally Bard City, founded in 1906.

14.1 miles (**ATN31**) - Pavement.

15.7 miles (**N135**) - San Jon.

OPTION TWO

Return to I-40 westbound and exit at 361 for Endee (**N138**). Follow frontage road (Old 66) 14.9 miles into San Jon.

At the 10.9 mile mark (**N137**), look to your left and you will see the dirt road visible south of I-40 that is the option 1 alignment from above. Also, on your left at this point, you will be able to see the crossover pattern (through I-40, ahead on your left) of the final alignment as it entered San Jon.

At San Jon, turn left onto NM 39 from the frontage road (**N136**), cross I-40 to the south into the center of town.

SAN JON (*San Hone*)

First building went up in 1902 in anticipation of the railroad, which arrived in 1904. The resulting boom was responsible for the town. Name is possibly an Americanization of the Spanish *zanhon* - deep gully.

East end of town shows how the Interstate can destroy a community, with the ruins of the closed gas stations and motels crumbling to dust.

At the center of town, at junction with NM 39 (**N135**), turn right and

ZERO ODOMETER

The road traverses a variety of landscape as it swings away from the Interstate. As you travel this section, it becomes obvious why, with heavy traffic, the old highway was called "Bloody 66."

8.5 miles - Remains of an old station on the right.

9.0 miles (**N134**) - Revuelto Creek.

9.7 miles (**N133**) - Plaza Larga Creek.

up for sale. The Antique Ranch and Café as you enter town from the east has great barbeque, combined with a chance to do some antique shopping.

46.9 miles (T002) - Must enter I-40. Frontage road deadends 1.3 miles ahead.
Remain on Interstate to Exit 0 - Glenrio **(T001)**.

Chicago to Santa Monica

2.0 miles - The Route 66 Antique Mall on the left.
2.4 miles - On the right an old gas station.
2.6 miles (T017) - Curve to left off of 6th Ave.
2.8 miles - Cross Western. Amarillo Country Club on right.
3.3 miles (T016) - Curve to right, now on 9th.
4.0 miles (T015) - Intersection of 9th and Amarillo Blvd. Make a left turn onto Amarillo Blvd.

After turn the large VA Hospital will be on the right. Notice all of the older motels along road on left - The Broncho, Sunset and Skyline all date to the 1950's.

5.2 miles - Curve to right and continue west.
At the Soncy Blvd intersection **(T014)**,

ZERO ODOMETER

2.0 miles (T013) - Make a left onto Hope Blvd - which is past Helium Road - but neither is well marked. This is a sidetrip to the Cadillac Ranch.
2.3 miles (T012) - Cross I-40 and turn right.
2.7 miles - Cross over I-40 eastbound off-ramp.
3.1 miles (T011) - Cadillac Ranch is one of those sites that must be visited and photographed. The idea of Stanley Marsh 3 (*yep, "3"*) and executed by The Ant Farm, Inc. the Ranch is a curious homage to the great finned beasts of the 1950s.
4.5 miles (T010) - Right on Arnot Road at I-40 interchange (Exit 60). Drive under I-40 and turn left onto the north frontage road (old 66).
7.6 miles (T009) - Grain elevators and

BUSHLAND

Named for W. H. Bush, landowner, and C. B. Bush, postmaster. Original name was Bush, but changed in 1908 when W. H. took a new wife. She thought Bushland sounded better and when the train station was repainted insisted the new name be placed on the building.

8.4 miles - On left is the Wind Generator Research Farm.
11.6 miles - Frying Pan Ranch Road.
12.7 miles - Cross under bridge.
14.2 miles - Curve to left. A major stock feeding operation is across Interstate to left.
13.1 miles (T008) - Wildorado - pronounced Will-doe-ray-doe. The old Jessie's Café (on the south frontage road) has reopened as Randy's (closed Sunday and Monday) and the plethora of pick-ups in the parking lot are a good indicator this a great place to eat. Stop in for lunch or dinner where you will be pleasantly surprised by a menu that is upscale with fresh seafood or steak specials that include a true taste of Texas. Nice folks, good food and a wonderful example of another Route 66 location brought back to life.
17.8 miles - Cross under bridge.
20.0 miles - Binford Ranch Road on right.
27.3 miles - Road becomes four-lane.
29.0 miles (T007) -

VEGA - The Heart of Route 66, halfway between Chicago and Los Angeles.

A store founded in 1903 was the first building in Vega. A. M. Miller, the stores owner, submitted the name Vega, along with Gusben (for his sons Gus and Stephen). The name Vega, Spanish for meadow, was chosen because it reflected the level land of the countryside.

LODGING: Best Western Country Inn - a 1960's motel, very nicely maintained. A full buffet breakfast at the café next door comes with the room (the cafe burned in 2002, but may be rebuilt by the time you read this). The Vega Motel - small, 1940's vintage with nicely restored rooms. Modern motel: Comfort Inn - exit 35 on I-40.

Another great place to photograph the old buildings of a Route 66 town. Also check out Dot's Mini-Museum. North on Hwy 385 is Cal Farley's Boys Ranch.

33.3 miles (T006) - Curve around rest area.
36.7 miles (T005) - Landergin. Shows on some older maps, but was never more than a railroad work camp with a few buildings and no tourist facilities.
42.8 miles (T004) -

ADRIAN

Adrian is full of surprises for the photographer in search of old buildings. Look for the Bent Door Cafe, currently closed, but

Chicago to Santa Monica

1.1 miles - Left is entrance to old Amarillo Air Terminal.

3.7 miles - On the left is the old Triangle Motel **(T025)**.

For the dedicated Roadie, a left here onto Triangle Road will let you explore the 1940's alignment of Route 66. As you make the run, look for Buster's on the right. The corner of Triangle Road and Amarillo Blvd was the original junction of Hwy 60 and 66. This road will go 0.4 mile and stop at Lakeside **(T026)**. At the Lakeside frontage road, make a right (this is the only turn possible), continue to the stop sign **(T027)**, cross Lakeside and make a left on east-side frontage road. At Triangle Road **(T028)** make a right and

ZERO ODOMETER

1.0 miles (T030) - Intersection with Folsom Road. "Dead End" on sign, because it will.

1.3 miles (T029) - Road ends at airport. The original road went across what are now runways and taxiways. Directly across the runways and beyond the hangers is the section of road you saw by the Air Force Base.

To return to Amarillo Blvd, backtrack 0.3 miles to Folsom Road **(T030)**, make a right and head north past the KOA to the stop sign. Make a left at Amarillo Blvd **(T031)** and continue on toward town, back past Triangle Road **(T025)**.

As you drive along Amarillo Blvd, take note of the many older motels and buildings along this stretch of road.

AMARILLO

The Spanish word for "yellow" (*pronounced AHM-A-REE-O in Spanish, but AM-A-RILL-O in Texan*) was laid out by Henry B. Sanborn in 1887 near Amarillo Lake. The name came from the yellow color of the lake banks, and the many yellow flowers growing in the area. Sanborn originally named the townsite Oneida, but changed it when the town was designated as the county seat in an election where he promised cowboys a town lot each if they would vote for his town.

Prior to Sanborn the area was rife with buffalo. Ragtown, as the camp was known, prided itself on a hotel constructed of buffalo hides - including walls and roof. With the demise of the local buffalo, the grinding and selling of bleached buffalo bones for fertilizer became a big business.

Cattlemen were the next to settle the area. The mighty XIT Ranch, formed from the sale of over 3,000,000 acres of land to finance the State Capitol at Austin, brought in cowboys, ranchers and settlers. Amarillo has served as a shipping point for cattle, farm products, oil and gas over the years. Amarillo is also the primary source for the majority of the worlds helium supply.

A local rancher, J. F. Glidden, invented and patented barbed wire. He and H. B. Sanborn were the first to use the wire to fence their ranch properties in 1882. Prior to that time the wire was used to prevent cattle from straying south during the winter.

Today, Amarillo is a thriving city, confidently facing the future, while still holding to the vestiges of the past.

Originally, The Big Texan Steak Ranch was located along this stretch of the old highway, just west of Eastern Ave. With the opening of I-40 on November 15, 1968 at 2 PM, Bob Lee's business went bust. He moved the Big Texan to its present location alongside the Interstate (west of Lakeside Road). In 1976, he had another set-back when the Big Texan burned to the ground, shutting down traffic on I-40 for over two hours. He rebuilt, added a motel with a Texas shaped swimming pool and was back in business. The Big Texan still serves a great steak at a reasonable price, and yes, they still offer the free 72 oz. steak, if you can eat it in an hour with all the trimmings - shrimp cocktail, salad, baked potato and buttered roll. It has been done by one local gent over twenty times, but be warned, it ain't as easy as it looks! When we were there in April of 2002 a dude finished the steak in 17 minutes and even commented, "I ate the gristle too!"

Lodging in Amarillo is pretty much like any good-sized city. Some of the older motels suffer from neglect. A few of my favorites: Best Western Amarillo Inn, 1610 Coulter, 806.358.7861. The Big Texan is fun with its Old West façade (*plus it ain't that far to walk, or be carried, after tackling that 72 ouncer!*), 806.372.5000. Comfort Suites, 2103 Lakeview Dr, 806.352.8300. Hampton Inn, 1700 I-40 East, 806.372.1425.

Dining offers just about anything you might want, a few of my favorites - The Big Texan (*of course*), Dyers Barbeque (*good sauce!*), Ruby Tequila's Mexican Kitchen (*kinda Gringo, but good*) and Calico County (*homestyle cookin'*).

Coming in from the east on Amarillo Blvd, make a left onto Pierce **(T024)** and follow it down to 6th Ave. (**Beware** - *there is a 6th Ave NE, that's not the one you want*). At 6th **(T023)**, make a right onto 6th Ave., off of Pierce. At Taylor and 6th,

ZERO ODOMETER

0.1 miles - Old brick pavement.

1.0 miles - Old, old motor court on left.

1.1 miles (T020) - Cross under Santa Fe tracks.

1.7 miles (T019) - Motor court on left, The Morning Star. The road makes a slight bend to the left here at McMasters and 6th.

1.8 miles - The Alamo Saloon is on the left. Great old building.

1.9 miles (T018) - At 2908 West 6th is the Golden Light Cafe, a great Roadie stop for a good old fashioned "slider with fries," be sure to order a Dr. Pepper to go with that burger (*but, damnit, they no longer have DP in bottles!*).

Chicago to Santa Monica

Turn south here for about one mile to a dirt road, make a right on the dirt road and this is the site of Jericho **(T048)**. The only thing left of Jericho are the remains of an old tourist court. One of the great stories of Jericho involves a man working at the gas station when a Model A pulls in, going in reverse. The driver asked for gas and the attendant asked if he was having transmission trouble. The driver said, "Nope, I'm just traveling Route 66 in reverse," got back in the car, put it in reverse and headed out on the highway. Tall story, Texas Tale, or fact?

This area was notorious in the days before the pavement for the gumbo mud that could grab and hold a semi-truck in its goo.

Re-join I-40 westbound **(T047)** to Exit 114 **(T046)**.

Left at stop sign and cross under I-40.

Right onto four lane into

GROOM

Named for Englishman Colonel B. B. Groom who established a ranch in the area. By the late 1910s, it was a booming community of farmers and ranchers. The area developed into cattle, wheat and maize country. Store fronts, motels and gas stations provide fine photo opportunities. The film *Leap of Faith*, with Steve Martin, was filmed in Groom, with The Movie Motel (on the west side of town, just east of TX 295) being used as a set. Site of largest cross in western hemisphere is here as well.

West side of town, at junction with Texas 295 **(T044)**,

ZERO ODOMETER

1.2 miles - Make a left, proceed past the I-40 off ramp (careful!) then right onto the old two-lane.

2.8 miles - Cross under bridge.

6.6 miles (T043) - Grain elevators and what is left of Lark.

6.9 miles - Cross under bridge.

9.9 miles - Cross under bridge.

11.9 miles - Cross under bridge.

13.9 miles (T042) - Junction with 207 (south) that goes to Claude. The 1926-27 alignment of Route 66 actually went east out of Amarillo on what is now Hwy 287 to Claude, then connected north to Conway.

14.8 miles (T041) - Junction with 207 (north) and

CONWAY

A small community with a great old gas station and tourist cabins.

A right on 207 (north) will take you to Panhandle (a short nine miles) to one of the more interesting museums we have visited in quite a while.

At the junction with 207 continue straight and

ZERO ODOMETER

20.3 miles - Curve right.

22.6 miles (T040) - Right and cross I-40 at TX 2161. This is Exit 81 on I-40.

22.9 miles - Left onto north frontage road.

25.4 miles - Curve around rest area.

27.1 miles (T038) - Durrett Road - Business Loop 40. (If you have chosen to run on I-40, this is Exit 85. Take this exit.) This is the far eastern end of Amarillo Blvd, the final alignment of Route 66 into Amarillo. A right on this will take you straight into Amarillo.

If you would like to drive the old alignment as mentioned in the Rittenhouse Guide, cross Durrett Road onto FM 2575 and

ZERO ODOMETER

1.7 miles - Farmhouse on right.

2.2 miles - Eight trees.

2.3 miles (T037) - Enter Potter County.

4.0 miles (T036) - Junction of FM 1912. Continue straight, this road becomes 1st Avenue. Watch for potholes.

5.0 miles (T035) - J Street, this is Amarillo Air Force Base J Street.

5.4 miles (T034) - Old entrance to Air Force Base as shown on page 65 of the Rittenhouse Guide.

5.8 miles (T033) - Road ends at gate. The old pavement can be seen continuing straight ahead and ending at the runways of Amarillo Airport.

Make a right on "B" Street. This will take you north to where you can join Amarillo Blvd (Hwy 60 and 66).

As you drive along "B" Street, you can see the hangers and training buildings of the old Air Force Base on the left. The Barracks buildings were on the right and have been removed.

7.2 miles (T032) - Join Amarillo Blvd and

ZERO ODOMETER

Chicago to Santa Monica

McLEAN

Established as a cattle-loading site around 1900. The townsite was donated by Alfred Rowe, an English rancher who died on board the Titanic. The town was named after W. P. McLean of the Railroad Commission.

McLean is the home of the Devils Rope & Route 66 Museum **(T058)**. The Route 66 section of the museum has some wonderful artifacts of the Mother Road and is well worth a visit, the Devils Rope section refers to barbed wire, and it is absolutely amazing how many variations of barbed wire there have been. Spend some time here, enjoy the exhibits and buy something in the gift shop. This entire museum was built by and is staffed by volunteers, so they can use your purchase to insure the continuing growth of the museum. Another project of the museum has been the restored Phillips 66 gas station **(T057)**. If your are lucky while visiting, you may meet Delbert or Ruth Trew, two of my special friends and very special friends of The Mother Road.

The Red River Steak House is a great place to eat, founded by the originator of the K-Bob chain. The Cactus Inn has been nicely restored, but because of numerous complaints concerning the owner we cannot recommend it.

East and north of McLean, during WW-II, was a prisoner of war camp where many Germans POW's were interred for the duration of the War. To experience a section of historic Route 66, use the following directions. If you would rather not, continue straight west out of town to join I-40 to Alanreed.

At the intersection of FM 273 on the west side of McLean (at the flashing light),

ZERO ODOMETER

0.3 miles (T056) - Time for a mini-Adventure Tour! Look to the left for the old, old alignment of the highway. For the adventurers, turn left to follow this old section of pavement (slow, can be rough in spots and/or bad weather) to where it ends at the stop sign near the I-40 under-crossing **(T053)**.

For the less adventurous, continue west on the 4-lane to the intersection with County Rd 26 **(T055)**. Turn left and follow the road south. Shortly, you will make a left **(T054)** towards the stop sign near the I-40 under-crossing **(T053)**.

Whichever way you came, go through the I-40 under-crossing and follow the road around to the right as it heads for Alanreed. Notice the old road veering to the left where it ends between two rows of trees **(T052)**. Could be worth a short hike to check it out.

5.5 miles - Intersection with Gray County Road 23 *(Don't be fooled! The road is black, not gray, because it's asphalt. The county name is Gray.)*

7.6 miles - Asphalt pavement. Stop sign for FM 291 (southbound). Cemetery on left (possibly the oldest cemetery on Route 66). Pavement narrows ahead for Alanreed.

ALANREED

A small quiet spot off the Interstate, Alanreed (*sometimes Allanreed*) has the distinction of having had more names than any other Texas Route 66 town. First known as Eldridge (1886) it became Spring Tank, then Springtown because of a large water tank fed by local springs. For a time it was known as Prairie Dog Town after a large colony of the critters nearby.

But the most interesting name has to be Gouge Eye. A local tale explains the name as follows. A pair of cowboys were having a violent fight in one of the local saloons. This saloon provided a free buffet and in the course of the fight the food was knocked off the bar. Grapes were a featured item and they spread out across the floor. After the fight broke up, a traveler stopped at the saloon, and, seeing the grapes on the floor, asked what they were. He was told there had been a terrible fight, and these were the eyes that had been gouged out during the melee. True? Who knows, but a thank you to that great storyteller Delbert Trew for sharing it with us.

It was named Allenreed (1902) in honor of a contracting firm Allen and Reed who were in business when the Rock Island Railroad came into the area and finally settled on Alanreed (*but no one knows why!*).

In the center of town is a nicely restored gas station, thanks to efforts of the volunteers from the Old Historic Route 66 Association of Texas. A right at this intersection will take you north towards I-40. At the I-40 frontage road, 6th Avenue, a right will place you on the 1950's alignment. Just past the intersection is the location of the old Regal Reptile Ranch. If you saw a large snake that arched into the blue Texas sky at the Route 66 Museum in McLean, this is where is came from.

Return back to old 66, by the restored gas station, make a right and continue west to the intersection with FM 291 (northbound).

8.2 miles (T050) - Make a right onto FM 291 to return you to the I-40 frontage road. Make a left onto the frontage road to enter I-40 westbound and continue to Exit 124.

It should be mentioned the original route went down the hills to Jericho and then across to Groom **(T045)**. Much has been written about the Jericho Gap and how to follow it. I would like to mention that much of the old highway has been obliterated or exists on private and posted land. So we will not go into this routing at any great depth.

Exit 124 - JERICHO (T047)

Chicago to Santa Monica

TEXAS

WESTBOUND

IMPORTANT DRIVING NOTE: In Texas, exiting traffic from the Interstate has the right-of-way, so there will be a stop or yield sign for traffic on the frontage road. Since you will be on frontage roads quite a bit watch for traffic exiting and stop or yield as necessary.

Just west of Texola, Oklahoma you cross into Texas. The road along this stretch is old, four-lane, divided concrete Mother Nature is trying desperately to reclaim. A stop along here in the summer can bring back memories of when this road was a steady stream of cars, trucks, and buses. In the huge trees alongside the road can be heard the sound of the cicadas sending their dry, rasping message to the world. Toss a rock into a tree and they stop, but only briefly, then the serenade begins again.
At the Shamrock 15 (miles) sign,
ZERO ODOMETER
    4.7 miles - Road surface changes and curves around an Interstate picnic area.
    6.1 miles (T070) - Classic old bridge.
    6.6 miles - Concrete road surface.
    6.9 miles - Asphalt road surface.
As the road has been repaired over the years, the surface changes back and forth between asphalt and concrete. In some cases, the concrete had deteriorated to the point it could no longer be patched except with asphalt.
    7.2 miles - Asphalt and curve around I-40 on/off ramp.
    7.5 miles (T069) - Stop sign and Farm Road 1802. (*If you are curious about the "FM" designation on some road signs, it indicates a Farm to Market road*).
    9.6 miles (T068) - Cross Farm Road 2168.
    13.6 miles - Shamrock City Limits.

SHAMROCK
Named for good luck and courage by the first postmaster of the town, George Nickel, an Irish immigrant. Shamrock sits on the eastern edge of the Panhandle gas field and for years was known for the thick black clouds produced by the carbon black plants in the area.
As you drive through Shamrock, it is impossible to miss the U-Drop Inn and Tower Gas station, an art deco masterpiece. As we went to press, we have learned the U-Drop has been purchased by the city. Watch for the future preservation of this icon of the road. Many other buildings in town tried to join the U-Drop-Inn by having roof caps placed on them to simulate the deco look.
    LODGING: Irish Inn Motel and the Econo-Lodge.
    DINING: Mitchell Family Restaurant - go for the chicken fried steak, also a great salad bar. The Dairy Queen - typical Dairy Queen fare, but you have to experience a true Texas phenomenon. Virtually every town in Texas has a Dairy Queen and they are the hubs of local activity serving everything from breakfast to dinner.
    At the west end of town, where the road becomes four-lane **(T066)**,
ZERO ODOMETER
    Make a left to cross the Interstate off ramp and return to concrete road surface.
    3.7 miles (T065) - Lela.
    8.9 miles (T064) - Farm Road 453, continue straight.
    11.1 miles (T063) - The trees in the median of the highway are remainders of the staggered windbreaks described in Jack Rittenhouse's *A Guide Book to Highway 66*. The trees were planted to slow the northern wind and prevent erosion in the summer and snow drifting in the winter.
    12.1 miles - Asphalt and curve around rest area.
    13.0 miles (T062) - Turn right on Farm Road 1443 and cross I-40.
    13.2 miles (T061) - Left onto north frontage road.
    14.4 miles - More trees in the median.
    15.4 miles (T060) - Stop sign at County Line Road, continue straight.
    17.8 miles (T059) - Right at stop sign onto four-lane road.

0.9 miles (H008) - Cross bridge and travel parallel to I-40.

3.4 miles - I-40 veers away.

3.6 miles - Curve left (*do not go straight or you will need a new grille and bumper*). Along here on the north side are abandoned sections of Route 66. This was once a four-lane road between Sayre and Erick.

8.8 miles (H007) - Four-lane returns.

11.2 miles - Curve right.

13.0 miles (H006) - Enter Erick, as highway reduces to two lanes.

ERICK

Founded in 1901 and named after Beeks Erick, a member of the founding townsite company. Erick straddles the 100th Meridian (*once considered as the eastern boundary of Texas*). In the mid- to late-1800s, banks would not loan money to farmers west of the 100th Meridian because that was considered the start of the Great American Desert.

Erick is known for the intersection of Roger Miller Boulevard (Old 66) and Sheb Wooley Avenue (formerly Main Street) **(H005)**. At this location, the buildings on all four corners had diagonal doors facing the intersection, the only place on Route 66 where this occurs. The reason for diagonal doors was to make the building, and thus the business, appear more inviting and friendly for the patron of the store, hotel or bank. There are now only three buildings remaining at this intersection.

Be sure to stop and see Harley and Annabelle at the Sandhills Curiosity Shop, one block south of 66 on Sheb Wooley Ave, two of the most fun lovin' people along the road.

When the road returns to four lanes **(H004)**,

ZERO ODOMETER

1.6 miles (H003) - Cross bridge.

2.0 miles - Turnoff for I-40, continue straight.

3.6 miles - Old alignment is across the gully and along the tree line.

6.6 miles - Texola.

TEXOLA

Bounced back and forth between Texas and Oklahoma, the town now rests a half-of-mile east of Texas (*Nope, it does not straddle the stateline. See Glenrio, Texas - out on the New Mexico line - if you've gotta have a straddler right away*). Originally granted to the Choctaw Tribe in 1820, it became part of Greer County, Texas in 1860. Settlement began in the 1880s and an 1896 Supreme Court decision made it a part of Oklahoma. Over the years the town has had three names - Texokla, Texoma, and Texola.

A photographers dream with many old store fronts, abandoned buildings and just north of 66 on Main Street the territorial jail - a dismal building for the criminal with nothing but bars between the miscreant and the elements.

7.2 miles (H001) - Leave Texola and Oklahoma.

Chicago to Santa Monica

   24.2 miles (**H026**) - Right turn and cross I-40.
   24.6 miles (**H025**) - Pass over I-40 and make a left onto north frontage road.
   27.0 miles - Stop sign, continue straight, freeway is on your left.
   27.2 miles (**H024**) - Asphalt pavement and stop sign at the junction with OK 34. (There is Love's Station on the corner.) Make a left, then an immediate right to turn onto Business Loop 40.
   28.6 miles - Curve to left.
   29.4 miles - Curve to right.
   29.5 miles - Cross river.
   29.6 miles - Downtown area of

ELK CITY

Original name was to be Crone, in honor of a local settler, but the application was mis-read and the town was named Crowe in 1899 at a location three miles south of the present downtown. The name was to be changed to Busch in 1901 in hopes of wooing the St. Louis beer magnate, Adolphus Busch, to build a brewery in the community (or at least make a contribution to the growing town). Many members of the town hated the fact their town name was to be derived from a beer label. When the railroad arrived, angry citizens threatened to push the ladder from beneath the sign painter who was putting the hated name on the station. Local residents called the town Elk City, but the name was not officially recognized until 1907.

Throughout the 1930s, 40s and 50s, Route 66 was a major force in the community as thousands of travelers discovered Elk City as a great place to stop for the night. The many motels along 3rd Street (old 66, now BL 40) attest to the popularity of Elk City as a continuing overnight stopping place.

LODGING: Best Western Elk City Inn (405.225.2331), Knights Inn (405.225.2241), Holiday Inn (405.225.6637).

While in Elk City visit the Old Town Museum complex on the west side of town where the National Route 66 Museum is located. The oil drum Kachinas out front were originally located at the old Queenan Trading Post. Downtown be sure to visit the Anadarko Basin Museum of Natural History in the historic Casa Grande Hotel. Behind the museum is the Parker Rig #114. At 179 feet it is the world's tallest, non-working oil rig.

On the west side of town, at Pioneer Road (**H023**),

ZERO ODOMETER

   1.6 miles - Curve to the left
   2.0 miles (**H022**) - OK 6 to right, stay on BL40 straight ahead.
   2.1 miles (**H021**) - Junction OK 34 and OK 6. There is a motor court and the vacant Queenan Trading Post on the right just past the intersection.
   4.5 miles (**H020**) - Right turn, followed by immediate left. Look for Historic Route 66 sign.
   9.2 miles (**H019**) - Asphalt road surface, right curve and stop sign. Make a left and cross I-40, then head right (**H018**).
   10.1 miles (**H017**) - Cross a yellow bridge. (Old Yeller, anyone?)
   10.9 miles (**H016**) - Turn right and cross I-40.
   11.1 miles (**H015**) - Left onto old road, just before Fina station.
   13.1 miles (**H014**) - Stop, right turn to enter

SAYRE

Founded in 1901 and named after Robert H. Sayre, a stockholder in the railroad.

The Courthouse and Main Street were used in filming *The Grapes of Wrath*. The scene is of the Joad's truck turning onto Main Street with the Courthouse in the background. Many people think this was a shot of the state capitol in Oklahoma City.

The famous boxer, Jess Willard, "The Great White Hope" once ran a rooming house here.

At the corner of 4th and Elm (**H012**) there appear to be a pair of storm cellars on either side of the highway. These are actually entrances to the underground pedestrian walkway that allowed people to cross what was once a busy Route 66 *(these were actually used at times as storm cellars during tornado alerts)*.

   14.6 miles (**H013**) - Stop sign, left to follow BL40.
   16.4 miles (**H010**) - Cross the North Fork of the Red River.
Until 1896, Texas claimed the land west from here. It took six years for the Supreme Court to decide Texas extended to the South Fork of the Red River and not the North Fork.

Watch carefully for the next turn (**H009**). Slow down and prepare to turn when you see the Flying J Truck Stop on the left. The right turn onto Rt 66 is unmarked and is a hard right, up a short rise. (*Note: This is a nasty little turn because there are no signs and it will catch you by surprise, dagnabit!*)

   17.8 miles (**H009**) - Right turn and
ZERO ODOMETER

Chicago to Santa Monica

0.6 miles (H050) - Arched bridge.
2.1 miles - Curve left and stop sign.
3.6 miles - Curve left and right.
4.1 miles (H049) - At top of the hill, make a right and cross I-40, make a left onto the north frontage road.
4.7 miles - Back on concrete road surface.
5.2 miles - Asphalt surface.
5.3 miles - Yield sign and four-lane into Clinton
5.4 miles (H047) - Turtle Creek Bridge.
6.4 miles (H046) - Rio Siesta Motel on right.
7.2 miles (H045) - Bridge across Washita River.

CLINTON

The land-rush crowd bypassed this area when the Cheyenne-Arapaho Reservation opened in 1892. Many felt the land was not worth staking out. The Frisco Railway built to the area in 1903 and Clinton was founded. Named after Federal Judge Clinton F. Irwin.

Clinton is the home of the first official state Route 66 Museum at 2229 W. Gary Blvd **(H044)**. Well worth a visit. (Note that the museum is not on Route 66, as described above in the text. You need to return to downtown to pick-up where you left off.)

Many sites to see here including McLain Rogers Park with its Route 66 themed miniature golf course. Recommended lodgings are Best Western Trade Winds (405.323.2610) and the Holiday Inn (405.323.5550), as with many towns the older motels suffer from neglect and disrepair. Dining is good at Branding Iron Restaurant for steaks and Lupita's for Mexican food.

Continue west bound through town to 10th Street **(H043)**. Turn left and follow the street down to I-40. When you cross under I-40,

ZERO ODOMETER

1.1 miles (H041) - Fork in road, bear right.
1.4 miles - Roadside park on left.
2.1 miles - Cross under railroad.
3.8 miles (H040) - Entrance to I-40 and abandoned building, continue straight. Parkersburg Cemetery is just ahead on the left.
5.0 miles - Cross bridge.
6.7 miles - Cross small bridge.
9.1 miles (H038) - Right and cross under I-40, then left onto north frontage road.
10.6 miles - Cross small bridge.
12.5 miles - Cross bridge.
13.0 miles - Cross bridge.
13.1 miles (H037) - Stop sign.

FOSS

Classified as an official Oklahoma Ghost Town. An abandoned gas station (Kobel's Place) is the only evidence of Route 66 days.

At the KOA, curve to the right, then left and stop.
16.1 miles (H036) - Left turn and cross I-40.
16.4 miles (H035) - On south side of I-40, make a right.
17.1 miles - Cross bridge.
18.2 miles (H034) - Left, right and stop, then right across I-40.
18.4 miles (H033) - Left onto north frontage road.
19.0 miles (H032) - Cross bridge.
20.6 miles (H031) - Curve right, left and stop, then left and cross I-40.
21.0 miles (H030) - Stop sign in middle of town. Turn right and continue west.

CANUTE

Founded in 1902 by a company that specialized in townsites. On the east end of town is the Catholic Cemetery where a hill is topped by a life-sized bronze of Christ on the cross and the Apostle John, Mary the mother of Jesus and Mary Magdalene.

21.7 miles (H029) - Cross railroad.
22.2 miles - Old pavement sweeps across toward the Interstate.

Chicago to Santa Monica

11.0 miles (H068) - Stop, then make left onto US 281.

PONY BRIDGE

11.5 miles (H066) - This is the 3,944 foot, historic 38 span, or "ponies," bridge across the Canadian River. Many stories are told as to why the bridge has 38 ponies, but the true story (*or so I've been told*) is the size of the ponies was the largest that could be handled by the road building equipment in the mid-1930s. "Road Test" hill is behind you, the road climbs 150 feet in one mile and was once used by new car owners to see if their car could climb the hill in high gear.

12.3 miles (H065) - Exit pony bridge.
13.3 miles - Cross bridge.
14.1 miles (H064) - This is Hinton Junction. Continue straight, Hwy 281 goes to the left.
15.9 miles (H063) - Abandoned motor court and turn-off for Bridgeport on the right.

A visit to Bridgeport is to see a modern day ghost town. As you travel the streets, you wonder about the people who lived here when it was a bustling town on the river and the old highway. A local legend has it that the newspaper in Geary told everyone in Bridgeport to move out because it was going to be a ghost town. So they did, and now it is.

17.8 miles - Cross bridge. It should be mentioned that portions of the road are in disrepair, particularly the bottoms of dips, so slow down to protect your suspension.
18.6 miles - Cross bridge.
23.0 miles - Single arch bridge.
24.4 miles - Cross bridge, lots of road patching here, watch your speed.

Once again, time seems to be suspended. What year is it? Who is the President? Look, up ahead, is that Rod Serling by the turn-off to a deserted gas station and motel? (*Or is really Anthony "Psycho" Perkins waiting to welcome you to the Bates Motel?*)

25.2 miles (H062) - Appears to be an old gas station converted to a private home.
25.7 miles - Cross bridge.
26.3 miles - Cross bridge.
26.6 miles - Exit ramp from the Interstate, watch for merging traffic.
27.5 miles (H061) - Junction of 58 and optional turn-off to Hydro. At this point (*or after returning from a sidetrip to Hydro*):
ZERO ODOMETER

HYDRO

An area noted for peanut production and a quiet stop on the old alignment as it is off the later alignment, and away from the Interstate. Be sure to park in the middle of the street - that's what it's there for.

Straight ahead on the Frontage Road at,

0.5 miles (H060) - Lucille's Historic Highway 66 Store and gas station on the right.
3.5 miles - Cross a bridge and pass under the railroad tracks. Notice the beautiful red rock on the sides of the cut.
4.6 miles (H059) - I-40 access, continue straight.
5.7 miles (H058) - Meet frontage road coming from the opposite direction - at an angle - on your left. Stay to the right and continue straight.
6.9 miles (H057) - Turn left on Washington.
7.6 miles (H056) - Right turn onto Main St.

WEATHERFORD

Founded in 1893 and named after US Marshal William J. Weatherford. Astronaut Thomas P. Stafford, commander of the 1975 Apollo-Soyuz mission, was born in Weatherford. A museum of NASA memorabilia is in town.

LODGING: Best Western Mark Motor Hotel (405.772.3325). **DINING:** City Diner at 1231 Main St, cool ambiance, good food.

8.2 miles (H055) - Business Loop 40 curves to the left. Continue straight across 7th Street.
8.9 miles (H054) - 4th Street, make a left onto OK 54.
9.1 miles (H053) - Cross railroad track and
ZERO ODOMETER

3.8 miles - Curve around an Interstate bridge.
6.2 miles - Road surface become asphalt. If you look across the Interstate, you can see the old alignment climbing the hill.
7.0 miles (H052) - Left turn and cross Interstate.
7.1 miles (H051) - Stop sign on the south side of the Interstate and
ZERO ODOMETER

A left here will take you east on the old alignment for about three-tenths of a mile. Make a right and continue west.

Chicago to Santa Monica

OPTION 1 - This option will take you on a loop north to Calumet, then west to Geary, and then south to the bridge, on a fully paved road.

OPTION 2 - This option follows the same route as Option #1 until you reach a turnoff just south of Geary where you join the old, old alignment to the pony bridge, with an optional sidetrip to see the old tollbridge crossing to Bridgeport. This alignment is a dirt road and is an Adventure Tour "Red Route."

OPTION 3 - This option takes you directly west to the pony bridge and bypasses Geary and Calumet altogether.

OPTION # 1

To follow the 1926 through 1933 alignment, make a right on 270 and head toward Calumet.

10.7 miles - Cross Six Mile Creek.
12.2 miles (H074) - Calumet - Route 66 Pizza is on the right. Hwy 270 heads west from Calumet.
12.7 miles - Curve left.
12.8 miles - Old building on left.
13.1 miles - Historic Route 66 sign.
13.7 miles - Cemetery on left.
17.8 miles - Cross bridge and curve to left.

GEARY

Named after Ed Guerrier, a pioneer, it soon became known as Geary. Established in 1898.

24.1 miles (H073) - Junction of 281 and 270 in Geary. Make a left. Continue straight on 281 south to the pony bridge **(H066)**, past the junction for the El Reno Cutoff **(H068)**. (*Keep an eye out for your mud-laden brethren from Option #2 who will be joining you on Hwy 281 just south of the El Reno Cutoff.*)

(Continue at the "Pony Bridge" listing, below.)

OPTION #2

To trace the old, old alignment, follow Option #1 to Geary. Then just south of Geary, OPTION TWO will take you on an Adventure Tour "Red Route." (Please read all admonitions regarding Adventure Tours at the front of this book.) OPTION TWO is a dirt road, slick and muddy in the winter, and following a rain. If you do not wish to travel on dirt, use OPTIONS ONE or THREE, which are paved all the way.

24.3 miles (H072) - Watch for a gravel road to the right. Make a right on this road. If it has been raining, be prepared for some slick, red, Oklahoma mud ahead.

This section is the 1925/26 original alignment of what was to become Route 66. The last portion of this road to Bridgeport was built in 1927 by businessmen from Geary who wanted the Route 66 traffic through their town.

25.4 miles - Road to left.
27.3 miles (H071) - Road to right (optional side trip). This will lead to the river and is part of the old alignment. The bridge across the river to Bridgeport is no longer there, but it is possible to see the old bridge pilings.
28.5 miles - Exit a literal tunnel of trees, the road curves to the left and suddenly you are in wide-open country.
29.8 miles (H070) - Stop sign. Make a right.
29.9 miles (H069) - Left turn.
30.3 miles (H067) - Right onto 66 and continue west towards the pony bridge.

(Continue at the "Pony Bridge" listing, below.)

EL RENO CUT-OFF

At junction of 270 and SH66
ZERO ODOMETER
Continue straight on SH66

0.1/0.2 miles - Notice the early rumble strips of asphalt in the eastbound lanes.
3.2 miles - "S" curve.
5.0 miles - Cross bridge.
6.1 miles - Cross bridge.
7.1 miles (H076) - Junction with new four-lane, Spur 281, make a right.
8.8 miles - Cross bridge.
9.4 miles (H075) - Left onto old Route 66. **(WATCH FOR THIS, it is NOT marked.)**
9.6 miles - Old gas station on right.
10.0 miles - Crest of the hill.

Chicago to Santa Monica

1.2 miles (H090) - Lakeview Pioneer Home, formerly the Lakeview Courts as shown in the 1945 AAA book.
1.4 miles - Cross bridge.
1.9 miles (H089) - Bear to the right at fork.
3.7 miles (H088) - Right, followed by left. This is a right onto Mustang Road, then an immediate left onto the 39th Expressway and
ZERO ODOMETER

YUKON

Home of Garth Brooks. Laid out by the Spencer brothers in 1891 and named after the Yukon River in Alaska. The nearby town of Frisco was virtually deserted when the railroad went through Yukon, and everyone moved to the new community.

If it is evening, check out the Yukon's Best Flour sign at the east end of town. The sign had been dark for years and became a matter of civic pride when it was re-lighted.

2.0 miles (H086) - Cross Garth Brooks Blvd. (also known as 11th St).
2.5 miles - Westport 66 housing development (left).
3.7 miles - Cross Shell Creek.
7.1 miles - Cross Purcell Creek.
7.6 miles - Three-lane road.
8.2 miles - El Reno city limits.
9.3 miles - Huge storage yard for drilling equipment.
11.1 miles -

EL RENO

Founded when the Rock Island Railroad arrived two months after the land run of 1889. El Reno was the western edge of the land rush. Reno City was originally located on the north side of the Canadian River. The city refused to pay the railroad the bonus it wanted to bring the tracks to the city, so the railroad built on the south side of the river. Then the town moved, buildings and all to the new site. One hotel was stranded for a short period in the middle of the river, but continued business as usual until it could be fully relocated.

July of 1901 saw the population of El Reno increase by 145,000 - in one day - when the Kiowa-Comanche Reservation was opened as the last chance for free territory land for settlers. Fortunately, most of the influx departed as soon as the lottery drawing for the land was completed.

The Dustin Hoffman, Tom Cruise hit film *Rain Man* was filmed at the Big 8 Motel on the east end of town, standing in for an Amarillo motel. A sign out front proclaimed it "Amarillo's Finest." Don't bother, new owners changed the name to Deluxe Inn (not even), trashed the sign and don't have a clue about any film being shot here.

LODGING: Best Western Inn at Hensley's (405.262.6490) and Days Inn (405.262.8720).

At the junction of 66 and Shepard Ave. **(H085)**
ZERO ODOMETER
Continue straight into El Reno, following the curve of the road.
0.8 miles - Pass the VFW hall with a WW-II bomber out front.
1.2 miles (H084) - Cross over railroad tracks. El Reno water tower is on left ahead.
As you go through town, move to left lane for turn coming up.
2.0 miles (H083) - Turn left onto Wade Street (40 BUS) and move into right lane.
2.1 miles (H082) - Make a right onto Choctaw Avenue and move to left lane for a left turn.
2.2 miles (H081) Left onto Sunset Drive.
2.6 miles (H080) - Cross railroad tracks.
When you cross Four Mile Creek **(H079)**,
ZERO ODOMETER
0.5 miles - Curve to left. Older motels along here.
3.5 miles (H078) - Fort Reno turn-off. Make a right here, but do not enter the fort grounds. The road straight ahead joins the Interstate.
6.6 miles - Cross small creek.
8.2 miles (H077) - Junction with 270. An old station is at this corner and well worth a photo stop.

NOTE: Options lie ahead as to how to follow various Route 66 alignments. It is strongly suggested you take some time to read all of the information from this point to the pony bridge near Bridgeport **(H066)** (22 miles west). From the junction of 66 and 270, there are three options for reaching the pony bridge.

Chicago to Santa Monica

26.4 miles - Cross bridge
28.1 miles **(H113)** - Rejoin 66, make a right and
ZERO ODOMETER
   5.0 miles **(H112)** - Luther city limits. Old station and store on left.
   5.7 miles - Cross railroad.
   8.9 miles - Little Brother's Gas Station on right.
   9.1 miles - Historical marker marks the east boundary of the Oklahoma Land Rush of 1889.
  10.7 miles **(H111)** - Right, a great example of a 20's type gas station;
  13.1 miles -

ARCADIA (H110)
Noted for the Round Barn, built in 1898 by William Odor, and restored by the Arcadia Preservation and Historical Society. HillBillie's Bar-B-Que as you enter town is well worth the stop and the Old Store is worth a photo or two.
From here to Edmond, the road is under construction and changing rapidly. Not much to see as suburbia moves into the area.
  19.7 miles **(H109)** - Cross Interstate 35.
If you want to avoid traffic hassles you can take I-35 south, this was the 1954 routing of Route 66 (*so you aren't cheating!*), connect to I-44 westbound, and exit at Lincoln **(H100)** (*see below for routing from Lincoln*).
  19.9 miles - Enter

EDMOND
Founded in 1887 as a coal and watering stop for the railroad. Named for a railroad official. Edmond is the site of Central State University and is primarily a college town and bedroom community for Oklahoma City.
  23.1 miles **(H108)** - Intersection with Broadway and make a left.
South on Broadway, exit at Memorial **(H107)**, left turn onto Memorial **(H106)** under Broadway and an immediate right onto Kelley **(H103)**. Follow Kelley south towards I-44. At 63rd St., a left will take you to the Cowboy Hall of Fame **(H102)** and the County Line Restaurant (*great bar-b-que!*). Enter westbound I-44 **(H101)**, STAY RIGHT to almost immediately exit onto Lincoln **(H100)**, then south to the state capitol.
Lincoln used to be Motel Row - but today all that can be seen are blocks of vacant lots as the city tries to renew itself. Lincoln will curve around the State Capitol **(H094)**, one of the few Capitol buildings without a dome. Be sure you are in the right lane to make a right onto NE 23rd St.

OKLAHOMA CITY
Oklahoma has the distinction of having the only state capitol building on Route 66 (post-1937 Route 66). It is also one of the few towns in the state with no Indian heritage, having started out as a pioneer town.
Many towns are said to have sprung up overnight, but Oklahoma City did so in thirty minutes. At noon, on April 22, 1889, the signal was given thirty miles away for the start of the Great Oklahoma Land Rush, and within fifteen minutes men of the Seminole Land and Town Company were dragging chains on a run. To be honest over a thousand people camped along the Santa Fe track at the projected townsite. This early preparation led to the nickname "Sooner" being given to the early settlers (*Which seems to be another way of saying cheaters*).
LODGING: I will admit to an aversion to large cities, but Oklahoma City appears to be a relatively "safe" city and I have not heard of a major area of crime against tourists. There are hundreds of properties available in the city and my suggestion is to stick to a major chain. My personal favorite is the Residence Inn at 4361 W. Reno (405.942.4500).
There were numerous routes of 66 through Oklahoma City. To get through the city we will follow the 1936 route. Always keep a watch for the Oklahoma Historic Route 66 signs to help guide you.
Go west on NE 23rd and make a right at Classen **(H095)**.
Turn left onto NW 39th **(H096)** and proceed west on NW 39th.
Make a left turn on Frankford Ave. and go one block to NW 38th **(H097)**.
Turn right onto NW 38th **(H098)**.
Turn right onto May Avenue **(H099)** and be prepared for an immediate left onto the westbound I-44 on-ramp. Continue west, and join the 39th Expressway into Bethany.
Just past Council Road make a left to rejoin the old alignment **(H091)**. Make a right and continue toward the steel truss bridge. At the east end of the bridge,
ZERO ODOMETER
   0.5 miles - Curve to the left, then right. Lake Overholser is on the left, named for Mayor Ed Overholser (1915-18). If you travel with a picnic lunch, there are many great places to stop and enjoy the breeze off the lake.

Chicago to Santa Monica

this turn may be unreliable and local road conditions should be checked.

5.0 miles (H130) - Early road sidetrip rejoins final alignment.
5.2 miles (H129) - Cross Camp Creek.
5.5 miles (H128) - You can see where the old road crossed over what is now the new alignment.
5.7 miles (H127) - Rejoin old road surface.
6.7 miles (H126) - Old road curves off to right.
7.7 miles (H125) - Access to old alignment.
8.2 miles (H124) - Cross Salt Creek and look for old bridge off to right through trees; can be accessed on a short road to the right.
8.8 miles (H123) - Both early and final alignments come together as you cross Allied Road entering

STROUD (H122)

This was one hell-raising town before statehood, with nine saloons dispensing to the many cowboys who brought cattle to Stroud for shipment on the railroad. After statehood, Stroud became a "dry" town and a trading center for the farmers of the area.

An interesting side note - from here to Bristow lies Oklahoma's largest natural gas storage area with more than 75 billion cubic feet deposited in a depleted underground natural gas field.

On the east side of town, don't miss The Rock Café (lunch and dinner only, Tuesday through Saturday), a local classic built from native stone.

9.7 miles - The Rock Cafe on the left.
At the junction with OK 99 **(H121)**,

ZERO ODOMETER

3.3 miles - Cross Dosie Creek.
5.3 miles - Cross Dry Creek.
5.9 miles - Curve left into

DAVENPORT (H120)

Founded by Southern Methodists in 1903 with the purchase of a farm and the laying out of a townsite. Oil was discovered in 1924 and the town attempted to grow, but discovery of the Seminole Field doomed expansion. Main Street is paved with bricks from the local brick plant and is locally known as "Snuff Street" - drive a block and take a dip. Also the site of the world's first round oil tank, built in 1925.

7.1 miles - Curve right.
11.3 miles -

CHANDLER

Founded in 1891 and named for George Chandler, Assistant Secretary of State under President Harrison. Chandler is an example of a "tough" town. Virtually every building in town was destroyed by a tornado in 1897. With the loss of fourteen lives and destruction of all of the community buildings, reconstruction began immediately. The last old-west style gunfight took place here in 1924, and cost the life of lawman Bill Tilghman. He is buried in the cemetery west of town.

As you go past the intersection of 7th and Manvel (Manvel is Rt. 66), check out the restored Phillips service station. Great old brick building, getting plenty of care.

13.2 miles (H119) - The Lincoln Motel on the right, built in 1939 and still operating.
14.6 miles (H118) - Hard right.
14.8 miles - Cross Bell Cow Creek.
21.4 miles (H117) - Town of Warwick. Old station on the right.
21.7 miles - Cross railroad.
22.2 miles - (H116) - Cross Deep Fork of the Canadian River.
22.7 miles - Junction with 177.
24.2 miles - Cross under Interstate.
24.7 miles (H115) - Pioneer Barbecue on right. Curve right to follow old (1925/26) alignment.
25.9 miles -

WELLSTON (H114)

When bypassed in 1933, the town took their case to the Supreme Court to keep the town on Route 66, they lost. Founded in 1880 as a trading post by Christian T. Wells on the Kickapoo Indian Reservation. Look for Pioneer Camp with its original sign and marble-eyed Totems.

Chicago to Santa Monica

5.4 miles (H151) - Old highway to right. Make right turn and,
ZERO ODOMETER
   This road meanders through the trees and over the hills, following the topography. It is one of those sections that drove the moms of this country crazy, yelling at the old man: "You don't HAVE to pass EVERY truck on the road!"
   1.7 miles (H150) - Rejoin highway and make a right.
   Another tricky turn ahead. (*For laughs, watch for the "Bob Moore" mailbox on the left side of the road at the point the highway curves to the left.*) The old alignment is visible straight ahead.
   2.3 miles (H149) - Right turn, up a slight rise, then a left to join old alignment, at this turn:
ZERO ODOMETER
   0.2 miles (H148) - Stop sign, continue straight.
   2.0 miles (H147) - Stop sign and highway. Now, pay close attention. The barbecue place should be on your right, a house is on the hill to your left and slightly behind you. **IMPORTANT** - the main road in front of you is NOT 66, it is Oklahoma 48. Make a left and
ZERO ODOMETER
   1.2 miles (H146) - Just past the T-intersection sign, and just before the STOP AHEAD sign, make a right followed immediately by a left and you're back on old pavement.
   1.5 miles (H145) - Curve right off old pavement, climb slightly to meet highway (this was a new alignment of Route 66). Go straight across and make a left followed immediately by a right to rejoin old 66. Road surface is pitted and a bit rough, but passable.
   2.4 miles - Curve and culvert.
   3.0 miles (H144) - Cross rusted arch bridge, stop sign, straight ahead, then right to rejoin Route 66.
   3.1 miles (H143) - Stop sign, make left to go into Bristow.
   3.6 miles (H142) - Cross under I-44.
   4.1 miles (H141) - Cross Sand Creek and

BRISTOW
   Began in 1897 as a trading post on Creek land in the Indian Territory. The railroad pushed west from Sapulpa and assisted in the development of Bristow. Town was founded in 1901 and named after J.L. Bristow, fourth Assistant Postmaster General. Bristow was also the site of Oklahoma's first radio station, KRFU, which became known as the "Voice of Oklahoma." The call letters were changed to reflect the nickname and became KVOO. In 1927, the station moved to Tulsa where it still pumps a strong signal across the plains.
   4.9 miles (H140) - OK 66 west makes a right. Check out the Goodyear store as you come around corner, it is on the right.
   5.4 miles (H139) - Curve left.
   6.1 miles - Old station on left.
   Cross Catfish Creek **(H138)** and
ZERO ODOMETER
   4.0 miles (H137) - Curve to left, the road straight ahead is NOT Route 66.
   4.8 miles (H136) - Cross Little Deep Creek.
   6.5 miles (H135) - Turn left for old alignment through Depew. Strongly suggest you make this loop into Depew, some of the finest examples of old, preserved architecture are here.
   6.7 miles - Right onto Main Street. Notice the old gas station and other buildings.
   6.9 miles - Check out the NAPA Auto Parts building on left.
   7.0 miles - Right turn off of Main St.
   7.3 miles (H134) - Back to 1939 alignment, make a left and:
ZERO ODOMETER
   0.2 miles - Old alignment on right. Blocked at both ends, cannot be driven.
   0.6 miles (H133) - Right, then left to join old road and
ZERO ODOMETER
   0.3 miles - Fork in road, bear left.
   0.5 miles (H132) - Intersection and sign for Oakdale Cemetery to your right. Make a left and rejoin OK 66 and,
ZERO ODOMETER
   The old road can be seen continuing over the hills ahead. It is blocked at various points and some bridges have been removed but parts of it are accessible. There are many short connectors between the old road and the final alignment you're driving on (OK 66).
   2.8 miles (H131) - Sidetrip! You can drive on the early alignment by making a left at the junction. **Note:** The markings for

Chicago to Santa Monica

was moved to Oklahoma during the relocation of the 1880s.

First Post Office was established in 1879. Railroad arrived in 1882 and the large cattle drives that used to go to Vinita for loading were brought to Tulsa.

LODGING: As with any large city, Tulsa has lodging options stretching from cheap to deluxe. Also, as with any large city I would recommend staying at a major chain hotel. Many of the older motels are run-down and neglected. A few of my personal choices are: Best Western Trade Winds Central Inn (918.749.5561); Microtel Inn, (918.234.9100); Residence Inn (918.664.7241).

DINING: Many fine restaurants throughout Tulsa. Favorites, Cattlemen's Steakhouse - what else? Good steaks; Chimi's Mexican Restaurant - good food in a casual atmosphere; Ruby's for good home-style cooking, a Tulsa favorite for 30 years.

To drive the original alignment, just past I-44 (you will cross under) make a right onto Mingo, go one mile north to the traffic circle and left onto Admiral Place. Stay on Admiral Place for 6.8 miles (one way west) to Lewis, then make a left onto Lewis and go one mile back to 11th. A right on 11th will put you back on Route 66.

Continuing west, when you reach downtown, 11th Street swings right and becomes 10th **(H170)**. 10th then curves back and becomes 11th again **(H169)**. (*Whew! Anyone home in the public works department?*)

Make certain you are in the left-hand lane for the next transition: Proceed west on 11th two blocks to 12th, where you make a left **(H168)** and follow 12th down a small hill, and make a left onto Southwest Blvd **(H167)**. You will cross a big river bridge immediately. Stay on Southwest out of town.

Cruising west on Southwest Blvd there is more evidence of old motels.

At the Frankoma Pottery Outlet (left) **(H166)**,
ZERO ODOMETER

SAPULPA

Founded by, and named for, Chief Sapulpa, a Creek Indian, who ran a store and farmed in the mid-1800s about a mile southeast of the present town site. With the arrival of the Frisco Railroad in 1886 Sapulpa became an important cattle shipping and loading center.

1.0 miles (H165) - Right turn onto Mission.
1.9 miles (H164) - Right onto Dewey.
2.7 miles (H163) - Rock Creek. The original road crossed this at creek level, the pavement can be seen to the right and down.
3.8 miles (H162) - Sign on right "Ozark Trail" (*on top of side road stop sign*). Make a right here and
ZERO ODOMETER

Just ahead is the historic Rock Creek Bridge **(H161)**. Built in 1921, this bridge is a classic. The pavement on the bridge surface is red brick and makes for some excellent color photographs. (*If the road across the bridge is closed continue on the main hwy to the VFW parking lot, make a right, cross the parking lot, then a left onto the old highway*).

0.3 miles (H160) - The closed TeePee Drive-in on the left.

This is one of the best "frozen-in-time" stretches of the Mother Road, as you drive this section, it is almost as if time has stood still. There is little to remind you that you're in the new millennium. The old highway and overhanging mantel of trees remind you of a time when this was the highway through the area. The only thing missing is the massive amount of traffic that traveled this road in its heyday. (*Certain high-quality Route 66 maps will show you that, at times, you're less than 100 yards from the freeway madness of I-44 as you cruise through this section. But you will feel like you're a hundred miles and a hundred years away...*)

2.6 miles (H159) - Cross beneath a 1925 railroad bridge. Road ahead is rough.
3.4 miles (H158) - Rejoin highway and turn right.
4.2 miles (H157) - Old store and cabins at turnout.
5.2 miles - Right curve.
6.1 miles - Kellyville.
6.4 miles - Old alignment on left. Not driveable.
7.2 miles (H156) At the Heyburn Lake turn-off, in Kellyville:
ZERO ODOMETER

0.9 miles (H155) - Four-lane. Cross Little Polecat Creek. A large rolling mill is on the left.
1.0 miles - Two-lane.
1.7 miles - Curve to right.
2.1 miles (H154) - On the right, in front of the Cripple Creek Antique Mall, is a section of old pavement.
3.2 miles - Curve to left.
4.0 miles (H153) - Cross Polecat Creek.
4.8 miles (H152) - Cross I-44.
HEADS UP, KIDS! WATCH FOR THE NEXT MILE-POINT AND TURN - THE ROAD IS NOT MARKED.

<h1 style="text-align: center;">Chicago to Santa Monica</h1>

CLAREMORE

The town found its beginning as an Osage Indian community early in the 19th century. It was named after the Osage chief who founded the town. Claremore was known for more than fifty years for its artesian spring water, discovered by accident in a 1903 during a test drilling for oil.

Claremore is noted as the hometown of Will Rogers, although Rogers stated he was born "half-way between Claremore and Oologah." The Will Rogers Memorial is west of Route 66, (turn left on Will Rogers Blvd).

Claremore was also the home of Andy Payne, the winner of the famous (or infamous) Bunion Derby, actually it was called the Great Transcontinental Footrace of 1928. Payne had entered the race to win the $25,000 grand prize. After nearly three months, 55 of the original 275 runners limped into Madison Square Garden with Andy Payne in the lead. The winners had to wait for nearly a week for the promoter, C. C. Pyle, to make good on the prize money.

LODGING: Microtel Inn, (918.343.2868.)

DINING: Hammett House, good down-home cooking and great pies and rolls.

Go through town on Lynn Riggs Blvd if you want to follow the newer alignment. To follow the historic alignment, turn right onto Stuart Roosa **(H187)**, and:

ZERO ODOMETER

This curves left and becomes J.M. Davis Blvd through town.

1.3 miles (H186) - For the gun collector the J.M. Davis Gun Museum, with over 6,000 weapons on display, is a must visit

1.4 miles (H185) - Cross Will Rogers Blvd (Memorial is about ten blocks to the right). Across the street, the Dayton Tire Store is an old gas station and garage - nicely preserved. GOOD WORK!

1.7 miles (H184) - Road curves to the left and intersects with Lynn Riggs Blvd. Turn right.

At the junction of OK 66 and the 266 over-crossing **(H183)**, west of town:

ZERO ODOMETER

1.2 miles (H182) - Verdigris.

3.4 miles (H181) - Cross Ship Channel. A great looking railroad bridge is on your right.

4.0 miles (H180) - Cross the Verdigris River on an ornate arched bridge.

To experience an old section of Route 66, it will be necessary to do some creative driving at this point, so follow along carefully, boys and girls. Make certain you are in the left lane and at the WEST end of the bridge, and as you pass the last small arch,

ZERO ODOMETER

0.4 miles (H179) - There is a paved crossover in the median. Use this crossover to make a U-turn and head back east. Make certain you are in the right lane after completing the turn.

0.7 miles (H178) - A road will intersect on the right at a reverse angle. Turn onto this road, it is a hard right cutting back to the southwest.

1.2 miles (H177) - Road curves to the right. Watch for an old store on the left. There will be a mobile-home park on the right.

1.6 miles (H176) - The Arrowwood Trading Post. Directly across the main road from the trading post is the closed water park with its famous Big Blue Whale. The park was built by a man for his wife who liked to collect whales.

1.7 miles (H175) - Continue down the hill and you will rejoin the highway to continue west.

2.1 miles (H174) - Cross Spunky Creek. To the left was the former site of Fort Spunky. As you cross the creek,

ZERO ODOMETER

0.6 miles (H173) - Right on Antry, followed by a left onto Cherokee. (This is the old alignment.)

CATOOSA

Named after "Old Catoos" the rounded hill just west of town. The name is supposedly a derivation of *Gi-tu-zi* - Cherokee for "Here lives the people of the light" who met on the summit of the hill. The Port of Catoosa (three miles north) is the largest inland seaport in the nation. It is situated at the head of the McClellan-Kerr Arkansas Navigation System and links Tulsa to the world by way of the Mississippi River to New Orleans.

1.8 miles (H172) - Hard right, followed by a left at the stop sign onto 193rd East Ave. Straight ahead is the Interstate, and as you cross under,

ZERO ODOMETER

1.0 miles (H171) - Make a right onto 11th, on the southwest corner is a swap meet and a sign for the Route 66 Bar-B-Que.

2.2 miles - A rock house and old station on the right.

Continue on 11th to downtown Tulsa. This is a distance of approximately 12 miles.

TULSA

Originally called Tulsey Town after the Creek Tribe of the Tallasse or Tulsey community. Originally from Alabama the tribe

Chicago to Santa Monica

13.4 miles (H203) - Cross Little Cabin Creek - Arched bridge.
14.5 miles (H202) - Cross under I-44 turnpike.
14.9 miles - Down hill into Vinita.
15.2 miles (H201) - Cross Bull Creek.

VINITA

Named after Miss Vinnie Ream, a sculptor commissioned to model the life sized statue of Lincoln in Washington D. C. Vinita is one of the oldest towns in Oklahoma. Original settlement was called Downingville and the name was changed in 1871 with the arrival of the M-K-T and Atlantic and Pacific railroads.

For people interested in such things, the worlds largest McDonald's restaurant (*second largest, now, I believe*) is built on a bridge that spans I-44 a few miles from Vinita, (*worth looking at, but the service is terrible and the rest rooms stink*).

Make a left turn at the intersection of Wilson and Illinois **(H200)**. Curve to the right at the south end of town. Quite a few older motels along this stretch. As you complete the curve, in front of the River Dam Authority building **(H199)**,

ZERO ODOMETER

0.5 miles - Cross Big Cabin Creek.
3.0 miles (H198) - Junction with Hwy 69. A left turn here will take you to Big Cabin, nice motels and a great truck stop at the turnpike interchange. Ask for Peggy in the gift shop/store.
4.2 miles (H197) - Junction of 60 & Oklahoma 66. Go straight on OK 66.
5.7 miles (H196) - White Oak.
8.3 miles - Curve to right.
9.8 miles - Curve.
9.9 miles - Long hill.
11.1 miles - Four-lane road.
12.5 miles (H195) - Country Court motel on right. A motel set in the country to provide a respite for the traveler who may have traveled farther in one day than anticipated.
15.9 miles - Cemetery on right.
16.6 miles (H194) - Cross Prior Creek and enter

CHELSEA

Oil was first discovered in Oklahoma Indian Territory just west of here in 1899 and changed the industry of the community forever. Prior to oil, Chelsea had been a prairie hay shipping and cattle grazing town.
18.0 miles (H193) - Roadside park on left.
21.1 miles (H192) - Culvert crossing - WPA/CCC bridge.
22.6 miles (H191) - Culvert crossing - WPA/CCC bridge.
22.7 miles - Four-lane road and

BUSHYHEAD

Named for a chief of the Cherokee Nation.
23.5 miles - Old gas station on left.
26.0 miles -

FOYIL

An interesting side trip is to Galloway Park four miles east on Hwy 28A. Ed Galloway built a ninety-foot tall Totem pole and other examples of Oklahoma folk art.

To go through Foyil, make a left onto Andy Payne Blvd **(H190)** and:

ZERO ODOMETER

0.2 miles - Curve to left.
0.35 miles - Stop sign, continue straight.
0.8 miles - Curve left.
1.0 miles - Andy Payne Memorial.

At the west end of town where old Route 66 meets the new four-lane alignment **(H189)** (*look for the statue of Andy Payne in the small park*), turn left onto highway and

ZERO ODOMETER

3.4 miles (H188) - Sequoyah.
7.8 miles -

Chicago to Santa Monica

the criteria of this guidebook is that the designated Route 66 must be an all-weather road.
If you do not wish to travel on the narrow road, use **OPTION TWO**.

OPTION #1 - Driving the "Sidewalk Highway"
At the corner of Main and Steve Owens Blvd **(H219)** in Miami,
ZERO ODOMETER
Continue south on Main across the Neosho River. The road will become E Street SW.
  2.9 miles (H218) - Make a right turn at the "T" intersection of E Street SW and E 130 Rd.
The road surface is becoming well worn so "Slow" is order of the day.
  3.8 miles - Begin first nine foot section.
  4.4 miles (H217) - Curve to the left.
  5.4 miles (H216) - Curve to the right.
  6.4 miles (H215) - Left turn onto Hwy 69 and head south through Narcissa.
  12.5 miles (H212) - Right turn onto E 200 Road at the Technical Institute.
  12.7 miles - Start of 9 foot roadway. Watch your speed, road surface is badly pitted.
  13.5 miles (H211) - Curve to left.
  14.3 miles (H210) - Cross over I-44. Rough pavement.
  15.3 miles (H209) - Grade crossing at railroad. Turn off radio, roll down windows, (*stop arguing about driving on dirt roads!*) and proceed with caution.
  15.5 miles (H208) - Right onto highway to continue to Afton.

OPTION #2 - Skipping past the "Sidewalk Highway"
At the corner of Main and Steve Owens Blvd **(H219)** in Miami, make a right on Steve Owens Blvd and
ZERO ODOMETER
As you approach the Neosho River, make certain you are in the left lane to cross the bridge.
  1.2 miles - Curve to left.
  1.3 miles - Old Motor Court on right.
  1.4 miles - Old garage on left.
  1.6 miles - Route 66 Steel Building Company and the Frontier Motel. Also intersection with Oklahoma 10 - continue straight.
  2.0 miles - Cross railroad.
  2.5 miles - Curve right.
  3.7 miles - Small store on left.
  4.4 miles - Curve left.
  4.8 miles - Curve left.
  5.9 miles - Narcissa
  6.0 miles - Intersection with Oklahoma 25 - old garage and gas station.
  11.3 miles - Cross under I-44.
  11.8 miles (H214) - 60 East turns, continue on 59, 60, & 69.
  12.2 miles - Cross over railroad bridge.
  12.4 miles (H213) - Site of the Buffalo Ranch. In business from 1953 until 1997, as a tourist stop. Just ahead, Hwy 59 turns south, you continue around the curve towards Afton.
  14.0 miles (H207) - Curve to the left and cross Horse Creek. Notice the pedestrian walkways on either side of the bridge.
At Horse Creek Bridge,
ZERO ODOMETER

AFTON
Named after the river Afton from the Robert Burns poem. Some great examples of 1920's architecture here. Notice the bridge on the east end of town with its unique pedestrian walkways, built in 1929.
  0.3 miles (H206) - Rest Haven Motel on the right.
  1.1 miles - Old tourist cabins on right.
  1.6 miles - Road curves to left.
  5.5 miles (H205) - Dead Man's Corner - Old station and garage on right.
  8.8 miles - Cross stream.
  10.2 miles (H204) - Junction with OK 82, continue straight.

Chicago to Santa Monica

OKLAHOMA

WESTBOUND

Four miles south of Baxter Springs, Kansas, Highway 69A crosses the state line **(H227)** and a large sign welcomes you to Oklahoma. At this sign,
ZERO ODOMETER
    0.3 miles - Road curves to the right. Along the roadside can be seen many large mounds. These are piles of debris from zinc mining in the area and are called "chat."
    0.8 miles - Nothing to see, but beneath the roadway is part of an abandoned lead mine that once yielded more than $10 million to its owners.
    1.3 miles - Cross culvert.
    2.1 miles - Curve to right.
    3.6 miles - Small lake on right.
    4.1 miles

QUAPAW
Named for the Quapaw Tribe, who originally resided in Arkansas. At the turn of the century, this was a major hay-shipping center. With an abundance of tall prairie grass the area later became popular for cattle grazing. Around 1907, zinc mining became a mainstay of the area when ore from the Dark Horse Mine began paying off.
Today, Quapaw is quiet, but busy. Many of the buildings have great murals painted on them. One garage has a painting of an old-style gas station, if you frame your photo just right, it looks real.
    4.8 miles (H226) - Curve to right.
    6.1 miles - Cross under railroad.
    7.3 miles (H225) - Divided road and junction with Hwy 69. The road now becomes Hwy 69 and 69A ends.
    7.4 miles - Return to two-lane.
    8.6 miles (H224) - Cross Tar Creek.
    9.3 miles (H223) - Curve left. In many locations, you will experience this type of curve. If you look closely, you will see the original road went straight, then had a hard turn to the right or left. Later alignments added the curves.
    9.6 miles - Commerce, Oklahoma.
    11.0 miles (H222) - Short section of divided highway. To your right you will see the home of the fantastic Newell Motor Coach, the real way to travel Route 66. If you have the pocket change, I would appreciate it if you would pick one up for me ($750,000 and up) - I'll pay the gas money for delivery.
    11.7 miles (H221) - Just to the west is the Miami Municipal Airport which, beginning in early 1941, was home to British Flying Training School #3 where RAF pilots trained during WWII. Those killed during training are buried in the Grand Army of the Republic cemetery, which lays between Route 66 and the airport.

MIAMI
For those not familiar with Native American names, this is *MY-AM-UH*. Originally a trading post called Jimtown, it was home to four farmers named Jim (hence the name). A post office was established by Jim Palmer in 1890 and named Miami in honor of Palmer's wife, a Miami Indian.
    LODGING: Best Western Inn of Miami (918.542.6681).
    To follow Route 66 through Miami, go south on Route 69 (Main Street) to Steve Owens Blvd **(H219)**. *(Note: a Route 66 purist would have you jog over one block to A St NW and follow it south to Steve Owens Blvd and then jog back, but then you would miss the Coleman Theatre!)*
    14.3 miles (H220) - The Coleman Theater, built in 1929, at the corner of 1st and Main is an excellent example of restoration.
    On the south side of Miami, you have the highly recommended option of experiencing two extremely rare sections of nine-foot roadway. Yes, Virginia, the Mother Road is only NINE feet wide (sometimes less!) along these stretches.
    If you want to drive "The Sidewalk Highway," as it is known, use **OPTION ONE**, which is an Adventure Tour "Red Route." (Please read all admonitions regarding Adventure Tours at the front of this book.)
    OPTION ONE is partially a dirt road, slick and muddy in the winter, and following a rain. However, unlike some of the adventure tours in the Far West, this tour is more like "Adventure Tour Lite" because you are never isolated away from a nearby paved road. The only reason it is an adventure tour is because the old roadway doesn't tolerate wet weather very well, and one of

James G. Blunt approached Baxter Springs en route to his new posting at Fort Gibson. With him where his staff, a detachment of troops and a regimental band. Blunt mistook the departing Quantrill troops for an escort and was soon surrounded and captured. Quantrill sent a message to the garrison asking for an exchange of prisoners. Witnesses claim Quantrill had already killed all of the captives by the time the messenger was dispatched to the garrison.

General Blunt who, with eight men, had escaped Quantrill's band, found eighty-seven of his men dead by gunshots to the back of the head. In Baxter Springs National Cemetery (2 miles west on 166), a monument is dedicated to the men who fell that October day. *(Quantrill was later driven east into Kentucky where he died after a standoff with Union troops in the spring of 1865.)*

10.9 miles (K005) - Cross bridge. Baxter Springs Museum is one block east, to the left.
10.7 miles - Downtown Baxter Springs.
11.3 miles (K004) - Junction with Hwy 166. Continue straight on Hwy 69.
12.2 miles (K002) - Left turn off Military for old highway.
12.6 miles (K003) - Left turn back onto Military.
13.1 miles (K001) - The Oklahoma state line.

Chicago to Santa Monica

KANSAS

WESTBOUND

A brief trip across Kansas whets the appetite for what beauty lies beyond the short thirteen miles of the Sunflower State. At State Line Road **(K016)**,
ZERO ODOMETER
 The road crosses open country briefly before entering Galena. A green, tree-studded area, quite different from the chat-covered landscape to the north. You will be entering Galena on Front Street, which intersects with Main. **(H015)**. Make a left onto Main Street.

GALENA
Lead mines caused an explosion in population in 1877 as Galena was born. Over three thousand people moved here in the space of two months. The "hurry-up" factor combined with slag heaps made for a less than attractive town.

One of the more interesting stories is the rivalry between Galena and Empire City. A log wall was built between the two towns to keep the good citizens of Empire City from venturing to the rough-and-tumble Galena (*or was it the other way around?*). The people of Galena watched as the wall was painstakingly built, and when it was completed, proceeded to burn it to the ground.

The Post Office was established in 1877.

1.7 miles (K014) - The downtown area and intersection with 7th Street (US 26/K-66), make a right.

A couple of blocks west is Katy's Cafe (*a good place for lunch*) and the Galena Museum, it's on the right, by the "Old 66" sign. The museum is housed in a restored railroad depot that was moved to this site.

4.8 miles (K013) - Cross the Spring River. There used to be a marvelous bridge here, the Marsh Rainbow Arch Bridge, which was taken down in 1986. See Michael Wallis', *Route 66 - The Mother Road,* page 82 for a picture of this beauty.

On the right, as you cross the river, is the Spring River Inn, and on the left is the Empire District Hydroelectric Power Plant. This is one of those building you might expect to see in a 1930's Universal Pictures horror film.

RIVERTON
A river town situated on the west bank of the Spring River. Post office established in 1919.

5.3 miles - Kansas 66 ends here. Continue straight on Kansas 69 (designated as S-Alt 69). Riverton is the home of the Kansas Historic Route 66 Association. They are located in the old Eisler Bros. Store building **(K012)**. When you are in Riverton stop and say "Hi" to Scott Nelson, the president of the Kansas Association.

6.0 miles (K011) - Stop sign and cross Kansas Alt 400.

6.4 miles (K010) - Stop sign, continue straight.

7.3 miles - Road curves to the left.

7.5 miles (K009) - Stop and check out the Rainbow Arch bridge on the right, on the old alignment. There has been much controversy over the loss of the old arched bridges throughout Kansas. Heavy lobbying of the Kansas Department of Transportation has resulted in the saving of one and the losing of one in this area.

8.2 miles (K008) - Cross bridge

10.3 miles (K007) - Road veers to the left around a long curve.

10.6 miles (K006) - Stop sign and intersection with newer alignment, make a right turn.

BAXTER SPRINGS
A pleasant and bustling community with a busy downtown area. Baxter Springs takes pride in billing itself as "The First Cowtown in Kansas." The cowtown legacy goes back to the 1860s when cattlemen and cowboys from Texas would drive thousands of longhorns to feed on the abundant grasslands of the area. During 1867 and 1868, a boom hit the area as huge cattle drives brought cowboys in unprecedented numbers. With the arrival of the railroad, this seemingly quiet community became the "toughest town on earth" and a wide-open, hell-raisin' cowtown.

Once the railroad pushed on to the west, Baxter Springs returned to a quieter life.

Prior to the great cattle drives Baxter Springs was the site of a darker piece of history. On October 6, 1863, the Baxter Springs Massacre took place at what is now the eastern end of 7th Street. During that morning the Federal Garrison, consisting of one company of cavalrymen and 65 to 70 black infantrymen, was attacked by forces led by William Clarke Quantrill, a Confederate guerrilla fighter and pre-war criminal whose "troops" included Jesse James and his brother, Frank. After less than half-an-hour Quantrill's men withdrew, leaving two of their men dead and nine Federal soldiers mortally wounded. Later, on the same day, Major General

Chicago to Santa Monica

Chicago to Santa Monica

(417.624.7600).
DINING: Jim Bob's Steak and Ribs; Golden Ox.
Other routes through the city were known as "City 66" and "Alternate 66." The *Missouri US 66 Tour Book* by Skip Curtis covers these other routes in detail.

14.9 miles (M002) - Right turn onto to Old 66.
15.5 miles (M001) - Stateline Road and Kansas straight ahead.

Chicago to Santa Monica

34.9 miles (M031) - Remains of Shadyside Camp, all stone buildings and cabins.
37.2 miles (M030) - Plew. Named in 1893 for a local family. Sometimes found on old maps as Plewtite.
38.7 miles (M029) - Remains of Log City.
39.4 miles (M028) - Remains of Stone City.
40.4 miles (M027) - Cross White Oak Creek.
41.3 miles (M026) - Remains of White Oak Cabins.
42.4 miles (M025) - Avila. Quite a few old buildings.
44.8 miles - Log home on left appears to have had a store or gas station at one time.
46.3 miles (M024) - Small, white gas station on right.
50.2 miles (M023) - Left turn onto CR 118.
51.7 miles (M022) - Left onto MO96 where County Road V joins.
52.4 miles (M021) - Cross Spring River.
52.9 miles (M020) - Cross RR bridge and veer to the right onto Central.
53.3 miles (M019) - Left onto Garrison.
53.6 miles (M018) - Right on Oak.
53.8 miles (M017) - Cool bridge!

CARTHAGE

Platted in 1842 and named for the ancient commercial center in North Africa. In 1864, guerrillas of the Confederacy burned the courthouse, the business section and most of the private residences.
At the west end of Carthage:
55.2 miles (M016) - Left turn.
56.7 miles (M015) - Route 66 Drive-in.
58.1 miles (M014) - Right turn and cross MO71.
58.4 miles (M013) - Left at "T" intersection.
60.2 miles (M012) - Left at Carterville Cemetery onto Pine St. and
ZERO ODOMETER

CARTERVILLE & WEBB CITY

Carterville and Webb City were platted in 1875. Both were major lead and zinc producers until the demand dropped at the end of WWI.
1.2 miles (M011) - Right turn onto Main in Carterville.
1.9 miles (M010) - Left onto Carter St for two blocks, then follow around to the right onto Lewis St. which becomes Broadway in Webb City.
2.4 miles (M009) - Veer left onto Broadway.
2.8 miles (M007) - Broadway jogs to the left for 1/2 block on Webb St.
3.4 miles (M006) - Left on Madison.
5.7 miles (M005) - Right on Zora.
6.2 miles - Left on Florida.
6.5 miles - Right on Utica.
6.7 miles - Left on Euclid.
7.3 miles - Left on St. Louis.
8.5 miles (M003) - Right onto 7th Street westbound (MO 66).

JOPLIN

Beneath the city is a labyrinth of mine tunnels that have been filled with water to support the city above.
Originally settled by John C. Cox in 1838, along the banks of Turkey Creek. In 1841, he named the settlement that had expanded around his store, Blythville, after Billy Blythe, a popular Cherokee. In 1871, Patrick Murphy of Carthage purchased forty acres west of Joplin Creek and platted the town of Murphysburg. A few weeks later, John Cox, now Judge Cox, platted the city of Joplin on the east side of Joplin Creek. A rivalry developed between the two towns, so intense that children would stand on opposite sides of the creek and throw rocks at each other.
In March of 1872, the court was petitioned to combine the two cities under a common charter and call it Union City. More problems ensued and in March of 1873, the State General Assembly merged the two towns as the City of Joplin.
NOTE: If planning an overnight in Joplin, Range Line at I-44 is where many chain motels will be found.
LODGING: Hampton Inn (417.659.9900); Best Western Hallmark Motor Inn (417.624.8400); Thunderbird Motel

19.0 miles (M059) - Junction of 38 and "OO." Turn left onto "OO."
24.0 miles (M058) - Stop sign, without warning, at junction with "B," go straight - stay on "OO."
24.7 miles (M057) - Red Top Court was here.
27.7 miles (M056) - Holman.
31.1 miles - Strafford - Check out Grandaddy's BBQ at 101 E. Pine St (one block north of Route 66). Good food, friendly people. In Strafford, where 125 joins "OO" **(M055)**,
ZERO ODOMETER
1.2 miles (M054) - 125 turns to the left, stay on "OO."
3.7 miles - Roadway Freight lines terminal on the right.
4.2 miles (M053) - 744 joins "OO."
4.5 miles - Enter Springfield. Coming in to town, the Holiday Drive-in is on your right **(M052)**, about 1.5 miles before the intersection of Kearney and Glenstone.

SPRINGFIELD
Earliest settlement was by Thomas Patterson in 1821. In 1822, the Delaware tribe claimed the government had given them the lands of Southwestern Missouri. The courts upheld their claim and all the white settlers left the area. In 1830, John Polk Campbell and his brother established a cabin approximately 400 yards north of the present town square.

Like other western Missouri towns Springfield sided with the Confederacy during the Civil War. In August of 1861, the South won the battle of Wilson's Creek and held the city until February of 1862, when Union forces took it back.

LODGING: Best Western Sycamore Inn (Rail Haven) (417.866.1963); Park Inn (417.882.1113); Skyline Motel (417.866.4356). Plus many chain motels, a lot of the older motels suffer from neglect, disrepair or weekly tenets.

DINING: Hemingway's Blue Water Cafe (*check out the aquarium!*); Trotter's Bar-B-Q; The Shady Inn.

There are three routes through Springfield.
City Route - The 1925 to 1935 route takes Kearney to Glenstone, then left to St. Louis, right on St. Louis around the square, then College to the Chestnut Expressway.

Alternate 66 is left on SR 125, right on Division to Glenstone, right on St Louis and follow as above.

By-pass 66 (1936) is Kearney straight past the intersection with Glenstone **(M051)** through to US 160 (the west By-Pass) **(M050)** and left to the Chestnut Expressway (M049), then right towards I-44.

West of the intersection of the Chestnut Expressway and the West By-Pass, you will cross under I-44 **(M048)** to continue west on 266 and:
ZERO ODOMETER
4.0 miles - Old gas station foundation on left.
7.4 miles (M047) - Junction with "T." Old gas station on right.
9.5 miles (M046) - Plano and intersection with Farm Road 45. Large stone building on NW corner.
11.4 miles - Junction with "F."
13.9 miles (M045) - Halltown. Quite a few antique shops here. Interestingly, Jack Rittenhouse also mentioned antique shop here in his classic 1946 *Guidebook to Highway 66*.
16.4 miles (M044) - Stop sign, continue straight. Old station on left.
17.0 miles (M043) - Paris Spring Junction.
17.3 miles (M042) - Turnback Creek Bridge.
17.7 miles (M041) - Intersection with MO 96. For a taste of the old road, continue straight, across 96, onto "N."
18.3 miles (M040) - **UNMARKED TURN**: Make a right onto Farm Road 2062 and cross an old truss bridge.
18.4 miles (M039) - The buildings here are the remains of Spencer. Named in 1868, buildings here date to 1920s.
19.4 miles - Road jogs to the right, you can see where the old pavement went straight and is now under the fill for Highway 96.
19.5 miles (M038) - Cross 96 and turn left onto north side frontage road - Farm Road 2059.
20.1 miles (M037) - Cross "M" at stop sign.
21.5 miles (M036) - Forced to join 96, make a right onto 96.
23.6 miles (M035) - Heatonville. The Castle Rock Cabins were here.
25.9 miles - Another old station.
26.3 miles (M034) - Albatross. Named for the Albatross Bus Line that stopped at this spot. Founded in 1926. Junction with MO 39.
27.8 miles - Old road to the right, over the hill and rejoin at 28.0 miles.
29.6 miles (M033) - Phelps.
34.1 miles (M032) - Rescue.

Chicago to Santa Monica

routing to Lacquey and bring you back to the main highway farther west.

8.9 miles (M081) - Junction of 17 and "AB." Go straight on "AB." Do not follow 17 as it turns left, heading south.

9.3 miles (M080) - Junction of "AB" and "AA." Continue straight on "AB." The sidetrip from Lacquey rejoins the main highway here.

14.7 miles (M079) - Dadtown - Named for "Dad" Lewis who built a general store here in 1903. First silent movies in the area were shown in a large tent.

15.3 miles (M078) - Gascozark.

15.4 miles - Junction with 133. "AB" becomes Heartwood Road. Continue straight west.

16.6 miles (M077)

HAZELGREEN

Post office established in 1858. Once a bustling tourist town, the "new" four-lane Route 66 was built through town. Post Office closed in 1958.

18.1 miles (M076) - Bridge across the Gasconade.

20.1 miles (M075) - Junction of Heartwood Road. and "N." Go straight on "N." (Do not follow "N" to the south.)

21.3 miles (M074) - Junction of "N," "T," and Glacierpoint Road. Go straight on Glacierpoint. ("T" runs north to the right and "N" ends.)

26.2 miles (M073) - Right onto "F" and cross over I-44.

26.7 miles (M072) - Left onto old 66, north side of I-44.

32.1 miles (M071) - At stop sign.

ZERO ODOMETER

LEBANON

Founded with the forming of Leclede County in October of 1849. An example of a city moved because of the railroad. The railroad refused to build in town when the city refused to give them free land for the depot. They built the station one mile from town. The town picked up and moved to the new location, away from the well-drained original site to the mud-flats chosen by the railroad.

The Best Western Wyota Inn (417.532.6171) and the Hampton Inn (417.533.3100) are good bets for lodging, for a classic Route 6 motel, the Munger Moss on the east end of town, right on old 66. Stonegate Station is good for both American and Italian specialties.

0.2 miles (M070) - Road veers left.

1.0 miles (M069) - Cross Jefferson.

1.7 miles (M068) - Road curves left.

2.9 miles (M067) - Junction with "W," **NO WARNING**, make a short right, followed by a curve to left.

12.9 miles (M066) - End of "W," turn left onto "C" and cross I-44 to south side.

13.4 miles (M065) - Junction of "C" and "CC," make a right onto "CC" and

ZERO ODOMETER

2.7 miles - Road turns away from the Interstate (sharp turn).

4.8 miles (M064) - Conway, small main street area to the left. Junction with "J," stay on "CC."

The railroad begins to parallel the highway and suddenly you get a sense of being on the wrong road. The feeling is actually caused by being on an old section of The Mother Road. It is a feeling of contentment at putting the hustle and hassle of the Interstate behind you. You're not lost, you're not in the Twilight Zone, you're cruisin' on 66!

9.4 miles (M063) - Sampson and junction with "HH."

11.9 miles (M062) - The Abbylee Court is on the left. This was Niangua.

12.5 miles (M061) - Junction with "M," stay on "CC."

13.5 miles - Rock cut for highway.

14.8 miles - Truss bridge.

16.7 miles -

MARSHFIELD

Platted in 1856 and named after Daniel Webster's home in Massachusetts. The centerpiece of the town is the courthouse, built in 1870. In town, "CC" is also known as Hubble Drive, named for Edwin Hubble, a local boy, who was the first man to prove there were other galaxies. (*His name is also on the Hubble Space Observatory, which has had a somewhat checkered history.*)

18.8 miles (M060) - Junction of "CC" and 38. Go straight on 38 one long block to junction of "OO." (*Wake-up! We know you're tired of the alphabet soup road numbering system but this a busy five-way junction!*)

22

Chicago to Santa Monica

forcing them back into the traffic lanes. A unique concept that failed miserably. The curbs resulted in cars being tipped over. The road narrows along here and the trees encroaching on either side give a feeling of being transported back in time.

2.2 miles (M105) - Martin Spring.
2.9 miles (M104) - Cross one-lane bridge.
3.9 miles -

DOOLITTLE
Originally Centerville it was renamed in 1946 to honor General Jimmy Doolittle, Medal of Honor winner and WWII hero.
5.7 miles (M103) - Intersection with "T" in Doolittle.
9.1 miles (M099) - It will be necessary to get on I-44 West here, but first there's a sidetrip to explore the two dead-end sections that present themselves here.

The south frontage road road (known locally as the Arlington Outer Road or the Outer Road West) will take you 2.9 miles from here to Arlington **(M102)** where the road dead-ends. This section is a nice piece of old highway, the pavement is narrow and there are a couple of steep grades to make it interesting. Cross under I-44 just before Arlington, one of those places that seems to have had trouble finding itself. Through a seemingly endless process of redrawing county lines, Arlington, has been in St. Louis, Gasconade, Crawford, Pulaski, and Phelps Counties. The main street was cut off by the new highway in the 40s, and in 1946 Arlington was sold to Rowe Crey of Rolla for $10,000. He had plans of developing it into a resort. Today, Arlington sits quietly beneath the Interstate as a fishing and camping spot for those lucky enough to know where it is.

The north frontage road (known locally as the Sugartree Outer Road) dead-ends 2.1 miles down at an old motel that is now a private residence **(M101)**. For an interesting photo opportunity, drive just past Vernell's Motel to the long abandoned "John's Modern Cabins" **(M100)** which has been the subject of preservation efforts.

When you're ready, enter I-44, cross the bridge and take the first exit (#172 - Jerome) **(M098)**. The remains of Stony Dell resort are here.

Make a left after exiting the Interstate and follow the North Outer Road East (*say that fast six times!*) until it junctions with "J" at the I-44 crossover **(M096)**. Make a left, cross the Interstate, and make right onto "Z" and

ZERO ODOMETER
0.5 miles (M095) - Road becomes four-lane (*rough road!*).
1.4 miles (M094) - Right turn-off for

HOOKER
Originally Pine Bluff, renamed for a local family. Post office established 1900.
2.3 miles (M093) - Pass through the massive Hooker Cut.

This four-lane section of the Mother Road was the last piece of Route 66 to be replaced by I-44 in Missouri. What a great and magnificent demonstration of the art of road building.

2.8 miles (M092) - Left turn to visit the Devil's Elbow. (*Going straight would keep you on the final alignment, but it isn't nearly as much fun!*)
3.2 miles (M091) - The "Elbow Inn." A nice to place to stop for eats or a soda.
3.4 miles (M090) - Village of Devils Elbow.
3.9 miles (M089) - Vista Point.
4.8 miles (M088) - Grandview Courts on your right.
5.1 miles (M087) - Make left to rejoin four-lane highway and
ZERO ODOMETER
2.8 miles (M086) - Junction with MO 28. "Z" ends. Go straight onto BL 44.
3.7 miles - Cross I-44.
4.3 miles (M085) - St. Robert.
5.7 miles -

WAYNESVILLE
Jake Bates opened a store here in 1835 and in 1839 the townsite was platted. Named for Revolutionary War General "Mad Anthony" Wayne.
At the large county courthouse in the center of Waynesville **(M084)**,
ZERO ODOMETER
Follow business Loop 44 through town, and Hwy 17 South, out of town.
5.5 miles (M083) - Left and cross the interstate, then right onto MO 17.
7.0 miles (M082) - Junction of 17, "P," and "NN." Time for a sidetrip! A right turn onto "P" will take you along the 1927

gunpowder factory at Saltpeter Cave (Meramec Caverns). Some say that Sullivan was saved and lived to an old age.

BOURBON

During the 1850s, Richard Turner sold whiskey to railroad crews from his store. The place was called the Bourbon Store and in time the townsite took on the name.

5.2 miles (M126) - Cross junction with "N" and "J" in Bourbon.
5.9 miles (M125) - Cross junction with "C" and "N" in Bourbon.
10.9 miles (M124) - Cross junction with "H." Oak Grove Wayside Park on left.
14.2 miles (M123) - Remains of Hofflins.
17.2 miles (M122) - The Wagon Wheel Motel.
17.9 miles (M121) -

CUBA

Founded in 1857 as a farming village and railroad shipping point. The town virtually abandoned its original location near the tracks and moved up to the highway in the 1930s. Between here and Rolla, the highway crosses the Big Prairie.

Classic lodging at the Wagon Wheel Motel (573.885.3411), contemporary lodging at Best Western Cuba Inn (573.885.7707).

20.7 miles (M120) - Cross junction with "KK."
21.9 miles (M119) - Fanning.
22.8 miles (M118) - Junction of "ZZ" and "F". Go straight on "ZZ."
25.1 miles (M117) - Junction of "KK" and "ZZ." "ZZ" ends. Go straight onto "KK." "KK" also turns south, to the left.

This is the Rosati area, more a sprawling community of farms rather than a town. Italians settled area around the turn of the century.

Near Rosati, watch for cars stopping along the interstate and the people crossing over to old 66 *(See how smart you are to be traveling on the Mother Road instead of Insipid-state 44!)* to visit the numerous grape stands along here.

25.6 miles - Classic Car showroom on the left.
26.8 miles (M116) - Junction of "KK" and "U." Go straight on "KK."
35.1 miles

ST. JAMES

Originally platted in 1859 by James Wood and was known as Scioto. The name was changed in a matter of months to St. James. The main business district runs at a right angle to the highway.

You are still on "KK" when you enter St. James, where "KK" is also named E James Blvd. The main cross-street you will encounter is Jefferson St. (US 68). At the corner of "KK" and Jefferson **(M114)**, turn right.

Follow Jefferson north across the Interstate **(M113)**.

Take an immediate left onto the "Old Highway 66 Outer Road" and

ZERO ODOMETER

ROLLA

Founded in 1855 by a group of contractors who were building the railroad. In 1857, Phelps County was organized and Rolla was selected as the county seat. The town was named, according to legend, when John Webber wanted to call it Hardscrabble. E. W. Bishop, a railroad official wanted to call it Phelps Center. George Coppedge won out with the request it be named after his North Carolina home of Raleigh. However, the name wound up being spelled as Coppedge pronounced it, Rolla (*Raw-la*).

LODGING: Best Western Coachlight Inn (573.341.2511); Zeno's Motel (573.364.1301).
DINING: Johnny's Smoke Stak - great barbeque; Zeno's Steakhouse.
Downtown is the Uptown Theater (*sorry, I just kind of liked that!*).
This is the end of the Big Prairie country. The Ozarks begin here.

4.6 miles (M112) - Route 66 Motors and General Store. Classic cars and things for the person who is crazy about cars.

Continue for 1.5 miles to "V" **(M111)**. Cross "V." You will be joining Road 2020, continue west for 3.4 miles to Road 2000 **(M110)**.

Make an angled right turn onto Road 2000 and follow it (a short distance) to Bishop Ave. (US 63) **(M109)**.

Make a left on Bishop and follow it as it crosses I-44 **(M108)** to Kingshighway **(M107)**.

Make a right onto Kingshighway (BL 44). Follow it to the west side of town where Kingshighway meets I-44 Exit 184 **(M106)**, veer left onto Martin Spring Drive (Road 7100) and

ZERO ODOMETER

Traveling west out of Rolla, take note of the half-curbs alongside the road. These were designed to keep cars on the road by

Chicago to Santa Monica

and
ZERO ODOMETER

The Diamonds Restaurant and Motel are located here. This is the "new" Diamonds, the original diamonds is now a truck stop about two miles west. The Diamonds was started by Spencer Groof and was once billed as the world's largest restaurant.

0.4 miles (M147) - The Gardenway Motel, a classic Route 66 motel.
1.3 miles (M146) - Cross I-44. Bridge only - no interchange.
2.0 miles (M145) - Villa Ridge, cross MO 100 and go straight ahead on "AT."
2.3 miles (M144) - The Tri-County Restaurant and Truck Stop is the old Diamonds. The building you see here was built after a tremendous fire in 1948 that destroyed the original building. The fire was so intense that all traffic on Route 66 was stopped for hours.
3.3 miles (M143) - The Sunset Motel.
5.0 miles (M142) - Junction with Hwy "M." "M" joins "AT" at this point. Go straight.
6.0 miles (M141) - Junction with Hwy "O." Go straight.
6.7 miles (M140) - Junction of Hwy 50. Cross 50 and go straight ahead on the North Outer Road.
NOTE: THIS MANEUVER REQUIRES YOUR UTMOST ATTENTION BECAUSE YOU ARE CROSSING FOUR LANES OF A BUSY HIGH-SPEED DIVIDED HIGHWAY. BE CAREFUL! (*The producers of certain high-quality Route 66 maps almost met their Maker at this intersection!*)
7.8 miles (M139) - Do not cross Interstate here. (This is a crossover bridge to the South Outer Road.) Stay on north side of I-44.
8.8 miles (M138) - Hall's Place.
11.9 miles (M137) - I-44 Exit 242. Cross over the interstate to the South Outer Road, turn right and continue into St. Clair where 66 becomes Commercial Ave.
14.4 miles (M136) - "TT" turns south, to the left. Go straight
14.9 miles (M135) - Hwy 47 will merge into 66. Go straight.

ST. CLAIR

Once known as Travelers Repose, the name was changed in 1859 when the town citizens grew tired of the town being thought of as a pioneer cemetery or a tavern. Named for a civil engineer of the Frisco Railroad.

15.6 miles (M134) - West of town, Hwys 30 and 47 split, turning south to the left. Go straight and follow 66 to the I-44 interchange at Exit 239.
15.7 miles (M133) - Turn right and cross the Interstate.
15.9 miles (M132) - On the north side of I-44, take "WW" to the left.
17.3 miles (M131) - "WW" turns right, you continue straight on Outer Service Road East going west and
ZERO ODOMETER
1.5 miles - Road curves away from I-44.
3.2 miles (M130) - Junction with St. Louis Inn Road.
7.4 miles -

STANTON

Originally Reedville, renamed for Peter Stanton who ran a powder mill here during the 1850s. (*And who, like fellow Confederate gunpowder maker Stephen Sullivan, also ended up on the business end of a noose run by the Union troops.*)

Many great "tourist traps" along here. Check out the Antique Toy Museum, the Jesse James Museum and of course, Meramec Caverns.

The Caverns opened in 1930 as a commercial enterprise of Lester Dill. When originally opened, the caverns had parking for 300 cars, electric lighting and a dance pavilion all within the first room. The caverns are located about 3-1/2 miles to the right on "W."

Cross I-44 **(M129)**, then make a right onto the south frontage road. At this point, as you turn onto 66,
ZERO ODOMETER
Continue south out of Stanton toward Sullivan.
1.6 miles - Huge pottery shop on the left.
4.1 miles (M128) - Stop light at junction with MO185.

SULLIVAN

Founded as Mt. Helicon in 1856 and renamed in honor of Stephen Sullivan who donated the railroad right-of-way through the village. As a confederate sympathizer, he was hanged along with John Stanton (after whom Stanton is named) for operating the

Chicago to Santa Monica

Things went pretty much straight down hill from there. Besides suffering the decay of a typical un-maintained piece of urban infrastructure, there was a 1999 audit that revealed a fortune in "diverted" tolls and the City of St. Louis put a property tax lien on the bridge portion on the Missouri side and threatened to auction it off. Had enough? Well, there's more. There are $4 million in bonds still owed by Venice and the State of Illinois closed the bridge in October of 2001 because it was unsafe.

Okay, now for some good news. Pending a complicated list of negotiations, the bridge is going to be taken over by the State of Illinois and rebuilt as a toll-free bridge to be maintained by the Missouri DOT and the Illinois DOT. It will have only two traffic lanes, with bicycle lanes along the outside, and will have a connection with I-70 in St. Louis. However, the work - if it starts and is done on schedule - will not be complete until 2006.

Use Salisbury Street to return from the McKinley Bridge. Cross Florissant **(M168)** to Natural Bridge (*also marked as Palm Street*) **(M167)** and make a left.

Go four blocks and make a right back onto Florissant. **(M166)**. *(We know: picky, picky - but you want to follow the true Mother Road, don't you?)*

Continue on Florissant - it will curve to the left **(M165)** and briefly follow 13th Street before joining Tucker Blvd. Follow Tucker through downtown, it will become 12th Street, and as it passes under the I-55 interchange **(M164)**, Tucker becomes Gravois (pronounced *Grav-oy*).

Proceed on Gravois to Chippewa **(M163)** where you make an angled right. Follow Chippewa about 3 miles to 6726 Chippewa where you can visit a Route 66 landmark: Ted Drewes Frozen Custard **(M162)**. Stop in for an original treat!

Continue on Chippewa, and at the St. Louis city limit **(M161)**, Chippewa becomes Watson Road. Cross under the Frisco Railroad bridge.

About 2 miles west of Ted Drewes, at 7755 Watson Rd. in the village of Marlborough, is the site of a very famous Route 66 landmark, the Coral Court Motel. **(M160)**. Although now replaced by a housing subdivision, the Coral Court was a great place in its heyday, both architecturally and socially. You can read everything you'd ever like to know about the Coral Court in Shellee Graham's fine book of stories and photographs, *Tales from the Coral Court* (ISBN 1-891442-08-2 or visit www.coralcourt.com). Note: If you are using a contemporary map to supplement your travels, the Coral Court was located where Watson Road is intersected by Oak Knoll Manor Drive.

Proceed on Watson Road for 5 more miles, join I-44 west at the MO 366/Watson Rd interchange **(M159)**, and
ZERO ODOMETER

As you drop off the hill and cross the Meramec, you are at the site of Sylvan Beach, a once popular recreational and amusement site for St. Louis residents.

2.1 miles - Chrysler plant on the left.
5.2 miles - Frontage road on the right is old 66. It dead-ends.
10.1 miles (M158) - The Lewis Road exit will take you to Times Beach.

Times Beach can be seen off to the left. Visit the Route 66 State Park and Museum here. Times Beach was a summer get-away for the St. Louis crowd. It developed as a promotional stunt by the St. Louis Star-Times in 1925. If you bought a lot for a home, you were given a six-month subscription to the paper. Contests were held with additional lots being awarded as prizes.

In 1982, Times Beach was declared contaminated by the EPA because dioxin laced oil had been used on the dirt roads in the early 1970's. By 1986, the buy-out of the town was complete, bringing to an end Times Beach.

Return to I-44 and exit Interstate at exit 261 **(M157)**. Make a left, then a right on Old 66 and
ZERO ODOMETER

1.0 miles (M155) - A bridge followed by a major rock cut for the highway.
1.3 miles (M154) - Remains of the Beacon Motel.
2.0 miles (M153) - The Eastern Missouri Correctional Center. Don't pick up hitchhikers!
3.5 miles (M152) - Red Cedar Inn, a local favorite since 1934.
4.5 miles (M151) - Monroe's 66 Diner - nice 66 atmosphere and good food.
5.8 miles (M150)

PACIFIC

Originally named Franklin when founded in 1852. Renamed in 1854 for the ultimate destination of the railroad. Lots of coal trains pass through here. Many silica mines in the area provide fine sand for glassware.
LODGING: Holiday Inn Express (314.257.8400).
DINING: Sheffield's Grill and Cafe; Monroe's 66 Diner; The Red Cedar Inn.

8.6 miles (M149) - Highway bridge over the railroad tracks. The tracks run in a deep cut through here and in the distance can be seen the entrance to the tunnel that runs beneath Gray Summit.

9.3 miles (M148) - Join Highway 100 (**NOTE:** This is a dangerous intersection, traffic exiting the interstate does not stop!)

Chicago to Santa Monica

MISSOURI

WESTBOUND

Long known as the "Show Me" State, Missouri will share some wonderful sights along Route 66. A bridge with a bend in the middle, the Great Arch, and The Ozarks are just a sampling of what lies ahead.

ST. LOUIS
Town site was laid out in 1764 by Pierre Laclede and dedicated to St. Louis IX, the name-saint of King Louis XV of France. The first group to use the area were fur trappers followed by settlers from New Orleans. The 1840s saw the city virtually wiped out by fire, flood and a major cholera epidemic. In 1857, the railroad reached St. Louis bringing in the European immigrants to establish the character of the city. 1904 brought the Louisiana Purchase Exposition to the city and America was introduced to a plethora of new products, including the Hot Dog, Ice Cream Cones and Iced Tea. This is the largest city between Chicago and Los Angeles on 66.

LODGING: As with any large city St. Louis offers literally hundreds of lodging choices. I must admit the only hotel I have stayed at in the city is the Hyatt Regency St. Louis At Union Station, a very nice hotel, centrally located with so many amenities you virtually never have to leave the property. Suggestion is to stay at one of the major chains, many of the older motels I have inspected suffer from neglect.

DINING: Excellent dining in all parts of the city, personal favorites are Tony's for great Italian at 410 Market St; Ike's Smokehouse for great barbeque (2841 Hwy 100); and for something different the 94th Aero Squadron at 5933 McDonnell Blvd (excellent Sunday brunch). And of course for a real treat, Ted Drewe's Frozen Custard on Chippewa Street.

Route 66 found its way across St. Louis in a number of different alignments. We will start our Missouri tour where the Chain of Rocks Bridge crossed the Mississippi on the 1936 alignment, which at that time skirted the city.

Following the Bridge route, you would make a jog to the right on the Missouri side, then a left as you headed up the hill from the river bottom. This section of Old 66 now lies beneath I-270 from this point to Lindbergh Blvd. At Lindbergh, turn south and follow the road through to Kirkwood where you will meet up with Hwy 366 (Watson Road). Although known locally as By-Pass 66, this was the official Route 66 shown on various maps dating from 1933.

Other routings are also available. City 66 and Optional 66. Both routes start at Mitchell, Illinois and use Route 67. The routes separated at Broadway and 4th Street in Venice. For detailed information on the various routings, we suggest *The Missouri Route 66 Tour Book* by Skip Curtis.

VARIOUS ROUTINGS THROUGH ST. LOUIS

> **NOTE: THREE ROUTES OF 66 EXIST IN ST. LOUIS. THIS BOOK COVERS WHAT WAS KNOWN AS "CITY 66", THE ROUTE USED FROM 1933 ON. THE OTHER ROUTES ARE COVERED EXTENSIVELY IN THE MISSOURI ROUTE 66 TOUR BOOK BY SKIP CURTIS. ISBN 0-9633863-4-4 OR VISIT HTTP://WWW.BIRTHPLACEOFROUTE66.COM/**

Because of problems with the McKinley Bridge (*see below*), you will need to use one of the interstate freeway bridges to cross the Mississippi.

The recommended route is to use I-270 because it is closest to the Chain of Rocks Bridge where the Illinois chapter of the guidebook ended. I-270 can be used to get you to downtown St. Louis where you can pick up Route 66 on the other end of the McKinley Bridge, or you can use I-270 to go completely around St. Louis and join I-44 near Watson Road **(M159)**.

To get to downtown, take I-270 to the Florissant Road exit, which is about five miles WEST after crossing the Mississippi. Take Florissant south about nine miles. (*If you're mad for freeways, take I-270 to I-170, south to I-70, east to Florissant Rd south.*) Go to Salisbury Street **(M168)** and turn left. Follow Salisbury to the McKinley Bridge. (M169).

Now, about the McKinley Bridge. It was built in 1910 by the Illinois Traction System to connect its freight and passenger electric interurban network with St. Louis, and was named for William B. McKinley, the president of the company, not the assassinated president of the United States. (!) The bridge was later converted for railroad and highway traffic and became owned by the city of Venice, Illinois.

Chicago to Santa Monica

land extends nearly a hundred miles along the river from Alton on the north to Chester on the south.

14.1 miles (L011) - Old, small station on left.

14.4 miles - Cross bridge.

As we near Mitchell, it is obvious we are near a large city. Many of the older buildings - so carefully preserved in the rural locations - are being allowed to rot. Many 50's era motels stand alongside the road, their glittery signs harking back to a time when this was "The Road."

17.0 miles (L010) - Intersection with Illinois 111.

The abandoned Bel Air Drive-In is across intersection on right and the Hen House Restaurant is on the left. (*Try THAT place on for size if you want a dining adventure, particularly on all-you-can-eat fish Friday's!*)

Next to the Hen House is the Best Western Camelot Inn (618.391.2262).

As you cross the intersection,

ZERO ODOMETER

There are many older motels along this stretch.

1.1 miles (L009) - The Luna Cafe.

1.3 miles (L008) - Curve to the left for Illinois 203, also known locally as Nameoki Road. Immediately make a left to join I-270 westbound **(L007)**, but don't settle into your seat just yet because you're getting off immediately. (*Meaning NOW! The only reason for the freeway hopping is to get you across the Wabash Railroad tracks.*)

After you come around the curve of the exit, make a right onto Old Alton Road and cross beneath the Interstate. Then take the first road to your right **(L006)** (you are southbound) for the continuation of Chain of Rocks Road. The road is NOT marked at the intersection. About a tenth of mile west is the first sign telling you it is the Chain of Rocks Road. This area is great for photographing old motel signs.

The road will curve to the left and you will arrive at Route 3 **(L005)**. Cross over to continue west on Chain of Rocks Road. You will cross over the Chain of Rocks Ship Canal **(L004)** as you follow the road to the Chain of Rocks Bridge **(L003)**. The small dirt road a quarter of a mile back to the left will lead to the river **(L002)** and a great waterside view of the bridge and St. Louis across the Mississippi River.

Constructed in 1929, the Old Chain of Rocks Bridge was financed by tolls. The most obvious feature of the bridge is the 22-degree bend in the middle, a compromise between river traffic and the natural geology of the river (*no, it was not caused by Missouri and Illinois engineers making a mathematical error*!). Had the bridge been built straight, it would have wound up in an area where there was not solid bedrock for the foundation. The Chain of Rocks below the bridge were a hazard to river navigation until the construction of the Chain of Rocks Canal to bypass the danger. The two castle-like structures, visible to the south of the bridge, are water intake towers for the Chain of Rocks Water Treatment Facility constructed in 1894 (*and still in use*).

The bridge is now a great walking and bike tour adventure, and, at a mile in length, is the longest pedestrian/bike bridge in the world. TrailNet deserves major kudos for their efforts at restoration and the re-opening of this classic. The bridge was used in the making of the film *Escape From New York* where it became the 69th Street Bridge. Watch for it toward the end of the film.

Return to Route 3 **(L005)** and make a left, going north to I-270 **(L001)** where you join the interstate westbound to St. Louis.

As you cross the river, you are entering Missouri and our next state along the Mother Road.

Chicago to Santa Monica

OPTION 2 - This option follows the early alignment, taking you through Staunton but bypassing Livingston. (*Hey, you can't have everything, but there is a doctor there, I presume...*)

OPTION #1

At the junction of Staunton Road and old 66 (**L026**), make a left turn. Go straight ahead to the intersection with the west frontage road (**L025**) and turn right to Livingston. (*At this writing there was a detour in place affecting the route. If the detour is still in place, you will need to join I-55 here and continue south to the next exit. There you can re-join 66 in Livingston.*)

4.5 miles - Livingston. The frontage road curves to the right and becomes Church St. At the intersection with Park St., make a left and go straight ahead to the stop (**L023**). Continue straight, which will take you along the west side of I-55.

8.0 miles (L022) - Stop sign at junction with IL 4. Go straight ahead onto Possum Hill Road. (This is where the final alignment crosses the early alignment, which is coming from the right on IL 4 and continues past you on the left to Hamel.)

8.1 miles (L021) - Intersection with frontage road. Make a left and head south into Hamel to the junction with IL 140 (**L018**).

North of Hamel is the St. Paul's Cemetery (**L019**) and St. Paul's Church (**L020**). The cemetery is notable for its lack of a fence and the church is a very nice Gothic design.

To continue, jump to the text below labeled "HAMEL."

OPTION #2

At the junction of Staunton Road and old 66 (**L026**), go straight ahead.

0.3 miles -

STAUNTON

First cabin built here in 1817 by John Wood. The town was platted in 1835.

Stay on East Main through town.

1.7 miles (L030) - Junction with IL 4, make a left onto Hibbard Street, which is a continuation of IL 4.
1.8 miles - Right onto Pearl.
2.0 miles - Make a left on Hackman St.
2.7 miles - Curve to right.
2.9 miles (L029) - Curve to left, following IL 4 to the south.
4.1 miles - Cross railroad tracks.
4.7 miles - Old roadhouse on right.
5.6 miles - Curve right.
7.8 miles (L022) - Stop sign at junction with Possum Hill Road. Go straight ahead on IL 4 to continue traveling on the early alignment to Hamel. (This is where the early alignment crosses the final alignment, which is coming from the right on Possum Hill Road and continues past you on the left to Livingston.)
8.0 miles (L028) - Cross I-55.
11.1 miles (L027) - Junction of IL 4 and IL 140, make a right onto 140, which will take you to into Hamel where you make a left turn in town to join the final alignment (**L018**).

HAMEL

At the intersection of Route 66 and IL 140 (**L018**),
ZERO ODOMETER
2.9 miles - Curve right.
3.3 miles - Curve left.
6.9 miles - Truck lane as you climb hill. (*Nice paving job!*)
7.1 miles - End of truck lane.
7.5 miles - Edwardsville.
8.1 miles (L017) - Make a right and stay on Illinois 157.
8.6 miles (L016) - Cross downtown intersection with IL 143/IL 159 and continue on IL 157.
9.0 miles (L015) - Left on IL 157.
9.2 miles (L014) - Curve right.
9.7 miles (L013) - Under railroad bridge
13.3 miles - Top a rise and begin descent into the Mississippi River valley.
13.6 miles (L012) - Cross 4-lane highway onto Chain of Rocks Road.

This area, at the base of the bluffs, is the eastern edge of the American Bottom, classed as "flat as a table top." This bottom-

Chicago to Santa Monica

Leave I-55 at Exit 80 - Divernon **(L049)**.
At the stop sign at the end of the off ramp **(L048)**,
ZERO ODOMETER
Right toward Divernon
  0.1 miles (L047) - Left, return to frontage road.
  9.0 miles (L046) - Curve right - Farmersville, continue straight.
  13.7 miles (L045) - Waggoner road - straight on.
  15.6 miles - Curve to right around rest area.
  17.0 miles (L044) - Our Lady of the Highway monument.
  17.9 miles (L043) - Stop at junction with IL 48/ IL127, continue straight.
  21.2 miles (L041) - Junction with IL 108 (to Carlinville), go straight. Just before the junction is a very unique Holiday Inn **(L042)** - it has a lake and a steamboat!
  24.4 miles (L040) - Curve right, make left and cross I-55.
  24.4 miles - Right onto east frontage road.
  25.9 miles (L039) - Cross under railroad. On the left you can see old pavement. There would have been a grade crossing here on the old highway.
  27.3 miles - Old section to the left, DO NOT take, stay on four-lane. (*Tempting, though...*)
  27.6 miles - Cross bridge.
  27.7 miles (L038) - Intersection and enter Litchfield to left.

LITCHFIELD

An old mining town and the center of a coal field that lies beneath six counties. In 1882, Litchfield became the site of the first commercial oil production in Illinois. The small pocket of oil was soon exhausted, but not before guaranteeing Litchfield a place in the history books.

At intersection of old 66 and Illinois 16 **(L037)**, go straight ahead and
ZERO ODOMETER
The Ariston will be on your right. A fine place to dine with excellent food, a wonderful ambiance and great service. Nick Adam is your host.
  0.2 miles - Cross tracks (*slow, it's a rough crossing*).
  0.7 miles - Route 66 Cafe on right.
Once the site of an old tourist court, the Route 66 Cafe has the look of a 30's cafe, both inside and out. The food is good and the interior a deco influenced eye pleaser.
  2.3 miles (L036) - Road 1000/Kruse Road. There is an asphalt plant at this junction, make a left turn onto the final alignment.
  6.7 miles (L035) - Left turn onto early alignment into Mt. Olive. (*Like Litchfield, the final alignment goes straight ahead, bypassing Mt. Olive, but is uninteresting.*) The road curves right onto 5th Street and then curves left.

MT. OLIVE

This small, quiet town was the center of coal mining and union activities in the late 1800s and early 1900s. Mt. Olive is the final resting place of Mary Harris, better known as "Mother Jones." Her simple headstone is at the base of the tall monument in the Union Miner's Cemetery on the northwestern edge of town. Mother Jones was a fierce fighter for the rights of miners and children, having once led a march of children on the city of New York protesting child labor.
  9.0 miles (L034) - Intersection with Illinois 138. Go straight ahead.
  9.1 miles (L033) - Russell Soulsby's Shell Station. Now closed, but restored by the Illinois Route 66 Association. Was in constant operation from 1926 to 1992.
  11.1 miles (L032) - Left turn onto final alignment. (Old alignment visible on the left.)
  11.3 miles - Four lanes narrows to two lanes to cross under railroad.
  11.8 miles (L031) - Right onto old 66.
  12.0 miles - Cross over I-55.
  13.0 miles (L026) - Junction of old 66 and Staunton Road, which is also the access road to I-55, and
ZERO ODOMETER
Sidetrip! (This one is kind of neat because one option crosses the other. That allows you to mix and match between the two, if you want!)
OPTION 1 - This option follows the final Rt 66 alignment (1940-1977) and parallels the interstate, taking you through Livingston but bypassing Staunton.

Chicago to Santa Monica

10.0 miles (L062)

ELKHART
At north end of Elkhart the old road can be reached and followed back for about a mile. This section curves coming into town and crosses the four lane and winds close to the tracks before dumping you back on the four-lane. This short drive can give you a real feel for the old highway.

There are also sections of abandoned four-lane along here. In the center of Elkhart, at the intersection with Kennedy Road **(L062)**,
ZERO ODOMETER
    4.5 miles - Slight turn to the right. Old pavement to the left (very short section). Stay on four-lane.
    5.8 miles (L061) -

WILLIAMSVILLE
Williamsville has to be one of the most attractive of the small towns encountered on our Route 66 journey. Downtown is pleasantly maintained with nice shops and storefronts. Route 66 does not go into Williamsville, so if you chose to visit, return to the off ramp and continue south from there.

It will be necessary to enter I-55 here at exit 109 **(L060)**.

Continue on I-55 and leave the interstate at Exit 105. This is the north end of Springfield. At the end of the ramp **(L059)**, make a right and
ZERO ODOMETER
    0.4 miles - Old pavement to left.
    2.5 miles - Cross Sangammon River.
    3.5 miles - Curve to right. Pioneer Motel on right.
    4.5 miles - Cross under railroad tracks and immediately make a left, following BL 55 south on Peoria Road. Then make an immediate right onto Taintor Road **(L058)**.
    5.4 miles - Pass Illinois State Fairgrounds.
    6.0 miles - Curve left onto 5th Street.
    10.1 miles - Curve left onto 6th Street.

SPRINGFIELD
The state capital of Illinois did not exist when the state was admitted to the Union in 1818. That was the year Elisha Kelly arrived in the Sangammon River Valley in search of game. Impressed with the fertile soil and abundance of game, he returned home and convinced his brother and father to return with him to Illinois. They established a small settlement, and in 1821 when Sangammon County was created it was determined the Kelly settlement was the only place large enough to provide board and lodging for country officials. The name Springfield came from nearby Spring Creek and one of Kelly's fields.

Springfield is the site of the only home Abraham Lincoln ever owned. The National Parks Service maintains the home in a restored 19th century neighborhood. The area provides a step back in time allowing a visit to the homes and streets of a much simpler America.

LODGING: Best Western Lincoln Plaza Hotel (217.523.5661); Hampton Inn (217.529.1100); Mansion View Inn (217.544.7411); Red Roof Inn (217.753.4302).

DINING: The Cozy Dog (*of course*); Chesapeake Seafood House; Cancun Mexican Restaurant (*not bad Mexican food for Illinois.*)

Continue south on 6th street and enter I-55 at Exit 92 **(L057)** and head south four miles across the Lake Springfield to exit 88, Chatham/East Lakeshore Drive.

Lake Springfield was a section of Historic Route 66 until the creation of Lake Springfield in the 1930s which pushed the old highway underwater. It was not only the highway that wound up underwater - Dominic Tarro, owner of the Coliseum Ballroom in Benld, IL had been indicted by grand jury in 1930 - escaping trial by being discovered at the bottom of new Lake Springfield with concrete blocks strapped to his body.

At the end of the off ramp at Exit 88, Chatham/East Lakeshore Drive **(L055)**, turn right and
ZERO ODOMETER
    1.0 miles - Two-lane road.
    4.1 miles (L054) - Glenarm.
    5.2 miles (L053) - Cross at stop sign.
    6.8 miles (L052) - At stop sign, turn left and enter I-55 south. This is Exit 82 and the on-ramp is U-shaped.
Approaching exit 80, you can see the old highway to the right. It dead-ends about milepost 82.

Chicago to Santa Monica

7.3 miles - Curve right, then left to enter

McLEAN

8.3 miles (L078) - Curve left onto N. Steward Road.
8.5 miles - Right onto E. Carlisle Street and go one block.
8.6 miles - Intersection with Main Street, make a left and go two blocks.
9.0 miles - Junction of Main Street and US 136.

At this intersection is the well-known Dixie Truckers Home **(L077)**, unfortunately service and food quality has declined in the past few years. Route 66 Museum is across the street in the old McLean railroad depot.

From the junction, make a right and

ZERO ODOMETER

0.2 miles (L076) - Just before the railroad tracks, make a left.
1.0 miles - Curve left, then right.
3.0 miles - Change in road surface.
3.1 miles - Cross bridge.
4.2 miles (L075) - Turn right onto Atlanta Road.

ATLANTA

Another town that moved to meet the railroad. In 1854, the village of Newcastle was a mile away from the tracks and a station stop simply known as Zenia. The town packed up and moved. In 1855, the name Atlanta was adopted.

The Public Library is a unique eight-sided white granite building of Neo-Classic design. Built as the library in 1873, it became a museum in 1979. A tall, granite clock tower stands on the corner. The clock, a 1909 Seth Thomas mechanism, was originally the High School clock. An observation window allows you to see the clock mechanism.

On leaving Atlanta,

ZERO ODOMETER

0.6 miles (L074) - Curve to left - Stop sign, right turn onto frontage road.
1.4 miles (L073) - Large block culvert on the right is used by farmers for moving wagons and tractors from the fields.
2.7 miles - Cross bridge.
4.8 miles - Four-lane road.
6.2 miles - Cross under interstate.

LINCOLN

The only town named for Abraham Lincoln with his knowledge and consent. He warned the founders that he "never knew anything named Lincoln that amounted to much." The original settlement, west of the present site, was named Potsville. The arrival of the railroad brought both a location and name change.

To take the route through town, make a left onto Kickapoo Street off BL 55 **(L072)**. Go to Keokuk **(L071)** and make a right to Logan **(L070)**, where you make a left. Follow Logan to where it veers onto 5th Street **(L069)**. Follow 5th Street to Washington **(L068)** and make a left. Follow Washington to Stringer Ave., which will join Washington from an angle on the right. Follow Stringer to the junction with the parkway **(L067)** where you make a left.

LODGING: Comfort Inn (217.735.3960).

If you want to take the parkway around the city, continue straight ahead. After passing the junction with the "through-town" route **(L068)**, you will see a section of old pavement on right, two-tenths of mile in length. The parkway will then pass under railroad tracks and curve around to the left.

When the parkway meets the junction with the "through-town" route, at Stringer Ave. **(L067)**,

ZERO ODOMETER

0.5 miles - Cross Salt Creek.
2.1 miles (L066) - Left at the "Frontage Road Entrance." This will curve around on new pavement, then rejoin Old 66.
5.7 miles (L065) - Left turn to stay on 66.
5.9 miles (L064) -

BROADWELL

The Pig Hip Restaurant is on the right **(L063)**. A Route 66 landmark that closed in 1992 but the subject of ongoing restoration work by the Illinois Route 66 Association folks. The Pioneer Motel and gas station also stand abandoned, a monument to the passing of the great highway.

9.0 miles - Old alignment on left.

Chicago to Santa Monica

You have three choices for your trip through Bloomington - Normal:
OPTION 1: Follow the old route all the way through town.
OPTION 2: Take the "in-town" bypass: Veterans Parkway.
OPTION 3: Go completely around the city on I-55.

BLOOMINGTON - NORMAL
A pair of cities that share a common Main Street, only one like it in the country. A university is at each end of Main Street - Illinois State University at the Normal end and Illinois Weslayan at the Bloomington end.

This site was known as Keg Grove when the first settlers arrived in 1822, after a party of trappers hid a keg of whiskey here, and wound up playing absentee hosts to a group of Native Americans who found the booty. Because of the profusion of flowers in the area, the name was changed to Blooming Grove, a far better name than the inevitable Keg Town toward which it was heading. *(We're sure the students at both schools do their best to keep the Keg Town spirit alive every Saturday night!)*

LODGING: Hampton Inn (309.662.2800); Jumer's Chateau (309.662.2020); Eastland Suites Hotel (309.662.0000)
DINING: Steak 'N' Shake; Central Station Cafe.

OPTION #1:
Continue straight ahead from the Towanda junction. You will be on Shelbourne Road.
4.8 miles (L091) - Intersection with Henry Street. Make a left onto Henry. There is is a curving right ahead.
5.2 miles (L090) - Intersection with Pine Street. Make a right onto Pine.
6.0 miles (L089) - Intersection with Linden Street. Make a left onto Linden.
6.2 miles (L088) - Intersection with Willow Street. Make a right onto Willow.
6.9 miles (L087) - Intersection of Willow and Main Street. Make a left onto Main and head into downtown. Main will curve to the right and become one-way on Kingsley Street, then becoming Center Street. Center will rejoin Main just before Veterans Parkway.
10.7 miles (L086) - Junction of Main Street and Veterans Parkway. Make a right to one nasty little intersection.
11.4 miles (L085) - Right onto Morris, then left onto Springfield. This one is extremely tricky. Springfield Road lies almost directly across the intersection from Veterans Parkway and Morris. The best way to handle this is to go north on Morris for a block or so, make a U-turn and return to the intersection then make a right onto Springfield.
12.1 miles (L084) - Intersection with Beich Road. Turn right, following Beich Road across I-55.
12.7 miles (L083) - Immediately after crossing I-55, make a left onto the continuation of Beich Road and continue parallel to the interstate to the Shirley Road junction (**L080**) where you go straight ahead.
(Text continues at "SHIRLEY ROAD JUNCTION" below.)

OPTION #2:
Make a right at the Towanda junction (**L094**) and join the interstate at Exit 171 (**L093**).
Stay on I-55 to Veterans Parkway (Exit 167) (**L092**).
Take the parkway through the city (11 miles) to Exit 157 (**L082**).
Join I-55 south to Exit 154 (Shirley Road) (**L081**) and leave the interstate.
Make a right at the end of the ramp and go to the junction with Route 66 (**L080**) and make a left.
(Text continues at "SHIRLEY ROAD JUNCTION" below.)

OPTION #3:
Make a right at the Towanda junction (**L094**) and join the interstate at Exit 171 (**L093**).
Stay on I-55 to Exit 154 (Shirley Road) (**L081**).
Make a right at the end of the ramp and go to the junction with Route 66 (**L080**) and make a left.

SHIRLEY ROAD JUNCTION
At the Shirley Road junction (**L080**),
ZERO ODOMETER
On the south side of Shirley Road, east of our route lies some old pavement. It is possible to drive about a half to three-quarters of a mile on this section of the old road before it dead-ends at I-55. This is part of Old 66, although it appears to swing too far east. In examining the WPA guide, it mentions Funks Grove as being 3 miles from the highway. The present alignment puts Funks at less than 0.5 miles off the highway.
4.0 miles (L079) - Funk's Grove - The home of pure Maple Sirup, yep, that spelling is correct. The more common syrup indicates sugar has been added to the mixture.

Chicago to Santa Monica

The two-lane highway bypassed Odell early on. Probably because of the proximity of the downtown section to the railroad tracks.

Make a left onto the old alignment at the north end of town **(L110)**.

Go straight ahead to Prairie Street and make a right.

Go two blocks and turn left on West Street. The famous restored Standard Service Station **(L109)** is at the corner of West and Deer Streets.

Continue on West St. to join modern 66 on the south end of town **(L108)** where you make a left and

ZERO ODOMETER

0.8 miles - Road becomes two-lane.

1.8 miles - Interesting bridge across railroad on left side.

3.9 miles - Four-lane returns.

4.5 miles (L107) - Small bridge and to the right a barn has an ad for Meramec Caverns in Missouri painted on the side. (*There is a turnout here built by the Illinois Association for taking photos of the barn painting*).

4.8 miles - Bridge on the left crosses the tracks to Cayuga.

5.2 miles - Cemetery on the right.

PONTIAC

Founded in 1887 by James Fell and named for the chief of the Ottawa tribe.

On the north end of town is the Old Log Cabin Inn **(L106)**. The building faces the newer alignment of Route 66, but this was not always the case. Originally it faced the old highway (*which lies behind the building*). After construction of the new alignment the building was lifted and turned 180 degrees and set back down, facing the new alignment of the highway.

8.4 miles (L105) - Left onto old 66 to enter Pontiac.

Follow a long curve to the right to the left turn onto Division Street.

Continue straight on Division to West Lincoln Ave., just past the North Creek Bridge **(L104)**.

Follow the right curve on West Lincoln Ave to a left curve onto Ladd Street **(L103)** and go straight about 10 blocks. The street will angle right and you will cross the Vermillion River.

Go five blocks to the intersection with Reynolds Street **(L102)**.

Turn right on Reynolds and go to two blocks.

10.7 miles (L101) - Reynolds Street and modern 66 is the south end junction of old 66 in Pontiac. Turn left.

CHENOA

Name is Indian for White Dove. Town grew along alignments of the Peoria & Oquawka and the Chicago & Mississippi railroads that met at a four-way crossing in town. Town was laid out by Matthew Scott in 1856.

DINING: Chenoa Family Restaurant

21.7 miles (L100) - Town center turn-off.

Where old alignment joins at south end of town **(L099)**,

ZERO ODOMETER

7.6 miles (L097) Left off highway onto Main Street in

LEXINGTON

Named for the battlefield in Massachusetts and first settled in 1828.

There is an old alignment north of town that can be walked, but not driven. The town uses it for the annual Taste of Country Fair in July. Vintage looking billboards have been erected, making for an interesting walk. Hungry? There's good food and a fun atmosphere at the Shake Shack on Main St.

7.7 miles (L096) - Right on Grove.

8.2 miles (L095) - Angled left onto highway at the end of Grove St.

8.6 miles - Old bridge, rough road.

10.0 miles - Merge into two-lane.

11.2 miles - Cross bridge into Towanda.

TOWANDA

Indian for *Where we bury our dead*. Very small town.

At the stop in the center of town **(L094)**,

ZERO ODOMETER

Chicago to Santa Monica

0.2 miles - Notice the row of houses on the left, they are on old Chicago Road that was original alignment of the highway.

An experiment in farm rehabilitation by Arthur States began in 1924, resulting in ten of the twelve participants purchasing their own farms with proceeds from farm income.

In Elwood, turn left on Douglas **(L120)** and continue south out of town.

Notice along here the southbound lanes of the divided highway are the original Route 66. The southbound lanes follow the topography more than the northbound and are also closest to the railroad tracks.

7.8 miles (L119) - Back to two lane.

8.7 miles - Johnson & Johnson plant on right.

9.3 miles - Curve to right and enter.

WILMINGTON

Founded by Thomas Fox as Winchester, but because of a dispute over the name became Wilmington in 1854.

9.5 miles (L118) - The Launching Pad Cafe with large Gemini giant statue.

10.0 miles - Water Street and Junction with Illinois 102. Continue straight.

10.3 miles - Cross Kankakee River.

10.7 miles - Bear left and continue south.

12.2 miles - Coal City Road. Continue south.

14.4 miles -

BRAIDWOOD

In 1865, William Henneberry hit a rich vein of coal while sinking a well. By 1880, the population had swelled to 9,000 and long coal trains, up to six a day, pulled out of Braidwood. A few of the older tourist courts and mine structures can still be seen in the area.

Hungry? Check out the Polka Dot Drive-In **(L117)**.

16.6 miles (L116) - Godley.

Once a thriving mining community with twenty-one mines in operation within a mile and half of town, by 1906, all were shut down.

18.5 miles (L115) - Braceville.

The same story as Godley. Once a booming mining town, now all that are left are the overgrown slag heaps left by the mine operations.

20.4 miles - A long arched bridge is across the tracks on the "other 66."

22.0 miles - Curve to left.

GARDNER

As you enter Gardner, the Historic 66 signs will guide you onto IL 53. This route is a "mini-bypass" of Gardner. Go straight ahead from the intersection of IL 53 and Main Street **(L114)**. Follow IL 53 for one long block and make a right. Do not go straight ahead on IL 50. After the turn, go straight to the intersection with the frontage road **(L113)** and make a left.

If you would like to drive on Main Street, which was a very early routing, make a right at the intersection of IL 53 and Main Street **(L114)**. Go to the second stop sign and turn left onto the frontage road.

At the intersection of IL 53 and the frontage road **(L113)**,

ZERO ODOMETER

Continue south, keeping I-55 on your right. Road surface is good, with little traffic.

6.5 miles -

DWIGHT

Left onto the two-lane alignment at the north end of town **(L112)**.

7.4 miles - Y-intersection. Make a left onto IL 47, which joins from the right at the Y.

7.7 miles - Cross east-west railroad tracks.

8.2 miles - Make an angled right onto Waupansie Street.

9.2 miles - Road curves to left.

9.3 miles - Junction with IL 17. Continue straight. The well-known Route 66 Service Station is on the northeast corner.

9.9 miles - Curve to right. (Behind you is the 1918 alignment.)

Make a left onto four-lane alignment at the south end of town **(L111)**.

ODELL

Chicago to Santa Monica

13.3 miles - Route 66 Cafe & Grill on right.
14.2 miles - "Flicks on 66" video store, right.
14.6 miles - Bear left, cross Wolf Road and under I-294.
16.7 miles **(L137)** - Join I-55 (no choice) and continue out of Chicago for eight miles to Joliet.

Side trip! If you're hungry and want to enjoy a genuine Route 66 culinary tradition, stop at Del Rhea's Chicken Basket in Willowbrook on your way out of Chicago. Take the IL 83 North/Kingery Rd exit from I-55. (It's 2 miles west of where you joined the interstate.) Go north from the freeway 1/2 mile to Midway Drive and make a right to the T-intersection at Quincy. Make a right and go straight ahead to the frontage road. The Chicken Basket is just to your right at 645 Joliet Road **(L136)**.

Leave I-55 at Joliet Road, exit 269 **(L135)**. Position yourself for the LEFT side exit lanes to head south on Joliet Road.
As you pass under the bridge marked 14' 10",
ZERO ODOMETER
0.4 miles - Flea market on the right.
1.4 miles - Johnson & Johnson plant on right.
2.0 miles - White Fence Farm restaurant on right.
2.5 miles **(L134)** - Junction with Illinois 53, continue straight (south).
7.2 miles - Lewis University on right.
8.1 miles - Junction with Illinois 7.
9.0 miles - Division Street. State Police Headquarters on right.
9.3 miles **(L133)** - Hold it! That's not a picnic park on your right. It's Statesville Prison! (*No picnic there...*)
10.0 miles - Crest Hill.

JOLIET
The first settler was Charles Reed in 1831 and by 1834 a townsite was platted. The town was known as Juliet, after the Shakespeare character, for a number of years, but became Joliet after it was assumed (*and we know what that means*) the town was named for French explorer Louis Joliet.
In April of 1848, the first ship arrived on the newly constructed canal and was met by the entire town. Joliet became known for its limestone and shipped blocks as far as New York. In 1852, the railroad reached Joliet followed shortly thereafter by the steel industry.
LODGING: Hampton Inn (815.725.3110); Comfort Inn-North (815.436.5141).
At Broadway and Ruby **(L131)**
ZERO ODOMETER
Make a left turn onto Ruby. (*This is a busy intersection!*) Go down the hill one block and cross the bridge over the Des Plaines River.
Turn right onto Chicago Street **(L130)**.
As you cross Ohio Street, follow the slight curve to the right onto Ottawa Street **(L128)**.
Go straight to Jackson Street **(L127)** where you make a hard right followed immediately by a left onto the continuation of Ottawa. (*"Immediately" is an understatement!*)
1.2 miles **(L125)** - Intersection with Allen Street. Bear to the left one block onto Chicago Road **(L124)**. Follow the highway through a gentle S-curve and under an interstate.
2.2 miles **(L123)** - Route 52 and 53 split. Continue on 53, sign says "To Wilmington."
South of Joliet the road becomes four lane. In 1943, the State authorized construction of what would be considered a high speed, divided highway between Chicago and St. Louis that would by-pass the towns and provide a faster, more direct route. In a lot of areas, we will leave the four-lane for a more interesting route through the town along the road.
7.7 miles **(L122)** - Manhattan Road, at this point,
ZERO ODOMETER
Make a left and cross over the northbound lane. There is a row of houses extending N/S. Notice the old pole line. Make an immediate right and you are on Old 66 (Chicago Road).
0.4 miles **(L121)** - Road curves to the right. This is Mississippi Road.
2.2 miles - Curve to left.
2.6 miles - Curve to right.
2.7 miles - Stop sign. This is intersection with Illinois 53 (new 66). Straight ahead into Elwood.

ELWOOD

Chicago to Santa Monica

ILLINOIS

WESTBOUND

Credit must be given to the Illinois Route 66 Association for having done an excellent job of marking the old highway through the state. Not just the better-known alignments are marked, but the early and optional routes as well. If you are unsure of any of the directions that follow, just look for a Historic Route 66 marker.

CHICAGO

First explorers to the area were Louis Joliet and Jacques Marquette in 1673. Juan Batiste Point de Sable built the first cabin here in 1779 with Fort Dearborn being established in 1804. The town site of modern Chicago was laid out in 1830. With the coming of the railroad connecting to San Francisco in 1869 the city began a boom that never stopped - except for the setback caused by the Great Chicago Fire of 1871 which destroyed virtually the entire city. Rebuilt upon the ashes the city has never looked back.

Chicago is a giant city and as such has giant city problems. Parking is a horror with lots charging outrageous rates (up to $10 an hour) and traffic can be a positive nightmare. My suggestion for starting that Route 66 trip is to stay outside of the city, then drive in early on a Sunday morning to enjoy a few photo ops (*but then we all know how I feel about cities*).

LODGING (in the city): Chicago Hilton (312.922.4400); Four Seasons Hotel (312.280.8800); Days Inn Lake Shore Drive (312.943.9200); Residence Inn (312.943.9800). As with any large city, the majority of the older motels have fallen into disrepair, stick with a major chain (*and even that can be a problem at times*).

DINING: Lou Mitchell's (a Roadie classic); Ed Debevic's; Season's Restaurant (in the Four Season); Su Casa (good Mexican food), plus thousands of other choices!

The Mother Road begins at Adams and Michigan Avenue **(L154)**. (Adams does not go through to Lakeshore Drive). There is a Historic Route 66 sign here to help you begin the journey. The odometer will not be set as there is going to be considerable traffic and it would be too distracting to attempt to track the mileage.

Proceed west on Adams to where it intersects with Ogden Avenue **(L152)**. Ogden is a diagonal street running southwest/northeast. Make a left onto Ogden and

ZERO ODOMETER

0.3 miles (L150) - Cook County Hospital on left.
1.3 miles (L149) - Intersection of Ogden and Western (Western runs north/south), bear to the right and stay on Ogden.
5.3 miles - Large inter-modal railroad facility on the right.
7.5 miles (L148) - Straight through the large intersection of Cermak Road/Harding Ave./Ogden Ave. (*This is a very large intersection!*)

CICERO AND BERWYN

It is difficult to tell when you leave one and enter the other. The giant Western electric plant once provided employment for thousands in the area. Berwyn was actually founded as a bedroom community for Chicago in 1890 by a visionary real estate promoter.

6.6 miles (L147) - This was the site of Bunyon's Cafe on the right.
8.1 miles (L146) - Left on Harlem.
8.4 miles (L145) - A sweeping right onto Joliet Road.
8.9 miles (L144) - Cross the Des Plaines River.
9.0 miles -

LYONS

Standing at the edge of one of the earliest sites in the state - the portage between the Chicago and Des Plaines Rivers used by Indians and the explorers Marquette and Joliet.

9.3 miles - Route 66 Realty on the left. Road will bear left along here onto Prescott **(L143)**.
9.8 miles (L142) - Intersection with 47th Street. Bear to the right.
10.5 miles - Cross under Interstate. Ignore the "To I-55" sign. Continue past shopping center.
11.2 miles (L141) - Veer right onto 55th Street. This is a detour around a quarry.
12.1 miles (L140) - Left onto East Avenue.
12.7 miles (L139) - Right onto Joliet Road.

Chicago to Santa Monica

ADVENTURE TOURS

In various parts of the book will be sections designated as ADVENTURE TOURS. These are sections of the road chosen for their historical interest. However, in virtually all cases these sections are very rough, usually dirt or extremely damaged pavement and as such are not suggested for the Roadie traveling in a classic (or even new) Corvette.

It should be pointed out that each of these sections will cover all of the problems to be encountered with recommendations for four-wheel drive if necessary.

Conditions can vary from dirt to sand, to extreme hills and, in times of severe weather, deep mud.

When you see the designation ADVENTURE TOUR, read the entire section before deciding to drive it, understand all of the problems that may be encountered, and, if the suggestion for four-wheel drive only is provided, take it seriously.

Now for the stuff that keeps the attorneys happy:

> **SOME OF THE ALIGNMENTS DESCRIBED AS ADVENTURE TOURS MAY REQUIRE OFF-PAVEMENT DRIVING AND MAY NOT BE SUITABLE FOR A STANDARD AUTOMOBILE. SUCH AREAS WILL BE FULLY DOCUMENTED AND ALL CAUTIONS AND POTENTIAL HAZARDS SHOULD BE CAREFULLY OBSERVED BY THE READER. THE AUTHORS, ROUTE 66 MAGAZINE, ITS AGENTS OR ASSIGNEES WILL ASSUME NO RESPONSIBILITY FOR DAMAGE TO EITHER VEHICLES OR INDIVIDUALS WHO CHOSE TO PARTAKE IN ANY OF THE ADVENTURE TOURS OUTLINED IN THIS PUBLICATION.**

HIGHWAY NOTE

As we were going to press, information was received that California is joining the rest of the nation with a uniform numbering system of interstate exits. These numbers will be presented in a south-to-north and west-to-east manner beginning at where the interstate originates in California; for example I-5 will be numbered from the Mexican border north to the Oregon state line. Preliminary information received from CalTrans has been included in the guidebook indicating exit numbers on Interstates 10, 15 and 40 where required. Please note, this project is not due for completion until 2005 and although shown in the guidebook, the exits may not yet be posted.

NOTES FOR THE READER ABOUT MAKING THE GUIDEBOOK AND THE ATLAS WORK TOGETHER:

- The Guidebook text contains hundreds of map references that look like this: **(N117)** or **(A012)**. These references are the ID numbers of waypoints that appear on the maps in the Atlas, so you can read the text and follow your progress (or keep from getting lost!) by using the Atlas.
- Waypoint ID's are prefixed by the first letter of the respective state, except Oklahoma and Illinois which are prefixed by "H" and "L" respectively. This is because of a policy decision not to begin a waypoint with the letters "O" or "I," in order to avoid confusion with the numerals "0" and "1."
- If you can't figure out what map page a waypoint appears on, just look up the waypoint in the table of contents in the Atlas. It lists all the maps and the range of waypoints appearing on each.
- The waypoint numbers are only identification numbers, they are not sequential indicators. The correct sequence for travelers is described in the Guidebook so just follow that. A waypoint shown on the map that doesn't appear in the text you're reading applies to the other direction of travel.

Chicago to Santa Monica

INTRODUCTION

It should be pointed out that this Guidebook is for the Roadies of the world in an attempt to help them find their way along what has been termed The Most Famous Highway in America.

This book is designed to present the road from West-to-East, a new concept in Route 66 Guidebooks, and one that has long been requested, while also providing the traditional East-to-West format.

In traveling the road, I attempt to do so as anonymously as possible. I do not announce myself when I enter an establishment (besides, would anyone know me anyway?) - in this fashion I receive the same service and attention as any other "off the highway" Roadie. This allows for an honest evaluation of food, service, and accommodations. I do not accept "comps" or freebies for two reasons:
One, it prevents coloring an evaluation based on receiving something for nothing.
Two, the business owners along the road are there to make money - not give away their product or services.
I have been told about other writers and members of various organizations who not only demand they be comp'ed, but go so far as to threaten a bad review if they are not properly taken care of. In my opinion, this is despicable behavior and if you experience this kind of activity I would like to hear about it.
In this edition, there will also be more recommendations for dining and lodging. These are truly subjective recommendations based on my personal experience. You may notice quite a few Best Western properties mentioned, this is because in many smaller towns the Best Western is the best place in town - this determination is based on my staying in many of the other motels in a community and finding the B/W to be tops. Please remember that Best Western properties are individually owned and must meet strict standards to maintain the Best Western logo. Up and coming in the world of budget motels is the Microtel Inn chain - offering new, clean rooms in a pleasant atmosphere, you will find some of them recommended as well. Although I do not have extremely high standards - seeking only a clean room, decent service and good food - I nonetheless will point out when a place is unpleasant or if we have received multiple complaints.

A few general hints about traveling the old road.
1. Watch for low gas prices and take advantage of them. Virtually, all gas sold in this country is inspected for quality (only one state, Oregon, does not have a gasoline quality inspection program). So, for all intents and purposes, gas is gas.
2. Use the octane rating for your vehicle. Check the operators manual and you may be surprised to find you can use a lower octane fuel than you thought. I drive a GMC Yukon XL and the manual recommends 87octane (i.e. regular). I have never had a problem running this fuel. Don't pay for a higher octane than you need - it will do nothing to improve performance.
3. Food is another area that can become extremely subjective - what I like in the way of food you may not. But service is another matter. Over the past few years, I have stopped at a lot of Denny's and found the service has gone straight down the toilet. This observation covers locations throughout California, Nevada, Arizona and all of the Route 66 states. For that reason alone, I cannot recommend any of these restaurants. For breakfast I suggest seeking out a local café with a parking lot packed with local cars - or better yet - pick-ups, this is where you'll want to eat.
4. If you have a positive, or negative, experience at a Route 66 café, motel, or gas station drop me a line and let me know about it. I will check into it and when this book is updated will make use of the information.

The places rated or suggested in this book have been personally visited by yours truly and meet with my standards (such as they are) for a good Route 66 establishment. I do not go on the word of others (although positive or negative word-of-mouth will suggest a visit). A few places may receive negative reviews in these pages, this has been brought about by personal experience, or complaints I've received and followed up on to make my own decision. I do not use a check-list. (Is the menu pretty? Did the door open without a squeak? Etc.). I base my opinions on the quality of service, quality of the food, or the cleanliness of the accommodations. As a rule, most Route 66 businesses are great, but there are a few bad apples and if they are really bad, they will be mentioned. The fact an establishment does not appear in these pages is not indicative of a problem - most likely I have never stopped there - but please remember I have been traveling the Road since 1989 and have watched many places go downhill, or in some cases never come up. Now, for the lawyer's part: These are my personal observations and opinions and may not reflect the opinion of the publisher, editor or any other individual involved in the production of this volume.

So, with all of that explained, let's walk to the end of the Navy Pier and get a shot of Lake Michigan, because tomorrow morning, bright and early, we're ON THE ROAD!

FORWARD!

My dad loved cars.

Cars were a large part of his life.

When I was a kid, Dad had Packard's, Cadillac's, Imperial's, Lincoln's, Studebaker's, and step-down Hudson's - during the time when Hudson's were the top stock-car on the racing circuit. He once participated, as a mechanic, in the famous Carrera Panamericana, or the Mexican Road Race as it was popularly known, under the Lincoln banner. There was a time when our Southern California driveway and carport were home to the Raymond Lowey designed Studebakers. That was during the period when Dad drove the South Bend beauties in the Mobil Economy Run - a balloon-foot exercise in the name of good gas mileage.

But soon he returned to the behemoths he fondly called, "Great road cars." It was important to him how well a car handled out on the road. When he wasn't driving the highways of North America or Mexico, he was an ace mechanic, fixing the internal ills of all types of Detroit iron. Through his innate mechanical skills he learned which cars were well-built, and which were off-the-assembly-line junk.

I was in my teens when I discovered - on my own - that Dad's love affair with the automobile had very little to do with the cars themselves. I found myself, almost mystically, reliving many of the things he had done. During a period when I had no wheels of my own, I spent months hitchhiking from one end of the country to the other - south to north and back, then west to east and back. When wheels were mine once again I discovered the equation:

Car + gas ÷ (Road-out-town) x Map = Going Somewhere

To a hard-core Roadie "going somewhere" is all that matters. Destinations are important only in the context of being someplace to turn around. Roadies seek out maps, highways, and roads, much as coin collectors seek out the elusive 1943 steel penny.

To the Roadie, Route 66 is a major attraction. Along the 2448 miles of the Mother Road from Lake Michigan to the Pacific Ocean there are sights rarely seen on other highways. The Road is an adventure and along the road are thousands of cafes, motels and tourist stops demanding to be seen and investigated.

The Road offers views of a world missed on the Interstate, as it explores and celebrates the two-lane world of single-story motels, small cafes and stations where gas is still pumped by a guy with BOB stitched on a grease stained blue shirt.

Buckle your seat-belt and leave a big tip as we pull out of that lucky parking spot in front of Lou Mitchell's and onto the pavement of The Road. Journey with us along Route 66 as we seek out the well-known, the little-known, and the unknown in the world of the Mother Road.

Dad, this one's for you!

Bob Moore

DEDICATED TO THE MEMORY OF
JACK D. RITTENHOUSE,
WHO SHOWED US THE WAY

ISBN 0-9701423-1-5

Copyright © 2003
Route 66 Magazine
PO Box 66
Laughlin NV 89028

All rights reserved.
Without limiting the rights under copyright reserved above,
no part of this publication may be reproduced, stored in a
retrieval system, or transmitted in any form or by any means,
electronic, mechanical, photocopied, recorded, or otherwise
without written permission of the copyright owner.

All odometer readings are accurate for the vehicle used, however
actual readings may vary from vehicle to vehicle. The authors and/or the
Route 66 Magazine Publishing Company will not accept any responsibility
for damage to vehicles or individuals following the directions included herein.
The Road is a living entity and as such listed places may change over time.
Recommendations as to lodging or dining are strictly the opinion of the writer and
do not necessarily reflect the opinion of the publisher or Route 66 Magazine.

FIRST EDITION

5 4 3 2 1

THE COMPLETE GUIDEBOOK TO ROUTE 66

CHICAGO TO SANTA MONICA

By BOB MOORE &
RICH CUNNINGHAM

A Route 66 Magazine Publication